New Feminist Discourses

This collection of new feminist essays represents the work of young critics researching and teaching in British universities. Aiming to set the agenda for feminist criticism in the nineties, the essays debate themes crucial to the development of feminist thought: among them, the problems of gendered knowledge and the implications of accounts of gendered language, cultural restraints on the representation of sexuality, women's agency, cultural and political change, a feminist aesthetics and new readings of race and class. This variety is given coherence by a unity of aim – to forge new feminist discourses by addressing conceptual and cultural questions central to problems of gender and sexual differences.

The topics of discussion range from matrilinear thought to seventeenth-century prophecy; the poetry of Amelia Lanyer to Julia Margaret Cameron's photographs; from Dorothy Richardson and Virginia Woolf to eighteenth-century colonial painting of the South Pacific; from medieval romance to feminist epistemology. The essays utilise and question the disciplines of literary criticism, art history, photography, psychoanalysis, Marxist history and post-structuralist theory.

Isobel Armstrong is Professor of English at Birkbeck College, London, and co-editor of *Women: A Cultural Review*.

Contributors: Ros Ballaster, Rachel Bowlby, Harriet Guest, Lorna Hutson, Elaine Jordan, Kadiatu Kanneh, Catherine LaFarge, Angela Leighton, Laura Marcus, Josephine McDonagh, Jane Moore, Lynn Nead, Suzanne Raitt, Lindsay Smith, Carol Watts, Linda Williams, Sue Wiseman.

New Feminist Discourses

Critical Essays on Theories and Texts

Edited by Isobel Armstrong

London and New York

First published 1992
by Routledge
11 New Fetter Lane, London EC4P 4EE

Simultaneously published in the USA and Canada
by Routledge
a division of Routledge, Chapman and Hall, Inc.
29 West 35th Street, New York, NY 10001

Set in 10/12pt Times
Printed and bound in Great Britain by
Butler & Tanner Ltd

British Library Cataloguing-in-Publication Data
New feminist discourses: critical essays on
 theories and texts.
 I. Armstrong, Isobel
 305.42

Library of Congress Cataloging-in-Publication Data
New feminist discourses : essays in literature, criticism, and theory
 / edited by Isobel Armstrong.
p. cm.
Includes bibliographical references and index.
1. English literature–Women authors–History and criticism.
2. English literature–History and criticism–Theory, etc.
3. Feminism and literature–Great Britain. 4. Women and literature–
Great Britain. 5. Feminist criticism–Great Britain. 6. Sex role
in literature. I. Armstrong, Isobel.
PR119.N49 1992
820′.9′9287–dc20 91-22363

ISBN 0 415 06740–5
ISBN 0 415 06741–3 pbk

Contents

Plates

Contributors

Ros Ballaster is a lecturer in the Department of English Literature in the School of English and American Studies at the University of East Anglia, Norwich.

Rachel Bowlby is a senior lecturer in the Department of English at the University of Sussex.

Harriet Guest is a lecturer in the Department of English and Related Literature at the University of York.

Lorna Hutson is a lecturer in the Department of English at Queen Mary and Westfield College, University of London.

Elaine Jordan is a lecturer in the Department of Literature at the University of Essex.

Kadiatu Kanneh is a tutorial fellow in English in the School of African and Asian Studies at the University of Sussex.

Catherine LaFarge is a lecturer in the Department of English at Birkbeck College, London.

Angela Leighton is a lecturer in the Department of English at the University of Hull.

Laura Marcus is a lecturer in the Department of English and Humanities at Birkbeck College, London.

Josephine McDonagh is a lecturer in the Department of English at the University of Essex.

Jane Moore is a lecturer in the Centre for Critical and Cultural Theory at the University of Wales College of Cardiff.

Lynda Nead is a lecturer in the History of Art at Birkbeck College, London.

Suzanne Raitt is a lecturer in English at Queen Mary and Westfield College, University of London.

Lindsay Smith is a lecturer in the School of English and American Studies at the University of Sussex.

Carol Watts is a lecturer in English at Birkbeck College, London.

Linda R. Williams is a lecturer in the Department of English at the University of Liverpool.

Sue Wiseman is a lecturer in English at the University of Kent, Canterbury.

Acknowledgements

This book had its origins in a conference at Southampton in 1988. Maude Ellmann and Ken Hirschkop helped to originate this conference. Warm thanks to them both for helping to lay the foundations for *New Feminist Discourses*.

Chapter 1

Introduction

Isobel Armstrong

Feminist theory and criticism of the last twenty years has been fertile. In Britain and America, in France and other areas of Europe, a creative phase of thought continues and, indeed, changes and expands its interests almost yearly. The history of this phase is already being written, a movement characterized by a criticism which is both interdisciplinary and international. This is what one would expect of a form of thought founded on the recognition that a new category of discussion, the category of gender, transforms and reconfigures the categories of the disciplines it addresses. Given the spirit in which feminism works, therefore, it may seem something of an anomaly that the essays in this book are all by women working and writing in Britain. This was not actually intended as a principle of unity, though it does indicate the kinds of thinking young feminists, most of them at the beginning of their careers, are undertaking in this country. A more important enterprise, however, concerned with the formulation and exploration of new concepts and methods in feminist criticism, motivates these essays. A few words about the origin of this book will provide a context for its project.

Feminist Criticism: The Next Decade? was the title of a conference mounted by the English Department of the University of Southampton in the late 1980s. The conference was organized largely by graduate students. It was an international conference and we invited speakers from both America and Europe to take part. We also wanted to give opportunities for young speakers at the start of their careers to show how their thinking about feminist criticism in the nineties was developing. The aim was to set an agenda for the nineties and to consider what kinds of criticism and theory would be needed in the next decade. When we came to publish the conference proceedings we found that many of the papers were already committed to journals or in the process of publication. We extended our collection of essays by inviting contributions from young feminist critics and theorists working in Britain, stressing the speculative nature of the volume. Thus these essays challenge and reflect upon what has been done before, both in Europe and in America. They evolve new categories of thought and methods of investigation for a feminist criticism – or, one should say, *feminisms* – of the late twentieth century. As we move into the post-modern era of late capitalism there are undoubtedly new and vexing problems to address. Hence there is debate and disagreement in these essays, as they define new problems for feminist discussion.

The nature of these problems can best be understood by asking a question: what's new about these feminist discourses? Feminist criticism no longer needs to struggle to make claims for itself as a legitimate discipline. The enabling struggles of precursors to write feminist history, to retrieve lost or invisible texts by women for contemporary discussion, to challenge patriarchal constructions of experience, have prepared the ground for a very sophisticated debate and opened up a field of speculative thought. Feminist criticism takes for granted the importance of the founding category of gender, and in order to explore further its importance has responded to psychoanalysis, Marxist thought and cultural theory, post-structuralist thought, linguistics and the new semiotic disciplines. But this interdisciplinary confidence eschews eclecticism. Feminism is highly self-conscious about the sexual politics and the politics implied in different forms of thought. Feminist criticism today is characterized by disagreement and debate, by a capacity to reflect on its past history and the differences within itself. It is a presupposition of the essays in this book that feminist criticism is not a homogenized entity, that the practice of feminist *criticisms* is a necessary and proper one. As new configurations of thought are made, ideological challenges and faultlines open up. What's new about these essays is their willingness to remake categories and reconceptualize the disciplinary structures which have organized thought, and their recognition that debate is intrinsic to a feminist criticism which does not conceive itself as unitary and monolithic.

The commitment to feminist criticisms and the abandonment of the notion of homogeneity has meant that new projects and new debates have emerged. It is necessary to organize feminist criticism around different categories. Earlier ways of describing and structuring discussions of gender and sexual difference prove to be limiting or misleading. For instance, many of the essays in this book respond to psychoanalysis or Marxism or both but precisely because they cut across the customary boundaries of these forms of thought it is impossible to 'classify' them in terms of a Marxist or psychoanalytical feminism, for the terms themselves are being interrogated. Similarly, though these essays range from the medieval and early modern periods to the eighteenth, nineteenth and twentieth centuries, it would be misleading to arrange them in historical sequence, for they are not written to confirm and consolidate conventional periodizations of the literary text. In the same way, these essays do not belong to the different disciplines of literary criticism, history and art history as traditionally conceived, though painting, photography, extra-literary documents and literary texts are the objects of analysis. The sexual politics of these essays share a number of preoccupations – with power and class, colonialism, the family. But it would have been misleading to organize the volume round a series of problematical themes, for it is the project of feminist criticism to redefine topoi as objects of study. It is in the very nature of feminist thought to disinvest customary orderings of their unity and authority by transforming them. Gender is not a category simply to be added to an existing body of knowledge – 'women/gender and ...' – but the intervention of the category of gender radically changes discourse.

Accordingly, I have organized this volume round a series of debates which interrogate categories, including those of feminist discourses themselves. They are interconnected, of course, but nevertheless form distinctive though related discussions. The five areas of debate which are crucial to contemporary feminism and to thinking in the future are described here under the terms Knowledges, Subjectivities, Languages, Representations, Others. 'Knowledges' as a title conceptualizes and engenders what is a fundamental feminist debate, an enquiry into and contest for a feminist epistemology and its implications. Allied with this is an enquiry into the possibility of a feminist aesthetic. In what ways can we think of a gendered epistemology which will change our cognitive experience and our social relations? 'Subjectivities', following on from the question of epistemology, is an exploration of women's agency and its possibility. Gendered subjectivities constructed at particular historical moments in particular cultural circumstances through particular texts provide a starting-point for investigating the possibility of change and the conditions of change. Perhaps it is no accident that the texts under discussion here are all modernist or post-modernist in tendency; the twentieth century has been the site of explorations of gendered identity, and debates on the possibility of transformation and contending accounts of it are at their most urgent in the modernist movement. It is this fascination with the constructed subjectivity rather than their common concern with the twentieth century which determined the grouping of the essays here. In 'Languages' the nature of women's entry into language, the part played by language in the construction of subjectivity, the problem of essentialist accounts of language which advocate the isolationalism of *écriture féminine* outside the symbolic order, these questions are at the sharpest edge of feminist debate. However, language and politics, language and ideology, and the relation of these to a gendered discourse have been far less prominent concerns. These are addressed here. Questions of language open out into the following section, 'Representations'. The visual and verbal forms in which we construct experience and relationships of gender are crucial for controlling and limiting accounts and explorations of sexual difference. How it is possible to analyse and deconstruct gendered representations and categories, and how both to re-represent and to reconstruct these without a specious objectivity, provides a problematical enterprise which creates both methodological and conceptual difficulties requiring solution. Finally, 'Others': the space of the feminine as other has often prompted writers and theorists to align the oppressed other, whether in race or class structures, with women's oppression. The challenge to that homology and a more precise and unsentimental analysis of oppression is one of feminism's most important political projects.

Just as feminism today is plural and necessarily engenders conflict, so the categories of discourse which organize the grouping of these essays have been pluralized. There is more than one account of gendered knowledge, more than one account of gendered subjectivity, one analysis of representation, one analysis of the other. Accordingly, analysis within and between these groups of essays is often in disagreement. The post-structuralist epistemology explored in Jane Moore's essay, for instance, works against Carol Watts's feminist materialism and vice versa.

What now follows is a brief discussion of the essays grouped under the five categories of debate. Just as there is no single position ideologically in these essays, so there is no uniform understanding about the object of study in feminist critique – painting, photography, poems, fictions, aesthetics and rhetoric form the subject of analysis. The real consensus, however, comes through an agreement about the important problems in feminist criticism and about the priority of debating the five categories round which these essays are organized.

Linda R. Williams, Jane Moore, Rachel Bowlby and Laura Marcus develop different strategies for theorizing gendered knowledge. In 'Happy Families? Feminist Reproduction and Matrilineal Thought', Linda R. Williams considers the basis of both opposing epistemological paradigms for feminist knowledge, sisterhood and the sado-masochistic model of mastery and victim, unsatisfactory. She considers the revisionary strategies necessary for escaping from these models. Laura Marcus, using Rita Felski's work on aesthetics as a starting-point, explores the cognitive claims of the aesthetic as a way of changing experience in her 'Feminist Aesthetics and the New Realism'. Jane Moore, on the other hand, in her 'An Other Space: A Future for Feminism', considers the multiple, fragmented post-modernist consciousness as a model for feminist epistemology and celebrates the breakdown of traditional (male) monolithic knowledge.The problem of re-forming the feminine subject (or perhaps it should be called the subject of femininity) is taken up again by Rachel Bowlby in relation to Virginia Woolf and the new transgressive freedom of the city achieved by the feminine subject, the *flâneuse*. This gave Woolf the opportunity of reconceptualizing gender and sexual difference as changing commodity relations released new ways of thinking sexuality. When we move from 'Knowledges' to 'Subjectivities', we find Carol Watts arguing for a very different position: in 'Releasing Possibility into Form' she asks, as against the discontinuous subjectivity of the post-modern condition, to what extent gender identity is both culturally formed and volitional. Dorothy Richardson's difficult relation to modernist aesthetics and the problem of agency is taken as an example through which to explore this question. The critique of coercive accounts of the feminine subject continues in the last two essays in this group. In 'Fakes and Femininity: Vita Sackville-West and her

Mother', Suzanne Raitt considers the inadequacy of Freud's account of feminine subjectivity and the mother (particularly his failure to think beyond infancy into age), and uses the Sackville-West mother/daughter relationship as an example of his failure to theorize a crucial relationship. Angela Carter's challenge to stereotypical accounts of the feminine subject and her reinvention of alternatives is the theme of Elaine Jordan's 'The Dangers of Angela Carter'.

Kadiatu Kanneh's essay, 'Love, Mourning and Metaphor: Terms of Identity', begins the 'Languages' section of this linked debate on gender. She attacks French feminist accounts of language (particularly those of Hélène Cixous) for its justification of a feminist erotics of language through explicitly colonial and racist metaphor and looks for alternative feminist discourses which do not predicate themselves on the experience of woman as the dark continent. How women writers at another historical moment than ours might actually gain access to the economy of male rhetoric and subvert it or appropriate its form is at issue in Lorna Hutson's study of Aemelia Lanyer, 'Why the Lady's Eyes are Nothing Like the Sun'. Hutson explores Lanyer's strategies for both exploiting and circumventing the principles of Renaissance rhetoric to produce a critique of male practice. Not intrinsically gendered as male but culturally privileged as male, the discourses of the past provide an arena for exploring how women negotiate such heavily gender-marked forms and linguistic practices. The devious linguistic and textual strategies women undertook to justify their entry into the language of prophecy in the seventeenth century is the subject of Sue Wiseman's 'Unsilent Instruments and the Devil's Cushions: Authority in Seventeenth-century Women's Prophetic Discourse'. Language and ideology are bound up with one another. In a similar way politics and representation are inseparable. Under 'Representations' Lynda Nead considers the discourse of the Kantian and post-Kantian sublime as a discourse of power and control in relation to the painting of the female nude from the eighteenth century onwards. The contradictions of 'sublime' representations of the feminine produce a highly problematical gender politics which resonate beyond the aesthetic, she argues in 'Getting Down to Basics: Art, Obscenity and the Female Nude'. The control of representations of the feminine is also the subject of Josephine McDonagh's essay on De Quincey, 'Do or Die: Problems of Agency and Gender in the Aesthetic of Murder'. She engages with and challenges contemporary feminist analyses of sexual murder as a form of the unrepresentable sublime and argues that a truly feminist history must put sexuality and violence within and not beyond the representable in order that they can be understood. De Quincey's attempt to control the representation of feminine agency through his aesthetic of murder is an instance of such feminist history. Lindsay Smith's 'The Politics of Focus: Feminism and Photography Theory' considers the way in which focus and depth of field is theorized and gendered in the nineteenth century and contrasts the masculine control of focus in Carroll's photography with the strategies of representation which evade mastery in Julia Margaret Cameron's work. How to discover subtle and historically precise ways of analysing and deconstructing representation in male texts is an increasingly problematical enterprise. Catherine LaFarge explores Malory's discomfort with and failure to represent adultery and sexual transgression in 'The Hand of the Huntress: Repetition and Malory's Morte Darthur'. Repressed but perpetually reintroduced, the feminine and the transgressive actually orders the narrative structure of the poem and its narrative form as repetition both conceals and reveals the fact of adultery. The gender paradigms and politics at one level of the text are in conflict with those of another.

'Others' comprises three essays on class and colonialism in literary and pictorial texts which problematize the relation of gender to these categories. In 'New Hystericism: Aphra Behn's *Oroonoko*: the Body, the Text and the Feminist Critic', R. M. Ballaster argues that the female 'other' and the colonial subject cannot be easily identified in texts by women and explores Behn's repressive treatment of the black female 'subject' to demonstrate that the easy identification of black/woman made in recent new historicist criticism is fallacious. Following upon this recognition of complexity Harriet Guest analyses the ambiguous iconography of race and gender in 'The Great Distinction: Figures of the Exotic in the Work of William Hodges'. In Hodges's paintings of Tahiti the exotic and the erotic shift and redefine their relationship in the visual field of the painting, so that the non-European other is sometimes in identity with and sometimes in a relationship of difference with the Western feminine. Finally, from Enlightenment colonialism to the nineteenth century, Angela Leighton argues against traditional readings of the women poets and their response to prostitution. She suggests that this is a complex moment where class and gender can be read together because of a mutual relationship of transgression. Rather than an antithetical and antipathetic figure the fallen woman was the poet's double, an aspect of her own otherness.

Running across all these essays is a concern with change, a concern with the possibility of changing long-held gender roles and the structures to which they belong. A corollary is the necessity to understand and describe the violence which has sustained them. Two seminal but very different essays of the 1980s posed questions about the nature of consciousness and gender in the post-modern condition. Julia Kristeva's 'Women's Time' saw the female terrorist as a model of women's condition of damaged narcissism – only a more extreme version of the male terrorist, since all fixed roles are coercive – unless a structural redefinition of gender roles could be achieved in our culture.[1] Starting from the other side of the question, with women's assumption of the role of victim, Donna Haraway's 'A Manifesto for Cyborgs' urged women to abandon passivity and to celebrate the new possibilities being inscribed on our bodies, on time and space, by electronics and the microchip.[2] Women could embrace the discontinuous consciousness, fragmented identity and porous boundaries made possible by modern technology because it offers them release from prescribed gender roles and a new politics. The essays in this book implicitly address the questions about change which are proffered in these important discussions. In the process of addressing one set of questions, new ones begin to be formulated. Hence this book is part of a debate which is self-perpetuating.

NOTES

1 Julia Kristeva, 'Women's Time' (1979), first translated in *Signs* 7, no. 1 (Autumn 1981), pp. 13–35.
2 Donna Haraway, 'A Manifesto for Cyborgs: Science, Technology, and Socialist Feminism in the 1980s', *Socialist Review* 15, no. 80 (1985), pp. 65–107.

Part I

Knowledges

Chapter 2

Feminist aesthetics and the new realism

Laura Marcus

It is only recently that feminist accounts of women's writing have been centrally concerned with contemporary feminist fiction, after the work already carried out on earlier women writers, analyses of the social function of popular genres such as romantic fiction and explorations of a so-called feminine aesthetic. This new attention to contemporary writing gives a sharper edge to two familiar questions: the longstanding theme of the relationship between literary/aesthetic questions and political commitment, in this case feminist, and the more specific issue of the alleged opposition between 'experimental writing' and 'realism'. Whereas a prevalent theme for some time has been the assertion of an affinity between women's writing and literary modernism or avant-gardism, a number of recent studies have attempted to redeem literary realism from its negative place in left literary theory over the last two decades. Studies such as Rita Felski's *Beyond Feminist Aesthetics*, Paulina Palmer's *Contemporary Women's Fiction* and Anne Cranny-Francis's *Feminist Fiction* share a strong reaction against the lures of *écriture féminine*, avant-gardism and abstract accounts of a gendered language and literature, and a desire to explore what the majority of feminists are 'in reality' writing and reading and why.

The issue of political commitment arises at the very beginning, with the distinction between women's writing in general and feminist writing in particular. For present purposes, I shall borrow Rita Felski's definition of 'feminist literature' as 'encompass[ing] all those texts that reveal a critical awareness of women's subordinate position and of gender as a problematic category, however this is expressed'.[1] Felski is concerned with feminist writing of the last twenty or so years, written since the re-emergence of the women's movement in the late 1960s, and with the ways in which the emergence of 'new plots for women' in the literary arena are related to the 'emancipatory narratives' which characterize feminism as a social movement. She argues against the concept of a 'feminist aesthetic' on the grounds that it is impossible to locate or demonstrate the existence of either a 'unifying consciousness' in women's writing *or* a distinctive female form or genre; more specifically, she suggests that the conflation of this (illusory) aesthetic and 'modernist' or 'avant-gardist' literary practice has resulted in a failure to understand the cultural and political significances of the bulk of contemporary feminist fiction. (One potential source of confusion here is Felski's conflation of 'feminine' and 'feminist' in the context of the aesthetic. I would argue that a 'feminist' aesthetic does involve evaluations of the relationship between women's writing and feminist politics; while 'feminine' or 'female' refers to a whole set of characteristics making up women's 'difference', 'feminist' connotes an overtly political stance.) Given the 'dominant status of realism within contemporary women's writing',[2] Felski argues, it is counter-productive (within the terms of a feminist criticism) to reject 'realism' as an outmoded or conservative form. While Felski points to the reductiveness of a purely strategic and 'instrumental' approach to the 'politics of literature', she states explicitly that the politics of feminist fiction can only be adequately addressed 'by relating literary practices to the goals and interests of the women's movement, rather than relying upon an abstract fetishization of aesthetic modernism as a source of subversion'.[3]

The troubling relationship between art and politics is particularly acute in feminism, which, it could be argued, has existed in part as a cultural movement, has certainly been largely expressed, mediated and represented through its (often literary) texts and is, in Sara Maitland's words, 'deeply dependent' on them. One way of representing this relationship, in a necessarily simplified form, is through the contrast between perspectives in which literary/aesthetic questions are made primary and those, such as Felski's, which posit the primacy of the social/political. This dichotomy can then be seen to interrelate with a variety of 'aesthetic' options, of which the most important in this context are modernism/avant-gardism and realism.

MODERNISM AND REALISM

The so-called Brecht/Lukács debates have often been used by feminist critics to represent a modernist/realist dichotomy, with Brechtian accounts of the political efficacy of experimental techniques in 'modernist' art and of the need for a new aesthetic advocated in opposition to Lukács' 'naive realism' and his rejection of modernism as decadent. (In fact, the arguments are rather broader than this account would suggest, since, as we shall see later, Brecht was arguing against 'merely formal literary criteria for realism',[4] and not against the idea that the function of literature is to represent reality.)

Feminist debates have given a particular inflection to this opposition, with the claim that a 'feminine aesthetic' is intrinsically modernist or avant-garde. Among the diverse usages of the term 'modernism', one can distinguish two in particular: (1) a focus on subjectivity and the complex workings of consciousness, with the often related claim that subjectivity is intrinsically fragmented; (2) modernist writing as linguistically innovative, self-reflexive and subversive of received wisdoms and traditional narratives. (A further important usage, central to feminist critiques of modernism, defines it in relation to theories of authorial 'impersonality' and 'autonomy theories' of art.) The claim that there is an affinity between modernism in the first sense and a feminine aesthetic is too familiar to require illustration; the alleged connection between 'the feminine' and modernism-as-avant-gardism is rather more complex and contestable. Andreas Huyssen, for example, criticizes Julia Kristeva and other exponents of what has come to be known as 'French feminism' for equating femininity and modernism:

> Even though the French readings of modernism's 'feminine' side have opened up fascinating questions about gender and sexuality which can be turned critically against more dominant accounts of modernism, it seems fairly obvious that the wholesale theorization of modernist writing as feminine simply ignores the powerful masculinist and misogynist current within the trajectory of modernism.[5]

On the other hand, Huyssen recognizes an affinity between avant-gardism and feminism in the period of the late 1950s and early 1960s, following the decades associated with 'High Modernism':

> the avantgarde's attack on the autonomy aesthetic, its politically motivated critique of the highness of high art, and its urge to validate other, formerly neglected or ostracized forms of cultural expression created an aesthetic climate in which the political aesthetic of feminism could thrive and develop its critique of patriarchal gazing and penmanship.[6]

While this account contextualizes women's art and writing in relation to feminism as a political movement and invokes the important concept of feminism's 'political aesthetic' – to which I will return – Huyssen, who himself distinguishes between the 'Mallarmé–Lautréamont–Joyce axis of modernism' stressed by Kristeva and his own 'Flaubert–Thomas Mann–Eliot axis', passes over recent re-readings of literary modernism which have attempted to redefine it as a substantially female movement. Recent feminist studies have created, to borrow Huyssen's terms, a 'Woolf–Richardson–Stein axis' in an attempt to shift accounts of literary modernism dependent upon either of the 'axes' Huyssen describes. Although this is not an issue I wish to discuss here, it is a useful reminder that modernism can be constructed in very different ways and that particular exclusions can be reversed through a redefinition and not only through a rejection of the modernist aesthetic. Moreover, although such studies have tended to focus on the coterie aspects and the 'exotic' lives of 'modernist women' at the expense of broader cultural *or* textual issues, there has been an important focus on the *institutions* of literary modernism and the roles played by women writers and patrons in these.

Arguments for modernism also appear in the form of critiques of realism:

> We often seem tied to the notion of realistic presentation as if the umbilical cord between fiction and what we think of as reality must never be cut.

> ... A theory or practice of writing based on realism has an indirectly sinister (and, in the long run, debilitating) effect: it denies the real forces that go into the making of literature, the social and psychological pressures that function alongside the craft of the individual writer.[7]

This passage from Moira Monteith's introduction to the collection *Women's Writing* is one example amongst many of the ways in which 'literary realism' has come to be associated with crude, simplistic and in this account even 'sinister' critical approaches. This perception covers literature and literary criticism: 'realism' becomes synonymous with 'empiricism', the latter becoming synonymous with 'anti-theoreticism' and naive demands for authenticity. This is not to say that feminist critics of an anti-realist persuasion have bracketed 'reality' off altogether; in Monteith's view there are 'real forces' at work beneath appearances, realities which a so-called 'realism' fails to represent. Toril Moi discusses this issue at greater length:

> In *Images of Women in Fiction*, the double rejection of 'modernist' literature and 'formalist' criticism highlights the deep realist bias of Anglo-American feminist criticism. An insistence on authenticity and truthful reproduction of the 'real world' as the highest literary values inevitably makes the feminist critic hostile to non-realist forms of writing. There is nevertheless no automatic connection between demands for a full reproduction of the totality of the 'real' and what is known as a 'realist' fiction. At least two famous literary attempts at capturing reality in its totality, *Tristram Shandy* and *Ulysses*, end up by mischievously transgressing traditional realism in the most radical fashion precisely *because* of their doomed attempt to be all-inclusive.[8]

In Moi's account, as in others, it is modernism (including its precursors such as *Tristram Shandy*), which is at times made the true realism; literary realism as conventionally understood is presented as an empiricism which contents itself with immediate perceptions. Modernism is a true realism in the sense that it attempts to go behind surface appearances; it is radical in showing that mimetic theories of the literary reproduction of reality are pursuing a chimera. Thus the advocate of realism is doubly misguided – in making 'realism' a value and in believing that it will be embodied within the 'realist' text.

THE REALIST DEFENCE: TWO REALISMS

If, as feminist critics, we are being asked either to re-evaluate or to reject literary realism, it will be useful to examine in more detail what is meant by the term. Most fundamental is the contrast between theories of literary realism and the variety of ontological and epistemological doctrines which also describe themselves as realist. Penny Boumelha, in an otherwise excellent article on nineteenth-century literary realism, 'Realism and the Ends of

Feminism', having rightly criticized 'the collapse into and on to one another of realism as an epistemology and realism as a mode of writing',[9] seems to treat the former as the property of 'bourgeois humanists or misogynistic reactionaries' and reassures her readers that the value of realist literature is uncontaminated by epistemological realism (whatever she thinks this to be). Terry Lovell, one of the few critics to have attempted to sort out this relationship in her *Pictures of Reality*, also denies the evidence of any such connection, while arguing strongly *for* epistemological realism in the context of developing a sociology of art informed by Marxist cultural theory. For Lovell, a non-empiricist philosophical realism is essential, at least for a criticism wishing to call itself Marxist, while literary realism is an aesthetic choice largely distinct from this. Whereas literary realism raises issues of the nature of representation which are the concern of ontological and epistemological realism, these do not entail literary realism or any other aesthetic doctrine. Of realist theory and practice in art she states:

> There is no concept in the history of aesthetics which has generated more confusions, and no area, from the point of view of developing a sociology of art, where greater clarity is required. To investigate realism in art is immediately to enter into philosophical territory – into questions of ontology and epistemology: of what exists in the world, and how that world can be known.[10]

Lovell distinguishes three critiques of realism. The first, associated with the work of Brecht, is directed against the *formal conventions* of aesthetic realism but not against the view that it is the task of art 'to show things as they really are'. The second, opposed position is mounted from a conventionalist position in the philosophy of science, according to which the representational relation between theories and reality is broken: theory-choice is governed by considerations of internal coherence and even 'aesthetic' criteria. This approach was incorporated into British Marxism and hence into cultural studies via Althusser and his British followers. Its implications for aesthetic theory are a wholesale rejection, not only of realist conventions in art and of the belief that it is the role of art to represent reality, but more fundamentally of the idea that:

> external reality can be represented at all, that it is something which is in principle knowable. The conventionalist objection therefore to the conventions of realism is that realism pretends to be able to do something which cannot be done, and that it succeeds in creating the dangerous *illusion* that it *has* succeeded in representing the real, in 'showing things as they really are'.[11]

Lovell illustrates this position as upheld in literary and cultural theory using Colin MacCabe's now (in)famous account of the 'classic realist text', exemplified by George Eliot's novels. The classic realist text, briefly, is said to perform the work of 'ideology' through features which are both formal and ideologically motivated. The meanings of the text are carried by a 'dominant discourse' which, whether it appears overtly in the form of authorial commentary or covertly in the narrative structure, serves to construct the illusion of reality. Second, the classic realist text relies on an 'identification' between implied reader and character:

> the moment of ideological recognition – that this is indeed the way things are – only occurs when the reader accepts the position offered by the text. In so doing the reader is constituted as a subject and the work of ideological production is complete.[12]

The realist text is said to be 'closed', generating fixed and limited meanings, which the reader can only passively consume.

Against this text is set, as Lovell notes, 'a "progressive", or even "revolutionary", text which bears all the marks of modernism, and is opposed in every respect to the characteristics of the realist text'. Lovell criticizes this position not from a sense of its inadequacies and simplifications, but because it fails to take account of the fact that the modernist and avant-gardist aesthetic it valorizes are 'the exclusive preserve of an intellectual elite encapsulated within existing social relations'. Thus although Lovell states that there is no *necessary* relationship between a specific politics and its (contingently) corresponding aesthetic, current social relations have created a correspondence between class and cultural position and specific aesthetic forms.

The third critique of realism, and the one most fully endorsed by Lovell, includes an acceptance of the epistemological realism shared by Marx, Lukács and Brecht (the view that reality exists independently of our theories about it and that knowledge is the representation of that reality) but challenges the assumption that the realist goal of 'showing things as they really are' follows from Marxist epistemological realism and materialism. Lovell asserts that there is no necessary relationship between epistemological realism and realism in art. She does not, as I have suggested, propose the substitution of a modernist or avant-gardist practice. This, she argues, has created an elitism in art theory and practice while, conversely, the valorization of modernist and avant-gardist aesthetics in cultural theory has fed back into a regrettable, in Lovell's view, redefinition of Marxism as a conventionalist rather than a realist philosophy. Rather than advocating a particular aesthetic to accompany a Marxist politics, she shifts the debate to a questioning of the notion that the functions of art are primarily 'cognitive', reproducing a familiar opposition between the kinds of knowledge produced by art and science respectively and opting for a greater emphasis on what she describes as the 'social pleasures' afforded by cultural forms.

Finally, then, the link between epistemological realism and realism in art is broken by the claim that 'the cognitive functions of art are secondary to it', 'the status of its truths *as* valid knowledge is determined elsewhere than in art, in the univocal language of science and history rather than the polysemic language of art'.[13] Art should not be defined in terms of its 'ideas' but its 'social pleasures', the understanding of which will enrich Marxist approaches to art and culture. The demand is thus for a grounded and referential science and history (whose language is 'univocal') and a mobile aesthetics (whose language is 'polysemic'). Related to this is Lovell's account of scientific and philosophical realism as a given position, whose 'first premiss' can be unequivocally named ('there is an external world which exists independently of consciousness and knowledge of it'), whereas literary realisms are plural and defined contingently, arising in specific historical circumstances and taking their meaning from the practices to which they were and are opposed. Although Lovell, I would argue, draws a crucially important distinction between the varieties of realism, she treats literature, in a rather traditional gesture, as a sphere whose cognitive function, if any, is marginal. She also shifts from the 'nature' of the realist text, whose lineaments remain indistinct, to the ostensible function of literature in general, a move which omits any detailed analysis of realist conventions.

What are the implications of Lovell's book, published some ten years ago against the background of '*Screen* structuralist' approaches to cultural studies, for the relationship between a *feminist* politics and literature? Given that Marxism has largely set the terms for discussion of the politics of literature and the relationship between politics and aesthetics, it has inevitably prestructured subsequent feminist accounts of these relationships. Marxism itself, as Lovell has shown, is polarized between realist and conventionalist metatheories. Feminist theories could be classified in terms of the same dichotomy; where this *has* been done, however, 'realism' has been understood as an empirical realism, rather than one oriented to the structures and mechanisms which may be said to underlie observable phenomena. Like 'Western Marxism', recent feminism has shown a growing preoccupation with the cultural 'superstructure'; as noted above, this has tended to go along with conventionalist forms of Marxism.

Over and above these affinities and influences, important as they may be, there is the more fundamental question whether the mechanisms of women's oppression, to which feminism is a response, are essentially cultural-ideological. To the extent that this is the case, the determination of superstructure by base, a relation attenuated sometimes to the point of disappearance in Western Marxism, is even more problematic. As a corollary, the 'active role of the superstructure' would take on a particular importance in even the most orthodox Marxist feminism. This can be taken to mean either that the 'superstructure' is more than relatively independent and even free-floating, as implied in Lovell's conception of textual and cultural pleasure, or, conversely, that a particular importance attaches to cultural production in the women's movement and feminist politics.

REALISM AND FEMINIST FICTION

Rita Felski's *Beyond Feminist Aesthetics* addresses at length the nature of the links between contemporary fiction and feminism. Her excellent study also demonstrates the move in recent feminist criticism, with which I began, to redeem 'realism' as a critical category and 'realist writing' as a literary practice. Finally, as her title suggests, Felski is writing against the supposition of the 'unifying theory' of a feminist aesthetic which, she argues, has in recent years derived from 'an antirealist aesthetics of textuality'. Reiterating some by now well-rehearsed critical oppositions between Anglo-American and French feminisms, linked, as in Toril Moi's *Sexual/Textual Politics*, with earlier debates between exponents of 'realism' and 'modernism', Felski criticizes the association or equation of the avant-garde and the 'feminine', and asks whether experimental writing can any longer be defined as marginal or subversive. First, like Lovell, she denies the existence of any necessary connection between a specific aesthetic and a politics. Second, however, she suggests that the 'critical negativity' characteristic of modernist and avant-garde writing may be an inappropriate vehicle for a movement like feminism which is strongly oriented to a politics of identity in which literature has a crucial 'affirmative' function.

Here Felski argues that a feminist literary theory must be dependent upon a feminist social theory. Drawing upon the theories of Jürgen Habermas and Anthony Giddens, Felski explores first the concept of a feminist counter-public sphere as a 'discursive community' and second Giddens's account of the 'duality of structure' – the idea, developed in his critique of theories of structural determination, that social structures enable as well as constrain, and that individuals act upon systems at the same time as systems set the terms of selfhood. Felski defines women's writing in relation to the recent women's movement and contemporary feminist politics; the literature she discusses has all been written within this context and is viewed primarily as a mediation of feminism characterized, in Habermasian terms, as a 'new social movement'.

Felski examines two genres – or sub-genres – which she argues are central to contemporary women's fiction – the confession and the novel of self-discovery, one of whose forms is the female *Bildungsroman*, or novel of self-development. She argues that an identity politics such as that of the women's movement will find its most popular forms in literature which foregrounds questions of self-discovery and personal identity. Novels such as Marge Piercy's *Small Changes* and Marilyn French's *The Women's Room* are related to changes at both the social and the symbolic level and demonstrate the significance of women's autonomy and the process of separation for the women's movement. Felski is more critical of her second category of novels of self-development – those, like Atwood's *Surfacing*, whose narrative represents what she sees as a return to Romantic individualism, and the location of the female self in nature and the primitive.

What links all the modes of feminist fiction which Felski discusses is their focus on subjectivity, which she views as central to women's writing and as 'a fundamental category of feminist discourse'.[14] In her account female subjectivity becomes a category produced by a feminist politics. She writes:

> The fact that feminism constitutes an example of a subject-based political movement does not mean that it offers an unfiltered account of female subjectivity. There is no archetypal female subject which provides an ultimate grounding for feminist knowledge; rather, feminist discourse itself constructs a necessarily streamlined conception of subjectivity which can address the politics of gender as relevant to its particular strategic concerns.[15]

This post-Althusserian account of female subjectivity as a 'streamlined' conception – that is, functional and pragmatic in relation to a feminist politics – becomes linked to a correlation between 'subjectivity' and a realist aesthetic. In the 1970s, Felski asserts, after the more overtly politicized culture of the 1960s, 'the problem of self-identity re-emerges as a major cultural preoccupation within Western society':

> Largely because of the influence of feminism, women's writing has been one of the most important recent forums for self-analysis and autobiographical narrative. Insofar as this search for identity is often articulated through texts which attempt the 'close rendering of ordinary experience', and which tend to avoid irony, self-reflexivity and other markers of self-consciously literary discourse, many examples of feminist writing can be described as embracing a form of realism. It is, however, a 'subjective' autobiographical realism which possesses few of the features of the nineteenth century novel. ... The stress is on internal rather than external self, upon the exploration of conflict and ambivalences in relation to the problematics of self-identity ... [it is] centered upon the experiencing consciousness.[16]

A number of points emerge here. First, Felski seems at times to favour a somewhat limited account of modernism, characterized by purely linguistic features. Second, through the focus on the self which is taken as defining modernism (in the 'subjectivist' sense) as well as contemporary realism, the distinction between modernism and realism becomes blurred.[17] Her definitions of contemporary realism are strongly reminiscent of particular definitions of modernist writing, that is, subjectivist and attempting the 'close rendering of ordinary experience'. And, finally, she defines 'literariness' in the same terms as 'literary modernism', now seen in its ironic and self-reflexive manifestations. What she seems to be concerned with is not so much the alleged opposition between realism and modernism *per se* (whether defined as formal conventions or, as elsewhere in Felski's account, as structures of reception) but rather the contrast between a literature in which subjectivity and self-consciousness play a major part and one in which literary or linguistic structures merely play with themselves.

Felski, like Lovell, points to the dangers of asserting any natural relationship between particular literary or aesthetic conventions and a 'radical' politics, although, as I have suggested, she does not discuss the ways in which 'experimental', 'avant-garde' or 'modernist' writing could be a suitable vehicle for a feminist politics. What is being discounted is any link between those 'oppositional' groups in the early twentieth century associated with modernist or avant-gardist writings, and the 'identity politics' of the late twentieth century. She endorses Evelyn Keitel's claim that the oppositional sub-cultures that emerged in the 1970s and 1980s – centred on, for example, feminist or gay politics – 'reclaim[ed] for literary discourse a representative and mimetic function which has been rendered increasingly problematic since modernism. Much of this literature is primarily concerned not with negation but rather with the affirmation of oppositional values and experiences.'[18] This point is repeated throughout Felski's study:

> the current resurgence of Romanticism is to be grasped not merely as a regressive yearning for an idealized past ... but also as a critical exposure of and response to the hegemony of dominant modernist culture which has fetishized constant innovation and change and has effectively repressed all considerations or questions of community, tradition and symbolic identity. The point here is not to argue that it is either possible or desirable to return to the moral or epistemological certainties of a past age, but to develop an alternative account of feminist literature and culture which is able to explain the function of identity and affirmation as well as negativity and critique in the development of an oppositional feminist culture.[19]

The 'new look' at realist fiction supports the concept of an affirmative literature, implicitly or explicitly opposed to Adorno's concept of art as negation or a Kristevan 'negativity'. Once again, however, the terms of the realism/modernism opposition seem to repeat the concepts of those theorists, such as Adorno, from whom Felski and others wish to distance themselves, at least in her stress on the affirmation of opposition. It is unclear, given this distancing, why Felski should seem to echo Adorno's modernism/negativity, realism/affirmation equivalences, reversing the values attached to these rather than questioning the equivalences themselves. Why, for example, is it so difficult to imagine feminist art or literature which is both 'experimental' and 'affirmative' of alternative projects and identities? Moreover, despite her repeated strictures against associating a specific aesthetic with a particular politics, Felski is surely making some such association between realism (however loosely defined) and a politics of identity, even though this link is made against a background of repeated emphases on context and contingency.

FICTION AND FEMINISM

The connection between feminist literature and politics is more emphatically asserted at a narrative and discursive level, in the form of a correspondence, or indeed homology, between feminist fiction and the narratives of the women's movement *per se*. For example, Felski demonstrates 'a number of illuminating parallels between the structure of recent fictions of female identity and narratives of emancipation shaping feminist ideology itself'.[20] In addition to the narrative conjuncture of feminist fictions and political narratives, women's lives and women's plots are associated via the concept of 'symbolic fictions'. The mediation of the women's movement makes new plots possible, while 'the emergence of new plots for women which emphasize autonomy rather than dependence is to be welcomed as an indication of feminism upon the cultural and ideological domain'.[21] Where previous discussions of a feminine/feminist aesthetic and its political correlatives have tended to focus on the style, shape and contour of discrete linguistic/literary units, Felski and others are concerned with the broader dimensions of plot and narrative which, Felski argues, are gendered in a way in which literary 'style' cannot be.

A different perspective is offered by Sara Maitland in her recent essay 'Futures in Feminist Fiction'. Maitland addresses at length the issue of the contribution that feminist fiction can make to feminist politics: 'We do have to ask whether imaginative works are vehicles of social revolution, or time out from the struggle.'[22] She notes that despite earlier attempts to write a new feminist fiction, for example on a collective basis, most feminist novels have not been

> particularly innovative structurally. They have certainly not generated anything that could be seen as a new genre. ... Feminist fiction has been immensely successful in terms of pushing the boundaries of traditional genres out enough to include our interests and our concerns. ... [But] we have failed to do what we believed we would inevitably do which was forge a genre which was *ipso facto* feminist.[23]

(Felski also claims that a 'feminist aesthetic' would be a valid concept only if women writers had created an autonomous form or genre – but she, unlike Maitland, implies that this concept is itself the product of an untenable fantasy of pure difference.) Maitland argues that, given this failure to create 'a genre, a literary discourse of our own', feminist writers now find themselves far more dependent both on what happens to fiction generally and on 'what happens culturally and politically at large'.[24] Whereas 'a form of one's own' might have given feminist fiction a certain independence from both (general) literary and social determinations, its absence means that feminist writers find themselves caught in 'the cultural mainstream', and subject to the same pressures, including the threat of censorship and the current homophobia, as other groups of writers.

These are in many ways curious arguments, and perhaps stem from Maitland's conviction that feminism would be destroyed by assimilation and the loss of oppositional status. The interest of her essay for present purposes is the symbiotic relationship she posits between feminism and its literature: 'since we are and have always been a movement, for quite demonstrable historic reasons, deeply dependent on our printed texts'. Thus the 'cultural failure in feminism ... must reflect a political failure within feminism'.

The literature of feminism is thus endowed, or burdened, with a very large role in sustaining the women's movement. In Maitland's argument, feminist fiction has failed to create the wholly new forms required by the movement. Elsewhere, however, it has been claimed that a weakness of feminism is that it has become overly reliant on its fictions. Paulina Palmer discusses this at the close of her 'radical feminist' study, *Contemporary Women's Fiction*. First, she states,

> the vitality of women's fiction may well indicate, as Freeman implies in her comments on feminist publications, the decline of the Women's Movement from a political organization which seeks to improve women's social and material circumstances to one which is predominantly cultural in nature. Women's feelings of disquiet and anxiety at this decline are reflected, in fact, in works of fiction published in the 1980's.

For Palmer, 'fiction appears to flourish in opposition to, or even perhaps at the expense of, effective political action in the social and material areas of life'.[25] Feminist fiction reveals, in Palmer's view, 'feelings of frustration and irritation at the ineffectualness and fragmentation of *the Women's Movement itself*' – rather than being written 'out of anger at patriarchal oppression and injustice and with the hope of promoting political change'. This seems to imply, rather strangely, that a fiction with political effects would somehow make the movement *less* 'cultural' – although surely it could be argued that the more powerful and effective the fiction, the *more* 'cultural' the movement.

Sara Maitland, in her pursuit of the female future, makes a correlation between 'open-ended texts' (she, like the critics of 'classic realism', inveighs against narrative closure, particularly as it is enforced by 'genre expectations') and the limitless, unrealized possibilities for feminism, which social pressures have curtailed in the same way that the conventions of genre put an end to the story. Thus despite strictures against a so-called social realism, and against a fixed and determinate relationship between a specific aesthetics and politics, Maitland and others are making very strong claims for a homology between fictional form and the shape of the women's movement. 'Futures in Feminist Fiction' must, then, be understood (financial jargon aside) as a question not only about possible literary developments but about the ways in which feminist fiction will or will not prove enabling for the future of feminism itself. A number of critics, indeed, viewing feminism 'futuristically', have opted, against realism, for science-fiction as the most enabling genre for feminism.

The preoccupation with fictional forms is, I would argue, more fundamentally a concern with the shape and form of feminism itself. The attitudes adopted towards the nature of these forms will differ, however. Maitland opts for a collectivism – literary and political – and for the 'transformation' of conventional genres. In other arguments the repudiation of a 'modernist' aesthetic – characterized as fragmentary, self-reflexive and ironic – may derive from a belief that these are not viable characteristics of a political movement and that the 'fragmentations' within the 'movement' must be countermanded at the aesthetic/cultural level, even if they appear incurable in political reality.

This may in part explain, I would suggest, the demand for a literature of integration and affirmation. In other models, however, it has been argued that the anti-chronological and disjunctive forms of the 'female' narrative have always reflected the fragmentariness of women's lives, but in the modern era may well be sustained as positive markers of 'female difference'. Hence the valorization, for example, of such 'diurnal' forms of writing as letters, diaries and journals. Yet the celebration of diversity, plurality and an aesthetic which refuses the traditional ideal of coherence and unity contrasts with the assertion of the coherence of women's shared experience. Questions of a female or feminist aesthetic which are so largely centred on issues of coherence versus fragmentation, unity versus diversity, are not simply a feminist critique of a traditional 'male' aesthetic, but implicitly address concerns about the women's movement itself, and about the difficulty of reconciling increasing demands for the recognition of cultural diversity and women's 'multiple identifications' with a 'coherent politics'. The question then becomes less that of a 'feminist aesthetic' than of what the aesthetic – the narrative form – of feminism might be.

CONCLUSION

Discussions of the relationship between the politics and aesthetics of feminism have been complicated by the cross-cutting opposition between aesthetic options, in particular 'realism' and 'modernism/avant-gardism'. As we have seen, these terms have no single precise sense, and there seems little doubt that the fixation on this alleged opposition, which feminism has inherited from a largely Marxist context of argumentation, has unnecessarily burdened these discussions. Terry Lovell's useful clarification of these issues in relation to Marxist aesthetics has not been fully exploited by subsequent feminist writing. Whereas Lovell showed that a realist ontology did not entail an option for realism as a literary form, many feminist critics have simply assumed the opposite relation, in which any progressive politics, in this case a feminist one, requires a 'progressive' and therefore modernist/avant-gardist aesthetic. Felski's demolition of this assumption and her cautious rehabilitation of literary realism provides a welcome counter to this received wisdom. All of these discussions, however, are insufficiently sensitive to the variety of ways in which one can understand literary representations of the world. Lovell's Marxist *laissez-faire* approach relies to a considerable degree on downplaying the cognitive role of literature. Felski, too, in her exemplary analyses of the social functions of feminist fiction, does not go as far as she might into asking just how realist literature of the kind she favours, or for that matter any literature, can or might represent an external reality.

A second burden on our attempts to clarify the relationship between feminist politics and aesthetics, as in the case of Marxism, lies in the polarization of the two terms; a reductionist and instrumentalist conception of the political role of literature, criticized by Lovell and Felski, and an aesthetics which has tended towards a glib rejection of the very concept of representation as reference. Against this extreme polarization the desired mediation between the two terms has taken the mythical form of an aestheticization of the political, in this case the shape and narrative of the women's movement, itself represented in a developmental form with clear analogies to the novel. As I have attempted to show, strictures against the correlation between a specific politics and a particular aesthetic (modernism/radicalism, realism/conservatism) have not prevented a number of critics from producing at least two new correlations: first, the association of 'realism' and an identity politics, and second, and perhaps more interestingly, the homology between novelistic structures and the narrative of feminism. We should exercise, I would suggest, no less caution in relation to these more precise connections than we should in re-examining those which have pervaded both Marxist and feminist aesthetics.

NOTES

1 Rita Felski, *Beyond Feminist Aesthetics: Feminist Literature and Social Change* (London: Hutchinson Radius, 1989), p. 14.
2 ibid., p. 80.
3 ibid., p. 179.
4 Ernst Bloch, Theodor Adorno, Walter Benjamin, Bertolt Brecht and Georg Lukács, *Aesthetics and Politics* (London: New Left Books, 1977), p. 82.
5 Andreas Huyssen, *After the Great Divide: Modernism, Mass Culture and Postmodernism* (London: Macmillan, 1986), p. 49.
6 ibid., p. 61.
7 Moira Monteith, *Women's Writing: A Challenge to Theory* (Brighton: Harvester Press 1986), pp. 2–3.
8 Toril Moi, *Sexual/Textual Politics: Feminist Literary Theory* (London: Methuen, 1985), p. 47.
9 Penny Boumelha, 'Realism and the Ends of Feminism' in *Grafts: Feminist Cultural Criticism*, ed. Susan Sheridan (London: Verso, 1988), p. 81.
10 Terry Lovell, *Pictures of Reality: Aesthetics, Politics, Pleasure* (London: British Film Institute, 1980), p. 6.

11 ibid., p. 84.
12 ibid., p. 85.
13 ibid., p. 91.
14 Felski, op. cit., p. 71.
15 ibid., p. 73.
16 ibid., p. 82.
17 ibid., p. 81.
18 ibid., p. 94.
19 ibid., p. 153.
20 ibid., p. 122.
21 ibid., p. 152.
22 Sara Maitland, 'Futures in Feminist Fiction' in *From My Guy to Sci-Fi: Genre and Women's Writing in the Postmodern World*, ed. Helen Carr (London: Pandora, 1989), p. 195.
23 ibid., pp. 197–8.
24 ibid., p. 199.
25 Paulina Palmer, *Contemporary Women's Fiction: Narrative Practice and Feminist Theory* (Hemel Hempstead: Harvester Wheatsheaf, 1989), p. 164.

Chapter 3

Walking, women and writing
Virginia Woolf as *flâneuse*

Rachel Bowlby

PRE-AMBLE

Since this piece is about walking it seems reasonable to start out with a footnote. This will be covered, later on, by a bootnote. A footnote should be at the end; this one, right at the start, takes us back, to Plato's *Symposium*, to the speech of Aristophanes in that text, and its recounting of an unfinished history of walking – in fact of the prehistory of walking, a sort of pre-walk, recounted by Aristophanes, which will be my pre-amble.[1] *The Symposium* is anyway constructed around a walk (the narrator got it from his friend as they strolled into Athens), and this walk partly involves the recounting of another walk (at the beginning, Socrates goes with his companion to a drinking party). Aristophanes' tale is about the pre-walk and pre-women (and pre-men too) that make their later variants look strange, make the image of normality (upright men and women) seem deviant, a humorous wrong turning, in relation to the beings from which they originated.

Plato's Aristophanes tells the story of how humans were first of all divided into three, not two sexes: the male, the female and the male-female, known as the androgyne or hermaphrodite. Each of these, from the later perspective, are double: they have two heads facing outwards, two arms, two legs, and so on. Punishing them for aiming too high and trying to climb up to heaven (ambition is the first urging), Zeus has them all cut in half: the all-males divide into two males, the all-females into two females and the androgyne into male and female. Having lost their other half, literally, all these creatures long to be reunited with it. This is the origin of desire, as a wish to restore an earlier state of things. It is also the origin of male and female homosexuality (the desires of the halves of all-males and the halves of all-females) and of heterosexuality (the desire of each half of the former male-female, the androgyne).

In the twentieth century, in the context of the widespread and newly 'scientific' interest in questions of sexual tendencies and the differences of the sexes, this part of *The Symposium* has been a constant source of fascination, and in particular it offers a myth of the equal naturalness of homosexual and heterosexual tendencies – or at least for none being more natural than the others. Freud alludes to the story several times – in the context of the death drive (the wish to restore an earlier state) and also in relation to sexuality. In the *Three Essays on the Theory of Sexuality*, he uses it when introducing to his readers the idea that not all sexual desire is between the two sexes:

> The popular view of the sexual instinct is beautifully reflected in the poetic fable which tells how the original human beings were cut up into two halves – man and woman – and how these are always striving to unite again in love. It comes as a great surprise therefore to learn that there are men whose sexual object is a man and not a woman, and women whose sexual object is a woman and not a man.[2]

But what comes as an even greater surprise here is that Freud has mis-remembered the myth to which he is referring. He takes it as solidly het-erosexual, in order to reinforce the norm he is going to surprise his readers by disturbing, whereas in fact the existence of homosexuality, of what the next sentence calls – in inverted commas – 'inversion' is exactly what Aristophanes' story would lead us to assume.

This misremembering of Plato – Freud lights on exactly the right spot to prove his point but inverts its significance – is surprisingly common. Freud forgets the homosexual pairs all the better to produce them as a scandalous novelty; other readers develop an opposite tendency, remembering only the naturalization of homosexuality and omitting the heterosexual member of the trio, equally natural in the myth of origin. Sometimes, the hybrid her-maphrodite alone is remembered, but taken as an image of original perversity, whereas it is in fact this creature, who looks most monstrous to modern eyes, which is the origin of the norm, male and female heterosexuality. And it follows from this too that far from being a paragon of polymorphousness or promiscuity, as it is often taken to be, the post-hermaphrodite, and the other two kinds as well, are probably the most unswervingly monogamous creatures that ever walked the earth: they all want nothing better and nothing more than to rejoin forever their one and only lost other half.

But to use the terms heterosexual and homosexual is already to distort again. For in a sense all three sexual types are both homosexual and het-erosexual. They all seek to reunite with someone of the same sex (man to man from the all-male, woman to woman from the all-woman, man to woman from the hermaphrodite). And they all seek to form a couple: the 'hetero-' preposition has nothing to do with male and female but simply means 'the other of two'. These disorientations of view then suggest some further speculations about the categorical blinkers through which we tend to talk about homosexuality and heterosexuality, as about men and women. Freud is not yet using the terms 'homosexual' and 'heterosexual' when he writes the *Three Essays* in 1905; later on, he does. The words are new constructions of his time, consciously formed from Greek roots as so many scientific terms were at the time. Freud does not see male and female homosexuality as parallel formations united in the same difference from heterosexuality. But yoking the two forms of homosexuality under the same word, as our language now does, reinforces a dual opposition between heterosexuality and homosexuality; and it fixes the perspective in advance by implying that they have more in common with each other than they do with heterosexuality.

Later, as I said, these three inconceivable figures may return to haunt us or kick us in a bootnote, in the form of some other odd trios which disturb the securely dual vision of the difference between the sexes and their respective orientations. For now, though, it is time to move forward to a later, more familiar episode in the history of walking and sexuality.

THE FLANEUR

I am going to talk about walking and my paper, perhaps inevitably, will be a bit of a ramble. I shall be focusing for much of the time on writing by Woolf, after first looking at some texts by Baudelaire and Proust. The title 'Walking, women and writing' is not only meant to allude to the questions Woolf raises all the time, in her novels and in her essays, about the relations between women and writing, art and sex, fiction and femininity, and to the way in which she has been taken up as a key source for enlightenment on such issues; it is also intended to recall the expression 'wine, women and song'. Not to suggest that the pleasures of wine are replaced for Woolf by the perhaps less obvious pleasures of the obligatory constitutional: after all, it is she who, in *A Room of One's Own*, having experienced the differences in dining facilities between two 'Oxbridge' colleges, one for each sex, demands 'Why did men drink wine and women water?',[3] suggesting the benefits of wine for inspiration. Instead, the change of words is supposed to evoke the way in which Woolf puts in question the traditional status of women as at once the inspiration of literature and its object: as represented, but not themselves writers.

In thinking about women's writing there is a tension which comes back again and again between, on the one hand, narratives of straightforward advance, whereby modern women are taken to be slowly putting past restrictions behind them, getting to stand on their own two feet and write what they want; and, on the other, the description of formal structures of exclusion, whereby what does not go along with a norm defined as masculine is taken as disruptive of established spaces and in a certain sense feminine. The distinction is between access to something regarded as neutral, and subversion of something defined as both normative and masculine. This tension is explored throughout Woolf's own writing about women's writing. Sometimes she talks of 'impediments' – literally what stands in the way of the feet – obstacles without which women would be able to move on. And sometimes she talks of the outsider's place, the position of exclusion, as the origin of a difference of view which is valuable precisely in that it does not fit in with and thereby challenges the standard. Following this line, certain or not, we could simplify the two alternatives as between two sorts of walk or step – progressive, or the forward step in a given direction; and transgressive, or the walk that crosses and challenges set lines of demarcation, a step from a place represented as beyond the pale, out of bounds.

Let us start, however, from the male walker or writer from whom the woman has to take one of her leads, whether to follow him or to throw him off course. The figure of the *flâneur* epitomizes a distinctive nineteenth-century conception of the writer as walker, a sort of man about town with ample leisure and money to roam the city and look about him.

A PASSANTE

The place of the walker as writer is marked out as a masculine identity which places women already as part of the representation. Before thinking of or passing to other possibilities, we may cast a glance at her whose generic name brings together all the characteristics shared by the women viewed by the *flâneur*: the *passante* or 'passing woman', who is at once anonymous, elusive and of the city. Baudelaire's poem 'A une passante', 'To a Passing Woman' (1860) is perhaps the classical evocation of this figure:

> La rue assourdissante autour de moi hurlait.
> Longue, mince, en grand deuil, douleur majestueuse,
> Une femme passa, d'une main fastueuse
> Soulevant, balançant le feston et l'ourlet;
>
> Agile et noble, avec sa jambe de statue.
> Moi, je buvais, crispé comme un extravagant,
> Dans son oeil, ciel livide où germe l'ouragan,
> La douceur qui fascine et le plaisir qui tue.
>
> Un éclair ... puis la nuit! – Fugitive beauté
> Dont le regard m'a fait soudainement renaître,
> Ne te verrai-je plus que dans l'éternité?
>
> Ailleurs, bien loin d'ici! trop tard! *jamais* peut-être!
> Car j'ignore où tu fuis, tu ne sais où je vais,
> O toi que j'eusse aimée, o toi qui le savais![4]

Amid the clatter and din of the street, there she is; or there she was, no sooner there than gone, vanishing, disappearing, here only in what is now the loss of her. But the poem brings her back: gone/here, *fort/da*: brings her back fixed and no longer fleeing, but fixed as one who flees, 'fugitive', runaway, 'tu fuis'.

He looked, she looked; I looked, you looked; there was an instant, it could have been for ever, it is past.

You knew, 'toi qui le savais', you didn't say. Silent woman who knows, whom he sees knowing, who will not or cannot say.

He looks at her, she looks at him. Two looks, his at her and hers at him? Two looks fusing into one? Or two looks, different? Or one look, his that sees her seeing him (seeing her (seeing him . . .))?

She brought new life ('m'a fait soudainement renaître'), and is also a murderer ('le plaisir qui tue') coming in funeral garments, who fled away free ('Fugitive beauté', 'tu fuis'). In mourning, she has lost someone; she transmits her loss to him, leaving him marked by her passing. Death-dealer and life-giver, a mother.

A twofold mother: 'Moi, je buvais', 'I was drinking', in her eye, nourishing eye and evil eye, 'la douceur qui fascine et le plaisir qui tue'.

Anonymous: any woman, 'une femme'. And also the one and only, the unique woman, love eternal, at first and last sight.[5]

Two women seen in one. She is 'noble', 'majestueuse', a queen or goddess with her statuesque leg; unavailable, inaccessible, she is not to be approached. At the same time the woman of the street, the street-walker. A fast ('fugitive') lady. The whore, undomesticated, whose home is the *maison de passe*, the street inside.

From the third person, 'une femme', to the second, 'toi', addressed at the end. 'Ô toi que j'eusse aimée!', you whom I would have loved, past unfulfilled conditional – if what? No answer: she disappeared, never to return, con-secrated in the restoration of the imaginary moment when it might have been that she was there. Unconditional love: under no conditions could it be, its possibility is past, ruled out, from the start; and also without interference from external conditions of space and time, in eternity.

The timing puts her definitively in the past, bygone, as the one who passed, irrevocably, and yet will have marked him forever. She is out of time, no sooner here than gone, represented only in her absence. And out of time because only 'in eternity', in the timeless, will he see her again. There was a flash of light, 'un éclair', then darkness, 'puis la nuit'. The snapshot of what looked like a woman, caught, taken, in an instant, remaining only in an image, the picture of her.

In the distance between them, only their eyes 'meet'; otherwise they are apart. He is fixed, transfixed ('crispé'); it is she who moves, 'passa' across the field of his vision. On this separation between them, in space as in time, depends her perfection, and the unconditional quality of the love.

THE PASSANTE

But we have not seen the last of this *passante*, a *passante*. She turns up again, and repeatedly, in Proust's vast novel. Here is one such occasion:

> Les charmes de la passante sont généralement en relation directe avec la
> rapidité du passage. Pour peu que la nuit tombe et que la voiture aille vite,

à la campagne, dans une ville, il n'y a pas un torse féminin, mutilé comme un marbre antique par la vitesse qui nous entraîne et le crépuscule qui le noie, qui ne tire sur notre coeur, à chaque coin de route, au fond de chaque boutique, les flêches de la Beauté, de la Beauté dont on serait parfois tenté de se demander si elle est en ce monde autre chose que la partie de complément qu'ajoute à une passante fragmentaire et fugitive notre imagination surexcitée par le regret.[6]

Proust's *passante* might be a direct descendant of Baudelaire's. 'Fugitive' once more, she is the fleeting impression, only there in the moment that she is already gone. She is statuesque, 'comme un marbre antique', both noble and dead, her own monument, like the 'jambe de statue' of the sonnet. But the 'mutilated', 'fragmentary' nature of Proust's *passante* also, now, looking back, seems to have been shared by that 'statue's leg', just one leg, one part, singled out by Baudelaire. And the 'regret' here is similar to what is inferred from the poet's 'ô toi que j'eusse aimée', her loss the condition for the desire of her, and for the conditional being necessarily in the odd time of the 'past unfulfilled'.

The *passante* here seems to have moved on or away from her Baudelairean singularity, fixed now into a type: not '*une*', but '*la*' passante. There is not even a question, this time, of a look in return, from her. 'Fugitive' still, her fleeting appearance is not because she passes – she may be quite stationary, in the back of a shop – but because he does – or because 'we' do, a community of (masculine) readers invoked for the occasion as sharing in, recognizing, this as a commonplace experience, and the appeal to whom is a further reinforcement of the generalization of the scene. And if we ignore generic differences between lyric poetry and narrative prose, we could note that whereas the poem, in its title and in the concluding apostrophe ('ô toi ... ') is addressed to a particular *passante*, Proust's narrator addresses 'us' who are not *passantes* but viewers of *passantes*, on the subject of *passantes*, a general category. The generality of the experience, recognized as an example of a common type, removes its apparent uniqueness and irrevocability: one *passante* is like another in that she can be replaced, that another and another will figure in the same way, without there being any single, constitutive event, even in retrospect.

Putting the two together, Proust's spectator appears to extend and confirm what was only potentially there in the Baudelaire poem. Quite explicitly, the *passante* is now (in every sense) a mere projection from the spectator.[7] Her passing is really his, as he zooms by just catching sight of her; her partial and fleeting appearance belongs to the same phenomenon. Whence the hypothesis that Beauty might just be 'the complementary part added to a fragmentary and fugitive *passante* by our over-excited imagination'. The 'Beauty' is not out there, but born of 'our' own 'imagination surexcitée'; it is *added* as the missing, 'complementary' part to make a whole of what would otherwise be just the fragmentary vision. It is this addition, carried over to her from us, which completes her, raising her up to the heights of a capitalized essence. 'La Beauté' substantializes her fragmentariness and puts a stop to her disappearance, her passing ('fugitive'). It fits her to him, makes her in the image of his 'imagination surexcitée' prompted by her loss, 'le regret'.

Let us note, before leaving Proust's multiple *passantes*, that the mutation of this figure into pure projection, pure fantasy, may well mark an important turning-point in the unpredictable passage of or to women walking and writing. One moment in the course of *A la recherche du temps perdu* brings this sharply into focus. It is the single occasion on which the narrator makes the mistake of actually pursuing a passing woman:

> Je n'ai jamais rencontré dans la vie de filles aussi désirables que les jours où j'étais avec quelque grave personne que malgré les mille prétextes que j'inventais, je ne pouvais quitter: quelques années après celle où j'allais pour la première fois à Balbec, faisant à Paris une course en voiture avec un ami de mon père et ayant aperçu une femme qui marchait vite dans la nuit, je pensai qu'il était déraisonnable de perdre pour une raison de convenances, ma part de bonheur dans la seule vie qu'il y ait sans doute, et sautant à terre sans m'excuser, je me mis à la recherche de l'inconnue, la perdis au carrefour de deux rues, la retrouvai dans une troisième, et me trouvai enfin, tout essoufflé, sous un réverbère, en face de la vieille Mme Verdurin que j'évitais partout et qui, surprise et heureuse, s'écria: 'Oh! comme c'est aimable d'avoir couru pour me dire bonjour!'[8]

Neither beautiful, young nor anonymous, Mme Verdurin is the antithesis of every defining characteristic of the *passante*, quashing the enigma with the brutality of her all too familiar familiarity. Given that so many mistakes can be made which, in the normal course of things – when the narrator has the sense to keep his *passante* at an imaginary distance – go unnoticed and have no effect, we might consider dropping the only remaining attribute which links the actual and the imaginary *passante* here. For Mme Verdurin, whatever else she lacks or possesses, is, after all, still apparently a woman. But Proust could have gone even further. For if the *passante* is merely or mostly the man's projection, a creature of the masculine imagination, then the field, or rather the street, might be thought to have been left wide open for women to come along and walk in a way of their own – or for quite different, unrecognizable kinds of passer-by to appear.

WOOLF'S PASSANTE

Woolf's work contains extended explorations of the relations between women, walking and writing; so much, sometimes, does it appear that the three are natural companions for her that it is sometimes as if the figure of the masculine *flâneur* had been pushed off satirically down a cul-de-sac, as someone from whom the adventuring woman had nothing at all to fear (still less to desire), on the streets or on the page. Yet the street is not empty of men, of their way of representing women or of a woman's of seeing herself as represented by them.

Such an encounter is wittily enacted by a section from *Mrs Dalloway*. Peter Walsh, who has left Clarissa's house until the evening party, finds his attention diverted by a classical *passante*:

> But she's extraordinarily attractive, he thought, as, walking across Trafalgar Square in the direction of the Haymarket, came a young woman who, as she passed Gordon's statue, seemed, Peter Walsh thought (susceptible as he was), to shed veil after veil, until she became the very woman he had always had in mind; young, but stately; merry, but discreet; black, but enchanting.[9]

With its alternation of clichéd attributes of a certain version of ideal femininity, the 'shedding of veil after veil' to reveal not so much uniqueness as indistinctness, or rather uniqueness *as* indistinctness, a fantasy 'everywoman', the passage is already bordering on parodic literary stereotype. Woolf does not let go:

> Straightening himself and stealthily fingering his pocket-knife he started after her to follow this woman, this excitement, which seemed even with its back turned to shed on him a light which connected them, which singled him out, as if the random uproar of the traffic had whispered through hallowed hands his name, not Peter, but his private name which he called himself in his own thought. 'You,' she said, only 'you,' saying it with her white gloves and her shoulders. Then the thin long cloak which the wind stirred as she walked past Dent's shop in Cockspur Street blew out with an enveloping kindness, a mournful tenderness, as of arms that would open and take the tired –
>
> (*MD*, 48)

The paragraph, which ends with just this uncertain and hasty dash, continues the satire, most blatantly with the fingered pocket-knife, but then with the neutralization of 'this woman, this excitement ... its back', and with the revelation of the 'most private' of names as the generally applicable 'you'. As in the Baudelaire poem, this woman becomes both an enfolding mother (her 'enveloping kindness', but with a hint of smothering) and a mourner.

In the next paragraph Peter wonders whether she is 'respectable'; then he imagines a meeting: '"Come and have an ice," he would say, and she would answer, perfectly simply, "Oh yes"' (*MD*, 49). This happy conclusion is followed by Peter's and her metamorphosis into hero and heroine of a romantic story. Their respective sexual qualities are drawn out, by distinction or assimilation, from the window displays in the shops they pass:

> He was an adventurer, reckless, he thought, swift, daring, indeed (landed

as he was last night from India) a romantic buccaneer, careless of all these damned proprieties, yellow dressing-gowns, pipes, fishing-rods, in the shop windows; wearing white slips beneath their waistcoats. He was a buccaneer. On and on she went, across Piccadilly, and up Regent Street, ahead of him, her cloak, her gloves, her shoulders combining with the fringes and the laces and the feather boas in the windows to make the spirit of finery and whimsy which dwindled out of the shops onto the pavement.

(*MD*, 49)

The displays in the luxury shops are sharply differentiated by sex. But whereas Peter's buccaneering identity is defined by its difference from the accoutrements of masculinity on display, the desirability of his quarry is seen precisely as an extension of the fetishistically feminine bits and pieces visible as they pass. Peter's proud display of himself as distinct from other men and their 'damned proprieties' is parodied in his pursuit of a femininity as predictable as the dull masculinity he is consciously refusing.

The outcome of Peter's pursuit of his *passante* is as embarrassing as that of Proust coming upon Mme Verdurin, but for a different reason:

Laughing and delightful, she had crossed Oxford Street and Great Portland Street and turned down one of the little streets, and now, and now, the great moment was approaching, for now she slackened, opened her bag, and with one look in his direction, but not at him, one look that bade farewell, summed up the whole situation and dismissed it triumphantly, for ever, had fitted her key, opened the door, and gone!

(*MD*, 49)

The passage works as the parody of the amorous clinch or climax that might have been expected: the three times culminating 'now' of 'and now, and now, the great moment was approaching, for now she slackened ...', as well as that of the *passante* encounter itself, with the girl's 'one look', twice named, signifying something else entirely from what the convention requires, what Peter desires. The *passante* narrative, in other words, still stands, as the dominant street story, but knowingly fictionalized: 'for it was half made up, as he knew very well; invented, this escapade with the girl; made up, as one makes up the better part of life' (*MD*, 50). Here, the look, not even at him, is nonetheless for him, indicating her understanding of the 'situation' she sums up. The inclusion of the *passante*'s angle of view has produced a parody of the genre whose conventions are clearly understood by both parties, transforming it into a gentle power game where she comes out with the victory, 'triumphantly', her bag containing a key more decisive and more serviceable than the pocket-knife, and which rapidly brings things to a close.

Peter's imaginary girl with her own latch-key and her playful rejection of standard femininity is a model New Woman; further on in *Mrs Dalloway*, Woolf offers us another version in 18-year-old Elizabeth Dalloway, whose foray on top of a bus brings her into close affinity with the daring masculinity adopted by Peter Walsh. For Elizabeth takes on the qualities of a buc-caneering bus, 'the impetuous creature – a pirate' (*MD*, 120), and does so by an overt distinction from the literary femininity in whose terms she is starting to be perceived: 'it was beginning. ... People were beginning to compare her to poplar trees, early dawn, hyacinths, fawns, running water, and garden lilies' (*MD*, 119–20). Elizabeth's adventure on a bus is an adolescent equivalent of the dismissal of the *passante* scene accomplished by Peter Walsh's girl, in which she becomes a sort of tomboy female pirate.

These vignettes might lead us to imagine that the street-walking scene is being surreptitiously shifted, moving the *passante* out of focus to make way for something like a feminine *flânerie*. Perhaps this explains the very first words of the novel's heroine: ' "I love walking in London", said Mrs Dallo-way. "Really, it's better than walking in the country" ' (*MD*, 7). What else, after all, would Clarissa's surname have led us to expect than, the woman who likes to dally along the way, the *flâneuse* herself?

A ROAD OF ONE'S OWN

It might seem outlandish to think of *A Room of One's Own*, which is all about the importance of an inside, personal space for the woman writer, as having any connection with the links between women, walking and writing in Woolf's work. Yet the book is structured throughout by an imaginary ramble (through 'Oxbridge', London and the British Museum, and through many byways of bookish history), leading up to the point at which the narrator represents herself sitting down to start writing what she has just recounted. The literal and the recorded walk thus overlay one another so as to play upon the difficulty of differentiating them. As with *A la recherche du temps perdu*, the circular structure is such that the end sends you straight back to the beginning; but Proust's novel is not set out, as is *A Room of One's Own*, as a *flânerie*. For Woolf, it is as though casual walking were the only possible way of dealing with such an intractable subject for a lecture as 'women and fiction'.

A Room of One's Own has many direct evocations of this fictional stroll: 'I had come at last, in the course of this rambling, to the shelves which hold books by the living' (*ROO*, 79); 'And with Mrs Behn, we turn a very important corner in the road' (*ROO*, 64); 'I spare you the twists and turns of my cogitations, for no conclusion was found on the road to Headingley' (*ROO*, 17). The figure of rambling serves to suggest the argument which turns into the narrative of its own lack of an ending:

> I have shirked the duty of coming to a conclusion upon these questions – women and fiction remain, so far as I am concerned, unsolved problems. But in order to make some amends I am going to do what I can to show you how I arrived at this opinion about the room and the money.
>
> (*ROO*, 6)

'How I arrived', in the context of the general language of strolling and rambling, exposes one of a whole clutch of metaphors which writers and readers normally pass by without a second glance. Introduction, digression, excursus, passage: it is as though the very grounds of rhetoric were made for walking on, measured out in properly poetical metres and feet.

But there are also stopping points in Woolf's text where the city walk provides a more elaborated analogy for the writer's stamping ground:

> There came to my mind's eye one of those long streets somewhere south of the river whose infinite rows are innumerably populated. With the eye of the imagination I saw a very ancient lady crossing the street on the arm of a middle-aged woman, her daughter, perhaps, both so respectably booted and furred that their dressing in the afternoon must be a ritual.
>
> (*ROO*, 88)

What starts here as a typical ('one of those') and imaginary ('in my mind's eye') street soon becomes specific and actual, with the narrator acting as though it were not in her own power to determine the description or meaning of the characters 'I saw'. The scene then becomes precisely a question of specification:

> The elder is close on eighty. . . . And if one asked her, longing to pin down the moment with date and season, But what were you doing on the fifth of April 1868, or the second of November 1875, she would look vague and say that she could remember nothing. For all the dinners are cooked; the plates and cups washed; the children sent to school and gone out into the world. Nothing remains of it all. All has vanished. No biography or history has a word to say about it. And the novels, without meaning to, inevitably lie.
>
> (*ROO*, 89–90)

The disingenuousness of this is blatant: the lady is a fictional invention to begin with – a projection, perhaps of the 'overexcited imagination' of the woman writer. But that is only to say that the usual fiction that the subject is not a fiction – as though the narrator had simply said 'I saw an old lady of eighty' – has here been shown up. Though the final sentences seem to deplore the absence of solid written evidence for the woman's everyday life, or else its distortion in the novels which 'inevitably lie', the self-consciously fictional framing of the argument undermines the possibility of differentiating the facts from the errors. This gives a quite distinct cast to the proposal for future writing projects:

> All these infinitely obscure lives remain to be recorded, I said . . . and went on in thought through the streets of London feeling in imagination the pressure of dumbness, the accumulation of unrecorded life, whether from the women at the street corners with their arms akimbo, and the rings embedded in their fat swollen fingers, talking with a gesticulation like the

swing of Shakespeare's words; or from the violet-sellers and match-sellers and old crones stationed under doorways; or from drifting girls whose faces, like waves in sun and cloud, signal the coming of men and women and the flickering lights of shop windows.

(*ROO*, 89)

Some very unexpected moves are going on here. It is a self-conscious poeticization of the never before recorded lives which first suggests itself, through the Shakespearean gestures or the girls with faces 'like waves in sun and cloud', as though Woolf were pointing out the risks of assuming that words could act as a pristine or undistorted medium for the new records demanded of them. And then, the unrecordedness of the lives is in the eyes or the 'feeling' of the beholder, who, as in the case of the old lady and her daughter, is only a beholder 'in imagination'. She hereby records what she declares at once unrecorded (a presumed fact) and fictional (her own invention). What looks to the eye of the reader like a predictable call for indiscriminate documentary detail is actually a passage which creates all sorts of complications about the claims of documentary writing and the claims or place of the documentary observer.

So when, elsewhere in *A Room of One's Own*, the narrator speaks of 'the fascination of the London street' (*ROO*, 94), or when she urges her audience of Newnham College students to 'loiter at street corners' as one of the means 'to write all kinds of books' (*ROO*, 107), she is advocating a form of female street-walking or street-writing which is clearly going to deviate from any expected routes. It is not so straightforward a matter to urge that women make up for lost ground and lost time, even though that is also part of the plea; and it is not evident that one woman can simply call for or advocate the representation of other women as though that were a neutral question of inclusion and access, as though the writer objectively picked out and covered a topic or subject that was simply there, awaiting but not to be modified by her attention.

'STREET HAUNTING'

In a diary entry from May 1928 Woolf wrote: 'London itself perpetually attracts, stimulates, gives me a play and a story and a poem, without any trouble save that of moving my legs through the streets.'[10] The essay entitled 'Street Haunting', written in 1930, is probably her most graphic development of this statement. The piece dramatizes the evening walk through the streets of London of a narrator constantly fabricating or recording the stories around her; walking the streets becomes, in effect, the background or ground for story-making (at once, and indistinguishably, its necessary preliminary or pre-amble and its milieu, the place of the story). At the outset – setting off – the narrator declares, disingenuously, that her sortie involves a purely spurious object, an 'excuse for walking half across London between tea and dinner' to justify the pleasure.[11] That object is nothing else than the purchase of a pencil, of the means of writing. At the end of the essay the appointed purchase is duly made, after the narrator has entered a stationer's for the purpose (the purpose of fulfilling the fake purpose). There are two other shops she goes into during the course of her wanderings. Given the connection made in the diary between writing and walking, and given that the pencil is already taken care of, it seems wholly fitting that one of these should be a boot shop. But we are getting ahead of ourselves and must first retrace our steps to the start of the essay/adventure.

Leaving the house is accompanied, for the narrator, by a loss of personal identity:

> We are no longer quite ourselves. As we step out of the house on a fine evening between four and six, we shed the self our friends know us by and become part of that vast republican army of anonymous trampers, whose society is so agreeable after the solitude of one's own room.
>
> (*CE*, 4: 155)

The move outside involves the removal of individuality for anonymity, and the shift from stability – one fixed place – to mobility, a peaceable 'army' on the move. Already there are some odd shifts here: 'ourselves' is equivocally identified with the projection or externalization of 'the self our friends know us by'. The friends are associated with the house that is being temporarily left; but then it turns out that pleasant companionship ('agreeable' 'society') is actually to be found out of doors and among the 'anonymous'. On the very threshold of her walk, the narrator has already effected some striking displacements which should serve as hints of what is to come.

This shedding of self will quickly be given another simile, another walking attribute:

> The shell-like covering which our souls have excreted to house themselves, to make for themselves a shape distinct from others, is broken, and there is left of all these wrinkles and roughnesses a central oyster of perceptiveness, an enormous eye. How beautiful a street is in winter!
>
> (*CE*, 4: 156)

A corollary, then, of the move from self to anonymity is the change from 'I' to eye, from pronoun to organ, the recording eye of 'a central oyster of perceptiveness'.[12] A little further on, we discover more of its attributes. First, this is an eye which looks to surfaces, not to an in-depth examination:

> But, after all, we are only gliding smoothly on the surface. The eye is not a miner, not a diver, not a seeker after buried treasure. It floats us smoothly down a stream; resting, pausing, the brain perhaps sleeps as it looks. ...
>
> But here we must stop peremptorily. We are in danger of digging deeper than the eye approves; we are impeding our passage down the smooth

stream by catching at some branch or root. . . . Let us dally a little longer, be content still with surfaces only.

(*CE*, 4: 156–7)

The surface looking advocated here does not imply that there is no depth, but that its evasion is part of what defines the pleasures of all-eye looking. Dallying is superficial, 'surfaces only'. To dig deeper, far from being an obligation, is a danger.

And this leads on to one final characteristic: the spontaneous aestheticism of this roving eye:

> For the eye has this strange property: it rests only on beauty; like a butterfly it seeks colour and basks in warmth. On a winter's night like this, when nature has been at pains to polish and preen herself, it brings back the prettiest trophies, breaks off little lumps of emerald and coral as if the whole earth were made of precious stone. The thing it cannot do (one is speaking of the average unprofessional eye) is to compose these trophies in such a way as to bring out the more obscure angles and relationships. Hence after a prolonged diet of this simple sugary fare, of beauty pure and uncomposed, we become conscious of satiety. We halt at the door of the boot shop . . .

(*CE*, 4: 157)

Here the eye has become a mouth, a consumer of sweet things, 'sugary fare'. There is a frivolity, an avowed superficiality, shared in common by the spectator (the eye 'like a butterfly') and the surface from which it takes its selection ('the prettiest trophies'). The flirtatiousness of nature, 'at pains to polish and preen herself' seems to rub off her synaesthetic sensuality on to the 'butterfly' eye which seeks not only colour but warmth and touch (it 'breaks off little lumps').

The superficial sauntering of this eye finds its most perfect expression or egression in window-shopping. The first example has already suggested this:

> Let us dally a little longer, be content still with surfaces only – the glossy brilliance of the motor omnibuses; the carnal splendour of the butchers' shops with their yellow flanks and purple steaks; the blue and red bunches of flowers burning so bravely through the plate glass of the florists' windows.

(*CE*, 4: 157)

Colour, the surface view, takes precedence over distinctions of substance, say between meat and flowers. The transparency of the plate-glass windows seems, like the glossy omnibuses, to go along with a deliberate indulgence in purely visual pleasures at the expense of all else.

At the expense, in fact, of expense: this process is extended even further when looking in shop windows is represented as a pleasurable end in itself, unconnected with a potential purchase:

> Passing, glimpsing, everything seems accidentally but miraculously sprin-
> kled with beauty, as if the tide of trade which deposits its burden so
> punctually and prosaically upon the shores of Oxford Street had this night
> cast up nothing but treasure. With no thought of buying, the eye is sportive
> and generous; it creates, it adorns; it enhances. Standing out in the street,
> one may build up all the chambers of an imaginary house and furnish
> them at one's will with sofa, table, carpet.
>
> (*CE*, 4: 160)

The 'treasure' here is not excavated, the depth beneath a surface, but 'cast
up' spontaneously. 'Passing, glimpsing', the *passante* has become the mobile
spectator herself, not the one who is glimpsed, her active looking making an
implicit contrast with what now appears to have been the passivity of the
woman seen by the masculine *flâneur*.

But this is not the only possible reading of 'Street Haunting'. To read it
like this involves just the same kind of selectivity as the eye is supposed to
perform, with its 'butterfly' flitting to and fro, alighting only on what pleases
it, or even imagining what suits it: 'it creates'. Pursuing a different trail, we
would see quite other things along the way of Woolf's essay. Its title, after
all, might suggest that there is more going on than a simple, naive delight.
'Haunting' is almost a homonym of one of the possible English words for
translating *flâner*: 'sauntering'. In a diary entry from a few years before,
Woolf had written: 'I like this London life in early summer – the street
sauntering & square haunting' (*D*, 3: 11; 20.4.1925), as if bringing the two
terms into complete synonymity, neighbours of sense as well as sound. But
'haunting', in its ordinary usage, is anything but a casual, strolling word. The
essay that so vehemently advocates looking only at surfaces is also, by that
very exaggeration, indicating that such an attitude may be hiding something
else too.

Reading with less accommodating eyes, we spot other details. At first,
indifferently, as we have seen, the narrator left her house and her 'self' to
'become part of that vast republican army of anonymous trampers, whose
society is so agreeable after the solitude of one's own room' (*CE*, 4: 155). A
few pages on, her companions have been metamorphosed into 'this maimed
company of the halt and the blind' (*CE*, 4: 159). The section immediately
prior to the passage on window-shopping reads as follows:

> They do not grudge us, we are musing, our prosperity; when, suddenly,
> turning the corner, we come upon a bearded Jew, wild, hunger-bitten,
> glaring out of his misery; or pass the humped body of an old woman flung
> abandoned on the step of a public building with a cloak over her like a
> hasty covering thrown over a dead horse or a donkey. At such sights the
> nerves of the spine seem to stand erect; a sudden flare is brandished in our
> eyes; a question is asked which is never answered.

At the beginning it looks as though the self-consciously reassuring suggestion that 'they' are content with their inferiority to the observer is to be turned into restatement of a clear-cut difference, but of another kind, as 'they' become desperate, even dead animals. But the grotesque is twisted in an unexpected direction here. The wildness of the 'sights' is reciprocated in the bestialization of the genteel spectator too, reduced or transformed to a body of instinctual responses: 'the nerves of the spine seem to stand erect'. The passage continues:

> Often enough these derelicts choose to lie not a stone's-throw from theatres, within hearing of barrel organs, almost, as night draws on, within touch of the sequined cloaks and bright legs of diners and dancers. They lie close to those shop-windows where commerce offers to a world of old women laid on doorsteps, of blind men, of hobbling dwarfs, sofas which are supported by the gilt necks of proud swans; tables inlaid with baskets of many-coloured fruit; sideboards paved with green marble the better to support the weight of boars' heads; and carpets so softened with age that their carnations have almost vanished in a pale-green sea.

> (*CE*, 4: 159–60)

Preceded by this extreme juxtaposition, the 'Passing, glimpsing' paragraph becomes open to, if it does not demand, other readings. It is going to haunt the harmless pleasures of window-shopping. One way of looking at the relationship, clearly, would be as that of an implicit reprimand to the luxury-loving spectator. But here again, as in the earlier section, there is not a contrast but a *rapprochement*, even an identification, and in more than one way. The 'derelicts' freely 'choose' their position, and it is to them that 'commerce offers' its exhibition. They are not beggars but ideal consumers. And the more prosperous narrator, by her own account, is not looking to buy, but only to look, using what is on view in the windows as a basis for pure fantasy: she is only going to buy a practical pencil. The curious individuals who 'choose to lie' near the theatres and shops are 'sights' for strolling eyes, but they are also themselves connoisseurs of the pleasures of spectacle for its own sake. And though the narrator does not see herself as seen by them, the path of her own description has had the effect of abolishing the difference it initially sets up.

From this perspective, we can turn to two particularly odd trios encountered *en route*. Inside the boot shop the casual walker is cut down to size:

> We halt at the door of the boot shop and make some little excuse, which has nothing to do with the real reason, for folding up the bright paraphernalia of the streets and withdrawing to some duskier chamber of the being where we may ask, as we raise our left foot obediently upon the stand: 'What, then, is it like to be a dwarf?'

> (*CE*, 4: 157)

Here the difference of indoors and outdoors makes the streets equivalent to the butterfly's wings, their display an extension of the walker who is at liberty to fold them up for her withdrawal inside. The interior of the shop is represented as a place of infantilization, of fitting conformity 'as we raise our left foot obediently', in which the footloose *flâneuse* is brought abruptly to a standstill. In this light, the question 'What is it like to be a dwarf?' acquires enough of a rationale for its literal explanation, in the next sentence, to come as a surprise:

> She came in escorted by two women who, being of normal size, looked like benevolent giants beside her. Smiling at the shop-girls, they seemed to be disclaiming any lot in her deformity and assuring her of their protection. She wore the peevish yet apologetic expression usual on the faces of the deformed. She needed their kindness, yet resented it.
>
> (*CE*, 4: 157–8)

So far, the female dwarf is still a curiosity, and also a type, wearing the 'expression usual on the faces of the deformed'. But then her pride in her feet alters the focus to hers as she stands unique among an undifferentiated audience of 'us':

> Look at that! Look at that! she seemed to demand of us all, as she thrust her foot out, for behold it was the shapely, perfectly proportioned foot of a well-grown woman. It was arched; it was aristocratic. ... Her manner became full of self-confidence. She sent for shoe after shoe. ... She got up and pirouetted before a glass which reflected the foot only in yellow shoes, in fawn shoes, in shoes of lizard-skin. ... She was thinking that, after all, feet are the most important part of the whole person; women, she said to herself, have been loved for their feet alone.
>
> (*CE*, 4: 158)

This is a wonderful turning upon ordinary viewpoints, as the female dwarf, already diminished in the common perception, is shown to aggrandize herself by an identification with an even slighter part, her feet alone, classic choice of male fetishism; and by means of what might be assumed to be her weakest point, the figure of the narcissistic woman, parading in front of the glass for her own admiration. Instead of a surface/depth structure, in which the appearance of abnormality or deficiency is represented as nonetheless concealing an inner virtue or beauty (the pure heart or soul within), the surface look which it might have been thought tactful to disregard is highlighted as the very image of perfection. Unerringly, the dwarf puts her best foot forward, thereby transforming the narrator's own view: 'she had changed the mood; she had called into being an atmosphere which, as we followed her out into the street, seemed actually to create the humped, the twisted, the deformed' (*CE*, 4: 158).

Woolf's transformation of the small woman into the epitome of a proud, sure-footed femininity perversely plays on other representations of the grotesque and of the feminine, the impact of the passage deriving from the way in which the negative connotations of each are dramatically inverted. The impression that Woolf is playing with distortions of sexual perspective is reinforced by the sighting, immediately on leaving the boot shop, of a second, equally bizarre, single-sex trio: 'Two bearded men, brothers, apparently, stone-blind, supporting themselves by resting a head on the small boy between them, marched down the street' (*CE*, 4: 158). There is something deliberately staged in the symmetrical contrasts here: two groups, one female, one male, formed to protect a disability, the one in the middle being the sufferer in the first case (the dwarf), and the support (the little boy) in the second. In the second group, the two on the outside are the blind, in the first group the 'outsider', the dwarf, is on the inside. But this focused formal perfection is not left as an aesthetic spectacle: it moves out to take over the onlookers as well:

> As they passed, holding straight on, the little convoy seemed to cleave asunder the passers-by, with the momentum of its silence, its directness, its disaster. Indeed, the dwarf had started a hobbling grotesque dance to which everybody in the street had now conformed; the stout lady tightly swathed in shiny seal-skin; the feeble-minded boy sucking the silver knob of his stick; the old man squatted on the doorstep as if, suddenly overcome by the absurdity of the human spectacle, he had sat down to look at it – all joined in the hobble and tap of the dwarf's dance.
>
> (*CE*, 4: 159)

This is a scene quite similar to the one in *Between the Acts* in which the audience of the village play is forced, by means of mirrors turned in their direction, to see themselves as part of the spectacle, not its comfortably external observers. The street 'scene' here becomes precisely the place where the simple stereotypical distinctions associated with anonymous encounters and visual judgements are broken down. Everyone is grotesque, just as all the seeming poor can turn out from one point of view to be equivalent to affluent consumers.

My suggestion here is not that Woolf is making a moral point about the harmony of all mankind, whether wealthy or impoverished, disabled or healthy, or, on the other hand, that she is wilfully disregarding the effects of social and physical differences; nor is she using a form of ironic assimilation to emphasize these differences all the more. All these possibilities are present in the way that the scenes are narrated, but they are exposed as limited, much as the artificially distinguished sexual groupings point by exaggeration to the inadequacies of the habitual binary division. Like Aristophanes' three sexes, Woolf's curious trios and types show up the normal orders in an unfamiliar light.

But there is a third shop entered along the narrator's way: a second-hand bookshop. Placed between the two other shop scenes, this episode has the function, by position as well as by subject matter, of a *mise en abîme* of this ambulatory inventiveness: 'Second-hand books are wild books, homeless books; they have come together in vast flocks of variegated feather, and have a charm which the domesticated volumes of the library lack' (*CE*, 4: 161). Most of the volumes randomly perused turn out to be accounts of foreign travel, 'so restless the English are' (*CE*, 4: 162), and their printed narratives, of which random fragments are gleaned here and there in a few minutes' browsing, are identified with the casual encounters of the walk in London:

> The number of books in the world is infinite, and one is forced to glimpse and nod and move on after a moment of talk, a flash of understanding, as, in the street outside, one catches a word in passing and from a chance phrase fabricates a lifetime.
>
> (*CE*, 4: 163)

The street here is one of words, just as the book is a passing street acquaintance, briefly sighted, from which we 'move on'. Woolf's essay is rounded off with the expected purchase of a lead pencil, having declared from the outset that this object is a mere excuse for the walk in which her narrator has meanwhile been indulging. But of course the point of the pencil is a sharper one than this allows. The shoes and the pencil suggest the connection between walking and writing, between strolling and story-making, which the other two shops, with their footwear and literary wares, reinforce: these boots are made for writing.

The essay ends with a celebration of walking as fantasy, as creative mobility:

> Walking home through the desolation one could tell oneself the story of the dwarf, of the blind men, of the party in the Mayfair mansion, of the quarrel in the stationer's shop. Into each of these lives one could penetrate a little way, far enough to give oneself the illusion that one is not tethered to a single mind, but can put on briefly for a few minutes the bodies and minds of others. ... And what greater delight and wonder can there be than to leave the straight lines of personality and deviate into those footpaths that lead beneath brambles and thick tree trunks into the heart of the forest where live those wild beasts, our fellow men?
>
> (*CE*, 4: 165)

This is not, once again, so easy an affirmation as it looks: 'those wild beasts, our fellow men' include the walker who knows she is only giving herself 'the illusion' of not being 'tethered to a single spot': her imaginative freedom is qualified as that of an animal in reality tied to its place, its imaginary other identifications starting from there. But the valorization of deviation over the straight line itself makes way for a transformation here of a conventional comparison. Covertly displacing the usual opposition between the artificial city and primitive country, it is the urban landscape which becomes a natural wilderness.

Before finishing with Woolf's walking text, let us just note in passing a moment in the 'Street Haunting' essay where the narrator seems to put the clamp on the open and fluid identifications she is elsewhere suggesting. The passage takes a very standard, direct-line route to the suburbs south of London:

> The main stream of walkers at this hour sweeps too fast to let us ask such questions. They are wrapt, in this short passage from work to home, in some narcotic dream, now that they are free from the desk and have the fresh air on their cheeks. They put on those bright clothes which they must hang up and lock the key upon all the rest of the day, and are great cricketers, famous actresses, soldiers who have saved their country at the hour of need. Dreaming, gesticulating, often muttering a few words aloud, they sweep over the Strand and across Waterloo Bridge whence they will be slung in long rattling trains, to some prim little villa in Barnes or Surbiton where the sight of the clock in the hall and the smell of the supper in the basement puncture the dream.
>
> (*CE*, 4: 163)

Woolf's representation of the commuter crowd takes a conventional distance, through its predictable representation of bourgeois conventionality. It first promises, as with the other encounters of the evening walk, to complicate the stereotype, making the rush-hour into a time of escape, of dreaming. But then the homogeneous crowd is swiftly dismissed into the standardized horrors of 'some prim little villa', where the narrator seems positively to turn up her nose at 'the smell of the supper in the basement'. If the habitual representations of the Victorian 'nether world' of the back streets of London can be successfully questioned and rendered differently, Woolf's narrator seems to stop short when it comes to imagining suburbia as other than a nightmare when viewed from what now becomes the safe preserve of the sophisticated inner-city gaze.

Near the beginning I drew a distinction between two approaches or walks toward a conception of women's writing: as a question of progress, forward along a given line, or a question of a transgressiveness implicit in the position outside that of masculine normality. In tracing a path that goes from Baudelaire to Proust to Woolf, I have been running or walking both these questions together. On the one hand, it will have seemed that all roads lead to Woolf, to the culmination of a certain tradition of writing about walking and women in the eventual arrival of the woman writer herself in the first part of the twentieth century. On the other hand, in suggesting that Woolf's writing upsets the perspectives of writing itself, and of the representation of the sexes, I have been implying that this questioning reaches no settled identity, but that there might be reasons for calling it feminine, in relation to what it exposes as a masculine norm.

I cannot conclude by smoothly bringing about a meeting between these two alternatives, and it may be their very tension which allows for some movement. At the same time, they are inadequate as alternatives, derived from conceptions of historical change and the difference of the sexes which decide the possible questions in advance, before the chance encounters of the walk. If, as I have been suggesting, there is no simple way forward for the *passante* as woman writer, nor is there an impasse, a block, a simple impediment. There may also be returns and double, even triple times and spaces of walking and writing. The ghosts that come back to trouble the familiar pictures of the modern street are a threat but also, perhaps, and for the same reason, a way of going somewhere else.

NOTES

An earlier version of this paper appeared in the journal *Tropismes* no. 5 (1991). Translations of French texts are my own.

1 See Plato, *The Symposium*, trans. Walter Hamilton (Harmondsworth: Penguin, 1951), pp. 58–65.

2 Sigmund Freud, *Three Essays on the Theory of Sexuality* (1905), Pelican Freud Library vol. 7 (Harmondsworth: Penguin, 1977), p. 46.

3 Virginia Woolf, *A Room of One's Own* (1929; reprinted Harmondsworth: Penguin, 1967), p. 26. Further references included in the text, as '*ROO*'.

4 Charles Baudelaire, *Les Fleurs du mal* (1861); reprinted in *Oeuvres complètes* (Paris: Seuil, 1968), p. 101

> The deafening street around me was shouting.
> Tall, slim, in heavy mourning, majestic grief,
> A woman passed, with a proud hand
> Lifting, balancing the garland and the hem;
>
> Agile and noble, with her statue's leg.
> Me, I was drinking, clenched like a madman,
> In her eye, livid sky where the hurricane germinates,
> The gentleness that fascinates and the pleasure that kills.
>
> One flash ... then night! Fugitive beauty.
> Whose look made me suddenly reborn,
> Will I see you no more but in eternity?
>
> Elsewhere, very far from here! too late! *never* perhaps!
> For I know not where you are fleeing, you know not where I am going,
>
> O you whom I would have loved, o you who knew it!

For a suggestive analysis of the *flâneur* in terms of women's exclusion from the newly formed 'public sphere' of modernity, see Janet Wolff, 'The Invisible Flâneuse', *Theory, Culture and Society* vol. 2, no. 3 (1985), pp. 37–46.

5 I borrow this phrase from Benjamin, who speaks in relation to this poem of 'eine Liebe nicht sowohl auf den ersten als auf den letzten Blick', a 'love not at first sight, but at last sight', in 'On Some Motifs in Baudelaire', *Illuminations*, trans. Harry Zohn (New York: Schocken, 1969), p. 169.

6 Marcel Proust, *A l'ombre des jeunes filles en fleur*, II (Paris: Garnier Flammarion, 1987), p. 87.

> The charms of the *passante* are generally directly related to the rapidity of the passing. It only takes night to be falling and the vehicle to be going fast, in the country, in a city, and there is not one female torso, mutilated like an ancient marble by the speed that carries us forward and the dusk which darkens it, which does not aim at our heart, at every corner on the way, in the depths of every shop, the arrows of Beauty, of beauty of which it might sometimes be tempting to wonder whether in this world it is anything else but the complementary part added to a fragmentary and fugitive *passante* by our imagination overexcited by regret.

7 Proust uses the word himself in another *passante* passage, referring to 'une projection ... un mirage du désir', *A l'ombre*, II, p. 182.
8 *A l'ombre* II, pp. 87–8.

> Never in my life have I encountered such desirable girls as the days when I was with some serious person whom, in spite of the thousands of pretexts I made up, I could not leave: some years after the one when I went for the first time to Balbec, in a vehicle doing an errand with a friend of my father's in Paris and having caught sight of a woman walking quickly in the night, I thought it was unreasonable to lose for reasons of propriety my share of happiness in what is no doubt the only life there is, and leaping down without a word of apology, I set off in search of the unknown woman, lost her at the crossroads of two streets, found her again in a third one, and found myself, finally, completely out of breath, under a lamp-post, opposite old Madame Verdurin whom I was avoiding everywhere and who, surprised and happy, exclaimed: 'Oh! how kind to have run up to say hello to me!'

9 Virginia Woolf, *Mrs Dalloway* (1925; reprinted London: Granada, 1976). p. 48. Further references will be included in the text as *'MD'*.
10 *The Diary of Virginia Woolf*, vol. 3 1925–30, ed. Anne Olivier Bell (1980; rpt. Harmondsworth: Penguin, 1982), p.186; entry for 31.5.1928. Further references will be included in the text as *'D'*.
11 Virginia Woolf, *Collected Essays*, ed. Leonard Woolf, vol. IV (London: Chatto & Windus, 1967), p. 155. Further references will be included in the text, as *'CE4'*.
12 This 'central oyster of perceptiveness' seems an extraordinarily enigmatic expression. Apart from the closeness of 'oy-eye-I', the oyster itself seems to include suggestions of sensory responsiveness (of the animal itself) and voluptuousness (the pleasures of the consumer). Webster's dictionary defines the oyster as,

> a marine bivalve mollusk (family Ostreidae) having a rough irregular shell closed by a single adductor muscle, the foot small or wanting, and no siphon, living free on the bottom or adhering to stones or other objects in shallow water along the seacoasts or in brackish water in the mouths of rivers, and feeding on minute plants or animals carried to them by the current.

The specification of 'the foot small or wanting' is not irrelevant to the theme of feminine strolling, and in particular to one of the episodes of Woolf's essay discussed below; that Woolf's street should be in a sense submarine accords with an insistent imagery that surfaces throughout her writing.

Chapter 4

Happy families? Feminist reproduction and matrilineal thought

Linda R. Williams

HEGEL AND THE PLANT-WOMEN

There is a point in *The Philosophy of Right* where Hegel's language takes a botanical turn, as he discusses a form of plant-life which he calls 'Women':

> Women are capable of education, but they are not made for activities which demand a universal faculty such as the more advanced sciences, philosophy, and certain forms of artistic production. Women may have happy ideas, taste, and elegance, but they cannot attain to the ideal. The difference between men and women is like that between animals and plants. Men correspond to animals, while women correspond to plants because their development is more placid and the principle that underlies it is the rather vague unity of feeling. When women hold the helm of government, the State is at once in jeopardy, because women regulate their actions not by the demands of universality, but by arbitrary inclinations and opinions. Women are educated – who knows how? – as it were by breathing in ideas, by living rather than by acquiring knowledge. The status of manhood, on the other hand, is attained only by the stress of thought and much technical exertion.[1]

It seems, then, that female conceptual life comes into being through a bizarre kind of immaculate conception, an osmosis of the mind, a process through which our porous brains find ideas quite literally 'absorbing'. Educationally we do not conquer, acquire something alien, or exert ourselves at all; by comparison Hegel's man seems to find thinking an awful lot of trouble. Mysteriously, women *live* knowledge and breathe it as atmosphere. Like air, ideas, it seems, are the stuff of our life and soaking them in is as natural as respiration.

But our minds aren't like gardens. We do not cultivate them – we cannot determine what can stay in and what must be kept out. The organic life of Hegel's plant-women is too chaotic to have meaning or purpose. We do not know the difference between wild weeds and precious plants, the wood from the trees; we lack the capacity of rational 'regulation'. We are, it seems, so inadequately differentiated from our surroundings that our surroundings absorb us through the undetermined 'principle of . . . vague unity of feeling'. Feminine nature for Hegel is then 'botanical nature bathed in the spirit of the times'.[2] And if we were to apply his caution about women and government to the specific case of the last prime minister of Britain, we would find that the State was apparently in jeopardy because Mrs Thatcher, as a woman, was and is 'arbitrarily inclined or opinionated' because she lacks the capacity to select or regulate the information and ideas that she osmotically absorbs. No doubt the more Hegelian members of the Labour party would have worked this out eventually.

It is uncanny how like Hegel's myth of plant-women are certain feminist theories of feminine knowledge, particularly the notion that the transmission of ideas between women occurs in the ostensibly unmediated manner of communication between a mother and infant daughter. This is Irigaray's (negative) notion that 'One doesn't stir without the Other';[3] the distinction between the two, between 'Me' (daughter) and 'Yourself' (mother), is blurred, and neither can move independently. Food, air, knowledge mingle between them and defy separation; experience is so intra-personal that individual identity and power are severely threatened. Mother and daughter mutually absorb each other, although the daughter who writes accuses the mother of being a phallically controlling and dominant mother. In Jane Gallop's words, 'the speaker . . . is paralyzed in an eternal minority': she is mummified by matrilineal containment.[4]

Sylvia Plath's mother calls this a 'flow of communication'[5] in her introduction to *Letters Home* – the fluid channels which, she argues, are there from the start of life are maintained and reinforced in mystical obscurity. As one who was undoubtedly tangibly responsible for part of her daughter's education (one common-sense answer to Hegel's question, in relation to Plath anyway), Schober Plath's statements about how knowledge and experience are transmitted between mother and daughter should clarify our understanding of the ways in which women learn, write, and communicate with each other. Yet even she – elsewhere eminently sensible and lucid – is committed to the language of feminine fluidity and unregulated or telepathic absorption:

> Between Sylvia and me there existed – as between my own mother and me – a sort of psychic osmosis which, at times, was very wonderful and comforting; at other times an unwelcome invasion of privacy.[6]

This notion of unmediated – if painful – communication can be placed in tandem with Toril Moi's discussion of feminist philosophers of science Evelyn Fox Keller and Susan Bordo in Moi's essay 'Patriarchal Thought and the Drive for Knowledge'. Moi writes of the positing of feminine 'ecstatic communion' against masculine 'control and domination',

> the problem with Keller's and Bordo's Chodorovian analysis of gender

and science and philosophy is not only its cultural essentialism, but the fact that the solution proposed ('commingling', 'union' of subject and object) remains curiously timid and flawed. If the 'union' proposed reinforces the separate identities of subject and object, their grand vision of 'female science' promises no more than a certain elasticity of boundaries between separate, self-identical essences.[7]

I want to clarify these rather obscure notions of consummate female thought in order to look more closely at how they feed into a larger, and for me more problematic, model: that of a specifically female history of ideas. This paper will address the persistence and attraction of the notion of unmediated feminine communication, which recurs across a range of writings by women as both a separatist ideal and an organizing metaphor for women's studies: the notion of a feminist, or at least female, matrilineage. I want to discuss the connection which feminist discourse has forged between the vague (and potentially pernicious) form of immaculate connection enshrined by Schober Plath, Keller and Bordo (as both 'a sort of psychic osmosis' and an 'ecstatic communion'), and the larger female matrilineage which feminist criticism has argued for since Woolf's 'We think back through our mothers if we are women'.[8] Alice Walker's deployment of Woolf's model as a pattern for understanding Afro-American women's traditions is perhaps the clearest example of this. *In Search of Our Mothers' Gardens*, which is finally a discussion of how it is possible to 'hand on the creative spark' when literacy is a punishable crime (as it was for Walker's slave ancestors), contains all of the elements which interest me here. She constructs a creative matrilineage which is held together by gardening metaphor and activity: quite materially, women had to actively inscribe themselves on their flower-beds as the only accessible outlet for the 'essential' creativity which Walker finally celebrates – her actual 'mother's garden' signalled by the essay title. But a more ideal 'flow of communication' is suggested, which keeps Walker's sense of a spirit of creativity alive against the grain of legislative denial:

> our mothers and grandmothers have, more often than not anonymously, handed on the creative spark, the seed of the flower they themselves never hoped to see: or like a sealed letter they could not plainly read.[9]

Whilst this may not seem 'ideal' in the everyday use of the term, the sense of passing on sealed packages of power without being able to engage with them materially is a curiously politicized refinement of Hegel's 'living rather than ... acquiring knowledge'; acquiring certain forms of knowledge was, for Walker's mothers and grandmothers, illegal. Thus women can only pass on an elemental sense of creativity to their daughters, lacking the power of literate or conventionally artistic germination themselves. Cross-generational connection is, therefore, a curious channel for Walker; the silent sense of passing wisdom down without consciously 'knowing' it yourself leads her into a discussion of more nebulous forms of knowing which permeates all of her works. Whilst there are specific historical conditions which shape Walker's re-reading of Woolf for the interpretation of black women's writing, the question of

How they knew what we
Must know
Without knowing a page
Of it
Themselves[10]

is strongly connected to the specifically feminine forms of 'unknowing' contact which other feminist writers celebrate. What, then, is at stake in the feminist desire to use an ideal but exclusive form of intra-subjective psychic contact as a model for literary history (or scientific knowledge) – the notion that down the historical chain of women's writing an ideal form of female creativity is communicated and regenerated?

The question 'who knows how?' persists, in a manner which uncannily echoes Freud's own late 'don't know' about femininity. Freud might reply to Hegel's question – to borrow a statement from the 'Dora' case – 'the mystery turns upon (the woman's) mother'.[11] Perhaps, feminism has argued, if we appreciated the importance of daughters' relationships with their mothers we would be able to *use* that pre-Oedipal power more fruitfully? Freud's 'don't know' famously runs thus:

We have ... long given up any expectation of a neat parallelism between male and female sexual development.

Our insight into this early, pre-Oedipus phase in girls comes to us as a surprise, like the discovery, in another field, of the Minoan–Mycenaean civilization behind the civilization of Greece.

Everything in the sphere of this first attachment to the mother seemed to me so difficult to grasp in analysis – so grey with age and shadowy and almost impossible to revivify.[12]

'This first attachment' has, then, formed the model for the notion that pre-Oedipal unity engenders writing creativity. The woman who understands and tunes into this space of unity writes, in Cixous's phrase, in 'that good mother's milk. She writes in white ink': 'Even if phallic mystification has generally contaminated good relationships, a woman is never far from her "mother".'[13] This communion is, then, the unrepressed moment of what Patricia Yaeger calls 'the "feminine" or "pre-oedipal" sublime', following Neil Hertz's reading of the sublime in Shelley as 'an oral, primordial desire to merge with (rather than to possess) the mother'.[14] For Yaeger this moment breaks open consciousness and is 'welcomed as a primary, healthful part of the writer's experience, as part of the motive for metaphor'; it is 'the initiating desire for the mother's inundation'.[15] Adrienne Rich (quoting Woolf's *To the Light-*

house) puts it another way, partly recognizing the desire for this sublimity from the fallen position of Oedipality:

> Psychic osmosis. Desperate defenses. The power of the bond often denied because it cracks consciousness, threatens at times to lead the daughter back into 'those secret chambers ... becoming, like waters poured into one jar, inextricably the same, one with the object one adored'.[16]

The founding position of matriarchal feminism is, then, that there is something *essentially positive* in the pre-Oedipal attachment between mother and daughter, in terms of which the unique flows and influences between women can be explained: 'Mothers and daughters have always exchanged with each other – beyond the verbally transmitted lore of female survival – a knowledge that is subliminal, subversive, preverbal.'[17] It is this 'exchange', this channel of fluidity, which prompts Hegel's question, 'women are educated – who knows how?'.

FEMINIST FAMILY ROMANCES

Mother/daughterhood is then one of the most persistent ways that feminism has articulated women's alternative networks of communication. As metaphor it has profoundly affected our reading of women's literary history, and I want to explore more closely what is at stake in this. It is, I think, not so simple. However strongly this 'pure' bond is asserted, however much it is seen to be a democratic exchange of feeling and information, its intervention as a controlling metaphor in feminist studies, and particularly in feminist criticism, needs to be challenged. From the premiss that women have access to purity of sublime or semiotic communication comes the notion that authentic female communication takes place through matriarchal and matrilineal networks, networks which are purified from the distortions of the symbolic. Hegel's women conceive immaculately because for them no defiling or politicized process of transmission takes place in thought. They 'gather' knowledge in an apparently unmediated way – it is 'exchanged' or absorbed, and therefore not subject to the problems of transmission.

Against this, and with Alice Jardine, I would

> like to avoid the mother/daughter paradigm here (so as not to succumb simply to miming the traditional father/son, master/disciple model), but it is difficult to avoid at this point being positioned by the institution as mothers and daughters. Structures of debt/gift (mothers and increasingly daughters control a lot of money and prestige in the university), structures of our new institutional power over each other, desires and demands for recognition and love – all of these are falling into place in rather familiar ways.[18]

Her 'Notes for an Analysis' is written in anticipation of a 'new kind of feminist intellectual' who 'fully inscribes herself within the ethics of impossibility', concluding by calling for the wiping away of 'the concept of "generation" altogether' when feminist women place themselves 'across the generations'. She suggests an embrace of intra-generational solidarity which would erase the power of differentials bound up in the relationship of debt between mothers and daughters, towards a totality of unified radical feminist intellectuals. It is a pity that such a complex analysis of the contemporaneity of feminism and psychoanalysis ends before suggesting how this embrace of generational forgetting is to take place, and at what point it would resist undifferentiated unity with a dynamic of different, *afamilial* powers.

How, then, can feminism interpret the transmission of ideas, knowledge, systems of thought outside of an Oedipal dynamic? With what language do we currently discuss the channels through which information is passed on? When Hegel writes the offhand 'Women are educated – who knows how?' he invites us to presume that the way in which men are educated is no problem at all. That's obvious – it's women who are the mystery. I want to ask a series of questions about how we pass on information to each other and what we want it to do. What is feminist transmission? Why do we so often employ familial metaphors to interpret our conceptual and scholarly relationships with each other? What are the power relations at stake in setting up feminist networks of thinking which rely on mother-daughter or sisterly ties? Why are we so reluctant to rid ourselves of the family? These questions focus not only on the problem of mother-daughter relations in history or psychoanalysis, but crucially on the way we have interpreted women's *literary* history as a *family* history, glued together by those 'unknowable' feminine relations discussed above: 'the unique bonds that link women in what we might call the secret sisterhood of their literary subculture'.[19] Thus it seems, ironically, that the very force which some writers have drawn upon to signal the breakdown of patriarchal family relations – a feminine communication which disrupts normal epistemologies – has then been used to make coherent an alternative Great (female) Tradition.

Virginia Woolf's famous statement, 'we think back through our mothers if we are women'[20] has engendered a whole family of feminisms dedicated to the recovery of an intellectual matriarchy. As Rachel Bowlby writes, 'Woolf has herself become foremother to a generation of feminists who "think back through our mothers".'[21] What Bowlby is indicating, then, isn't just that Woolf thought that there is a literary history which works matrilineally, but that this has in turn engendered a feminist critical family line. Matriarchal thinking has become a primary feminist characteristic, and its language acts as the freemason's handshake of Gilbert and Gubar's 'secret sisterhood'. I want briefly to outline here the arguments of a few kinswomen who display the family resemblances most strongly. Is it a happy family? I think not. Its members squabble constantly over who mother is. Is she Dale Spender's mother, stable source of a comfortable literary tradition, legitimized and authentic? Is she the sublime, pre-oedipal mother, with whom closeness opens up revolutionary possibilities of disruption?

Dale Spender's *Mothers of the Novel* – dedicated to the author's mother, presumably the grandmother of this text – is an unashamedly evangelical eulogy to 'our' literary matriarchs. Her project is to reclaim the 'treasure chest'[22] of 'women's traditions' which 'we have been missing'.[23] Indeed, her fervent championing of a tradition mothered and reproduced by women – 'it is my contention that women were the mothers of the novel and that any other version of its origin is but a myth of male creation' – is uncannily like that of F. R. Leavis who, in his early work, also occupied an inspired dissident position, championing the canonically repressed. And, like Leavis, what Spender wants to do is to produce an 'authentic' or 'legitimated female tradition',[24] thus exemplifying a feminist critical position which turns to the fecund mother figure as guarantor of a sense of stability and genealogical truth.

Gilbert and Gubar's *The Madwoman in the Attic* is perhaps a more interesting example of matriarchal reading. They take the problem of how creativity is engendered head-on, and partly inherit Harold Bloom's interpretation of literary movement as energized by the anxiety of influence. 'Criticism', for Bloom, 'is the art of knowing the hidden roads that go from poem to poem'[25] – it is the detection of the literary violation of fathers by sons. Writing that 'Poetry (Romance) is Family Romance',[26] Bloom rewrites literary history as the history of Oedipal conflict:

> True poetic history is the story of how poets as poets have suffered other poets, just as any true biography is the story of how anyone suffered his own family – or his own displacement of family into lovers and friends.
>
> Summary – Every poem is a misinterpretation of a parent poem.[27]

For Bloom, imagination is *mis*interpretation; creativity is the deliberate violation of what's come before. A feminism which would assemble all the fragments of women's literary history into 'the career of a single woman artist, a "mother of us all"',[28] which would conform in part to the notion that female imagination is osmotically communicated through that 'unique bond', would undoubtedly have enormous problems with such a violating tradition. What Gilbert and Gubar want to do is take Bloom's model and strip it of its anxiety as far as literary daughters and mothers are concerned, neatly retaining father as the bad relation. Patriarchal tradition takes on the image of the wicked stepfather in a romance of positive feminine relations: the father remains the one to be killed, and although today's women writers are 'the daughters of too few mothers', nevertheless a dedicated enough act of feminist critical genealogy can trace a whole matriarchal history, putting together the history of 'a woman whom patriarchal poetics dismembered and whom we have tried to remember'. Re-membering thus becomes a process dedicated to unity; fragments of written selves are made to undergo a rite of matrilineal coherence. Remembering phallically assembles fragments into a unity of 'membership'. If patriarchal history was the process of splitting women exogamically from each other, disseminating their powers and dismembering their tradition, certain feminist histories would bring the parts back into the organic whole again. Coherence, progress, growth, community, all combine to produce a stable tradition of women's literary history. The female artist can then begin the struggle which Gilbert and Gubar call 'the anxiety of authorship', 'only by actively seeking a female precursor who, far from representing a threatening force to be denied or killed, proves by example that a revolt against partriarchal literary authority is possible'.[29]

Furthermore, not only has the reintroduction of a sense of tradition restabilized our understanding of women's writing but ironically enough the very fact that women have been able to draw upon matrilineal metaphors has given that tradition the weight of genetic verification. To assert that paternity is undecidable whilst maternity is undeniable is a fairly commonplace idea; as Freud writes in *Moses and Monotheism*,

> this turning from the mother to the father points in addition to a victory of intellectuality over sensuality – that is, an advance in civilization, since maternity is proved by the evidence of the senses while paternity is a hypothesis, based on an inference and a premiss.[30]

Hélène Cixous, champion of fiction if ever there was one, is, however, quite prepared to denigrate it in contrast with this primary 'fact' of maternity: 'Paternity, which is a fiction, is fiction passing itself off as truth.'[31] To extend this into the metaphorics of writing generations, feminist literary history has reversed and rewritten Cixous' statement as: 'literary maternity, which is a fact, is fact which has historically been passed off as untruth'. Some feminist criticisms have challenged this 'historical passing off' in order to establish a framework within which feminist scholarship is meaningful. Thus in pursuit of matrilineal stability, feminism has been able to deploy the metaphor of the most concrete human given of all: the fact that one is the issue of one's mother. So, patriarchal literary tradition has acted only to render women writers temporary orphans; the happy ending of the family romance is that given sufficiently skilful sleuthing, the truth will out and our true mother will be found.

THE USES AND ABUSES OF TRADITION AND TRANSMISSION

Why should we need recourse to family structures to legitimize our work? Why should the metaphors of legitimate or verifiable generation be reproduced in each subsequent generation of feminist thinkers? As Rachel Bowlby implies, our relationships to each other's critical writings can be interpreted as reproducing those of women writers to each other; the interpretation of a literary historical pattern has been passed into the scholarly networks through which literature is then interpreted. In this section I want to discuss briefly how the power relations at work in the transmission of literary tradition are translated into the transference relationship of scholar and pupil. The issue of transmission becomes important here, in relation to the psychoanalytic notion of transference. Elizabeth Wright, in her essay 'Transmission in Psychoanalysis and Literature: Whose Text is it Anyway?', writes that 'transmission is generally thought to be of a fixed and unambiguous message through some intermediary from an authorized source to a passive recipient',[32] the transmission of radio signals through a transmitter being her example. However, in the balance between 'authorized source' and 'passive recipient' lurks a minefield of potential inequalities; an unequal power relation stakes one up against the other. One dictionary definition of 'transmission' offers: 'to send or pass on; to allow to pass through'. The first would be an equal or democratic dissemination of knowledge; the second state of 'allowing' is undoubtedly that which occurs between the author(ized) and the passive recipient. Or as Cixous puts it: 'Receivers are what they have received'.[33]

Thus with the idea of communication through transmission – a channel open to distortion and inequalities – rather than through osmotic absorption or exchange, the terrain of exchange shifts and warps under the problem of power. If we were to read women's communication or literary history as a process of transmission we would have to impose this master-slave relationship on to our idealized model of mothers and daughters, the mother being the 'authorized source' and the daughter being the 'passive recipient'. Or in more Nietzschean language, this epistemological exchange would be inherently subject to the will to truth of the mother. 'Pure' osmotic exchange is contaminated. Obviously this is a problem for those, happy to assert that thoughts between women transmigrate mystically, who want to posit the relation as one of non-threat and equality. With the notion of transmission, however, come many rather unpalatable problems.

The question of transmission is thus a place where our readings of literary history – the channels through which women writers communicate – and our readings of our own sexual political relationships, can come together through a discussion which is taking place over the transmission of psychoanalytic knowledge. Wright writes:

> The transmission of psychoanalytic theory and practice in the training of analysts may be taken as the problem paradigm for the transmission of any knowledge. 'Transmission' is a term currently in favour in French psychoanalytic discourse, where it has emerged as a key problem in the passing on of knowledge from teacher to student in the psychoanalytic institution. ... The key problem of the training analysis ... is that of the problem of any teaching/learning situation that takes place in an institution, in that the pupil/analysand is dependent on the teacher/analyst's

authority in a present that stretches almost interminably into the future. The situation is thus a real one, not one merely confined to the psychodrama of the classroom/consulting room, for it recreates and perpetuates the childhood situation where a child really depends for its future on its protectors. This amounts to a double-bind: the teacher/analyst is transmitting dependence on authority in practice whilst teaching emancipation from it in theory.[34]

Wright's position is, then, that transmission is intrinsically but paradoxically power-laden, between mother and child, and between the writer and those who have anxiously influenced her. To discuss this further the terms of questioning need to be opened up, so that transmission, transference and, consequently, the situation of mentor and discipleship can be used to read matrilineal thought. The process of transmission in training analysis is intimately bound up with the transference and counter-transference which takes place between the analyst and analysand, where 'false' or 'inauthentic' love plays at being the 'true' love between parent and child. From the problem of how knowledge is gathered or communicated in women, via some images of an immaculate communion between mother and daughter, we reach the position that transmission itself inevitably involves the inauthenticity of dependence and desire. In Catherine Clément's words, 'it is through the discourse of mastery that knowledge of the analytic act is transmitted'.[35] Or, as Lacan puts it, 'As soon as the subject who is supposed to know exists somewhere . . . [sujet supposé savoir], there is a transference.'[36]

One of the reasons I consider these questions so crucial is that at stake in this is the problem of how one creates one's future. In working toward new feminist positions we are undergoing a constant process of individuation from our predecessors. Perhaps this questioning of how one understands one's role means that I am just another ungrateful daughter. Perhaps this paper is in truth a symptom of what Lynn Sukenick calls matrophobia (in a reading of Doris Lessing); that is, in Adrienne Rich's words, 'the fear not of one's mother or of motherhood but of becoming one's mother'.[37] The problem is, how can the feminism of this generation begin to dismantle generational thinking?

Michèle Le Doeuff's brilliant essay 'Women and Philosophy' interprets the problem of the transmission of information as a problem of transference. For her the characteristic philosophical relationship is that of father and son, whereby a new position is reached, the relationship of transference is broken, when the master fails. Thus new positions in thought are arrived at only through an acknowledgement of the master's *lack*:

Let us recall for example the *Phaedo* or the *Discourse on Method*. In both cases we are given the account of a disappointment and a frustration in teaching: 'I imagined I had found the man who would teach me . . . but he disappointed me' (97c–99d). The disappointment begins the story of 'all the trouble I went to' in trying to fill the lack. There is nothing like this in the relationship of women of the past to their master's philosophy: he knows all, his philosophy has an answer to everything.[38]

Women philosophers, she says, inevitably fail in such a relationship, and thus fail to achieve anything philosophically of their own except a respectful position of scholarship, tending and nurturing the 'original thoughts' of others, because they have not been encouraged to feel sufficiently aggressive toward their mentors. The moment of breaking with the parent figure thus never comes. Le Doeuff's problem is how to articulate this more positively – how to 'go beyond' without first having to have posited the failures of one's teacher, without having dialectically to supersede the master's lack. In a sense this is Gilbert and Gubar's position – wanting to set up women's networks as spaces of *plenitude*, not as sequences of revolt – but the drama of overcoming still exists as a problem of rebellious reaction to patriarchal culture.

For Le Doeuff, then, the problem of creating new philosophical spaces for and by women is inherently a problem of transference, and the only solution would be one within which the transference relationship is itself altered to accommodate women's desires to become powerful without that meaning the occupation of a position of power over another – that is, without one necessarily having to become an object of transference oneself in order to cope with one's own unresolved transference relationship with one's mentor. Of course, feminism has no 'Great' figures, and this has been said to be one of its strengths, despite someone like Spender's attempts to create a Great Tradition of them. These problems of transmission and transference are variously analysed by Hélène Cixous and François Roustang, and I want briefly to look at their analyses of the kind of situations which Le Doeuff confronts and imagines.

Roustang offers the kind of sado-masochistic intellectual history, made flesh in the circle of Lacan and his disciples, which presumably all feminist 'schools' would want to avoid like the plague. For Roustang, both Freud and his circle, and Lacan and his followers, were locked into a system of stifling familial protection whereby master and disciples mutually stave off each other's potentially delirious – and creative – individualities. Mutual mastery and discipleship curbs the power of fantasy:

> The real problem is to understand why one becomes a disciple or, cor-relatively, why one has disciples. This double question can, in my opinion, be given a single answer: in order not to go mad. ... If he is a disciple it is basically because he is afraid of bearing his own name, of speaking in his own name, of thinking about his own fantasies and dreams or, in other words, of flying on a trapeze without a net.[39]

Whilst Le Doeuff would put this issue far less strongly, there is a sense in which she is addressing for feminism the same problem. Whoever one's ostensible master is, one needs to ask why such an abject relationship with a knowing system of thought is reinforced by one's participation. Her desire that women be able to take up freely an independent intellectual position – in Victor Tausk's phrase, 'independent because nobody depends on me, not a slave because I am not a master'[40] – is a position of healthy intellectual individuation. The problem is how one reaches such a position. Can some feminisms' reverence for the metaphorical mother be taken as a kind of discipleship – has feminism needed her as a disciple painfully relies upon his master, in order to establish a secure sense of a feminine past without recourse to a Bloomian moment of aggressive usurpation? At best it seems that these structures of mother- and daughterhood offer only Freud's possibility of 'independent disciples or faithful originators'.[41] Roustang writes, in fact, that 'Freud was looking for a brilliant pupil and not for a brilliant future leader'.[42] In the argument of *Dire Mastery* all relationships are contained within loose family structures, and so his problem of the progress of intellectual history becomes very like our problem of the pervasive nature of generational and family language. Critic of Roustang, Cornelius Castoriadis, writes: 'Roustang seems to regard as at once desirable and impossible the objective of "extricating oneself at all costs from the system of filiation and general reproduction which is the basis of any society".'[43]

Whilst it might be hard to discuss Lacan's circle without invoking the family in love or enraged – even Catherine Clément casts herself as one of Lacan's seduced daughters, who then relates stories of the father to her own daughter in *The Lives and Legends of Jacques Lacan*[44] – Castoriadis' point, like matrilineal feminism's, is that the family isn't all bad. For him the history of philosophy offers countless examples of great men being good mothers to their sons, positing a sensible, nurturing alternative to the anxiety of influence or to dire mastery, which would either provoke the son into killing the father or cause the son's 'imbecilic', 'Mad', 'psychotic' or 'delirious' impulses (all Roustang's words) to be constrained by the master:

> Socrates never stifled Plato, and Plato never presented Aristotle with the mere choice between repetition and silence. Fichte did not drive Schelling to suicide, and Schelling did nothing to prevent Hegel from taking up an independent standpoint. What Roustang presents as a necessity of the master–pupil relationship, the crazy wager which he sees in the latter's need to 'think his own thought within the thought of the master, or again to speak in his own name in strict accordance with the master's speech', the consequent reduction of the right to speak nothing but 'imbecilities, imbecilities which the master will stigmatise and correct' – this is an excellent description of the relation of Lacan to his 'pupils', but it has no general validity.[45]

For Le Doeuff, however, 'The game is far from being won ... the mandarins still need to be transference objects, and, moreover, they are not the only ones.'[46] Castoriadis' more charitable notion of the history of thought as a helpful passing on of support is not Le Doeuff's, who reads that history rather more as a tradition of violations:

> Everyone knows that the more of a philosopher one is, the more distorted one's reading of other philosophers. Think of ... Hegel's reading of Kant! They cannot respect the thought of the other: they are too engrossed in their own. Nietzsche said that a scientist's objectivity indicated his lack of instinct. How could a woman manhandle a text, or violate a discourse?[47]

Yet this irreverence is surely what Le Doeuff calls for, the crisis moment which fissures from incessant questioning, as in Roustang's notion of analytic breakthrough: 'Analytic work, theoretical as well as practical, presupposes that one stands by oneself at the moment of discovery.'[48] This is the position Le Doeuff advocates that women take in relation to established traditions: one must be prepared to react violently to one's philosophical antecedents, to destroy discipleship in our independence and to be utterly unfaithful in our originality. Indeed, there was much of this spirit at work in the early moments of feminist thought, recounted by many women in descriptions of their bitter struggles with the patriarchal critical establishment. The problem comes when that initial violence is distilled into an alternative and stable traditionalism, evidenced by the lexicon of familial relations at work, whilst the radical impulses of literary archaeology have, for Le Doeuff, stabilized into another form of nurturing female behaviour:

> The vestal of a discourse which time threatens to eclipse, the nurse of dismembered texts, the healer of works battered by false editions, the housewife whom one hopes will dust off the grey film that successive readings have left on the fine object, she takes on the upkeep of the monuments, the forms which man has deserted.[49]

NEWLY BORN FEMINISMS: ANTI-OEDIPAL INTERPRETATION

Looking back and looking forward should not be a question of looking back through one's foremothers or forward toward a reproduction of familial structures. Regenerating the family in our language seems to me to be a morbid de-generation. What is the feminism of this, of 'our generation', to become? Are we daughters of mothers who want us to become mothers ourselves, according to the means by which mothering is reproduced in Nancy Chodorow's model?[50] How is a new century to be engendered, for which we must write a differently gendered script? Surely one of the urgent problems is to rethink this language of generation, by unwriting the family structure of feminism.

What is at stake in this debate is, then, the problem of whether passing on information – about how one analyses a person or a text, about how one writes a literary text itself, about where it comes from – involves a dependence relation, and if so, how do we respond to this? The issue is crystallized in 'A Woman Mistress', part of the 'Exchange' between Catherine Clément and Hélène Cixous in *The Newly Born Woman*. Clément's position is clear:

> It has to be said straight out: for me mastery is fundamental and necessary. I don't particularly think one can transmit certain knowledges – *the* knowledges – except through mastery. That involves everything having to do with democratic transmission. Paradoxically, information contained in a system of knowledge cannot be transmitted outside of mastery. It is dependent upon the 'law' of the Symbolic.[51]

We could, perhaps, flip back to our original discussion of motherhood and pre-Oedipal communion to assert that the terrain which feminist criticism deals with has nothing to do with this understanding of systems of knowledge and mastery within the realm of the symbolic. However, since what is being transmitted via matrilineal channels is then used in service of an alternative, stable, 'legitimized' (thus 'dependent upon the law') *tradition*, its claims to evade mastery seem tenuous. Cixous' response looks forward to other possibilities and more imaginative alternatives:

> Your position, which I understand, disposes of a problem that is funda-mental and primary for me: how is one to think and struggle against what mastery inevitably entails as a form of repression? A mastery's contradiction, if it isn't thought differently, is that, far from transmitting knowledge, it makes it still more inaccessible, makes it sacred. That is Law's dirty trick.[52]

How, in that case, is one to 'think differently' powerful relationships of intellectual giving and creativity which don't involve one having power over another? Behind this is the problem of what would constitute an anti-Oedipal feminism, not necessarily in the anti-Freudian context in which Deleuze and Guattari use the term, but in a much more literal manner. Is it enough to shore up a relationship between women as mothers and daughters, because such a relationship doesn't work as neatly Oedipal? Do we perhaps use a patriarchal language when we talk of literary mothering, when we unearth a 'buried' matrilineage, when we nurture a female tradition? Or do we invent anti-Oedipal feminism just by loving our literary mothers more than our scholarly fathers? Is a pre-Oedipal feminism – with which we began – enough? I think not. We need to be able to think, and to think literature, in a way which doesn't recognize its importance, beauty and development in the 'Great Traditional' concepts of familial hierarchies.

In tandem with Hegel's description of plant-women comes this conclusive statement: 'Woman ... has her substantive destiny in the family, and to be imbued with family piety is her ethical frame of mind.'[53] I am concerned that feminism is 'imbued' with this Hegelian notion of 'family piety', or with an essentially womanly 'ethical frame of mind', when it maintains or reinvokes familial language in the way I have described. But the alternatives to the manner in which we currently articulate our coming into thought would inevitably be harsh. The literally anti-social claims which Roustang makes for psychoanalysis could be displaced on to feminism, but only if we also embrace a notion of psychosis in which 'There is no Oedipus, so a break severs the continuity from generation to generation':[54] 'if we consider its rigorous aims, if psychoanalysis exists to undo repression, then it should include no social formations, except as elements to be expelled'.[55] Some implications of anti-generational thinking might be these: to follow up Alice Jardine's call for 'an ethics of impossibility' we would need to question the network of support and solidarity, as well as the notion of a teleological history through which information is generously passed on, in order to learn how violently to inscribe on to the world the unimagined. Would we be willing to sacrifice that cherished economy of gratitude and its balance, moral debt, in order to affirm that in reality we *owe nothing*? An experimental irresponsibility which is not ungrateful because debt does not exist, and through which not only the notion of communication as unmediated osmosis is smashed, but also its mirror, the image of thought occurring in an equally mystical isolation. A position of *release*, where thinking takes place without a safety net.

NOTES

1 G.W.F. Hegel, *The Philosophy of Right* (1821), trans. T.M. Knox (Oxford, 1967), pp. 263–4, §107; also quoted in a different form by Michèle Le Doeuff in 'Women and Philosophy', in *French Feminist Thought: A Reader*, ed. Toril Moi (Oxford, 1987).
2 Le Doeuff, op. cit., p. 186.
3 Luce Irigaray, 'And the One Doesn't Stir without the Other', trans. Hélène Vivienne Wenzel, in *Signs*, Autumn 1981.
4 Jane Gallop, *Feminism and Psychoanalysis: The Daughter's Seduction* (London, 1982), p. 115.
5 Aurelia Schober Plath, introduction to Sylvia Plath's *Letters Home* (London, 1976), p. 33.
6 ibid., p. 32.
7 Toril Moi, 'Patriarchal Thought and the Drive for Knowledge', in *Between Feminism and Psychoanalysis*, ed. Teresa Brennan (London, 1989), p. 193.
8 Virginia Woolf, *A Room of One's Own* (1929) (St Albans, 1977), pp. 72–3.
9 Alice Walker, 'In Search of Our Mother's Gardens', in *In Search of Our Mother's Gardens and Other Essays* (London 1984), p. 240.
10 Alice Walker, 'Women', in *Revolutionary Petunias* (London, 1988), p. 5, my emphasis.
11 Sigmund Freud, 'Fragment of an Analysis of a Case of Hysteria ("Dora")' (1905 [1910]), in *Case Histories I*, Pelican Freud Library vol. 8 (Harmondsworth, 1980), p. 105.
12 Freud, 'Female Sexuality' (1931), in *On Sexuality* (Pelican Freud Library vol. 7), pp. 372–3.

13 Hélène Cixous, 'The Laugh of the Medusa', in *New French Feminisms*, ed. Elaine Marks and Isabelle de Courtivron (Brighton, 1981), p. 251.
14 Patricia Yaeger, 'Towards a Female Sublime' in *Gender and Theory*, ed. Linda Kaufmann (Oxford, 1989), p. 204.
15 ibid., pp. 204–5.
16 Adrienne Rich, *Of Woman Born, Motherhood as Experience and Institution* (London, 1977), p. 231.
17 ibid., p. 220.
18 Alice Jardine, 'Notes for an Analysis', in Brennan, op. cit., p. 77.
19 Sandra Gilbert and Susan Gubar, *The Madwoman in the Attic* (New Haven and London, 1979), p. 51.
20 Virginia Woolf, *A Room of One's Own* (1929) (St Albans, 1977), pp. 72–3.
21 Rachel Bowlby, *Virginia Woolf: Feminist Destinations* (Oxford, 1988), p. 25.
22 Dale Spender, *Mothers of the Novel: 100 Good Women Writers Before Jane Austen* (London, 1986), p. 2.
23 ibid., p. 6.
24 ibid., pp. 262–3.
25 Harold Bloom, *The Anxiety of Influence* (Oxford, 1973), p. 96.
26 ibid., p. 95.
27 Bloom, op. cit.
28 Gilbert and Gubar, op. cit., p. 101.
29 ibid., p. 49.
30 Freud, *Moses and Monotheism* (1939 [1934–8]), in Pelican Freud Library vol. 13, *The Origins of Religion*, p. 361.
31 Hélène Cixous and Catherine Clément, *The Newly Born Woman* (1975), trans. Betsy Wing (Manchester, 1986), p. 101.
32 Elizabeth Wright, 'Transmission in Psychoanalysis and Literature: Whose Text is it Anyway?', in *Discourse in Psychoanalysis and Literature*, ed. Shlomith Rimmon-Kenan (London and New York, 1978), p. 90.
33 Cixous and Clément, op. cit., p. 134.
34 Wright, op. cit., p. 93.
35 Cixous and Clément, op. cit., p. 139.
36 Jacques Lacan, quoted by François Roustang in *Dire Mastery: Discipleship from Freud to Lacan*, trans. Ned Lukacher (Baltimore, 1982).
37 Rich, op. cit., p. 235.
38 Le Doeuff, op. cit., p. 188.
39 Roustang, op. cit., p. 33.
40 Quoted by Roustang, op. cit., p. 81 from Paul Roazen's *Brother Animal: The Story of Freud and Tausk* (1969) (Harmondsworth, 1973).
41 Roustang, op. cit., pp. 114–15.
42 ibid. p. 39.
43 Cornelius Castoriadis, *Crossroads in the Labyrinth* (1978), trans. Kate Soper and Martin H. Ryle (Brighton, 1984), p. 86.
44 Catherine Clément, *The Lives and Legends of Jacques Lacan*, trans. Arthur Goldhammer (New York, 1983).
45 Castoriadis, op. cit., p. 64.
46 Le Doeuff, op. cit., p. 199.
47 ibid., pp. 205–6.
48 Roustang, op. cit., p. 68.
49 Le Doeuff, op. cit., p. 206.
50 Nancy Chodorow, *The Reproduction of Mothering: Psychoanalysis and the Sociology of Gender* (Berkeley, California, 1978).

51 Cixous and Clément, op. cit., p. 138.
52 ibid., p. 139.
53 Hegel, op. cit., p. 114, §166.
54 Roustang, op. cit., pp. 149–50.
55 ibid., p. 25.

Chapter 5

An other space: a future for feminism?

Jane Moore

I

Feminists have always written from an other position and from the position of the other.[1] But the project rising from this shared starting-point has not always been the same. Feminist writing of the 1970s commonly sought to make women and their texts visible within patriarchal culture, with the joint aim of stressing the difference of women's writing from men's, and procuring for women a position of full subjectivity on a par with that seen to be enjoyed by men.[2] In the 1980s, however, the emphasis has shifted from procuring full subjectivity for women to calling into question the possibility of its realization, for men as well as for women. This has led in many instances to a re-conceptualization of the relationship between the knower and the known. In Britain, work by Rachel Bowlby, Rosalind Coward and Chris Weedon, among others, has suggested that culture is the limit of our knowledge, and, in consequence, has revealed the impossibility of full unified subjectivity.[3] In America, Barbara Johnson, Jane Gallop, Alice Jardine, Gayatri Spivak and Shoshana Felman have separately explored the consequences for the future of feminism and sexual difference of refusing to continue to conceptualize ignorance as the subordinate and static binary opposite of knowledge, which is the privileged term.[4] Barbara Johnson writes: 'Much has been made of the fact that "knowledge" cannot be taken for granted. But perhaps rather than simply questioning the nature of knowledge, we should today re-evaluate the static, inert concept we have always had of ignorance. Ignorance, far more than knowledge, is what can never be taken for granted.'[5]

Precisely why ignorance can never be taken for granted is the subject of another of Johnson's essays, 'Teaching Ignorance'. In a reading of Molière's play *L'Ecole des femmes* Johnson analyses the gender politics of pedagogy, bringing to prominence the assumption in the history of Western (male) thought that to know is to master, and to be masterful is usually to be male.[6] Johnson's essay goes on to argue that although ignorance has historically been gendered as *feminine*, it is possible to argue that the concept of ignorance has strongly *feminist* connotations:

In this sense, paradoxically enough, it could be said that Plato's belief in Socrates' pedagogical mastery is an attempt to repress the inherent 'feminism' of Socrates' ignorance. And it is out of this repression of Socrates' feminism that Western pedagogy springs.[7]

French feminism, especially the work of Luce Irigaray, makes similar points about the repression of female 'ignorance' in Western philosophy.[8]

Alongside feminist forays into ignorance, but in a way that has sometimes been blind to its implications for the politics of gender, nowhere more so than in Jean-François Lyotard's book, *The Postmodern Condition*, post-modern theory has initiated a rethinking of the status of knowledge and of its relation to the knower.[9] *The Postmodern Condition* identifies a decline in the legitimating power of the grand narratives of history. One of the consequences of this decline has been to call into question the assumption that the speaking and writing subject generates and guarantees meaning, with the result that the very possibility of the subject ever fully knowing and mastering meaning is denied. But denying the possibility of an autonomous and unified knowing subject is not at all the same as abolishing the illusion that this is what we think we are. Neither is it coterminous with abolishing the will to master meaning and the desire for knowledge. My concern in this paper is with the future of feminism as what is at stake in either striving to sustain or working to disrupt the mastery accorded to the subject by what Terry Eagleton terms 'the Enlightenment's grand narrative of human eman-cipation'.[10]

My paper is thus shaped not only by feminist work on knowledge and ignorance – work that itself might easily be said to be produced at the interface of post-modernity – but also by some of the unfavourable responses that *The Postmodern Condition* itself has received. Here I am thinking in particular of Fredric Jameson's paper, 'Postmodernism, or The Cultural Logic of Late Capitalism', and of Terry Eagleton's follow-on piece, 'Capitalism, Modernism and Postmodernism'.[11]

Without, I hope, reducing Jameson's and Eagleton's lengthy arguments to the point of absurdity, I want to suggest that their essays effectively but prematurely close the post-modern debate in a way which renders *The Post-modern Condition* virtually unreadable as anything other than a reactionary manifesto that has nothing to say to socialists or feminists about political struggle and social change.

Both Eagleton's and Jameson's masterful, yet paradoxically elegiac nar-ratives, mourn the loss of the master Marxist narrative which enabled us to situate ourselves historically and thence to emancipate ourselves from what is taken to be the disempowering, decathected, dehistoricized, relativism of the post-modern condition.

The Postmodern Condition contends that meaning and history, or more aptly, histories, are produced 'within the domain of a general agonistics', that is, within relations of struggle and difference.[12] But Jameson's essay refuses to conceive of the possibility of a politics of struggle and change without the conceptual anchor of 'truth'. In a nostalgic quest for modernity which, unlike the post-modern condition, asserts the existence of true meaning and fixes it historically, the essay looks back to the past in a regressive move and mood that is everywhere apparent. The essay's subtitles, for example, throw into relief what is assumed to be the anti-humanist, even death-inducing nature of the post-modernist aesthetic. Some of these subtitles are: 'Pastiche Eclipses Parody', '"Historicism" Effaces History', 'The Fate of "Real History"' and 'Loss of the Radical Past'.[13]

Eagleton's essay goes along with Jameson's contention that in the post-modern condition style substitutes for struggle, pastiche replaces politics and representation eclipses the referent. In Jameson's account the historicity of post-modernity is defined as a 'random cannibalization of all the styles of the past', with the result that 'the past as "referent" finds itself gradually brack-eted, and then effaced altogether, *leaving us with nothing but texts*'[14] (my emphasis). This final phrase, 'leaving us with nothing but texts', is significant. It makes apparent the assumption running throughout Jameson's essay, and others written from a Marxist interest in defending the concept of 'truth', that words only make meanings work in the most passive of senses, that is to say, words transparently reflect and therefore facilitate access to the meanings *behind* them.[15] It supposes also, as David Simpson has noted, that the only alternative to telling the truth, is to 'celebrate pluralism or diversity as a matter of faith'.[16]

And this is the line that Eagleton's essay takes. Without a totalizing theory to explain and historicize meaning, without a theory grounded in historical event or truth, we are left only with the random plays of difference, which are no more than the effect of style. Hence, according to Eagleton, in *The Postmodern Condition*:

> Totalizing historical theories must yield to a 'pragmatics of narrative' ... there can be no real difference for Lyotard between truth, authority and rhetorical seductiveness: he who has the smoothest tongue or the raciest story has the power. ... Nor can there be any total social critique, since there is nothing left to be criticized. We are always caught up in one narrative or another, and can never catapult ourselves to some meta-linguistic vantage-point beyond them.[17]

Perhaps unsurprisingly Eagleton's essay never consciously draws attention to its own style, which is seamless: the voice of the essay is authoritative and unhesitating. For feminism, however, style is not only a political matter, but very often it is the matter of politics. For feminists narratives are not neutral, language is not transparent, style is not innocent. From a feminist perspective there is much to say about Eagleton's magisterial prose, but what is perhaps more significant – or at least more pertinent to this essay – is that his master-

"I think,
therefore
IBM."

IBM

ful style is neither sustainable nor sustained. Towards the end of the essay indecision intrudes into Eagleton's sure sentences, the authoritative voice falters and the seamless prose is fissured. What is remarkable about this intrusion is that it occurs at the precise moment when feminism appears on the post-modern scene, which happens as follows:

> there are few more intractable problems in the modern epoch than of distinguishing between those critiques of classical rationality which are potentially progressive, and those which are irrationalist in the worst sense. It is the choice, so to speak, between feminism and fascism.[18]

The challenge of feminism, it seems, is that it offers a critique of classical (male?) rationality that is potentially progressive. But this is a challenge that although named in Eagleton's essay is never seriously entertained. In place of an attention to feminist politics the essay turns to post-modern critiques of classical rationality, and turns on them because they produce what is taken to be a disempowering relativism, which potentially reproduces a barbarous, fascist type of irrationality. The price paid for this attack is the loss of what is earlier glimpsed in the essay as the appearance in our culture of 'a quite different rationality, which still newly emergent, is not even able to name itself', but is identified as feminist.[19]

It is precisely this 'quite different rationality' that I want to explore with respect to recent feminist writing. And I want to pick up on the almost off-hand suggestion in Eagleton's essay that feminism might currently be involved in the production of an other cognitive space – a space that occupies the realm of the unknown, which is the unpresentable of totalizing thought. However, I wish to add that post-modern theory is more implicated in this process than Eagleton allows. Following on from this, I want to raise the possibility that feminism offers a liberating way of reading *The Postmodern Condition*, which is to read it as a liberating text, and in doing so re-opens, or rather keeps open, the post-modernist debate.

II

As a way into 'the post-modern condition' I want briefly to look at an advertisement for IBM, which appeared in the *Guardian* newspaper on 20 May 1988, and which is reproduced on the following page. When I first came across the advertisement I read it in the manner in which presumably it was intended to be read, that is, as a joke, as a piece of Enlightenment tomfoolery which takes advantage of both the probable familiarity of *Guardian* readers with the Cartesian cogito and the capacity of the English language for punning and double meanings.[20] In this context, it is possible to interpret the sentence 'I think, therefore IBM' simply as a rewording of the initial cogito with emphasis added. That is to say, here the 'I am' of 'I think, therefore I am' is doubly affirmed in its reinscription as 'I B(e) and I (a)M'.

Yet despite trying to make sense of the advertisement in this way, which is to read it commonsensically, what such a reading has to repress in order to maintain the illusion of the centrality of the subject in the knowledge process is the paradox that the moment of the self's affirmation is also that of its petrification with respect to knowledge. Knowledge is located not in the corporeal human I, but in the non-human corporate body of IBM, into which the two separate affirmations of being – I B(e) and I (a)M – are collapsed.

In consequence, the sentence now works as a kind of post-modernist anti-cogito, which calls forth the mastering position granted to the knowing autonomous 'I' in the sum of the Cartesian cogito only to deny it. I write post-modernist, because what we are here presented with is possibly nothing less than the realization of a prediction made in Lyotard's *The Postmodern Condition* almost ten years ago. This was that in the context of the miniaturization of machines and the corresponding commercialization of knowledge we could expect 'a thorough exteriorization of knowledge with respect to the "knower"'.[21]

But what is striking about the sentence 'I think, therefore IBM' is that whether the sum of this cogito is interpreted as a double affirmation of self-mastery or as the loss of a mastering self, it is impossible entirely to dispose of the initial 'I' which mobilizes the sentence and which resists displacement into the sum of IBM. At the level of that initial 'I' the desire for mastery remains momentarily intact. And, by implication, so too does the unitary *male* subject.[22]

Jacques Lacan has written, 'we know that what begins at the level of the subject is never without consequence, on condition that we know what the term *subject* means'.[23] Catharine MacKinnon 'knows' what the term subject does not mean, and that is woman: 'A subject', writes Mackinnon, 'is a self. An object is other to that self. Anyone who is the least bit attentive to gender since reading Simone de Beauvoir knows that it is men, socially, who are subjects; women, socially, who are other, objects.'[24] If this is so, and if we know, to paraphrase Craig Owens, that 'the representational systems of the West [of which the Cartesian cogito is the most traditional] admit only one vision – that of the constitutive male subject – [and] posit the subject of representation as absolutely centered, unitary, masculine';[25] and if the consequence of the 'I' that begins the cogito is to re-inscribe the male subject's desire for total mastery of and total power over the discourse of itself and others, then it may be that one of the most strategically important questions addressed by feminist writing implicated in post-modernism is the question of the politics of style. Style is, among other things, a matter of inscribing the 'I' in writing; the politics of style, therefore, are the politics of gender also. And it is to the gender politics of style that I now want to turn.

III

Language is not transparent. The author is dead. These are the lessons of post-structuralism. They have taught us that style is not incidental, spontaneous or natural; it is not the property of a unique individual. It is culturally and historically produced; it is, therefore, always-already, but not essentially, gendered. Meanings, meanwhile, which are produced from the struggle between competing narratives, are not single or fixed, but multiple and unstable, always in process, and constantly changing. All of these post-structuralist precepts pertain to the post-modern condition where the grand narrative has lost its credibility. That is to say, those masterful and masterly accounts of the world, which claim to explain it, and which centre on 'Man, the Subject, Truth, History, Meaning' have been delegitimized and put into crisis.[26] In consequence, the subject who presumes to know has lost *his* authority.

The use of the masculine form is appropriate here. Alice Jardine has written in her book *Gynesis* that: 'The crises experienced by the major Western narratives have not ... been gender-neutral. They are crises in the narratives invented by men.'[27] This is not to say that women have never been complicit in these narratives; they have. Margaret Thatcher is the most obvious example. But then Margaret Thatcher is not a feminist. Alice Jardine, on the other hand, is. And it is a striking feature of *Gynesis* as well as of other recent feminist theory that loss of the legitimating function of master narratives and the consequent loss of a fixed place from which to speak is not mourned. On the contrary, such losses are commonly brought to prominence, even celebrated, in texts which continually draw the reader's attention to the precarious non-masterful position of their narrative voices.

In Jane Gallop's work, for example, a non-masterful style is used to disrupt and call into question the authority of patriarchal pretences to mastery. In *Feminism and Psychoanalysis* Gallop declares: 'In this book, the writer's viewpoint, the narrative voice, changes – from chapter to chapter, even within chapters.'[28] Gallop similarly begins her more recent book, *Reading Lacan*, by refusing to authorize her own narrative voice and by pleading guilty to the charge of ignorance: a reader's report accused her of having neither fully read, nor properly understood Lacan, and of having failed to master his texts.[29] Gallop doesn't dispute this charge, although she does question its implications as follows:

> The attempt to cover up one's inadequate command of Lacan's text necessitates a violent reduction of the contradictory plurality and ambiguity of that text, just as the assembling of a coherent self necessitates repression. I believe that the pretense of a masterful grasp of Lacan serves only to consolidate the oppressive mystification of the Lacanian institution. Lacan talks insightfully about the 'subject presumed to know'. I am trying to undo that illusion ... and therefore wish to write from some

other position. This project is profoundly feminist. It involves calling into question the phallic illusions of authority.[30]

Judged on the criterion of mastery, another 'failure' would presumably be Shoshana Felman whose book, *Jacques Lacan and the Adventure of Insight*, also relinquishes any pretence to having fully mastered that subject.[31] One interpretation of Gallop's and Felman's refusal to speak from a position of mastery over a text or even to be the masters of their own texts might be that these claims to relinquish the pretence to know are in themselves a pretence, perhaps even pretentious.[32]

But I want to suggest that it is impossible to accuse Gallop and Felman of writing in bad faith without simultaneously re-inscribing the subject who knows. And, anyway, even if it could be proved that, say, *Reading Lacan* bears the marks of mastery in its formation into sentences, paragraphs, chapters, etc., this wouldn't override the feminist project in hand. For it seems to me that what is offered in these texts is something more than coy disclaimers of authorial responsibility of the kind that women writing in the eighteenth century were expected to inscribe in the prefaces to their novels. That is to say, what is at work here is the production of an other knowledge from an other position, which is the position of the female other. It is, in other words, what Alice Jardine calls 'gynesis', 'the putting into discourse of "woman"'.[33]

IV

In the book *Gynesis* Jardine observes that throughout western history the master narratives that structure patriarchal culture have consistently marginalized women, thus placing them on the edge of reason, truth, meaning and certainty. If this was all Jardine had to offer then perhaps at best *Gynesis* would be saying nothing new, and at worst it would be reaffirming what men have always said about women: that women are less capable of reasoning objectively than men because, as is well known, they are less rational than men and have a less developed sense of judgement than men. But Jardine is saying something more and something quite different from this. Her book argues that the current post-modern crisis in legitimation 'has brought about, within the master narratives in the West, a vast self-exploration, a questioning and turning back upon their own discourse, in an attempt to create a new *space* or *spacing within themselves*'.[34] This space, notes Jardine, 'has been coded as *feminine*, as *woman*'.[35] What is more, its creation has resulted in 'the valorization of the feminine, woman, and her obligatory, that is, historical connotations, as somehow intrinsic to new and necessary [post-modern] modes of thinking, writing, speaking'.[36]

Now it seems to me that what is going on in Gallop's and Felman's repudiations of mastery and their consequent admissions of ignorance is precisely the production of the new and necessary ways of thinking, writing and speaking to which Jardine refers. These are ways of thinking that consciously begin to break up binary thought and potentially break out of an oppositional concept of sexual difference. For example, when Gallop, Felman and Johnson re-evaluate the status of ignorance, they not only produce an other form of cognition, they simultaneously unfix the binarism of knowledge/ignorance which has shaped the history of western thought and given credibility to patriarchal versions of it. Constantly wary of fixing ignorance as an essential attribute of the female sex, and careful not to reaffirm the old cultural opposition where femininity is aligned with frippery and ignorance and masculinity is aligned with mastery and knowledge, these writers bring to prominence the binary-breaking play of *différance*. Ignorance is thus revealed not as a totally other and, therefore, totalizing kind of knowledge, but as an integral part of the production of meaning and the process of knowing. In Felman's words, 'human knowledge is, by definition, that which is untotalizable, that which rules out any possibility of totalizing what it knows or of eradicating its own ignorance. ... Ignorance is thus no longer simply opposed to knowledge: it is itself a radical condition, an integral part of the very structure of knowledge.'[37]

The production of a conceptual space that pertains to the unknown, not the known, and to the knower, not knowledge, might be one way of summarizing gynesis. Yet, perhaps, not a very good one since the sentence is already structured by the binarism that gynesis unfixes and puts into process. What is illustrated by the sentence, however, is the ease with which it is possible to return to binary thinking; *Gynesis* itself has been criticized on exactly this count. Rachel Bowlby has argued that the 'anti-American tilt' of *Gynesis* manifests itself in cultural schematic opposition where:

> All the bad qualities associated with 'the west' [stasis, theme, pragmatism, realism] get attributed to the United States; and where non-western cultures [and their good qualities: process, text, theory, (post)modernism] figure as other in relation to the west, so Europe, and especially France, can come, bizarrely, perhaps, to stand in as the new or different departure from old and oppressive America.[38]

While Bowlby's argument with *Gynesis* illustrates well the seductive but dangerous hold binarism still has on our thinking, and therefore needs to be acknowledged, I want to urge making a less negative acknowledgement than Bowlby makes of Jardine's book in general and the effect of gynesis in particular.

Like Bowlby, I too situate *Gynesis* alongside work by Julia Kristeva and Jane Gallop, not because I want to privilege France above America – on the contrary, it is Americans, such as Felman, Jardine, Gallop and Johnson, who beautifully make French theory work *for* American and, I think, for British readers – but because the implications for the future of feminist and sexual politics of making those theories work, of putting them into process seem to me to be radical and exciting. As a process which puts *différance* to work, gynesis potentially offers the feminist reader a utopian space that goes beyond the history of sexual identity, which refuses essentialist versions of sexual difference and the binary oppositions which structure it, which goes beyond the ideological fixity of 'truth-in-experience', and which puts into discourse what Julia Kristeva, in her essay 'Women's Time', has termed the subject in process.[39]

To attempt fully to describe that space would in one sense be to divest it of its Utopian element, because this would involve colonizing it and appropriating it for a still patriarchal present, and a still binarily-structured society. I do not want, therefore, to finish this essay by attempting to describe the new spacing gynesis would map, and to supply the closure gynesis resists, but to offer instead the thought that if *The Postmodern Condition* is read alongside *Gynesis*, and alongside Kristeva's essay 'Women's Time', it becomes possible to read post-modernism differently.

'Women's Time' was published in France in 1979, which was also the year of publication of Lyotard's *La Condition postmoderne*. 'Women's Time' identifies two ways of thinking about time: linear and cyclical. Linear time is associated with the first generation of feminists and their attempt to secure women's rights within existing society, within the symbolic order. Cyclical time is associated with a second-generation feminism that stressed the difference between men and women, and led in some instances to a separatist politics. In place of both these generations and their corresponding ways of thinking about time, which 'Women's Time' resists because of their shared tendency to fix female identity, the essay proposes a third time-phase or, more properly, a new space, where the play of *différance*, of difference *and* deferral, is celebrated as the condition of all sexual identity, so that the cultural characteristics of both femininity and masculinity become the basis of all subjectivity. In this way sexual identity is released and exposed as unfixed, not timeless, always in process and always incomplete.

To place *The Postmodern Condition* in the context of the conceptual space occupied by the third generation of women in 'Women's Time', at the same time as reading it as a text, or con-text of that essay, is I suggest to begin to glimpse the possibility of reading Lyotard's book differently from some of its Marxist, as well as feminist, critics. This would be to read the post-modern condition as a potentially liberating one and to see there the possibility of creating a space where the sexual opposition masculine/feminine and the epistemological opposition knowledge/ignorance is undone.

Could it be, then, that this is the conceptual space where, to paraphrase Jane Gallop, identity is continually assumed and immediately called into question?[40] Could this be the space about which Kristeva asks: 'What can "identity", even "sexual identity", mean in a new theoretical ... space where the very notion of identity is challenged?'[41] And is it here with these pertinent political post-modern questions that the future of feminism lies?

NOTES

1 Although I describe the position of women in relation to men in patriarchal societies as 'other', and find the term useful because it invokes both the desire and the lack which characterize the relation between (male) subject and (female) other, the term is also problematic. It is problematic in the sense that 'the other' can quickly become a blanket-term for all that is outside the subject possessed of the power to name the other, for everything that is not self-same. In consequence, the effect of otherness can be the erasure of difference, so that, for example, all women – past and present – share the same ontological and epistemological space.

But, as Gayatri Spivak's work has stressed, not all women are equally subordinated, not all women have equal access to speech, and not all women will utter what white Western feminists may want to hear. Spivak's essays, 'Can the Subaltern Speak?' (in Cary Nelson and Lawrence Grossberg, eds, *Marxism and the Interpretation of Culture*, London: Macmillan, 1988, pp. 271–313) and 'Three Women's Texts and a Critique of Imperialism' (in Catherine Belsey and Jane Moore, eds, *The Feminist Reader: Essays in Gender and the Politics of Literary Criticism*, London: Macmillan and New York: Basil Blackwell, 1989, pp. 175–95), alert the reader to the way that Western imperialism has totalized a non-white other, adding that white Western feminist theory may inadvertently perpetuate that form of oppression by grafting their theoretical projects and knowledges on to non-Western texts. 'Three Women's Texts' points in its reading of *Jane Eyre* to the way that Bertha – the white colonial 'other' woman – is the price paid for Jane's purchase of an (illusory) full subject-identity. The essay adds that readings of *Jane Eyre* by Western feminists frequently forget the other woman in the same moment that they implicitly name her as other. The alternative, Spivak's work proposes, is not to bring back the other as fully individuated subject, since to do this is only to reaffirm a liberal-feminist individualism; but rather to insist on marking the *positionality* of the feminist critical investigator. Elsewhere, Spivak urges the feminist reader to ask 'not merely who am I? but who is the other woman? How am I naming her? How does she name me?' ('French Feminism in an International Frame', in Spivak, *In Other Worlds: Essays in Cultural Politics*, New York and London: Methuen, 1987, pp. 134–53, p. 150).

2 Three famous books published in the 1970s share the aim of making women's writing visible in patriarchal culture and distinguishing a female literary tradition: Elaine Showalter's *A Literature Of Their Own*, published in 1977, identifies a distinct female literary tradition and finds there the difference of women's experience from men's. In 1979 Sandra M. Gilbert and Susan Gubar published *The Madwoman in the Attic*. Like Showalter's book, *The Madwoman in the Attic* analyses fiction primarily as the expression of female experience, or more precisely, of the anxiety and anger, rage and misery, that women writing under patriarchy feel. The third book is Ellen Moers's *Literary Women*, published in 1977, which analyses the effect on women's writing of their marginal position in patriarchal societies.

3 See Rachel Bowlby, *Just Looking: Consumer Culture in Dreiser, Gissing and Zola* (New York and London: Methuen, 1982); Rosalind Coward, *Female Desire: Women's Sexuality Today* (London: Paladin, 1984) and Chris Weedon, *Feminist Practice and Poststructuralist Theory* (Oxford: Basil Blackwell, 1987).

4 See Barbara Johnson, *A World of Difference* (Baltimore and London: Johns Hopkins University Press, 1989); Jane Gallop, *Feminism and Psychoanalysis: The Daughter's Seduction* (London: Macmillan, 1986) and *Reading Lacan* (Ithaca and London: Cornell University Press, 1985); Alice Jardine, *Gynesis: Configurations of Woman and Modernity* (Ithaca and London: Cornell University Press, 1985);

Gayatri Spivak, *In Other Worlds: Essays in Cultural Politics*; Shoshana Felman, *Jacques Lacan and the Adventure of Insight: Psychoanalysis in Contemporary Culture* (Cambridge, Massachusetts and London: Harvard University Press, 1987).

5 Barbara Johnson, 'Nothing Fails Like Success', in *A World of Difference*, pp. 11–16, p. 16.

6 Barbara Johnson, 'Teaching Ignorance', in *A World of Difference*, pp. 68–85.

7 ibid., p. 85.

8 See Luce Irigaray, *Speculum of the Other Woman*, trans. Gillian C. Gill (Ithaca and New York: Cornell University Press, 1985). The book was originally published in France as *Speculum de l'autre femme* (Paris: Minuit, 1974). A simple, but crude, summary of *Speculum* might be that it comprises a series of essays which offer a critique of Freudian psychoanalysis in particular and of the history of western (patriarchal) philosophy in general – or at least from Plato to Hegel. But to say this much is to convey nothing at all of the remarkable stylistic verve (and nerve?) of *Speculum*. The style of *Speculum* goes beyond usual conceptions of what counts as knowledge in as much as it exceeds 'common-sense' understanding, renouncing the teleological chronology of the thesis format. As Irigaray herself has put it, 'Strictly speaking, *Speculum* has no beginning or end. The architectonics of the text, or texts, confounds the linearity of an outline, the teleology of a discourse, within which there is no possible place for the "feminine", except the traditional place of the repressed, the censured' (Irigaray, *This Sex Which is Not One*, trans. Catherine Porter with Carolyn Burke, Ithaca and New York: Cornell University Press, 1985, p. 68. *This Sex* first appeared in France as *Ce Sexe qui n'en est pas un* (Paris: Minuit, 1977). Part of the project of both *Speculum* and *This Sex* is to re-evaluate-as-knowledge the feminine discourse which men have historically called ignorance, thus calling into question the relation of knowledge and ignorance in Western history.

9 Jean-François Lyotard, *The Postmodern Condition: A Report on Knowledge*, trans. Geoff Bennington and Brian Massumi (Minneapolis: University of Minnesota Press, 1984 and Manchester: University of Manchester Press, 1987). The book was originally published in France as *La Condition postmoderne: rapport sur le savoir* (Paris: Minuit, 1979).

10 Terry Eagleton, 'Capitalism, Modernism and Postmodernism', *New Left Review* 152, 1985, pp. 60–73, p. 63.

11 Fredric Jameson, 'Postmodernism, or The Cultural Logic of Late Capitalism', *New Left Review* 146, 1984, pp. 53–92. See also Anders Stephanson, 'Regarding Postmodernism – A Conversation with Fredric Jameson', *Social Text* 17, 1987, pp. 29–54.

12 Lyotard, op. cit., p. 10.

13 Jameson, op. cit., pp. 64–5, 68–70.

14 Jameson, op. cit., pp. 5–6.

15 For further criticism of *The Postmodern Condition* from a Marxist-feminist perspective see Meaghan Morris's essay, 'Postmodernity and Lyotard's Sublime', included in her collected essays, *The Pirate's Fiancée: Feminism, Reading, Postmodernism* (London and New York: Verso, 1988), pp. 213–39. Like Eagleton's essay, Morris's criticism is delivered from a belief in the need to hang on to the concept of truth. Not only does Morris's essay support truth, it takes issue with *The Postmodern Condition*'s implication that truth really is under threat. The essay asserts that 'incredulity towards master (and/or meta-) narratives is not necessarily the kind of universal *fait accompli* ... Lyotard suggests' and proposes that even if a crisis in the credibility of master-narratives is occurring, it can, 'in context,

simply mean the disintegration of motivating arguments for intervening in any-thing at all', pp. 222, 233.

16 David Simpson, 'Literary Criticism and the Return to "History"', *Critical Inquiry* 14, 1988, pp. 721–47, p. 744.

17 Terry Eagleton, 'Awakening from Modernity', *Times Literary Supplement*, 20 February 1987, p. 194.

18 Eagleton, 'Capitalism, Modernism and Postmodernism', p. 70.

19 ibid., p. 70. In a review of Lyotard's *Le Postmoderne expliqué aux enfants* and *Just Gaming*, co-written with Jean-Loup Thébaud, Eagleton casts a similarly fleeting glance in the direction of feminism, here positioning feminism as the spectre which haunts post-modernity. One of the reasons why Eagleton criticizes Lyotard is because '[t]here is no comment in his recent work on the women's movement, which complicates his own view of Enlightenment by its simultaneous belief in emancipation and hostility to dominative rationality' ('Awakening From Modernity', p. 194).

20 The joke has recently been shared by Amstrad, at IBM's expense. An adver-tisement in the *Guardian* on 16 February 1989 compares IBM's 8086 Processor with Amstrad's. Needless to say, at half the price of the IBM model and with added extras, Amstrad comes off best. Bringing the intertextual allusion home is a caption which refashions the Cartesian cogito for a capitalist age as follows:

'I THINK MORE CAREFULLY
THEREFORE I AMSTRAD.'

21 Lyotard, op. cit., p. 4.

22 I interpret the Cartesian ego as symbolically unitary, masterful and male in spite of the well-known story that its author insisted on publishing not in Latin – the usual and almost exclusively male-learnt language of learning – but in French. Moreover, as Genevieve Lloyd, among others, has observed, 'Descartes saw his method as opening the way to a new egalitarianism in knowledge. In a letter written shortly after the publication of the *Discourse on Method*, he commented that his thoughts on method seemed to him appropriate to put in a book where he wished that "even women" might understand something' (Lloyd, *The Man of Reason: 'Male' and 'Female' in Western Philosophy* (London: Methuen, 1986), p. 44).

But Lloyd also observes that despite the egalitarian aims of Descartes's method, the social realities of women's lives precluded their full involvement in the collec-tive, scientific endeavour which was sparked off by Descartes's method and soon outstripped it (p. 49). In consequence, 'Women have been assigned responsibility for that realm of the sensuous which the Cartesian Man of Reason must transcend, if he is to have true knowledge of things' (p. 50).

Philosophers have, of course, raised doubts about the infallibility of the cogito, suggesting that the appeal to God as the author and guarantor of man's existence produces not deductive method but a theocentrically circular argument. See, for example, A. D. Lindsay's criticisms of the cogito in his introduction to *A Discourse on Method: Meditations and Principles*, trans. John Veitch (London: Dent, 1912; reprinted 1978), pp. vii–xxiv. For more recent criticism of the cogito, see Jonathan Rée, *Philosophical Tales: An Essay on Philosophy and Literature* (London and New York: Methuen, 1987). See especially chapter 1, 'Descartes' Comedy', pp. 5–30.

Yet despite these criticisms, to which I add that the subject, Descartes's, appeal to God, to the *grand autre*, is the means by which his identity is conferred and confirmed, with the result that the Cartesian ego loses its assumed autonomy and magisterial oneness, it is clear that the illusion of the knowing subject who is the site of all (self) knowledge is born with the cogito. Telling the story of the place of the Cartesian cogito in the history of philosophy, Rée writes:

> 'Here we finally reach home', as Hegel put it after surveying 2,000 years of philosophy leading up to Descartes, 'and like a mariner after a long voyage in a tempestuous sea, we can shout, "Land ho!"'; for with Descartes the culture and thought of modern times really begin.'

(p. 5)

23 Jacques Lacan, *The Four Fundamental Concepts of Psycho-Analysis*, ed. Jacques Alain Miller, trans. Alan Sheridan (Harmondsworth: Penguin, 1987), p. 37.
24 Catharine A. MacKinnon, 'Desire and Power: A Feminist Perspective', in Nelson and Grossberg, eds, *Marxism and the Interpretation of Culture*, pp. 105–16, p. 111.
25 Craig Owens, 'The Discourse of Others: Feminists and Postmodernism', in Hal Foster, ed., *The Anti-Aesthetic: Essays on Postmodern Culture* (Washington: Bay Press, 1985), pp. 65–90, p. 66.
26 Jardine, op. cit., p. 25.
27 ibid., p. 24.
28 Gallop, *Feminism and Psychoanalysis*, p. xi.
29 Gallop, *Reading Lacan*, pp. 18–21.
30 ibid., p. 20.
31 Felman, *Jacques Lacan and the Adventure of Insight*.
32 Another strategic interpretation is to subordinate Gallop's and Felman's work altogether, which is the strategy adopted by Geoffrey Bennington's essay, 'Deconstruction and the Philosophers (The Very Idea)', in Robert Young, ed., *Oxford Literary Review* 10, anniversary issue, 1988, pp. 73–130. Significantly enough, in an essay that implicitly defines knowledge as mastery and is clearly a masterful piece of prose, Lacanians like Gallop and Felman, who are also, of course, women, are relegated to the sidelines of the argument. Lacanian psychoanalytic theory is pushed into parenthesis as follows:

> Gasché's much-quoted 'Deconstruction as Criticism' told us what we feared: that we were philosophically naive or at least 'untrained'. . . . Not, of course, that *we* had ever really been guilty of the confusions Gasché so severely denounced, though we all knew someone who was. But as reproaches went, there was a disturbing difference between these and the sort we had got used to from the moralists such as Said or Jameson or Eagleton, who simply kept getting it wrong about reference or history or the political or the real (*best not even mention the Lacanians* [my emphasis]), and who could be easily enough refuted, however volubly they repeated their charges. Putting them right kept us going happily enough (though tended to give some people the unfortunate idea that something they kept calling a 'debate' was going on, or, even worse, that talk of 'agendas' was in order). This was different, and something of a threat: far from being someone we could laugh at and put right, Gasché clearly *knew better*.

(p. 74)

Is it only a coincidence that Gasché's – the philosopher's – readings of continental philosophy are privileged above the efforts of literary critics? Isn't it precisely because Gasché is a philosopher and therefore is taken to stand for 'scholarship' – read rigour, read mastery, read masculinity – that his work is positioned as the (philosophical) other, threat to literary criticism? Lacanians do not receive the same treatment; the threat posed by Lacanian theory which, given its large number of female advocates – Felman, Gallop, and, to a degree, Johnson and Spivak – is the threat of the (female) other, never receives the 'serious' consideration accorded to philosophy. Is the neglect of Lacanian feminists perhaps the sign of a greater threat to the history of patriarchal philosophical thought than the essay consciously concedes?

33 Jardine, *op. cit.*, p. 25.
34 ibid.
35 ibid.
36 ibid.
37 Felman, *Jacques Lacan and the Adventure of Insight*, p. 78.
38 Bowlby, 'Flight Reservations', in Robert Young, ed., *Oxford Literary Review* 10, pp. 61–72, p. 67.
39 Julia Kristeva, 'Women's Time', trans. Alice Jardine and Harry Blake, in Belsey and Moore, eds, *The Feminist Reader*, pp. 197–217. 'Women's Time' was originally published as 'Le Temps des femmes', in *33/44: Cahiers de recherche de sciences des textes et documents* 5, Winter 1979, pp. 5–19.
40 Gallop, *Feminism and Psychoanalysis*, p. xii.
41 Kristeva, op. cit., pp. 214–15.

Part II

Subjectivities

Chapter 6

Releasing possibility into form: cultural choice and the woman writer

Carol Watts

> The body of a woman is one of the essential elements in her situation in the world. But that body is not enough to define her as woman; there is no true living reality except as manifested by the conscious individual through activities and in the bosom of a society.
>
> (Simone de Beauvoir, *The Second Sex*)[1]

> Whereas a few men here and there are creators, originators, *artists*, women are this all the time.
>
> (Dorothy Richardson, *Pilgrimage*)[2]

In her familiar proposition, 'one is not born, but rather becomes, a woman',[3] Simone de Beauvoir asserts what has subsequently become for feminism an enabling distinction between 'natural' and culturally defined identity, between sex and gender. The physical fact of a woman's body is 'not enough' to define her, essentially, as a woman; rather such an identity is allotted to her within a continual process of acculturation that positions her in a restricting and defining set of cultural norms. In an original and suggestive essay, 'Variations on Sex and Gender', Judith Butler has extended the interpretation of Beauvoir's formulation, exploring the ambiguity in the notion of 'becoming' with its dual sense of both 'being constructed' and 'constructing oneself'. Becoming a woman is thus 'the acquisition of a skill' – in Sartrean terms a project 'to purposefully assume or embody' one's gender. In other words, gender identity is not simply a matter of cultural construction but also, significantly, a 'volitional set of acts', a matter of choice.[4]

Judith Butler's exploration in Beauvoir's work of a theory of gender that 'tries to make cultural sense of the existential doctrine of choice' (p. 128) may prove of value to feminist literary analysis, at a time when the nature of a feminist aesthetics is once again on the agenda. For it is clear that literature in its many forms is an important cultural site of gender construction, reinforcing and promoting social norms while also providing a forum where social experience can be worked through and to some extent collectively possessed, made manifest and conscious. In this sense the sphere of literature can be seen covertly to secure consent – unconscious 'choice' – from its participants in naturalizing social conventions which define gender roles; yet by the same token it can also show such 'norms' to be a matter of invention and interpretation, and thus open to alternative choices or possible change. The recent renewal of interest in the question of women's authorship and its relation to literary form, indicated by the number of 'gender and genre' articles, events and journals emerging over the last few years, suggests that generic formal constraints might also be seen to relate to the ways in which women writers and readers engage with their gendered identity. If, as Jeffrey Weeks has argued, 'Identity is not a destiny but a choice ... identities are not expressions of secret essences. They are self-creations, but they are creations on ground not freely chosen but laid out by history',[5] might not literary genres, conventions of representation, form part of that ground?

What role then does literature – its production and consumption – have to play in the process of 'choosing' a gender, 'becoming' a woman? Can Butler's approach help us define what we mean by women's writing? What follows is an attempt to sketch out possible lines of enquiry. After outlining those aspects of Butler's argument which seem especially productive I examine the kind of feminist cultural politics to which it gives rise. Such a politics is then related to current debates within feminist aesthetics, and by way of particular example, the use of modernist form in writing by women. What are the choices involved when the woman writer takes up the mode of impersonality associated with modernist form, and what are their consequences in terms of gender relations? Dorothy Richardson's extraordinary narrative *Pilgrimage* enables us to consider the process of gender acquisition as a formal project, and to begin to explore these questions.

THE CONCEPT OF GENDER AS CULTURAL CHOICE

How is it possible to bring together the notion of cultural choice with a theory of gender, without appearing vulnerable to the charge of voluntarism? After all, an individual is clearly not able to interpret her gender as she pleases in an act of free invention, but must comply with those social constraints – economic, patriarchal – which seek to define her unambiguously within binary gender norms. One such constraint, and an important site for the contestation of social norms, is of course the body itself. And it is upon this foundation that Beauvoir formulates the double ambiguity of 'becoming' a woman, and sets out her concept of choice.

In Butler's view, Simone de Beauvoir is not positing a free-floating Cartesian subject that is able to choose *prior* to its assumption of cultural, embodied life, since that agency is always already embodied; after all, 'it is our genders we become and not our bodies' (p. 129). Indeed, such a transcendent mode of autonomous subjectivity is one promoted by masculine gender norms, a mode that can only sustain itself by naming women as the corporeal other, immanent bearers of the bodily realm. Rather, she suggests,

Beauvoir is working with a different concept of autonomy which moves beyond binary gender distinctions in taking the Sartrean project at its 'non-Cartesian best'. Butler expands her argument as follows. For Sartre the body 'is a *point of departure* which I *am* and which at the same time I surpass'. The Cartesian moment is thus inscribed within consciousness itself, which is at once embodied and transcendent. If one can 'surpass' the body, one does not cut loose from it altogether, for 'the subversive paradox consists in the fact that the body itself is a surpassing':

> The body is not a static and self-identical phenomenon, but a mode of intentionality, a directional force and mode of desire. ... For Sartre, the body is lived and experienced as the context and medium for all human strivings. Because for Sartre all human beings strive after possibilities not yet realized, human beings are to some extent 'beyond' themselves. This *ek-static* condition is itself a corporeal experience; the body is thus experienced as a mode of becoming.
>
> (p. 130)

What Beauvoir achieves, in Butler's view, is a transposition of Sartre's 'mode of becoming' on to the realm of sex and gender, and thus a rendering of his formulation in concrete *cultural* terms. The repeatedly negotiated movement from the physical to the culturally defined body is analogous to that tension in being/surpassing the body: it is a movement that takes place within embodied life itself. If the body is thus conceived as a Sartrean 'situation', then Beauvoir moves beyond the binary distinctions of the masculine-transcendence/feminine-immanence gender model. The body is both a 'locus of cultural interpretations' which have been socially pre-established, *and* a 'field of interpretative possibilities' in which possible roles and identities proliferate: a nexus, then, of culture and choice. 'Becoming' a woman is thus a ceaseless activity, an 'active style of living one's body in the world' (p. 131). Consequently the issue of sex and gender becomes a thoroughly *cultural* affair.

While her argument usefully disengages the question of difference from an absolute link with biological sex, it is not clear whether Butler's prefiguring of a possible sexual pluralism can be said to have any material foundation at all, nor indeed how she is using her notion of culture. What is certain, as she points out, is that such an approach 'does not overcome the existential pitfalls of Sartrianism (*sic*) by the mere fact of its cultural application' (p. 139). In the interests of pushing her model of gender acquisition forward, this seems a risk Butler is prepared to take, in the name of an 'essential freedom' which she perceives at the heart of that process. For while 'the anguish and terror of leaving a prescribed gender or of trespassing upon another gender territory testifies to the social constraints upon gender interpretation', this at once is signal 'to the necessity that there be an interpretation, i.e. to the essential freedom at the origin of gender' (p. 132).

It is by keeping this 'essential freedom' in sight that the prospect of a proliferation of gender identities can be imagined, a transcending of binary structures through cultural innovation. Such a vision ties in with a familiar fantasy often invoked in feminist accounts of difference, for instance that encapsulated in Derrida's dream of 'a relationship to the other where the code of sexual marks would no longer be discriminating'.[6] The fact that this Utopian moment lacks a reality principle is acknowledged by Butler, who points out that from a psychoanalytical perspective such pre-Oedipal polymorphousness might appear to be outside culture altogether. Yet if such dreaming is the 'stuff of great literature' (p. 140), as she ruefully attests, her point is no less important: that the ways in which cultural fantasies inform and constitute new realities of gendering should be opened up and explored. This would seem a particularly difficult and necessary position to defend in the embattled 1990s, as the recent censorship furore in the United States over the exhibition of Robert Mapplethorpe's work might suggest.

I would like to retain Butler's productive notion of gender as cultural fantasy, without following her culturalist logic through to its conclusion in radical gender invention, and begin to define what culture might mean in this context. If, following Raymond Williams's materialist account, we take culture to consist of those forms and beliefs, myths, narratives and images that are rooted in social relationships and institutions, then the negotiation of identity becomes a rather more fraught and contradictory process than that which figures in Derrida's dream of 'the masses' as an 'indeterminable number of blended voices',[7] a process which vitally includes factors such as race and social class.

In raising the question of agency in gender acquisition, with its double sense of being constructed *by* social meaning and also a producer *of* it (a tension also present in Williams's notion of culture), Butler's Beauvoir establishes three related areas of direct interest to a feminist politics. First, she suggests that human subjects are not wholly subsumed by oppressive systems such as patriarchal power relations, which are themselves not uniformly repressive; rather such systems depend upon the reproductive practices of those 'consenting' subjects to maintain their ideological legitimacy, and can be acted upon and modified by such practices. In this way women are not to be seen as 'victims' of patriarchal structures, but indeed as having considerable room for political manoeuvre. Second, by regarding gender acquisition as an ongoing, active process of negotiating past, present and future norms – that is, by refusing an origin to psychic relations – it becomes possible to introduce into this process factors such as race, class, religion, even generation, which obtain at different levels, often contradictorily. And finally, it is clear that the 'burden of choice' (p. 132) involved in this process can itself become an important means of *coming-to-consciousness*. The unspoken, constant reinterpretation of cultural norms and social constraints may lead to self-realization and potentially a politicization of personal life. 'Choice' in this sense, then, seems less to refer to a radical act of self-creation than, in Judith Butler's words, 'a tacit project to renew a cultural history in one's own corporeal terms' (p. 131): a tacit project, that is, which may itself become manifest. If one is to consider gender as a cultural fantasy in this materially mediated sense, then it becomes essential, within a feminist framework, to relate such fantasies to the general question of women's position in society and culture, and to the conditions of their emancipation.

THEORETICAL CLAIMS

Kate Soper has remarked on 'the under-theorized relation between feminist theory and empirical social science' evident in the *Feminism as Critique* collection that contains Butler's essay, a relation which is becoming increasingly important as the meta-theoretical nature of feminist argument develops.[8] An analogous case could be made for the deficiency in feminist literary studies, where a variety of large claims have been made for the political – revolutionary – potential of certain, invariably modernist, forms of narrative whose 'feminine' disruption and textual play are regarded as an assault on the patriarchal order itself. Such claims are often validated with recourse to a semiosis of the woman's body, from Derrida's 'invaginated text' to the avowed materialism of relating text to clitoris, approaches which risk an essentialism antithetical to Beauvoir's formulation and which seem only to be held in place by metaphor and assertion. Thus 'feminine' textuality (disruption, unreason, the play of desire) becomes synonymous with a notion of *feminist* practice. Such a conflation reigns, for example, in Alice Jardine's *Gynesis*, where we are asked the necessary question 'to and for whom are feminist critics writing?', which has already been answered: 'this *gynema* is a reading effect, a woman-in-effect that is never stable and has no identity. Its appearance in a text is perhaps only noticed by the feminist reader.'[9] For the feminist reader, read informed semiotician, presumably; and it is not clear how Jardine's 'new feminist hermeneutics able to give up its quest for truth'[10] links with the wider question of women's emancipation.

If one believes, following Rita Felski and Alison Jaggar, that one can define as feminist 'all those forms of theory and practice that seek, no matter on what grounds and by what means, to end the subordination of women',[11] then 'giving up the quest for truth' seems at best premature. While it is evidently important to challenge the gender bias of particular forms of philosophical universalism, values such as reason, truth, freedom and objectivity are no less necessary to women's movements that organize in the name of justice and equality, knowing in their various ways the truths of oppression.

One answer to this problem of the purchase of feminist theoretical work would of course be to examine the position of feminism within the academic and publishing institutions, and its relation to the wider social movements. In literary studies this would also be to signal a revitalized sociology of literature, in the widest and richest – non-functionalist – sense. Yet one does not even need to embark upon detailed empirical research into the patterns of women's readership and literary reception – which would contribute to an understanding of the political value and uses of diverse literary forms – to realize that the vast range of forms and genres produced and consumed by women are in any case yet to be taken on by feminist criticism. Their inclusion would surely explode the now rather sterile Hobson's choice which has preoccupied feminist literary analysis for so long: on the one hand an Anglo-American model that retains the notion of female authorship in its focus on the realist text as an unmediated expression of experience, but which fails to deal with textual signification; on the other, a French modernist formalism that foregrounds literariness and issues of representation, but which erases the question of agency altogether.

That these models narrow and prescribe our options is increasingly clear, not least in the way that they rehearse a now inadequate opposition between an expressive 'bourgeois' realism and an experimental modernism. It is not self-evident that realist conventions are necessarily more complicit with patriarchal structures of representation, any more than textual indeterminacy is inherently subversive of them. And it is not an insignificant point that realist forms tend to reach a wider readership. As Rita Felski suggests, isn't the representation of female experience, by whatever narrative strategy, a legitimate cultural need?

> Literature does not merely constitute a self-referential and metalinguistic system, as some literary theorists believe, but it is also a medium which can profoundly influence individual and cultural self-understanding in the sphere of everyday life, charting the changing preoccupations of social groups through symbolic fictions by which they make sense of experience.[12]

The present critical 'discrimination of modernisms' – and indeed, reconsideration of realisms – may be seen as a response to a feminist critique of literary forms which is itself part of a wider attempt to rework our understanding of the social mediation of generic forms and strategies. The strict realism/modernism divide is breaking down, and with it any automatic assessment of a text's political value, or ideological effect, according to uncritical assumptions about literary form.

BECOMING A WOMAN WRITER

The observation that 'symbolic fictions' help us achieve a level of emancipation through self-understanding is central to Judith Butler's re-interpretation of Beauvoir: the formulation, that is, of a gendered cultural politics. If the process of 'becoming' a woman is seen as a 'tacit project to renew a cultural history in one's own corporeal terms', then literature is one cultural forum where such a renewal takes place. It is a site where both 'practical ideology' – accepted representations, images and modes of action – and new interpretative possibilities can be negotiated, contested and imagined. This is true not just for the reader of such fictions but also for their producer, the woman writer. Indeed the focus on gender as a volitional act, on the notion of 'becoming', allows us to approach the troubled question of female authorship from a perspective that will allow us to grasp the ways in which generic forms and strategies offer both constraints and enabling conditions for the process of gender acquisition. It becomes possible to speculate – only half-playfully – upon the notion that one is not born but rather becomes (in the full cultural-political sense) a woman *writer*.

If the authoring subject is seen to be unified, static and monodimensional – as is the case in certain forms of American feminist criticism – then we are led towards the question as to what constitutes that feminine consciousness, and also relatedly how those invariant psychic structures might account for the supposed distinctive features of women's writing, that it is fluid, spontaneous, and more intuitive in form, for example. But if we take on the more dynamic concept of the gendered subject as a mode of becoming, then a single notion of feminine experience can never be adequate to such a complex and often contradictory activity. Nor can we posit any privileged relation between gender and a particular literary form (nor indeed any one-to-one relation between an ideological position and literary form), since such an interactive process offers diverse possibilities, various positionalities, to the authoring subject, who may take up any number of them depending upon how her choice is constrained and the ways in which the forms are already culturally and institutionally defined and internalized by her.

One example of this, which I will develop in more detail later, is the mode of autonomy suggested in the notion of modernist impersonality. A woman writer may approach such a form by a quite different route than a male writer, whom patriarchal culture has already positioned with access to such a universalizing perspective; but questions of gender, class, race, access to education and so on will further complicate her engagement with this form. I do not want to invite a relativizing stress on difference but to draw both the literary producer and textual representation into a dynamic cultural materialism. This would take account of extra-literary factors – the debates concerning mass and high culture, the social position of the art institution, the stage of development of the women's movements and the place of women in society, say – when assessing the diverse modes in which women write.

When does a woman writer 'become' a Woman Writer, however? The answer, perhaps, is when that 'tacit project to renew a cultural history' gradually becomes manifest, for writer, reader, or for the critic. One of the important gains in using this model of gender as cultural choice is that the process of negotiation can itself become a *conscious* organization of cultural forms. This moves us away from what is, in one sense, a Romantic view of literary invention as a spontaneous overflow of expression, or indeed as an onomatopoeic writing to the body. While not denying the significance of unconscious processes in artistic invention, such a view acknowledges that writing also involves a mastery of technical skills, and an often conscious manipulation of symbolic forms. This is no less true for women writers, whose social positioning in terms of access to education, their class, or their domestic responsibilities, has frequently provoked an acute awareness of their rhetorical or generic positioning *as* women, before the male arbiters of convention and taste. If 'art demands what, to women, civilization won't give',[13] as Dorothy Richardson described, it is nevertheless in their engagement with the demands of literary structures, which act as a locus of established meanings and an arena for alternative interpretative possibilities, that women writers have achieved a measure of self-realization.

NEGOTIATIONS OF LITERARY FORM: THE IMPERSONAL TURN

Dorothy Richardson's narrative *Pilgrimage* can be read as a project which brings together questions of literary production with what it is to 'become' a woman, and it is here that I intend to examine the relation between women's writing and the kind of cultural materialism I have been sketching out. *Pilgrimage* is a text that defies, indeed goes into battle with, the neat closure of formal categorization. A woman's *Bildungsroman* – a novel of the protagonist's self-development and thus emancipation – it resists the seductive comforts of the romance plot that reinforces restrictive models of marriage and familial life, while drawing upon the fantasies and desires encoded within such conventions. The narrative pushes a realist premiss – 'the close rendering of ordinary experience'[14] – to its limits, the sheer inclusiveness of detail refusing the refuge of story, the phenomenal retentiveness of the heroine's consciousness forcing the apoplectic demise of any simple notion of character. With its realization that 'the torment of all [male] novels is what is left out',[15] the novel begins to write a notion of women's experience into the 'symbolic fictions' by which a dominant culture both reproduces and comes to know itself: the struggle with form is a process of coming to terms with the social construction of gender. Yet does this search for an adequate poetics tip the narrative over into modernism – which the evident stream-of-consciousness technique might suggest – or are we looking at a reworking of a form of 'subjective' realism? These questions are shown to be inadequate in relation to a narrative which avails itself freely of a number of 'realist' and 'modernist' strategies, bringing us to re-evaluate the very terms of our analysis. How, then, do the formal choices open to a writer like Dorothy Richardson connect with the process of 'becoming' a woman?

In order to follow the way a specific form is negotiated in Richardson's work, I want to return for a moment to the modernist concept of literary impersonality, and, in particular, how it is defined by Virginia Woolf. I suggested earlier that women writers might approach the question of impersonality by a route distinctive to them, that indeed it might *mean* something quite different depending on their cultural positioning. Dorothy Richardson, like Woolf, knew that 'nothing short of a dehumanized solitude will serve the woman at work',[16] but was anxious nevertheless at what such detachment would entail for that woman. If impersonality was an accepted precondition for the *practice* of art, it also involved, within one particular modernist ideology, a hidden cultural agenda: a 'dehumanizing' voyage out away from the soilure of the everyday social world, away from the political and historical demands of embodied life, into the autonomous realm of art. We recognize in this agenda the claims of a now increasingly unpersuasive aestheticist modernism, which would have us believe, in Ortega y Gasset's words, that a novel 'can be nothing beyond a novel'.[17]

In *Feminine Fictions*, Patricia Waugh argues that the model of selfhood which lies behind such an aesthetic is one based upon separation and over-differentiation, a male stance of rational individualism which, when it falls into crisis, produces the tortured, alienated double familiar to modernist narrative. Neither position, it seems, has much to offer a woman writer, as Waugh explains:

> My argument is that women writers, on the whole, have not felt comfort-able with an aesthetics of impersonality as it appears in many modernist and postmodernist manifestos. The reason for this is the overvaluation in the first instance of exclusive objectivity, of distance, autonomy, sep-arateness, discrete form, and the disappearance in the second instance of human communication via meaningful affection, communication, or ethical belief.[18]

Dorothy Richardson would seem to concur with this view when, in one of her letters, she suggests that Dostoevsky would have had a greater access to detachment 'writing against time on the corner of a kitchen table' than a woman writer no matter her position: 'Neither motherhood nor ... the simplest housekeeping can so effectively hamper her as the human demand besieging her wherever she is, for an inclusive awareness.'[19]

A familiar opposition thus presents itself, between a notion of masculine consciousness as a distanciated, autonomous ego and a posited feminine stress on an intersubjective model of identity and its corresponding ethics of care. We must be cautious, however, lest in rehearsing such a distinction it becomes reinforced and in some measure prescriptive. For it is also true that strategies of detachment are to be found in women's writing, not just connectedness or inclusiveness, strategies which do not always carry with them such unwelcome aestheticist baggage. Rita Felski notes, for example, that recent reworkings of the *Bildungsroman* have led to new forms of nar-rative plot whereby 'separation' is seen to be essential to any path towards a woman's self-discovery and thus emancipation. Waugh too points out that in Woolf's narratives distanciation is part of 'a concept of collective subjectivity which foregrounds the construction of identity *in relationship*', rather than the definition of an individual ego.[20] In assuming a more dynamic model of the authoring subject as a mode of intentionality and desire in a complicated, often conflictive, negotiation with cultural forms, it is to be hoped that we have moved beyond the binary categorization of this gender model. This is not to deny that it is powerfully inscribed within Western culture and deep within psychic structures themselves, nor is it to evade the need to contest it at every level. But it is to argue that while challenging a masculine stance of distanciation and the power relations it implies we retain the possibility of objective ways of relating; otherwise how is it possible for different groups of women to reach consensus, work toward new norms and realities, in any way at all? Similarly, while we might wish to acknowledge the representation of values such as nurturing, intimacy and connectedness as a specifically feminine mode – associated as they are with cohesive solidarity and affective strengths – it is clear that this could be used against women's interests by promoting the existing distinctions between social relations in the public and private spheres. The advantage of our model, drawn from Beauvoir's concept of becoming, is that it enables us to envisage diverse and often irregular modalities and alignments for the subject within embodied life itself. The urge towards transcendence or detachment is thus not *separate* from material existence, but *integral* to it, to the very process of gender acquisition itself. If we are to begin to understand the complex articulations of class, gender and ethnic identity which are masked within concepts such as 'alienation' and 'impersonality', we necessarily have to employ extra-literary forms of knowledge. To acknowledge this is to refuse to take one selective – but in literary studies very influential – modernist aesthetic at its own universalizing estimation: to read diverse forms of modernism in terms of their reaction to, and engagement with, a social formation.

Virginia Woolf welcomes the 'turn to the impersonal' in women's writing in her essay 'Women and Fiction'(1929), which exhibits the pressures and tensions around this concept of literary form in interesting ways. Impersonality is seen as a rhetorical position only recently secured for women by the successes of the women's movement and the demands of the market, though Woolf does not name the agent of this social transformation directly:

> The change which has turned the English woman from a nondescript influence, fluctuating and vague, to a voter, a wage-earner, a responsible citizen, has given her both in her life and in her art a turn towards the impersonal. Her relations now are not only emotional; they are intellectual, they are political.[21]

Testimony to the material boundedness and motivation of literary forms, Woolf's statement suggests that the 'turn to the impersonal' is enabling for women – a symptom of their newly enfranchised social status. Rather than a turn away from the demands of the social world it is a signal of a growing critical and political engagement with it, a broader perspective: 'their novels will deal with social evils and remedies. Their men and women will not be observed wholly in relation to each other but as they cohere and clash in groups and classes and races' (p. 51). No longer, according to Woolf, will women be constrained to write of their private frustrations and desires; having emerged from the dark 'underground' of the domestic realm they are freed, blinking, into the light of social day, now able to write *as* women, *for* women, writing 'of women as women have never been written of before' (p. 49).

This last statement catches a sense of the new ground opening up in such works, and with good reason. For the kind of autonomy described by Woolf was fought for by the pioneering women's movement, synonymous as it seemed to be with a notion of individual freedom, both political and economic, enjoyed by men in the public sphere. Indeed it was economic independence – the opening up of the professions, access to money and leisure – which allowed women, though not *all* women, to assume such an 'attitude'. However the risk of such an equation – of autonomy with freedom – is a devaluing of those affective and interpersonal relations which characterize the private realm of women's inhabiting, an impoverishing loss of connection or dehumanization, as Dorothy Richardson termed it. Modernist 'alienation' is thus recast as a potentiality in the actual forms of women's organization and struggle, in the process of 'becoming' a woman itself.

Isolated in a room of her own, then, the woman writer may achieve the necessary detachment to choose an adequate form, to make manifest that 'tacit project to renew a cultural history in one's own corporeal terms', in Judith Butler's words.[22] As Virginia Woolf explained in the *Times Literary Supplement*, 'to try the accepted forms, to discard the unfit, to create others which are more fitting, is a task that must be accomplished before there is freedom or achievement'.[23] Yet in this process of coming-to-consciousness through an engagement with cultural forms, she is courted by an aestheticist ideology which regards the material coordinates of such an activity as so many 'excrescences of history and fact' (p. 52). Paradoxically, the 'turn to the impersonal' enables the woman writer to develop politically, but also to split her politics away from her art; the poetic attitude will allow her to 'look *beyond* the personal and political to the wider questions which the poet tries to solve – of our destiny and the meaning of life' (my italics) (p. 51). The writer is thus seen to divide into two selves: artist and reformer, 'butterfly' and 'gadfly to the state', two modes of writing which seem increasingly incommensurate as Woolf's argument develops. The tension is nowhere more evident than in her discussion of feminist anger, which as an embodied and personal response to oppression is regarded as an explicable but nevertheless narrowing intrusion into the vision of an artistic work:

> In *Middlemarch* and *Jane Eyre* we are conscious not merely of the writer's character ... we are conscious of a woman's presence – of someone

resenting the treatment of her sex and pleading for its rights. This brings
into women's writing an element which is entirely absent from a man's,
unless, indeed, he happens to be a working-man, a Negro, or one who for
some other reason is conscious of disability. It introduces a distortion and
is frequently the cause of weakness. The desire to plead some personal
cause or to make a character the mouthpiece of some personal discontent
or grievance always has a distressing effect, as if the spot at which the
reader's attention is directed were suddenly twofold instead of single.

(p. 47)

By interpreting the objective reality of social oppression – whether it stems
from the experience of a woman, a 'working-man' or a 'Negro' – as the stuff
of *personal* 'grievance', Woolf upholds the public/private division which
informs her concept of autonomy. A liberation into the public world of the
responsible citizen, with its nominal formulation of equality, is thus double-
edged. If a woman writer is to write *as a woman* then, for Woolf, 'it is as one
who has forgotten this fact', as Patricia Waugh suggests. This is, she argues,
because Woolf resists the identity of a coherent, essential 'self' as a masculine
cultural norm, choosing rather to project an identity 'defined potentially
through relationship in a more equal society'.[24] There is, however, a certain
luxury to this 'forgetting': the woman writer may no longer be bitter or angry
but the solidarity and equality of her connections with those who do not
share the same serenity of status is questionable. Woolf's relational concept
of identity is in fact undermined by an all too familiar 'gender-blind' model
of autonomy. Indeed the twofold perspective that Woolf finds so distressing
is a product of her own concept of art, for by locating freedom in the realm
of art, in the literary text, as Pauline Johnson has argued, 'the merely
aesthetical character of this ideal means that her critique ultimately fails to
project a practical imperative'. As Johnson continues:

> The alternative vision proposed in her art functions as a compensatory,
> substitute gratification which siphons off and renders harmless the radical
> need for changed gender relations to which her works, in their passionate
> critique of existing relations between the sexes, also gives expression.[25]

We are thus presented with a familiar modernist paradox: that in the very
enactment of critique through its distance from social reality the very form
and structure of the literary work is voided of material life and motivation.
Woolf's social class, it might be argued, is one element that draws her into
aestheticism, her gender politicizes her aesthetics; this tension is not resolvable
and both positions are actively held at the same moment.

PILGRIMAGE AS 'PROJECT'

Formal characteristics such as literary impersonality can thus be read, in the words of Fredric Jameson, as 'a projected solution, on the aesthetic or imaginary level, to a genuinely contradictory situation in the concrete world of everyday social life',[26] less solving than configuring the conflicting social identities which are held simultaneously by the individual subject, a conflict enacted in that moment of 'choice'. Such contradictory allegiances are writ large in Dorothy Richardson's *Pilgrimage*, forming a late Victorian/Edwardian cultural landscape in which Miriam Henderson, the central and presiding consciousness, works to realize herself as a woman and – what is seen to amount to the same thing – a writer. Yet Richardson's narrative engages with the formal question of impersonality in a self-critical manner that promises a different form of resolution from Woolf's championing of the aesthetic.

Richardson's concern about the effects of artistic detachment on the woman writer who is sustained by the cohesion of her social relations has already been noted; the 'inclusiveness' she values is enacted in the wealth and agglomeration of discursive detail in *Pilgrimage* which forces the reader to experience the processes by which meanings are embodied and made objective. Yet Richardson is equally clear of the need for separation as a prerequisite for agency, of the value of self-realization as 'the moment of entry into life', as she put it in *The Dental Record*.[27] Miriam Henderson, so vitally a part of Dorothy Richardson's own self-discovery (*Pilgrimage* being a project which she worked on all her life and which she refused to draw to an end), brings the two positions together in her discussion of 'female art'. Women's art, she tells Hypo Wilson (a fictional H. G. Wells), is the creation of social life itself: a covert and continuous activity, a way of 'existing' social relations – to use the verb 'exist' in a transitive sense. Far from testifying to a woman's unknowing immersion in a world of social intimacy, however, such a process requires from her the 'maximum of detachment and control':

> Artists, well, and *literary* people, say they have to get away from everything at intervals. ... That is why so many women get nervy and break down. The only way they can rest is by being nothing to nobody, leaving off for a while giving out any atmosphere.

> Stop breathing.

> Yes. But if you laugh at that, you must laugh at artists, *and* literary people.

> I will. I *do*.

> Yes, but in general. You must see the identity of the two things for good or for bad. If people reverence men's art and feel their sacrifices are worth while, to *themselves*, as well as to other people, they must not just pity the art of women. ... Men, and the women who imitate them, bleat about

women 'finding their truest fulfilment in *self-sacrifice*'. In speaking of male art it is called *self-realization*. That's men all over. They get an illuminating theory – man must die, to live – and apply it only to themselves. If a theory is true you may be sure that it applies in a most thoroughgoing way to women. They don't stop dead at self-sacrifice. They reap ... freedom. Self-realization. Emancipation.[28]

In the narrative model of the *Bildungsroman* the newly self-possessed young male individual, after an initial separation from society, is finally reinserted into public life; for the woman protagonist, however, finding herself positioned differently, social self-realization poses a more ambivalent prospect. For while Miriam has necessarily to contend with the version of masculine autonomy associated with the public sphere, since, as we saw in the Virginia Woolf essay, it is what stands for a model of freedom, she *also* creates an alternative vision of autonomy which will allow her to discover herself *as a woman*. On the one hand, then, Miriam is propelled into identifying with such a masculine stance – regarding herself as her mother's 'son', and declaring 'I am like a man' (II, 261) – in order to gain her independence. Correspondingly, she vehemently rejects the conventional society of women for its claustrophobic domesticity: '"I hate women, and they've got to know it", she retorted with all her strength, hitting blindly out towards the sofa, feeling all the contrivances of toilet and coiffure fall in meaningless horrible detail under her blows' (I, 436). On the other hand, however, she is also repelled by such a position for what it denies or leaves out, growing to appreciate the 'shared being' of a love between women as restoring respect for 'the personal life in everybody' (IV, 245).

Subject to this process of psychic and social oscillation across familiar boundaries – private/public, woman/man, dependence/autonomy – Miriam is frustrated: 'positive and negative, north and south, male and female ... why *negative*?' (III, 51). She begins to reconfigure a mode of autonomy based upon the notion of 'becoming' that I explored earlier, one in which the movement towards detachment, towards 'surpassing' material life, is integral to embodied life itself. Thus, in her discussion with Hypo Wilson, Miriam reinterprets the formal question of male artistic detachment in terms of women's social agency, refusing Woolf's twofold perspective by locating freedom for women *as* women in social life itself. The voyage out is necessary, for 'leaving go, not going through life clenched, would mean losing oneself, passing through, not driving in, ceasing to affect and be affected'. It is also to reveal life as a set of possible choices, 'a game to be played, or even not played'. But the beauty of that voyage out depends upon a return journey that is inseparable from it, a reaffirming of connection. 'This new joy of going into life, the new beauty, on everything, was the certainty of coming back' (III, 135). And the price of the insertion of this movement into the pattern of the *Bildungsroman* is, very simply, its transformation: a liberation of its representation of self-development into an unceasing and uncompromising process of becoming, a narrative of emancipation.

Miriam's negotiation of these opposing constructions of autonomy is, as we might expect, complicated further in that it is also mapped against questions of class and national identity. Jean Radford, who has done much to bring the work of Dorothy Richardson to critical attention, argues usefully that *Pilgrimage* can be read against what Eric Hobsbawm, in his *The Age of Empire*, terms 'the uncertainties of the bourgeoisie'.[29] Forced out into the world to find employment after the bankruptcy of her father, Miriam undergoes a dislocation of class which brings about a keen awareness of her social positioning and, indeed, of the limitations of certain strategies, such as marriage, which would enable a return to that safe bourgeois world. As Jean Radford explains:

> Poised below the 'secure' rentier class of her childhood, and above the 'abyss' of the working classes, Miriam Henderson looks 'with the eyes of a stranger': with hatred and longing at the forms of class life she has left, with shame and anxiety at the shifts and deprivations of the lower middle class world she has joined.[30]

Miriam can no longer 'belong' to either world, nor indeed to that bohemian set of intellectuals who acknowledge her sense of difference. She thus experiences a form of alienation in class terms; even her Englishness, that curious detached 'mystery' of belonging, of being at the imperial centre, begins to be dislodged as she listens to the new voices, alternative cultures, which the London landscape opens to her, 'expanding the range of her being' (II, 272):

> For a while she would remain as she was. But even seeing England from his point of view, was being changed, a little. The past, up to the last few moments, was a life she had lived without knowing that it was a life lived in special circumstances, and from certain points of view. Now, perhaps moving away from it, these circumstances and points of view suddenly became a possession, full of fascinating interest. But she had lived blissfully. Something here and there in his talk threatened happiness.
>
> (III, 151)

These contradictory strands of identity are brought together in one of the most significant moments in *Pilgrimage*, when in a docklands cafe Miriam discusses the question of feminism with her Russian lover, Michael Shatov. 'Feminism' is a term new to her, and an identity he claims for himself; Miriam's first reaction is to resist it. To place her argument exactly would be to return to the suffragist discourses of the period, and to Dorothy Richardson's own writing in the anarchist and socialist journals of the time; there is no room for such a study here. It is enough to point out that her objections to 'women's rights people' consist in their reinforcing of the opposition between a concept of masculine culture as civilized and women as alterity, which feminism is seen to invite by stressing 'traditions of slavery for memory'. Miriam does not want a romance with marginality. Men, she argues, 'must leave off imagining themselves a race of gods fighting against chaos, and thinking of women as part of the chaos they have to civilize. There isn't any chaos. Never has been. It's the principal masculine illusion' (III, 219). Yet Miriam also realizes that such binary distinctions are inscribed within cultural and discursive structures at every level. And in attempting to change Shatov's mind by rational argument she will also be positioned in a dialogue based on a similarly false foundation, upholding yet another related position between public and private:

> Men did not admit their private discoveries in public. It was not enough to see and force the admittance of the holes in a theory privately, and leave the form of the words going on and on in the world perpetually parroted, infecting the sky. . . . A private reconstruction of standards with one person would not bring healing. It was history, literature, the way of stating records, reports, stories, the whole method of statement of things from the beginning that was on a false foundation.
>
> (III, 218)

With Miriam's realization comes the admission of a need for a cultural politics, in which the 'tacit project to renew cultural history in one's own corporeal terms' might become a collective aim. If, as she considers at an earlier moment in her development, 'all that has been said and known in the world is in *language*', then this fact introduces a certain indeterminacy, for 'no-one *knows* anything for certain', and cultural differentiation, since 'everything depends upon a way a thing is put, and that is a question of some particular civilization' (II, 99). Miriam, then, achieves an insight into the cultural contestation for meaning, the need to engage with those 'symbolic fictions' and narratives that both construct accepted models of identity and suggest alternative interpretative possibilities. She glimpses, too, the importance of a concept of difference in circumventing those dichotomies enshrined at the heart of Western culture.

The irony of this moment, however, is that just before Miriam's realization she has experienced an intense form of racial (and class, we suspect) disgust at the presence of a black docker who is eating at the next table. The 'alien' identity of her Russian companion is quite transformed; as a fellow European he becomes an honorary Englishman in contrast to the 'huge, bent, snorting and devouring figure':

> He was an Englishman in the fact that he and she could *not* sit eating in the neighbourhood of this marshy jungle. But they were, they had. They would have. Once away from this awful place she would never think of it again. Yet the man had hands and needs and feelings. Perhaps he could

sing. He was at a disadvantage, an outcast. There was something that ought to be said to him. She could not think what it was.

(III, 217)

At the moment, then, that Miriam becomes conscious of the value of differing points of view – begins to develop, in a sense, a concept of intersubjectivity that will enable her to challenge the 'false foundation' of discourse – she also affirms those subject-object relations that are at the heart of imperialist power relations, which lie behind the 'mystery' of Englishness and are internalized at a deep level within her.[31]

Miriam's coming-to-consciousness is thus an irregular process, a setting out of choices and contradictions that are not resolved but allowed to coexist in various stages of cognition and prejudice, only to be worked through and reconfigured once again. Her pilgrimage can be seen in a Sartrean light as a *project*, the activity of 'becoming' a woman at one situated moment in history. In discovering a concept of diversity – 'a million sides ... no questions, only sides ... always changing' (II, 189), Miriam releases possibility into a notion of women's experience that, in Judith Butler's words, refuses 'the reductive imposition of a substantializing nomenclature'.[32] A move beyond the distinctions of man/woman, public/private, autonomy/dependence, is clearly the condition of her entry as a self-possessed individual into the social realm, and the cultural fantasy of that future Utopian moment is no less potent for her than it is for contemporary valuers of difference; as Hypo tells her, 'there will be books – with all that cut out – him and her – all that sort of thing. The books of the future will be clear of that sort of thing' (II, 118).

Yet in *Pilgrimage* this fantasy demands what Pauline Johnson could not find in Woolf, that is, a 'practical imperative'.[33] Miriam is not to discover the freedom she seeks in the imaginative choices offered in art alone but has to make cultural forms and their available plots answerable to the conditions in which she finds herself, and, indeed, to women's position in general; the urge towards transcendence is no single leap into the autonomous realm of art but integral to an engagement with embodied life itself. One way Richardson might be seen to achieve this is by focusing so intently on Miriam's 'damned egotistical self'[34] as Woolf described her, not in order to suggest the complaint of an intrusive 'private' vision but as the voice of embodied, *gendered* choice, causing supposedly gender-neutral forms to yield their hidden, material histories that organize social identity. Thus, for example, impersonality might position the subject at the vantage-point of critique while underlining his/her impotence; it might represent a flight into the aesthetic, away from the social and political demands of the real; it might correspond with a notion of deracinated autonomy or be implicated in class or imperialist power relations; it might form a necessary stage in the process of self-realization enabling a subject to intervene as a social agent. The dominance of one or several of these interpretations is dependent upon their relation to the ideologies of the immediate moment, the position of the writer, and the text's historical distance from the reader or critic. *Pilgrimage* battles with a number of these interpretations in defining the nature of Miriam's cultural 'choice', without resolving the deeper contradictions they represent; in so doing the narrative projects an alternative model of 'becoming a woman' that is rooted in the conditions and desires of its historical moment. For 'what is called "creation", imaginative transformation, fantasy, invention, is only based upon reality' (IV, 657).

CONCLUSION

'Woman is not a completed reality, but rather a becoming . . . her *possibilities* should be defined', wrote Simone de Beauvoir.[35] Judith Butler's interpretation of Beauvoir's concept of 'becoming' a woman enables us to analyse the negotiation of generic forms and strategies as a process of cultural choice, whereby women writers engage with the social construction of gender. This is not to argue that the meaning of a literary work is to be wholly reduced to a narrow sociological reading of its function for a particular writer at a given historical moment. But it is to suggest that in such formal choices, to borrow a phrase from Seyla Benhabib, 'are intertwined the history of the self and the history of the collective'.[36] An embodied history, then, that registers the symbolic organization of gendered social identity, and the interrogation of its conventions, as part of 'a tacit project to renew cultural history in one's own corporeal terms', which has indeed become a collective aim in feminist cultural politics. This is a history that continually renews itself as the desires, needs and positions of women in society shift, as forms of mass and high culture change. It is by uncovering this 'literary' history – considering, as Rita Felski persuasively argues, 'the full range of literary forms written and read by women in relation to a broader theorization of women's position in culture and society'[37] – that we can begin to assess the political value of formal strategies in women's writing, and understand the ways in which cultural fantasies seek to constitute new realities of gendering. In discovering this history, we release possibility into form.

NOTES

1 Simone de Beauvoir, *The Second Sex* (Harmondsworth, 1983), p. 69.
2 Dorothy Richardson, *Pilgrimage* (London, 1979), III, 256.
3 Beauvoir, op. cit., p. 295.
4 Judith Butler, 'Variations on Sex and Gender', in Seyla Benhabib and Drucilla Cornell, eds, *Feminism as Critique* (Oxford, 1987). All subsequent references are included parenthetically in the text.
5 Jeffrey Weeks, *Sexuality and Its Discontents: Meanings, Myths and Modern Sexualities* (London, 1985), p. 209.
6 Jacques Derrida and Christie MacDonald, 'Choreographies', *Diacritics* 12(1982), · 76.

7 Derrida and MacDonald, op. cit., p. 76.
8 Kate Soper, 'Feminism as Critique', *New Left Review* 176(1989), p. 111.
9 Alice Jardine, *Gynesis: Configurations of Woman and Modernity* (Ithaca and London, 1985), p. 25.
10 ibid., p. 63.
11 Rita Felski, *Beyond Feminist Aesthetics* (London, 1989), p. 13. Felski is here following Alison Jaggar's formulation of a feminist critical practice.
12 ibid., p. 7. Felski's work has impressively opened the way to a re-evaluation of the feminist analysis of literary form.
13 Dorothy Richardson, quoted in Gillian E. Handscombe, *The Art of Life: Dorothy Richardson and the Development of Feminist Consciousness* (London and Boston, 1982), p. 165.
14 Damien Grant, *Realism* (London, 1970), p. 72.
15 Richardson, *Pilgrimage*, IV, 239.
16 Dorothy Richardson in a letter to Louise Theis, quoted in Handscombe, op. cit., pp. 164–5.
17 T. Ortega y Gasset, *The Dehumanization of Art* (Princeton, 1968), p. 94.
18 Patricia Waugh, *Feminine Fictions* (London, 1989), p. 20.
19 Dorothy Richardson, quoted in Handscombe, op. cit., p. 165.
20 Waugh, op. cit., p. 10.
21 Virginia Woolf, 'Women and Fiction', in Michèle Barrett, ed., *Virginia Woolf: Women and Writing* (London, 1979), p. 50. All subsequent references are included in the text.
22 Butler, op. cit., p. 131.
23 Virginia Woolf, 'Men and Women', in Barrett, op. cit., p. 67.
24 Waugh, op. cit., p. 10.
25 Pauline Johnson, 'From Virginia Woolf to the Post-Moderns: Developments in a Feminist Aesthetic', *Radical Philosophy* 45(1987), p. 29. See Felski, op. cit., pp. 160–3 for a discussion of Johnson's argument in the light of debates about the politics of a modernist aesthetics.
26 Fredric Jameson, *The Political Unconscious: Narrative as a Socially Symbolic Act* (London, 1981), p. 225.
27 Dorothy Richardson, quoted in Handscombe, op. cit., p. 86.
28 Richardson, *Pilgrimage*, III, p. 258. All subsequent references are included in the text as volume number followed by page number.
29 Eric Hobsbawm, *The Age of Empire 1875–1914* (London, 1987), p. 165.
30 Jean Radford, 'Coming to Terms: Dorothy Richardson, Modernism, and Women', *News from Nowhere* 7(1989), p. 32.
31 Dorothy Richardson's own position in relation to the debates on the question of race is yet to be established. As Julian Stallabrass has recently shown, questions of racial identity and notions of the primitive fed into a number of discourses at the time of the First World War, during a period of uncertainty for British colonialism – anthropology, art, theories of sexuality and the unconscious, formulations of social class, to name but a few. Wyndham Lewis's description of the 'negro' as 'racially a sort of Proletariat' would seem to echo this passage from *Pilgrimage*. The fear of such otherness thus expressed any threat perceived to undermine the 'civilized' order: colonial unrest, social revolution, sexuality, moral degeneracy, and so on. As an associate of Wyndham Lewis, Roy Campbell wrote, 'Nearly all modern writers are out to humiliate the conscious white "self" in favour of the savage, the woman, the child, or even the animal.' See Julian Stallabrass, 'The Idea of the Primitive: British Art and Anthropology 1918–1930', *New Left Review* 183(1990), pp. 95–115.

32 Butler, op. cit., p. 141.
33 Johnson, op. cit., p. 29.
34 Virginia Woolf, quoted in Handscombe, op. cit., p. 50.
35 Beauvoir, op. cit., p. 66.
36 Seyla Benhabib, 'The Generalized and the Concrete Other', in Benhabib and Cornell, op. cit., p. 94.
37 Felski, op. cit., p. 180.

Chapter 7

Fakes and femininity:
Vita Sackville-West and her mother

Suzanne Raitt

Lady Sackville loved fakes.[1] Particularly, she loved fake flowers.

> If she saw a gap in her border she would cheerfully stick in a group of delphiniums made of painted tin, on nice tall metal stalks. . . . Perhaps of all the odd corners of her garden the one she liked best was a sort of rockery entirely planted with flowers made of china.[2]

Nor did she stop at flowers. Honey Harris, a close friend of Lady Sackville's, was employed painting stair treads to look like shelves of books;[3] and Lady Sackville 'caused a most realistic half-crown to be painted on a stepping-stone'.[4]

Flowers, books and money. For Lady Sackville, all three were intimately bound up with her daughter Vita Sackville-West, her only child and a well-known gardener, writer and broadcaster. Lady Sackville wanted to rival (and to mock) her daughter's skills. Honey Harris recalls having to buy and plant £30 worth of artificial flowers on the day Vita came to lunch for the first time at Lady Sackville's Streatham house. According to Honey Harris, Vita 'said nothing, looked very grave and withering, and made no comment before she left'.[5]

The relationship between Lady Sackville and her daughter was a struggle for possession of authentic femininity. As we shall see, their most devastating quarrel saw Lady Sackville accusing Vita of stealing some of her diamonds, and of substituting them with fakes. Throughout their long and passionate intimacy there was a series of rows with a common theme: which of them was, as Virginia Woolf said of Vita, '(what I have never been) a real woman'?[6] The intensity of their rows demonstrates the high stakes for which they were playing (and Vita, when in Monte Carlo with her lesbian lover, loved to gamble). It is as though there is only a single possible position for femininity. Each woman is continually trying to drive the other out of it through a fear that, if both occupy it simultaneously, they will somehow become indistinguishable. The prize over which they fight is undisputed possession of authentic womanhood. In this paper I will show how the womanliness for which they are competing comes to be symbolized by the jewels which they repeatedly exchanged, claimed back, and, on one celebrated occasion, threw at each other in the street.[7]

These dramatic scenes have a more than anecdotal significance. Read alongside Freudian accounts of the development of femininity, they draw attention to the extent to which femininity is conceived psychoanalytically as a state of psychical and sexual impasse.[8] A close look at one specific and unusually well-documented relationship shows that femininity is of its essence something to be struggled over, fought for, defended and, in the last resort, stolen. The apparent pessimism of this, and the conclusion that women do not, necessarily, work together to produce themselves as women, but rather define themselves *against* other women, in competition with them, is not intended as a demonstration that women cannot, or never do, inspire or support each other. Rather, it is to show the consequences of male power for the possibilities for femininity in this society. To deny the dark side of being a woman, its freaks and its fantasies, would be to do men a favour. In Catharine A. Mackinnon's words, to gloss over the radical impossibility of femininity is to act:

> as if the purpose of speech is to say what we want reality to be like, as if it already is that way, as if that will help move reality to that place. This may work in fiction, but it won't work in theory. Rather, if this is reality, nothing needs changing: *this* is freedom; we choose *this*. To me, this answer is about denial and is the opposite of change.[9]

To face the sober truth of our psychical options is also to recognize the urgency with which they need to be altered.

For Freud, 'normal' femininity was like a distant winning post at the end of a very cluttered obstacle race. Two challenges, specific to women, stand out:

> We have long understood that the development of female sexuality is complicated by the fact that the girl has the task of giving up what was originally her leading genital zone – the clitoris – in favour of a new zone – the vagina. But it now seems to us that there is a second change of the same sort which is no less characteristic and important for the development of the female: the exchange of her original object – her mother – for her father. The way in which the two tasks are connected with each other is not yet clear to us.[10]

It is perhaps in this mysterious connection that the secret of femininity lies. For the little girl must not only change the emphasis in her object relations (substitute a man for a woman), she must also change the way she imagines and experiences her own body. With the change in genital zone comes a change in object: 'she slips – along the line of a symbolic equation, one might say – from the penis to a baby'.[11] But slipping is neither well controlled nor irrevocable. There is always a 'before' for femininity, a pre-body, a pre-history. We shall return to this later.

Femininity is also an end, a point of arrival. Freud was fond of the phrase 'final outcome' in his accounts of sexual life,[12] and in his late paper 'Femininity' (1933) he outlined three possible outcomes for women.

> The discovery that she is castrated is a turning-point in a girl's growth. Three possible lines of development start from it: one leads to sexual inhibition or to neurosis, the second to change of character in the sense of a masculinity complex, the third, finally, to normal femininity.[13]

The three possible outcomes – their exact details do not concern us at the moment – are presented as equally plausible alternatives; but only one is favoured with the prize-winning epithet 'femininity'. We must conclude then that there are a lot of females walking around who are not really feminine and, consequently, not really women: fakes.

This problem of feminine masquerade, in Joan Riviere's term,[14] is further complicated by an uncertainty in Freudian accounts of sexuality over the status of the word 'outcome'. Jacqueline Rose notes that although Freud's theory of femininity is 'at moments' developmental, it was not developmental – or teleological – enough for many of Freud's contemporaries.[15] Comparing the youthfulness of a 30-year-old man with the inflexibility of a woman of the same age, he remarks that she

> often frightens us with her psychical rigidity and unchangeability. Her libido has taken up final positions and seems incapable of exchanging them for others. There are no paths open to further development; it is as though the whole process had already run its course and remains thenceforward insusceptible to influence – as though, indeed, the difficult development to femininity had exhausted the possibilities of the person concerned.[16]

Harold Nicolson, Vita's husband, echoes Freud's metaphor in talking of Vita's mother's vindictiveness: 'it is the elasticity of her mind that is going wrong – it is hardening like old india-rubber'.[17] The prize of femininity can come to seem simply a dead end, an extremity.

This is one possible version. In another, femininity – and indeed subjecthood itself – is never finally achieved, is always slipping. Rose sees the strength of psychoanalysis to be the extent to which it conceives the failure of identity not as something to be regretted, or eschewed, but as 'something endlessly repeated and relived moment by moment throughout our individual histories'.[18] For femininity, the failure to arrive is specifically linked to the pre-Oedipal relation with the mother. 'A number of women remain arrested in their original attachment to their mother and never achieve a true change-over towards men.'[19] An inadequate femininity is thus connected with a repeated slipping back to that preliminary relation – the 'before' – that 'normal femininity' must surpass and repudiate. The coexistence in Freudian theory of one version of the sexual which involves a 'final outcome', an immobility, and of another version which envisages continued oscillation between pre-Oedipal and Oedipal positions, is encapsulated in one of Freud's own titles, 'Analysis Terminable and Interminable'.

It is in this same paper that Freud makes his famous statement about the repudiation of femininity. Here femininity is taken as the limit to psychoanalytic intervention:

> We often have the impression that with the wish for a penis and the masculine protest we have penetrated through all the psychological strata and have reached bedrock, and that thus our activities are at an end. This is probably true since, for the psychical field the biological field does in fact play the part of the underlying bedrock. The repudiation of femininity can be nothing else than a biological fact, a part of the great riddle of sex.[20]

Femininity is not only the limit to psychoanalysis as theory and as practice; it is also the boundary of identity. It does not in itself constitute a position. In 'Analysis Terminable and Interminable' it is not even a dead end. The closest we can get to it is to the achievement of its denial. In its positive state (that which is denied) it exists somewhere beyond sexual identity, beyond possibility. For women, the 'bedrock' of their identity is the repudiation of exactly that femininity towards which they are simultaneously striving. Freud himself demonstrates this contradiction in his *New Introductory Lectures on Psychoanalysis*. In 'Anxiety and Instinctual Life' he speaks of 'the entirely unfeminine wish to possess a penis'; in 'Femininity' of the 'wish for a penis as being *par excellence* a feminine one'.[21] To take this to its logical conclusion, the extreme of femininity would be to wish to be what you are not (masculine) in order to be what you can never quite achieve (feminine). As Rachel Bowlby has pointed out, 'there is no place of femininity at all'.[22]

Freud's metaphor for the pre-Oedipal period on which feminine identity is built, 'grey with age and shadowy and almost impossible to revivify',[23] emphasizes the shifting foundations, like an archaeological dig, on which women live: 'the discovery, in another field, of the Minoan-Mycenaean civilization behind the civilization of Greece'.[24] The unstable ground on which women must walk does not encourage trust. Vita noted that, in later years, 'suspicion, always latent in [my mother's] mind, had come to stay'.[25] The precariousness of feminine identity can foster paranoia: who is it who is making life so dangerous? Vita wrote of her mother:

> It meant, in effect, that she would never have her bedroom touched or dusted; it meant that the servants had to watch their moment while she was having her daily bath to dash in and make her bed; it meant that she

kept odds and ends of food standing on tables because she declared that if it were taken away it would be stolen.[26]

Lady Sackville, feeling under siege in her own home, resorted, as we shall see, to fantasies of being poisoned, attacked and robbed.

These responses are all predicted in psychoanalytic accounts of the mother-daughter relationship. Freud notes, somewhat parenthetically, in 'Femininity': 'the fear of being poisoned is also probably connected with the withdrawal of the breast'.[27] (The fear of being poisoned is of course an accusation as well as a phobia.) Freud comments further that in the pre-Oedipal 'dependence on the mother we have the germ of later paranoia in women. For this germ appears to be the surprising, yet regular, fear of being killed (?devoured) by the mother.'[28] This fear is associated by Freud with infant hygiene and the ministrations of the mother (we remember Lady Sackville's embargoes on cleaning, dusting and bedmaking): 'this fear [of being killed] corresponds to a hostility which develops in the child towards her mother in consequence of the manifold restrictions imposed by the latter in the course of training and bodily care'.[29] It is the fragile boundaries of the body which are felt to be dangerous: their instability is associated with an imperfectly defined and blurred identity. Lady Sackville was sure that Vita wanted to kill her. 'I am not going to let myself be ill again & play into her homicidal hands by dying through worry – *NO indeed*' (Lady Sackville's diary, notes for the week of 14 May 1928). 'And those parcels of food I receive! I wont touch any of them as once there was arsenic' (Lady Sackville's diary, 15 June 1928). Vita and Harold began to respond in kind. 'If she sends the boys chocolates don't let them eat them until you have had a look. She is quite capable of putting in weed-killer' (Harold to Vita, 23 April 1928).

Melanie Klein's analysis of anxiety in adult patients reaches an impasse at a point which is connected to the similar impasse Freud reached in 'Analysis Terminable and Interminable'. 'In states of great anxiety there seems to exist in the patient's mind no other alternative but that he is robbing or being robbed.'[30] 'No other alternative' is reminiscent of Freud's idea of the bedrock. The 'repudiation of femininity' is the essence of – but also the limit to – sexual identity, as the notion of robbery is the anxious obsession *par excellence*, but also the end to anxiety, its climax. Lady Sackville liked to steal: 'she would quite shamelessly purloin the stationery from an hotel if she stopped there for luncheon, and came away convinced that she had effected a real economy if she could stuff half a dozen envelopes into her bag without anybody noticing'.[31] Sometimes she wrote letters on toilet paper from Harrods Ladies Cloakroom.[32] If there is a significant link between femininity and robbery as the endpoints of identity and anxiety, its ramifications can be traced in the tortuous progress of the relationship between Lady Sackville and her daughter. For if femininity is never a secure possession – if it is always built on sand – then it seems logical to assume that its underlying pathology would be the fear of losing it altogether. Hence Lady Sackville's paranoia, her defensive accumulation of trifles (she wrote in her 'Book of Reminiscences' 'how I have complicated my life with these senseless accumulations!'[33]); and hence too perhaps the popular association of women and kleptomania.

The psychical mechanism that both Harold and Vita seem to have used to deal with Lady Sackville was close to that described by Melanie Klein as 'splitting'. In order to survive his or her ambivalent relation to the source of nourishment, the infant evolves two objects to which he or she relates: the 'good breast' and the 'bad breast'. This splitting is an essential part of the process of 'ego-integration'. Vita and Harold began to evolve a language of death and decay to deal with Lady Sackville's demands: 'the foetid atmosphere where she reigns supreme ... our youth & peace are being given blows like the blows of a vulture's beak' (Harold to Vita, 11 September 1914). But at other times they were euphoric in their descriptions of her. Vita wrote to Harold on arriving back in England in 1926 after a trip to see him in Teheran: 'never had anybody such charm as BM!' (Vita to Harold, 19 May 1926). Later, in September of the same year, Harold responded as though with amnesia of the difficult years:

> [BM] has been such an angel to me: when one gets far away one sees these things in perspective. And BM's goodness to me & her affection and her wisdom about us emerge as one of the dominant features in that gay and lovely landscape which dates from October 1 1913 [the date of his marriage].
>
> (Harold to Vita, 27 September 1926)

Klein comments that:

> A very deep split between the two aspects of the object indicates that it is not the good and bad object that are being kept apart but an idealized and an extremely bad one. So deep and sharp a division reveals that destructive impulses, envy, and persecutory anxiety are very strong and that idealization serves mainly as a defence against these emotions.[34]

The oscillation between dread of and adoration for Lady Sackville demonstrates the instability of the structure within which, by this time, all three were finding their identities.

It is hard not to sympathize with the changes in Vita's and Harold's attitudes to Lady Sackville. She herself was so wildly erratic – and her paranoia so manipulative – that she succeeded in the end in driving them in their turn into a paranoid state. It was she who dictated the terms of their relationships with each other, perhaps as part of an unconscious strategy to bind her daughter even more deeply into the exaggerated intensities of the Oedipal and the pre-Oedipal phases. She was arrogating to herself the place of the phallic mother whom Vita was supposed to have lost.

Freudian psychoanalysis has little time for the mother's side of things.

There is one brief acknowledgement that what is going on may be an exchange as much as a robbery:

> We find the little girl's aggressive oral and sadistic wishes in a form forced on them by early repression, as a fear of being killed by her mother – a fear which, in turn, justifies her death-wish against her mother, if that becomes conscious. It is impossible to say how often this fear of the mother is supported by an unconscious hostility on the mother's part which is sensed by the girl.[35]

It may be true that in the case of an unconscious hostility it is very difficult – or even impossible – to gauge its extent. In the case of the Sackville-West family, however, partly because of the pronounced nature of Lady Sackville's paranoia, and partly because so many letters were exchanged and have survived, it is possible to map the progression and eruption of these hostilities as they take place well in the realm of the conscious, even if the unconscious motivation is obscured. As the daughter grows up, the relationship between mother and daughter begins to mirror that between daughter and mother, so that envy, anxiety and paranoia are played out not only by the daughter in relation to the maternal breast, but reciprocally by the mother in relation to what we might call the filial breast. That this struggle has barely been touched on by psychoanalysis is part of its eclipsing of the process of ageing. If femininity always has a 'before', psychoanalysis *only* has a 'before'.

But if we read carefully we can see psychoanalysis forecasting the full circle which the mother–daughter relationship will describe. The structuring principle of femininity according to Freud is envy. When little girls see little boys' bodies, 'they are ready to recognize them immediately and are overcome by envy for the penis – an envy culminating in the wish, which is so important in its consequences, to be boys themselves'.[36] That wish, as we remember, is *par excellence* feminine, and from this quotation it is clear that the impulse behind the wish – with which femininity begins and by which it is sustained – is a feeling of envy. One of its consequences is accusation: 'in the end the girl's mother, who sent her into the world so insufficiently equipped, is almost always held responsible for her lack of a penis'.[37] The daughter, then, lives her femininity as a state of envy and of blame. As Freud half-recognized, the progression to 'normal femininity' and the wish for a penis-child bind women even more strongly into their antagonistic relation to their mothers – an antagonism that was already well developed in the pre-Oedipal phase. 'Her hostility to her mother, which did not need to be freshly created, is now greatly intensified', and this Oedipal hostility can seem like a 'haven of refuge': 'girls remain in it for an indeterminate length of time; they demolish it late and, even so, incompletely'.[38] Throughout adulthood women are assumed to remain in a state of envy of men and anger with the maternal figure, such that the 'repudiation of femininity' can seem synonymous with the repudiation of the mother.

But what happens to the mother's envy? When the daughter herself becomes a mother, a complicated pattern of envy and paranoia can be set in motion. Freud suggests this in passing:

> Under the influence of a woman's becoming a mother herself, an identification with her own mother may be revived, against which she had striven up till the time of her marriage, and this may attract all the available libido to itself, so that the compulsion to repeat reproduces an unhappy marriage between her parents.[39]

But now it is grandmothers who are ignored. For many women as they age, their daughters come to seem rivals and dangers as well as cherished and respected companions. Lady Sackville seems to have been one of these women.

Victoria, Lady Sackville (1862–1936) was the illegitimate daughter of British diplomat Lionel Sackville-West, and a Spanish flamenco dancer, Pepita de Oliva.[40] This liaison – never legitimized because Pepita was already married – continued discreetly for about twenty years, until Pepita's death in childbirth in 1871, and the couple had five surviving children, of whom Victoria was the second oldest. Victoria grew up in a villa which Lionel bought for Pepita at Arcachon in France. By all accounts she adored her mother, and remembered her dancing with castanets to amuse the children.[41] 'She often sang as she went about the house, and in the afternoons she would drive out to the sand-dunes with the children and laugh when they filled their drawers with the silvery sand, standing up to let it trickle out at their ankles.'[42] When Victoria was eight her mother died, and she was placed, at the age of eleven, in the convent of St Joseph, 17 Rue Monceau in Paris. She was to stay there, lonely, bored and confused, for the next seven years.

In 1881 Victoria went to Washington DC to act as hostess for her father, who had been appointed minister to the British legation there. But in 1888 Lionel's brother died and Lionel became Lord Sackville and master of Knole in Kent. Victoria, having managed the social affairs of the British legation in Washington, was now called upon to take up her duties as chatelaine of Knole. The house was vast, and Victoria managed it with all the zest and enthusiasm of which she was capable. 'The cook and the obliging Mrs Knox both came to her room for orders every morning, and in the afternoons she could rummage in the cupboards, discovering every kind of treasure, from Sèvres china to old lace.'[43] Soon she was to marry her own cousin, also named Lionel, in 1890 in the chapel at Knole.

Her happiness seemed complete. 'She had youth, beauty, wealth; Knole to rule over; an unobtrusive father; an adoring husband with whom she was now passionately in love; a child [Vita, born 1892] whom she alternately scolded and hugged, very much as Pepita herself had done.'[44] 'Normal femininity' seemed to have done Lady Sackville proud. At least one of the transitions described by Freud was apparently accomplished with remarkable efficiency. 'Baby', Lady Sackville's name for Lionel's penis, was extremely active in the early days of their marriage. 'Baby was very naughty this morning, we kept Mrs Knox waiting for forty minutes – awful of us' (Lady Sackville's diary, 13 September 1890). 'Tio [Lionel] was perfectly mad tonight – he kissed me passionately even in front of Amalia and Bertie, which ended in the most delicious love making. He really is a stallion – 4 times' (Lady Sackville's diary, 18 September 1890). 'Delirium. Afterwards Tio said, "Was it nice, Vicky?"' (Lady Sackville's diary, 28 November 1890).[45]

Vita's arrival into the midst of this does not seem to have been entirely welcome. 'She loved me when I was a baby, but I don't think she cared much for me as a child, nor do I blame her.'[46] (Vita didn't much like children herself.) Another of Freud's comments about the mother as a prohibiting figure in the child's life is echoed in Vita's remarks: 'I don't mean to imply that Mother neglected me, or wasn't good to me, but simply that she figured more as a restraint than anything else in my existence.'[47] She also noted that 'I liked [Dada] a great deal better than Mother, of whose quick temper I was frightened.'[48]

Vita grew up a solitary, awkward child. The passion between her parents began to fade. Lady Sackville was terrified of having another child, and her uninhibited delight in her husband's virility must have been compromised by her fear. By 1899 Lord Sackville had taken a mistress.

In 1912, Vita became romantically attached to a young diplomat called Harold Nicolson. By this time Lady Sackville was a wife only in name, and she dreaded losing Vita's companionship. She placed an embargo on Vita's and Harold's engagement and insisted that the sexual element be missing from their letters: 'they must not correspond as engaged people and no words of Dearest and Darling must be used!'[49] Terms of endearment are displaced in Vita's letters back to their original pre-Oedipal context. Writing to Harold, she enthused:

> Mother has been buying chefs, and gardeners, and people, it is such fun. She has bursts of opulence. Yes, she is a splendid person. ... She is more wonderful every day. She never grows monotonous, but Shakespeare has said all that better than I can, 'nor custom stale her infinite variety', which might have been written for her, mightn't it?
>
> (Vita to Harold, 16 February 1912)

The imperiousness that irked Vita when it was directed at her is a source of attraction when it confirms Lady Sackville as a commander of men, able to acquire and cast aside with all the caprice that was an essential part of her character. In this incarnation Lady Sackville is the *phallic mother*, restraining everyone but her daughter and fostering in her daughter's mind an impression of feminine power.[50] As Vita approached marriage – a state that she already anticipated as one of restraint (she wrote to Harold asking for a postponement because 'this is the first year I have lived at all ... and ... if I let you take me away this year it will all end', Vita to Harold 23 July 1912) – she became increasingly aware that her mother did not, in fact, have the freedom – the phallic power – with which Vita had been endowing her. It seems to have dawned on her simultaneously that her mother did not always get what she wanted and that, therefore, neither might she.

> There is another reason [for postponing the marriage]. The **B.M.** [their name for Lady Sackville] would simply *hate* it. I know you will think that if I wanted it sufficiently myself I should not stop to think about that, but you are wrong: she has been wonderfully good to us both, and we do owe her that.
>
> (Vita to Harold, 23 July 1912)

A sense of what she herself had to lose becomes almost indistinguishable from an awareness that her mother too will be deprived by her marriage. The vocabulary of debt and credit would take on an increasingly menacing aspect as Lady Sackville grew older.

The situation mirrors the scenario Freud proposed for the little girl's original entry into the Oedipus complex. Having perceived her own castration, the girl soon discovers that her mother lacks a penis as well. The consequent 'repudiation' covers not only her own body, but also that of her mother: 'as a result of the discovery of women's lack of a penis they are debased in value for girls just as they are for boys and later perhaps for men'.[51] Vita and her mother both conceive Vita's marriage as a rejection of Lady Sackville – a turning-away from women and castration, towards men and penis-babies. Lady Sackville's own dallyings with Lionel's 'Baby' had exemplified this perfectly.

For Lady Sackville, Vita's marriage is cast in terms not merely of castration, but of bereavement: the lonely widow. 'What a lonely life I shall lead without Vita. ... Enfin!! one must go on pluckily & one must hide one's sorrow and loneliness, I could be such a devoted wife & companion, but it's too late now, I do miss my Kidlet' (Lady Sackville's diary, 2 April 1913). On the day of the wedding she was menstruating and so did not appear. It is tempting to see some parallel between the loss of her daughter to a man, and the experience of herself as wounded and bleeding (she had unmanageably heavy periods). Not only grief but a renewed realization of castration is inscribed in both events.

Friends treated her as one bereaved. 'It was so good of [?] to write and condole & console me. So many people have written in that way' (Lady Sackville's diary, 2 October 1913). She was sitting to Rodin for a sculpture, and described his sympathy in terms not only of condolence but also of worship, reinstating herself as a centre of heterosexual magnetism: 'Rodin was so kind to me today when I broke down talking about Vita, & when he saw my eyes full of tears, he got up & came to me ... & knelt in front of me and said: Pauvre amie comme v. souffrez de son absence' (Lady Sackville's diary, 11 November 1913). The motif of jewels, which occurs throughout the relationship between the two women, appears first at this point: Lady Sackville gave Vita a lavish wedding gift of emeralds and diamonds, and wrote of one of Vita's letters to her: 'V. writes that she never thought she could be so happy; that every letter of the word "Happiness" shines brilliantly like the D^{ds} of my Catherine Parr's necklace' (Lady Sackville's diary, 3 October 1913). Vita's transition to active heterosexual femininity is marked by her adornment with jewels: she is crowned a woman.

Vita and Harold spent the first months of their marriage in Constantinople. They returned to England for the birth of their first child, Ben, who was born on 6 August 1914. At this point, Lady Sackville's anxiety and grief reached a sudden and explosive climax. She had felt rebuffed during the last months of the pregnancy, when Vita and Harold were in England: 'I am a little disappointed at her indifference to me, altho' I try to understand it; naturally H. is everything to her now & the baby – and I feel I am hardly wanted' (Lady Sackville's diary, 19 June 1914). She was fading from the heterosexual picture. In 1915 Lionel would install his mistress Olive Rubens and her husband at Knole; they were staying there on the night of Ben's birth. Lady Sackville already had to face one double: the usurping wife, in the shape of Olive Rubens. The terms of the dispute with Vita show that when Vita became a mother Lady Sackville felt herself eclipsed twice over. The uncertainty over what might happen to the pre-Oedipal intensity which had been so strong between the two women before Vita's marriage, once Vita herself became a mother and started to occupy the opposite position in the structure from the one in which Lady Sackville was used to seeing her, was intolerable.

The details of the birth itself were unpropitious. Harold came running into the ballroom, where Olive Rubens and Lady Sackville were sitting, to announce the birth of his son.

> He asked Olive to be extra godmother; I asked him if since last night (and I asked again tonight) if Vita had sent me any messages; I asked the same of Dr S and of the nice nurse Mrs Evans but they had to admit that altho she had thought of Olive as extra godmother, she had never expressed any wish to see me, or asked for me. It is quite heartbreaking to me to realize all this.
>
> (Lady Sackville's diary, 6 August 1914)

Lady Sackville is excluded entirely from the maternal scene – not even receiving an acknowledgement of her relationship with Vita. Instead Olive Rubens is promoted to a version of maternity in being asked to act as godmother. Lady Sackville's pre-Oedipal bond with her daughter is broken as Vita moves to take up the maternal position in her own family. The energy released by this severance fuels a series of manoeuvres by Lady Sackville designed to get herself reinstated as sole mother in the extended family.

The power to name a child, and to fix it taxonomically in a certain relation to its family history, is a privilege – or a burden – that traditionally in Western society belongs to its parents. Lady Sackville, with an anomalous relation to her own family history (sharing her father's title not by inheritance but through lateral marriage), named her child after herself. She in turn had been called by her mother's name, Pepita, until she entered the convent. To call her child Victoria was to ensure that the pre- and post-Oedipal identification between mother and daughter would be apparently guaranteed. Her choice of an unusual abbreviation for Vita's name, pounced on by Virginia Woolf in *Orlando* ('they come here, says the bird, and ask me what life is; Life, Life, Life!')[52] reaches back to her own mother's name and to her childhood self: 'Pepita'.

Lady Sackville's failure to bear a son – her physical horror of pregnancy and childbirth, and her decision not to have more than one child – meant that on her husband's death (which occurred in 1928) her family would have to leave Knole. She knew the fear of being dispossessed; during a lawsuit brought by her brother Henry she had faced the possibility that she might have to move out permanently. Vita's production of a son underlined her inadequacy and increased her envy. Freud comments in one of his case histories on the feelings of an adolescent girl whose mother bore a son late in life:

> [The girl] became keenly conscious of the wish to have a child, and a male one; that what she desired was her *father's* child and an image of *him*, her consciousness was not allowed to know. And what happened next? It was not *she* who bore the child, but her unconsciously hated rival, her mother.[53]

Lady Sackville, smarting at her rejection by her husband, seems to have started to relate to Vita as though Vita were the mother bearing the desired child, and she herself the spurned daughter.

Vita and Harold wanted to call the baby 'Benedict Lionel'. Lady Sackville wanted him to be called 'Lionel Benedict'. Vita was deeply wounded. Harold wrote to Lady Sackville at Vita's dictation (the handwriting of the letter itself marks the destruction of any untroubled pre-Oedipal relation):

> BM, all this is not an attack on you, it is an attempt to try & make you see that I have not refused this to you out of any petulant egoism, but out of a real mothers longing to call her own baby what pleases her [*sic*]. You say this is the only favour you have asked, but I answer that he is the only thing in life which is absolutely mine – mine through the pangs of hell – & that it is more than bitter for me to be called ungrateful, because I cling to the name I have chosen for him. Why you yourself say that you had called me Vita before I was born so you can't pretend now not to realise how much the chosen name of one's little baby means.
>
> (Vita to Lady Sackville, not dated, August 1914)

Of course Lady Sackville knew exactly how much it meant; that was why she was making an issue of it. The vocabulary of debt and gratitude is strong again. Earlier, Vita, almost giving in, had written: 'you have appealed to the great debt of gratitude I owe you & I cannot refuse' (Vita to Lady Sackville, not dated, August 1914). What Vita owes her mother – and what she has taken from her – is maternity.

It is hard to know how far elements of this exaggerated and distorted situation are present in a more subdued and routine manner in other relationships between adult daughters and their mothers. As we have seen, it is one of the *lacunae* of psychoanalysis that it has so little to say about ageing. But the fact that Lady Sackville's reactions are recognizable as factors in the psychoanalytic scenario suggests that as the infant–mother bond is shifted, snatches of it continue to echo throughout the development of adult relationships.

Nor are the names over which there was such debate, arbitrary. Lady Sackville's father and husband were both called Lionel; it is reasonable to suppose that any son she might have had would also have been called Lionel. In naming her grandson Lionel she sought to preserve an unbroken succession along the male line, and to write out of the genealogical tree her own failure to produce a son.

In January 1928 Vita's father died. Lady Sackville, having been forced out of Knole years earlier by Olive Rubens' presence there, was not present either during his illness or at his funeral. The result of this was an extremely violent backlash against Vita.

Vita, having pushed Harold's endurance as far as it would go during her affair with Violet Trefusis (1918–21), had pulled back just in time and was now enjoying the fruits of a tested and stable marriage, simultaneously with a series of passionate lesbian affairs that were condoned and even supported by the similarly occupied Harold. Vita had all the prizes of heterosexual femininity – wealth, children, respectability, a home – with few of its costs. Lady Sackville, on the other hand, innocent of any sexual misdemeanour, found herself excluded from her family house and even from her own husband's funeral. Harold wrote to Vita that

> we know that BM has had a complex about you not being a boy, & that this burst like a volcano when Dada died & you did not succeed, & has turned into malignant jealousy of you my sweet: – jealousy of your calm, & unworldliness, & of our love for each other.
>
> (Harold to Vita, 20 November 1928)

Lady Sackville saw Vita as a thief and a forger. Looking for somebody to blame, she held Vita responsible for her own loss of the symbols of adult femininity, and accused her of holding them in her own right under false pretences. Lady Sackville demanded the return of some of the Knole jewels – those touchstones of femininity.

What about my 4 big brilliants which [Vita] wrote might be 'paste'. It looks as if the brilliants had been changed with paste & the emeralds of the leaves Tiara ditto. And 4 beautiful brilliants are missing from my necklace. What is one to think, my God! with such dishonourable lying people, that *liar* who became executrix through such a deliberate lie, backed by both Pembertons [the family solicitors].

(Lady Sackville's diary, notes for the week of 14 May 1928)

Lady Sackville, convinced that Vita is actually a 'false' woman – adorned with the trappings of adult heterosexual femininity in spite of her active lesbianism – accuses her of forging jewels, taking more than her fair share, trying to pass fakes off as authentic. In the meantime Lady Sackville's own body speaks only of pain and mortality, the inescapable fact of the flesh. She produces a bizarre parody of the menstruation which kept her from Vita's wedding:

I have been so badly treated by H & V that I have written a decisive letter. I could not receive them now; it would open the flood gates of my tears again. And I am much frightened, as blood came mixed with my tears this evening.

(Lady Sackville's diary, 30 January 1928)

Their most melodramatic exchange involved the jewels of which Lady Sackville was so suspicious. On 18 April 1928 Vita was at the family lawyers in London, making arrangements for her father's estate. Unexpectedly, her mother burst into the office.

Darling, never, *never* have I heard such floods of the vilest abuse, aimed at both Pemberton and me. She was like a mad woman, screaming thief and liar, and shaking her fist at me till I thought she was going to hit me. It was quite impossible for either P. [the lawyer] or me to speak, and equally impossible to make out what it was all about, – the jewels, mostly.

(Vita to Harold, 18 April 1928)

Eventually Lady Sackville went out into the street, and then sent back a demand that Vita come with her to a jeweller to have twelve pearls cut from her necklace. Vita went out, and, standing by her mother's taxi, cut through the string of her necklace and handed over twelve pearls. 'She screamed that she hated me, & wished I would die, – wished indeed that I might be run over & killed that very day' (Vita to Harold, 18 April 1928). Furious and despairing, Vita hailed a taxi and left. She wrote to Harold that evening: 'this has torn it, & I feel the rupture is complete' (Vita to Harold, 18 April 1928).

Lady Sackville felt that she had done well. Her desire to obliterate Vita was coterminous with her fear of her own obliteration. In response to her feeling that, at her husband's funeral, 'I was treated as if I didn't exist' (Lady Sackville's diary, 15 February 1928), she wrote that 'I buried her [Vita] with him, altho' I had loved her so' (Lady Sackville's diary, notes for the week of

30 January 1928). On 26 February 1928 she referred to 'the burial of V. at Withyham'. Her unconscious consigned Vita to a kind of living death.

NOTES

1 I am very grateful to Teresa Brennan and Diana Hinds for reading and commenting on early drafts of this paper.
2 Vita Sackville-West, *Pepita*, 1937 (London: Virago, 1986), pp. 262, 264.
3 Susan Mary Alsop, *Lady Sackville: A Biography* (London: Weidenfeld & Nicolson, 1978), p. 217.
4 Sackville-West, op.cit., p. 265.
5 Alsop, op.cit., p. 217.
6 Virginia Woolf, *The Diary of Virginia Woolf*, ed. Anne Olivier Bell, 5 vols (London: Hogarth, 1977–84), III, p. 52, 21 December 1925.
7 See Victoria Glendinning, *Vita: The Life of V. Sackville-West* (London: Weidenfeld & Nicolson, 1983), pp. 192–4.
8 The long debate among feminists about the usefulness of psychoanalysis informs this paper's relation to Freudian theory. Some of Freud's remarks about women (for example, that they have inadequately developed super-egos, and are highly prone to jealousy) have led many women to reject his work outright – particularly, for instance, women working with incest survivors who object to Freud's contention that many women's accounts of incest abuse are in fact only fantasies. The relationship between Vita and her mother seems to bear out many of Freud's analyses, rather in the manner of an ideal case study.
9 Catharine A. Mackinnon, *Feminism Unmodified: Discourses on Life and Law* (Cambridge and London: Harvard University Press, 1987), p. 59.
10 Sigmund Freud, 'Female Sexuality' (1931), in *On Sexuality*, ed. Angela Richards, Pelican Freud Library, VII (Harmondsworth: Penguin, 1977), pp. 367–92, p. 371.
11 Sigmund Freud, 'The Dissolution of the Oedipus Complex' (1924), in *On Sexuality*, pp. 313–22, p. 321.
12 Sigmund Freud, 'Three Essays on the Theory of Sexuality' (1905), in *On Sexuality*, pp. 31–169; pp. 116, 128.
13 Sigmund Freud, 'Femininity', in *New Introductory Lectures on Psychoanalysis*, ed. James Strachey and Angela Richards, Pelican Freud Library, II (Harmondsworth: Penguin, 1973), pp. 145–69, p. 160.
14 Joan Riviere, 'Womanliness as Masquerade', in *Formations of Fantasy*, ed. Victor Burgin, James Donald and Cora Kaplan (London: Methuen, 1986).
15 Jacqueline Rose, 'Femininity and its Discontents', in *Sexuality in the Field of Vision* (London: Verso, 1986), pp. 83–103; p. 93.
16 Freud, 'Femininity', p. 169.
17 Harold Nicolson to Vita Sackville-West, 5 (misdated for 4) July 1928, Lilly Library, Bloomington, Indiana. All further references in the text to letters between Harold Nicolson and Vita Sackville-West, and to Lady Sackville's diaries, are to unpublished material in this archive. I am very grateful to Nigel Nicolson, and to the Lilly Library, for permission to quote extracts here.
18 Rose, op. cit., p. 91.
19 Freud, 'Female Sexuality', p. 372.
20 Sigmund Freud, 'Analysis Terminable and Interminable' (1937), *Standard Edition*, ed. James Strachey, XXIII, pp. 209–53; p. 252.
21 Sigmund Freud, 'Anxiety and Instinctual Life', in *New Introductory Lectures on Psychoanalysis*, pp. 113–44, p. 134; 'Femininity', p. 162.

22 Rachel Bowlby, 'Still Crazy After All These Years', in *Between Feminism and Psychoanalysis*, ed. Teresa Brennan (London: Routledge, 1989), pp. 40–59, p. 50.
23 Freud, 'Female Sexuality', p. 373.
24 ibid., p. 372.
25 Sackville-West, op. cit., p. 277.
26 ibid.
27 Freud, 'Femininity', p. 156.
28 Freud, 'Female Sexuality', p. 373.
29 ibid.
30 Melanie Klein, 'Envy and Gratitude' (1957), in *Envy and Gratitude and Other Works 1946–1963,* introduced by Hanna Segal (London: Virago, 1988), pp. 176–235, p. 222.
31 Sackville-West, op. cit., p. 205.
32 ibid., p. 206.
33 Victoria, Lady Sackville, 'Book of Reminiscences' (1922), in Alsop, op. cit., pp. 237–47, p. 243.
34 Klein, op. cit., p. 192.
35 Freud, 'Female Sexuality', p. 385.
36 Freud, 'Three Essays on the Theory of Sexuality', p. 114.
37 Freud, 'Some Psychological Consequences of the Anatomical Distinction between the Sexes' (1925), in *On Sexuality*, pp. 323–43, p. 338.
38 Freud, 'Femininity', p. 163.
39 ibid., pp. 167–8.
40 All biographical information in this paper is taken from the Lilly Library archive (including Lady Sackville's diaries); Alsop, op. cit., Sackville-West, op. cit., Glendinning, op. cit. and Nigel Nicolson, *Portrait of a Marriage* (London: Weidenfeld & Nicolson, 1973).
41 Sackville-West, op. cit., p. 132.
42 ibid., p. 142.
43 ibid., pp. 182–3.
44 ibid., p. 189.
45 These quotations are the fairly free translations into English given in Alsop, *Lady Sackville*, pp. 106–7. The originals are in a rather cryptic French.
46 Nicolson, op. cit., p. 20.
47 ibid.
48 ibid., p. 11.
49 Quoted in Glendinning, op. cit., p. 45.
50 Freud, 'Femininity', p. 160.
51 ibid., pp. 160–1.
52 Virginia Woolf, *Orlando* (London: Hogarth, 1928), p. 243.
53 Freud, 'The Psychogenesis of a Case of Homosexuality in a Woman' (1920), in *Case Histories II*, ed. Angela Richards, Pelican Freud Library, IX (Harmondsworth: Penguin, 1979), pp. 367–400, p. 383.

Chapter 8

The dangers of Angela Carter

Elaine Jordan

She felt young and tough and brave, giving away her relics.
The Magic Toyshop, p. 189.

The habit of sardonic contemplation is the hardest habit of all to break.
The Infernal Desire Machines of Dr Hoffman, p. 201.

The wisest thing – so the fairy tale taught mankind in olden times, and teaches children to this day – is to meet the forces of the mythical world with cunning and with high spirits.
Walter Benjamin, 'The Storyteller'
(*Illuminations*, Fontana Books, 1973, p. 102).

My title sounds as though I am joining the attack which in fact I mean to counter by offering this paper – riding to the rescue of a woman writer in danger. But, every Pauline her own saviour from Perils – Angela Carter doesn't need me. What gets me going is of course what Carter's critics (Patricia Duncker, Susanne Kappeler, Robert Clark) make of me as someone who not only loves reading her work, but put it on my reading lists and in the way of my teenage daughter, and my sons. Patricia Duncker here signifies lesbian, woman-identified criticism; Clark an old-fashioned if Althusserian Marxism that wants to articulate itself with the 'authentic experience of women'; Susanne Kappeler represents anti-pornographic feminism, although her larger argument in *The Pornography of Representation* knows that censorship from within the existing system is merely cosmetic: she challenges representation altogether.[1]

Reading back through Angela Carter's work from the sixties on, I had my moment of horror and cold feet at what I was letting myself in for. It's true (as she acknowledges in the Afterword to the reissued *Love*) that she started out writing as a kind-of male impersonator, with a strong streak of misogyny which is very much of the period and which, since it's directed against the taste of the proper little lady, the educated daughter of the bourgeoisie or the Welfare State, is preserved in her later writing as an assault on the confining codes of 'femininity'.

Does she offer a knowledge of patriarchy, Robert Clark asks, as if that were something that could be simply served up on a salver; or does she, as he thinks, simply repeat the 'self-alienation' imposed by the system of power relations condensed in that term? Inevitably, her work exposes a history, a process of change which involves a series of honourable attempts to be an agent of change – part of the solution, rather than contemplating a problem of which she is part – to be boldly and honestly materialist, atheist, anti-tyrannical and feminist. I'll please no-one, least of all her, by trying to say she's not offensive. Just about everything Carter gains in her writing is at a cost: to be immediately specific, to query the political value of speaking as a victim can be only a hairsbreadth away from blaming the victim. But that space does exist. I want to assert – although in a rather schematic form here – those things which I see as constructive, productive, positive, for women and feminism, in Angela Carter's writing:

1 The questioning throughout her work (but most quickly located in the figure of Justine in *The Sadeian Woman*), of the subject position of the virtuous victim, and its adequacy as a position from which to resist oppression. Justine's preservation of her purity and innocence in an awful world is not, Carter writes, 'the continuous exercise of a moral faculty' but 'a sentimental response to a world in which she always hopes her good behaviour will procure her some reward, some respite' (p. 54). This position needs, not just a sympathetic audience of other victims, but the supposition of some benign authority that can make it all better. Carter's position is a dangerous one, because given the actual situation of many women they are quite likely to speak or write against it as victims, in some degree. Nevertheless, she alerts us to the limitations of this mode of resisting the systems of power that produce suffering.

2 Conversely, she queries Juliette, the career woman of power who avoids slavery by embracing tyranny. In *The Pornography of Representation* Susanne Kappeler assumes that Angela Carter is offering Juliette as a model, and ignoring her complicity with a system that oppresses women. Carter is in fact stating a position like Kappeler's: 'A free woman in an unfree society will be a monster' (*The Sadeian Woman*, p. 27). Kappeler ignores this solidarity, as she ignores Carter's final rubbishing of Sade, once she's used his writing as a springboard for whatever she can get from it for women – that is, an analysis of the virtuous victim and the woman of power, as well as Sade's liberating refusal to consider sexual pleasure as secondary to the business of reproduction. Like Donally in *Heroes and Villains* and the Count in *The Infernal Desire Machines of Dr Hoffman*, Sade cannot abide reciprocity, or even the freedom he means to desire, 'still in complicity with the authority which he hates', *The Sadeian Woman*, pp. 132, 141, 136. Work like Carter's is crucial if we are to both use, and differentiate ourselves from, 'traditions' of liberation and the surreal.

The rejection of the types of behaviour figured in Justine and Juliette, and elaborated through twentieth-century instances, implies a general struggle towards something else, towards free and fair human relations, and love that can be 'a reciprocal pact of tenderness' (*The Sadeian Woman*, p. 8). This may involve acknowledging some of the advantages that are side-effects of subordination, and letting go some defences and justifications; and that is why Carter's writing can baffle, or be experienced as an assault. I was astonished to find some aspects of myself in both Justine and Juliette, which provoked me to question my ways of relating myself as I had never done before. In this respect I find it useful to lean on the idea of the discomposing or decomposition of the reader, in Linda Williams's paper in this volume, 'Happy Families? Feminist Reproduction and Matrilineal Thought'. If books can change lives at all, they must do so by unsettling identities and fixed positions. I plead, against Clark, Duncker and Kappeler, that readers should attend to the whole argument of Carter's fictions and at least think twice before deciding that there is nothing positive for them and for feminism, when their predispositions are offended. This does not mean that I am asking for passive submission to the author's goading; it is the moment of disturbance and anger which may produce a new consciousness and a new order of things.

3 One knowledge or exploration Carter does genuinely offer is of narcissistic desire, self-preoccupied fantasies which interfere in the possibility of relation between people who are other in themselves, not just projections of each other's desires. This is a particular concern of *Heroes and Villains*, where Marianne embodies her estranged desire in the Barbarian Jewel; it is implicated in the virgin births of Eve and Tristessa in *The Passion of New Eve*, and it is articulated in 'Flesh and the Mirror' in *Fireworks*, where, like Jewel, the man is objectified:

> I suppose I shall never know, now, (how he really looked) for he was plainly an object created in the mode of fantasy. His image was already present somewhere in my head and I was seeking to discover it in actuality, looking at every face I met in case it was the right face – that is, the face which corresponded to my notion of the face of the one I should love, a face created parthenogenetically by the rage to love which consumed me. So his self ... the thing he was to himself, was quite unknown to me. I created him solely in relation to myself, like a work of romantic art.
>
> (p. 67)

4 One of the things I'm very keen to get said is that, although such a passage may sound autobiographical, none of Carter's exploratory fictions are absolute versions of reality, although real relations – sexual, political, economic – are of immense concern to her. There are no naturalistically credible imitations of experience in her work and no role models either, not in any simple sense; choices of behaviour have to be read within a particular set-up. However much motifs are repeated from one end of her work to the other,

each project is tactical and specific within a general feminist and materialist strategy – you cannot lay a grid across her work and read off meanings from it, according to a law of the same, which is what I think Duncker, Kappeler and Clark try to do.[2] To offer one example of what I mean: Patricia Duncker assumes that the blindness of the piano tuner in 'The Bloody Chamber' is a symbolic castration, like Charlotte Brontë's mutilation of Mr Rochester in *Jane Eyre*. And indeed the piano tuner does function as a cipher, as anonymous as the princess that the prince may be awarded in a fairy tale. I want Carter and myself to be allowed a transient tactical liberation from the genuine enough theoretical import of such an interpretation (though it is never *more* than an interpretation). I can't speak for the blind, being at the moment abled in that respect, but I think that if I were blind I would by now be quite weary of this sort of interpretation. The blindness of the piano tuner, the alternative husband to Bluebeard, is produced by the needs of the story's argument. The bride has already been too much seduced by seeing herself as the object of an erotic gaze, so that any other lover must be marked as 'not like that', one who knows her in his heart, and can appreciate her skill as a musician. He must of course be disabled in some respect, so that it is the bride's mother not he who rescues her. But, the musical instrument which brings them together is 'perfectly in tune' ('The Bloody Chamber', p. 40).

Another example: in my experience readers often assume that Eve in *The Passion of New Eve* is a role model for a new woman (it is not Carter who misleads them but the desire for role models disseminated by the empire of US sociology).[3] The title's analogy with the passion of Christ the Messiah might also suggest such a reading – but this is blasphemous not authoritative; Carter is playing with alternative theologies of the power of virginity and the androgyny of God's son. Rather, Eve/Evelyn like Desiderio in *Hoffman*, is akin to the passive hero of Scott's novels, who is put through certain phases of action for the instruction of the reader. It is the action and the commentary on it which signify. In *The Passion of New Eve* these phases are modelled on those of the alchemical search: first *nigredo*, the melting of the metals, as in the chaos of New York where blackness actually holds a promise for the future as yet unseen; then the whitening phase in which elements separate out, as in the fragments of American lifestyles Eve encounters; and finally *rubedo*, the red fire of revolution which may produce pure gold. The Czech alchemist in New York is one pointer to such a reading; and given this story's concern with cinema, one model could have been Sergei Eisenstein's notion of combining alchemy with dialectical materialism, in montage.[4] So all this demands special knowledge? Yes, why not? Curiosity, as Charles Perrault said, is a charming passion. It is not essential for a feminist writer to assume naive readers, or for every reader to see all possible readings. In my mother's tenement there are many apartments, and that's not the only house there is. This may mislead readers who are not already politically aware, as

Clark fears? Get away – I'm not as daft as you think, my mother always says.

Carter's fictions are serial and episodic, not hierarchical and organic. That is, they work like the speculative fictions of the Enlightenment, like *Candide* or *Gulliver's Travels*, not like Romantic works of art in which the whole significance might be read off from any sample. Her typical narrative procedure is the refusal of nostalgia, *not* keeping the home fires burning for an escape route. She burns the boats or the brothel, crashes the train, or buries the last provisional family acquired under a landslide. There's no going back, her narratives insist; you have to go somewhere else, even become someone else: 'It just goes to show there's nothing like confidence', as Fevvers concludes (*Nights at the Circus*). On the one hand, that's a simple crude slogan, and Carter has a few of those, with which, as it happens, I sympathize; they manifest her general tendency unmistakably. Contrarily, it's not that simple. Confidence is a desideratum for any woman or any group in struggle, but Carter also means conning people. The rational truth teller is also a performance artiste, turning a penny or two.

That you have to let go, move on, give away your relics – the moral of all Carter's longer narratives – is violently in contradiction with the fact that in demythologizing she is also refurbishing old myths and symbols, setting them going again. And that strong linear drive of her fictions is never towards conclusion and resolution, only towards the assertion of certain principles or negations, in the light of which the struggle goes on. She has no time for Utopias or 'that great commune in the sky'. Confidence is all because life is struggle. 'There is no way out of time. We must learn to live in this world, to take it with sufficient seriousness, because it is the only world we will ever know' (*The Sadeian Woman*, p. 110). This maxim comes as the conclusion to her rejection of Woman or Mother as the last refuge of the concept of Eternity, of escape or appeal to some other level; to me it is poignant and invigorating. It is the heart of her demystifications.

Angela Carter is a writer of contradictions. Her style (that is, her self-production as a writer, her deliberate though often ironic position – not some showy extra, as Clark seems to think) yokes disparate effects: the banal and the extraordinary, the prim and the offensive, the baroque and the offhand. The unmistakable boldness of this style is produced by its collisions, its very active dependency on previous texts, which is a reader's rewriting and the rewriting of readers. It is not out of this world. I want to examine Carter's intertextual dialogues (or polylogues) through discussion of one short fiction, the title story of *The Bloody Chamber*. I have chosen this story because it also allows me to discuss the apparent contradiction between Carter's feminist 'line' and her exploitation of a dangerous reactionary fascination – heterosexual desire in thrall to soft pornography and sado-masochism.

The young pianist of 'The Bloody Chamber' is the willing bride of a Bluebeard, a connoisseur of juvenile and sadistic pornography, as well as of five centuries of European art. These are his things. Carter's writing here offers the excitement of erotic anticipation even while parodying it.[5] It parodies also the poignancy of the separation of mother and daughter, a pathos which constitutes part of the erotic excitement:

> my burning cheek pressed against the impeccable linen of the pillow and the pounding of my heart mimicking that of the great pistons ceaselessly thrusting the train that bore me through the night, away . . . from girlhood. . . . Oh! how he must want me!
>
> (*The Bloody Chamber*, pp. 7, 10)

The mother's regrets are imagined: 'folding up and putting away all my little relics', lingering over 'this torn ribbon and that faded photograph' (p. 7), while the bride herself is so seduced by the part she is playing that she does not regret 'the world of tartines and maman that now receded from me as if drawn away on a string, like a child's toy' (p. 13). In context, this wonderfully evokes the sensation of pulling out of a railway station, but also, in a wider context, grandfather Freud's game of Fort/Da, here and gone – the child's overcoming of separation from the mother by calling performance and language, signification, into play.

Carter's writing may simply be consumed but can also produce *wincing* from this fascination of the girl with being acquired and seduced by a knowing and powerful man who 'wants her so much' – a wincing recoil of the reader who has been at all seduced by the aroma, texture, dynamics, of erotic difference. 'Was it I who wanted this? Was it this that I wanted?' The rhetorical figure that's been on my mind as I've tried to characterize Carter's writing has been zeugma, the yoking together of different objects and effects within the same syntax – a comic and explosive device. Fascination and recoil are parts of the enticements of pornography, either way. One feminist position is to condemn any truck with such available fascinations altogether.[6] Another is to face the fascination – to spring forward *from* recoil, from wincing at an acknowledged desire. (*Who* is it that acknowledges? Either the sadistic or the masochistic subject, of whatever gender. To whatever degree.)

If I read Robert Clark right, he believes that sexuality is *only* made significant by prohibition, so that Carter's experiment with 'moral pornography' as a critique of current sexual relations is doomed to be part of what it criticizes: 'the illicitly desiring self pulls forwards, the censoring mind pulls back preaching an exemplary sermon'.[7] What then shall we do with our illicit desires? Flagellate ourselves? The notion of recoil can have an opposite value, one which does not deny or prohibit the energies of desire as they exist: a springing movement which may be experienced as active and productive, rather than a helpless captivation. Although the attitude of mind is perhaps already sufficiently widespread, I take the term recoil, or wincing, with its implication of self-overcoming ('Was it I? Was it this?'), from my notes of a particularly lively account by Charles Scott of Foucault's *Madness and Civilization* and *The Order of Things*, notes which continue:

> Genealogy is effective history, and curative science. It is not a coming to truth or health (concepts which can be used punitively and coercively), but to a knowledge of one's own contingent process, as in psychoanalysis. The curative aspect is in a knowledge that finds itself repeating and departing from the inheritance it describes. This is not true insight inspecting a false knowledge: it stays on the boundary, on the dangerous edge, as a therapeutic listening, the very opposite of a discipline of confinement.[8]

Repeating and departing from the inheritance described struck me as a good account of the processes of Carter's writing, and the strongest answer to the charge that she merely reinscribes patriarchy. Where else can you start from, if not from where you actually are? (as Voltaire wrote, and it still seems to me good political practice). Where we are may include fascinations from which a rational and ethical self recoils. My diction there gave me a long pause for thought – how many can I include in what I acknowledge about myself as a reader? 'I think I'm typical', Angela Carter said in an interview with Lorna Sage.[9] And yes, she does speak to my condition as a daughter of the Second World War and the Welfare State, who has done time in Yorkshire and South London, and been nourished by Eng. Lit. and centuries of European art and taste, or versions thereof. I do feel that I know better than Robert Clark what she's up against and up to. Where I start is with the languages of my education and the responses it produced: 'Kennst du das Land?' Is that song a nostalgic harking back, or a certainty that there is somewhere else to be?

I want to consider Carter's 'fiction as literary criticism', as putting the educated reader on the spot.[10] 'Read Angela Carter and re-read Culture?' 'The Bloody Chamber' rewrites a folk/fairy story, of Bluebeard's castle and bride. But Carter's tales in fact rarely rewrite one story only. 'Peter and the Wolf' in *Black Venus*, for example, suddenly reveals itself as not only a revision of Prokofiev's instruction of children but also as a blasphemous revision of Genesis, in which the gulf between human and animal is seen to yawn less wide than that between the perceived nakedness of male and female. This double gulf is bridged when the boy shocked by visible sexual difference into priesthood gets a second chance to recognize his peaceable kinship with the wolf-cousin who is simply a mother. So, the story of 'The Erl-King' in *The Bloody Chamber*, which Patricia Duncker dismisses briefly as a reworking of Goethe's ballad, *also* re-examines Hegel's dialectic of master and slave through medieval ballads such as 'The Cruel Mother' and a version of Blake's 'The Mental Traveller', which represents the cycle of mother/father and child – the rebel who becomes oppressive authority in her/his turn. 'The Erl-King' needs to be compared to the Red Riding Hood story that Clark has a go at, 'The Company of Wolves'. The dank but brilliantly lit atmosphere of

'The Erl-King' (which does for the vegetable, the 'natural', kingdom what other stories do for the 'wild' world of wolves) is evoked as a cage, a world without ambiguity: 'everything in the wood is exactly as it seems' (p. 113). The resolution, in which the captivated girl will turn on her captor, is in the future tense. The shifting of tense and of grammatical subject in this story (from 'always' to 'now' to 'will be', from 'anyone' to 'you' to 'I') ought to be read as twistings and turnings to escape the transparent, unambiguous world of experience, the world of Locke's enlightened linguistics in which ideas are derived simply from sense-perception. This is the Enlightenment, Locke's world of locks, cages and fixities from which Blake also wanted to get out:

> A young girl would go into the wood as trustingly as Red Riding Hood to her granny's house but this light admits of no ambiguities and, here, she will be trapped in her own illusion because everything in the wood is exactly as it seems.
>
> *(The Company of Wolves*, p. 113)

So, 'The Company of Wolves' must be read in the afterglow of this story, as producing a world where there are ambiguities, gaps between the signifier and the signified, so that the significance and the outcome can be changed. At some point the mother need not poison or consume her son, the girl need not kill her beloved and make him the instrument of her song of seduction and betrayal; conceivably she could just get into bed with him.

The Bloody Chamber, then, is not a coherent whole, but neither is it entirely heterogeneous and fragmentary. The fairy stories are played with and worked as different versions ('see what we can do with this one, then?' – or then, try again, as in the side-by-side versions of 'Beauty and the Beast', 'The Courtship of Mr Lyon' and 'The Tiger's Bride', reworked again with lots of other things in 'Wolf-Alice'). Carter's critics seem unable to keep up with her productive resourcefulness. The pleasure of innocent readers less disposed to disapprove may be a better guide. The next story to 'The Erl-King' is very disturbing, in representing a father's sexual penetration of his daughter, but it can be made less so when it is read in this deliberately placed succession, rather than in some assumed universally valid context; 'The Snow Child' follows on the argument of 'The Erl-King'. It has to do with breaking 'archetypal' cycles of oppression. It prefaces 'The Lady of the House of Love', which transforms a vampire *femme fatale*, suffering from her destined immortality which feeds on humanity, into a girl whose death establishes her reality: 'I am, because I can die like anyone else' and, 'because that is how I am, I desire'. This appalling She becomes a human subject, not someone else's fantasy. Her lovely young lover's successful attempt to revive the baleful rose which has been her symbol dooms him to the carnage of the First World War. He would have been better advised to accept her mortality along with her love for him, and to stay with his bicycle, the anti-Gothic sign of human rationality.

The daughter in 'The Snow Child' remains inhuman. She is what the father wants, as Snow White was the creature of her mother's desire. Like a customer in a brothel, sometimes he wants the virginal girl, sometimes he wants the corrupt queen, a role which the girl would take up in her turn, if she survived to age. The queen or rather Countess in 'The Snow Child' exposes the truth of such masculine desires: either the love-child is ephemeral as snow, or her sexuality when matured would threaten the man – the final rose that bites, of male terror. Go on imagining women in these ways and you will destroy or disempower women as human beings, and thereby annihilate love as a mutual pact of tender passion; that's the argument, as I read it. The killing of the object of desire in these stories is not a killing of women, but a killing of masculine representations, in which some women collude. To invert their ferocity, as at the promised end of 'The Erl-King' and in the threatening image of the genital rose with teeth, is one tactic but not the whole strategy. It doesn't have to be the only story that can be told.

Carter's rational arguments are produced by such strange yokings of representations. 'Bluebeard' has the dubious charm of the young-girl-at-risk – *that* story, as Anne Sexton put it in *Transformations*.[11] Carter's *ingénue* is not like the wife in Margaret Atwood's 'Bluebeard's Egg', who ends up knowing that she has been fooled about the secret life of a husband who is a specialist in women's bodies (a heart surgeon) and also that she has fooled herself – but doesn't know what to do about it.[12] Atwood's wife is exposed as a victim and remains so, to this reader's horror and her own. Carter's is always a girl of spirit, both an adventuress and a curious, knowing spectator of her own seductions and trials. Another comparison could be with the trials of Blanca in chapter 8 of Isabel Allende's *The House of the Spirits*.[13] Far from knowing, Allende's heroine nevertheless has the guts to get right out from there – the house of her husband's experiments in photographing sexual exploitation – even in an advanced stage of pregnancy, or probably because of that. The spiritedness of Carter's bride of Bluebeard derives from the *other* pre-text for 'The Bloody Chamber', that is, the homage it pays to the turn-of-the-century writing of Colette.

This may well be obvious, in terms of the bride's style and the phenomena she encounters, but some of the connections are very precise. This title story is one which Patricia Duncker exempts from her criticism of Carter's whole collection of revised fairy stories: that the bride is rescued not by her brothers but by an indomitable and loving mother, redeems it for Duncker from the captivated heterosexism of the rest. Nicole Ward Jouve has pointed out to me that the story can be read as a version of Colette's biography, for example of 'Mes apprentissages', of how her mother rescued her from her husband Willy, that titillating master of hack writers, and from the dissipations of urbane society which had made her ill; the mother, so the story goes, nursed her back to rude health in the country.

It was mean of Patricia Duncker, I think, to leave consideration of this story to the last in her article, since Carter deliberately put it first, possibly to disarm the kind of attack Duncker makes on the rest of *The Bloody Chamber*. 'She couldn't imagine Cinderella in bed with the Fairy Godmother', writes Duncker.[14] The love between Mignon and the Princess of Abyssinia in *Nights at the Circus* reads like a response to such complaints, a rich, multifocal, reparation, as the black woman finds a voice, and the victim girl of Europe, Mignon, becomes first a performing artist and then a composer, through their mutual love. It is an empowering lesbian idyll which also redeems and celebrates the ecstatic and revolutionary potential within European art. *Nights at the Circus* rewrites Yeats ('The Second Coming', 'Sailing to Byzantium' and 'The Circus Animals' Desertion'; Yeats for all his sins learned from Blake the artisan) and Hamlet's 'What a piece of work is man!', in deconstructing its sardonic observer, Jack Walser, and showing how the New Woman is constructed by Fevvers as the 'Winged Eros' which Alexandra Kollontai also wanted to make real.[15] In speaking of such a reparation, I'm thinking of the twice replayed scene where Blake's Tygers, set in gold like Yeats's sages, are enchanted by the two loving women's performance of Goethe's lyric 'Mignon', which begins 'Kennst du das Land?' Mignon did not yearn for that land because she was uncertain of its existence. Certainly, unlike her original, she could not have wanted to go back to what her life had been, her 'fatherland': Carter writes that 'she said that this new land existed, and only wanted to know if you knew it too' (*Nights at the Circus*, p. 247). This is a rare instance of idyll in Carter's work. Her Paradises usually have shit in them, horse shit, and even here it's not everyone's cup of tea; the Shaman and the Finno-Ugrian tribe don't like it, because they can't read it (although they do know more than they will yet speak).

The dialogic relation of *Nights at the Circus*, narratively speaking, is also (effectively) a strong mother–daughter relation, that of Fevvers and Lizzie, fond and ratty by turns. I think the tactic in 'The Bloody Chamber' which Patricia Duncker buys, is less whole-hearted, more a matter of giving them what they want to buy them off. Carter didn't after all buy Colette's late return to her mother's house (which I love) – 'all that obsessive gush about Sido' (*Nothing Sacred*, p. 175). It's the bad Colette, the narcissistic performer who began writing as her husband's creature and hack, that Carter said would do women good if they were exposed to her early enough. Carter will write in a fair do for gay women; but that's not the end of it, in *Nights at the Circus*, and that's not what she's really about. She is 'doing it from a feminist angle', 'trying to be radical' (to use her own offhand phrases from *Nothing Sacred* and the *Women's Review* interview with Anne Smith), but she writes from and for the difficult position of being heterosexual and feminist, and it's from that position that I value and want to use her work. I might also add that although Carter hardly ever complicates her story line in a modernist manner her conclusions may offer alternative options. So *Nights at the Circus* gives us optimistic versions of Justine/Marilyn Monroe, in Mignon's story, and of Juliette/Mae West in that of Fevvers – the woman of power who not only helps Mignon but becomes more shabby, less starry, before regaining her stride differently. So in *The Passion of New Eve*, 'Woman' leaves Myth and enters History, in the penultimate sequence which shows the black prostitute and victim Leilah/Lilith as a guerilla leader; but also a space is left for the fascination of what is not yet known, as the new Eve sails off to give birth to an unpredictable future.

Colette's *My Mother's House* was entitled *La Maison de Claudine* in the 1922 original, thereby linking memories of her childhood home that celebrate her mother, Sido, with the heroine of her first novels, Claudine, from whose home the mother was rigorously excised, in favour of a benignly neglectful father whose preoccupation with malacology leaves his spirited daughter free. Claudine was a version of Colette; Angela Carter's young bride, the pianist, is a version of both. If you read the first of the Claudine novels to be published in Colette's own name rather than that of her husband, *Claudine amoureuse* or *Claudine Married* (1902) you will find that the sensual feeling for Renaud, Claudine's husband (an idealization of Willy), has been evoked for the husband in 'The Bloody Chamber' – the masculine whiff of tobacco and Russian leather (or, most probably, soap and after-shave – 'Cuir de Russie' or Imperial Leather). Each offers his bride a ruby necklace also. Claudine sucks hers as if it were a sweetie; Angela Carter means to suggest the red neckband defiantly sported by aristocratic women facing the guillotine. Renaud fails to satisfy Claudine's desires. She wants to be deeply ravaged by passion, and is frustrated by his light-hearted licentiousness: 'Alas! Are you to remain your own mistress for ever, Claudine?', she asks herself. Perforce she must rest contented that 'If I have not found my master, I have found my friend and ally' (*Claudine Married*, pp. 334–5). What she has desired is the hero of romantic fiction, duplicated in soft pornography.

The strongest feminist reading of 'The Bloody Chamber' is not only in terms of a mother–daughter idyll, but as a quarrel with another, intensely admired, woman writer. The dynamic and the conclusion of that argument are identical to the moment of recoil articulated by Desiderio in *The Infernal Desire Machines of Dr Hoffman*, in response to the fantasies projected by himself and Hoffman's daughter Albertina, his beloved and his alter-ego, of dismemberment and gang rape: 'victims of unleashed, unknown desires, then die we must, for as long as those desires existed, we would finish by killing one another' (p. 191). 'The Bloody Chamber' is a strong answer to an existing representation, Colette/Claudine's desire to be ravaged by the other, saying 'I can see the fascination, but just look where it gets you – to a spread of pictures in the *Sun*, to a place in the series of defunct and mutilated brides.' Better the man who's friend and ally, the blind piano tuner.

One weakness I can see in my own reading is that something much the same could have been reached without recourse to *Claudine Married* (that in fact would be one answer to Clark's accusation that Carter's stories may be read one way by feminists, and otherwise by those who are not). But the invitation that is there to read 'The Bloody Chamber' in the light of Colette *underlines* as an active process something that has to be worked through if we are to change what we desire, the ways in which women can be complicit with what captivates and victimizes them, even or especially in their adventurousness. It underlines and undoes the captivation. What Carter does in 'The Bloody Chamber' didn't come home to me fully until I read *Claudine Married* in the light of it. My conviction that you have to go through it, and along the line of Carter's narrative arguments to evaluate them properly (that is, politically), needs to be argued by serious analysis of her longer fictions, which explore the real material world of fantastic appearances, of representation. To stop short at particular sensational instances is to reproduce the titillating censoriousness of newspapers.

The spiritedness of Colette and Angela Carter gets them into dangerous places. Both Patricia Duncker and Susanne Kappeler quote Andrea Dworkin against Carter; but on the 1987 publicity tour for her novel *Ice and Fire* Andrea Dworkin confessed that her models for writing were men, because of their boldness and freedom; 'feminine' modes and themes she found constricting. Like Atwood's 'Bluebeard's Egg', *Ice and Fire* ultimately represents women as victims of their own desire and that of others. What I want to celebrate finally about the work of Colette and Angela Carter is that you can't feel sorry for yourself, reading it. They may make you cross but anger animates.

NOTES

1 Patricia Duncker, 'Re-imagining the Fairy Tale: Angela Carter's Bloody Chambers', *Literature and History* X, 1, Spring 1984; Susanne Kappeler, *The Pornography of Representation* (London: Polity Press, 1986), pp. 133–7; Robert Clark, 'Angela Carter's Desire Machine', *Women's Studies* XIV, 2, 1987.

2 The notion of 'the same' – judgement according to universal criteria, so that whatever you look at you can only see mirror images of yourself and the present – is drawn from the work of Luce Irigaray.

3   One important function of bourgeois fiction is to teach people how to behave in social circles to which they think they might be able to aspire. ... But all this bores me stiff, in fact, because it no longer seems particularly relevant to instruct people as to how to behave in a changing society, *when one's very existence is instrumental in causing changes the results of which one can't begin to calculate* [my italics]. And I personally feel much more in common with certain Third World writers, both female and male, who are transforming actual fictional forms to both reflect and to precipitate changes in the way people feel about themselves.

Angela Carter, 'Notes from the Front Line', *On Gender and Writing*, ed. Michelene Wandor (London: Pandora Press, 1983) p.76

4 I'm indebted to conversation with Richard Crane about his play on Eisenstein, *Red Magic*, for this analogue (the play was presented at the Edinburgh Festival Fringe and at the South Bank Museum of the Moving Image in the Summer of 1988).

5 Though it's an article she might well want to revoke or renew, I'll cite here Susan Sontag's 'The Pornographic Imagination', to the effect that pornography is already so selective and ready-made that it *can't* parody itself or be parodied (*Styles of Radical Will*, London: Secker & Warburg, 1969, p. 51).

6 See Mandy Merck's comparison of Andrea Dworkin's *Intercourse* with the film *Fatal Attraction*, in *Feminist Review* XXX, Autumn 1988.

7 Clark, op. cit., p. 153.

8 Seminars at the University of Essex, May 1988.

9 Lorna Sage, 'A Savage Sideshow', *New Review* IV, 39/40, July 1977.

10 Interview with Anne Smith, 'Myths and the Erotic', *Women's Review* I, November 1985.

11 Anne Sexton, *Transformations* (London: Oxford University Press, 1972).

12 Margaret Atwood, 'Bluebeard's Egg' in her collection *Bluebeard's Egg* (London: Jonathan Cape, 1987).

13 Isabel Allende, *The House of the Spirits* (London: Jonathan Cape, 1985).

14 Duncker, op. cit., p. 8. (Contrast this with Carter's account of her grandmother's story-telling, in John Haffenden, 'Magical Mannerist', *The Literary Review*, November 1984.)

15 That's not, of course, the half of it. I would and would not like to produce the annotated edition of one page of *Nights at the Circus*. Which is not to say that Angela Carter is not a highly original writer.

I would like to acknowledge my debt to discussions with graduate students at the University of Essex, Manda Ilic and Sally Keenan, and with Dr Jane Heath.

Works by Angela Carter

The Magic Toyshop (London: Heinemann, 1967; Virago, 1981).

Several Perceptions (London: Heinemann, 1968; Pan, 1970).

Heroes and Villains (London: Heinemann, 1969; Harmondsworth: Penguin, 1981).

Love, Hart-Davis 1971 (London: Chatto & Windus, 1987 (revised)).

The Infernal Desire Machines of Dr Hoffman (London: Hart-Davis, 1972; Harmondsworth: Penguin, 1982).

The Passion of New Eve (London: Gollancz, 1977; Virago, 1982).

Nights at the Circus (London: Chatto & Windus, 1984; Pan, 1985).

The Sadeian Woman: An Exercise in Cultural History (London: Virago, 1979).

Nothing Sacred (London: Virago, 1982).

Fireworks (London: Quartet, 1974, Virago, 1987 (revised)).

The Bloody Chamber (London: Gollancz, 1979; Harmondsworth: Penguin, 1981).

Black Venus (London: Chatto & Windus, 1985; Pan, 1986).

Works by Colette

'Mes apprentissages', *Oeuvres de Colette* III (Paris: Flammarion, 1960) pp. 381–454.

My Mother's House (Harmondsworth: Penguin Books, 1966).

The Claudine Novels (Harmondsworth: Penguin Books, 1985).

Part III

Languages

Chapter 9

Love, mourning and metaphor: terms of identity

Kadiatu Kanneh

The obsession of feminist theories with the body as the conclusive image of identity and the site of political struggle has led to a proliferation of unspoken conflations, confusions and invisibilities in the field of gender studies. Where love is fractured by violence and subjectivity is an unstable and threatening arena, a keen and painful listening to the conflicting pasts and languages which constitute Woman seems an obvious and difficult imperative. Within the terms of experience and desire I envisage an ongoing feminist battle which demands consideration.

Focusing eclectically on a variety of feminisms – previous, current, white and black – I intend to scrutinize the role of the body as metaphor, how the fusion of desire and language theorizes and politicizes love and suffering. How does experience guarantee political authenticity and the ownership of identity?

Any literary, cultural or political theory, any movement towards the liberation of a community, a class or a nation must attempt to construct a detailed knowledge of its object of study and to deconstruct the frameworks within which it is trapped. No theory, therefore, can afford to ignore the vital consideration of language as an institution, a socio-cultural instrument and the formative moment of an individual and a collective self-consciousness. A wide range of political and theoretical positions includes or begins from a rigorous inquiry into the role of language as a principle of human identity, as the blueprint for structures of oppression, repression, self-understanding and subordination. From anthropology to psychoanalysis, from feminism to racism, language has found itself at the centre of a scene of brilliant illuminations and as the site of crucial and bitter struggle.

Feminist theory has not failed to privilege the language question and the role of language in creating discourses. Institutions which both construct femininity and oppress women have, in various ways, been approached and tackled. Dale Spender, in *Man Made Language*, for example, confronted the language of everyday spoken and written communication in terms of its function as a register of systemic sexual oppression. In her introduction, she provided a succinct account of just why it is that language should become a point of scrutiny for feminists in their attempts to analyse and change women's position in the social order: 'Language helps form the limits of our reality. It is our means of ordering, classifying and manipulating the world.'[1] In stating this Spender put forward the idea of language as the mediation between a human being and her social environment; it is a way of giving form to chaos, of producing a grid through which the outside filters into a specific order of comprehensibility. It is language, as an acquirement that needs to be learned, which brings into being both the social world and the human being by which that social world is perceived: 'For having learned a particular language and had access to being "humanized" we have also been "socialized" in the process.'[2]

However, Spender slides into tautology by making it clear that there is ample room for agency in the process. Any 'particular cultural World view' is the product of a dominant group that has been able to manipulate the 'real' in such a way as to dictate the boundaries of 'humanness' itself. There is, it would seem, a human being before a community, an existence before a culture and thought before meaning. The concept of agency is of vital political importance for Spender, precisely because it enables women to define unequivocally the identity and the territory of the enemy. At the beginning of her revised introduction she makes this identity and territory very plain:

> A patriarchal society is based on the belief that the male is the superior sex and many of the social institutions and much social practice is then organised to reflect this belief: in one sense a patriarchal society is organised so that the belief in male supremacy 'comes true'.[3]

For Spender, then, the chicken has unquestionably come before the egg: man, in order to convince a community of the 'truth' of male dominance, creates a society to prove it.

Here we confront the category of experience as the *sine qua non* of feminist insurrection rigidified in the body through language. This outdated theory of the biological, linguistic trap is taken up, radicalized and essentialized through the later French feminisms of, for example, Luce Irigaray and Hélène Cixous. These particular white feminist approaches to language prescribe not mere reformism but revolution, not a major reclamation of semantics but a spectacular annihilation of the existent logical order. To liberate women, the answer is not to do a little rearrangement of the system but to begin an explosion at the very iron roots of 'male' language, an explosion which will shatter the old way – not just of speaking and writing – but of the thinking behind it. The reverberations will begin a whole new refrain.

The writers who appear under the title *New French Feminisms*, such as Luce Irigaray and Hélène Cixous, claim that language has become so much a legacy of male power that for women to keep operating within it would mean a continuing and intolerable compromise of their femininity. This approach is tied into certain psychoanalytic conceptions of sexuality and language, where the unconscious is the site of the repressed self, the inner, private space in which each woman hears the rhythms of her own desire, the scattered mutterings of a body yearning to speak itself. Luce Irigaray ('This Sex Which Is Not One') suggests that: 'Woman's desire most likely does not speak the same language as man's desire'[4] and it is on this conceptualization that the cry for the new, free woman is based. Going further than Dale Spender, Irigaray and Cixous confront the language of patriarchy, the language which prescribes a strict grammatical code, the language of institutions and commerce, as being fundamentally at odds with the female subject. It is the construction of a history of male power, of a nationalistic and patriarchal economic system, of centuries of masculine logocentrism which slams cold grids against the subjectivities of male and female alike: 'it probably has been covered over by the logic that has dominated the West since the Greeks'.[5] Genderized, theorized, coded into trapped and rigid formulations of the feminine and the masculine, men cling to the concrete monolith of phallogocentrism, while women lie breathless beneath an oppression which denies them the power of their own speech and writing. Irigaray, referring to Freudian and Lacanian psychoanalysis, claims that: 'Female sexuality has always been theorised within masculine parameters',[6] which posits women as the site of a lack – she who does not possess the phallus which is the symbol of virility, activity and sexual potency. Caught always on the underside of the equation to have/have not, continually the reflection of the masculine libido and fated to act as the blank space within and against which masculinity can erect itself, woman can experience only a 'vicarious pleasure' which, in this state of affairs, 'is above all a masochistic prostitution of her body to a desire that is not her own and that leaves her in her well-known state of dependency'.[7] This is an 'Occidental sexuality', product of 'the dominant phallic economy', of language laws which were made to benefit the scoptophilic, one-sided drive of masculine eroticism.

Both Irigaray and Cixous throw splashes of light on to what they percieve to be the dark and shadowed area where lies the secret of female emancipation. Taking a leap from the Freudian/Lacanian psychoanalytic ground, their attention is focused on the Unconscious as the locus of the constantly self-refracting energy which is the feminine libido. Like an arrow of reflected light, feminine eroticism returns and turns in a glorious spectrum of pleasure and infinite beauty: 'Women's imaginary is inexhaustible, like music, painting, writing; their stream of phantasms is incredible.'[8] Taking up Lacan's maxim of the Unconscious being 'structured like a language',[9] Cixous concentrates on writing as being the focus of female revolution: 'writing is the very possibility of change, the space that can serve as a springboard for subversive thought, the precursory movement of a transformation of social and cultural structures'.[10] Such writing must follow the patterns of the Unconscious, which exists as the linguistic manifestation of an archaic sexuality to which women are more in tune due to their marginal existence 'beyond "culture"'. Luce

Irigaray describes the kind of language which can be specifically feminine: 'in her statements, woman retouches herself constantly. She just barely separates from herself some chatter, an exclamation, a half-secret, a sentence left in suspense.'[11] It is a language which lies outside the logic of institutionalized codes: 'They are already elsewhere than in this discursive machinery where you claim to take them by surprise.'[12] It is dream language, true to the deepest pulse of a rushing, rising, spreading desire, murmuring shades, sighs and shining edges of an auto-eroticism whose pleasure is spilled from the body: 'I, too, overflow; my desires have invented new desires, my body knows unheard-of songs. Time and again, I, too, have felt so full of luminous torrents that I could burst.'[13]

Both Luce Irigaray and Hélène Cixous claim a radical political rationale for their advocation of this feminine writing which will stain pages with an unchecked sexual love. It involves a massively significant reclamation of the vilification, the suppression and the imprisonment that women have suffered through history and continually through the development of their personal lives. Cixous claims that, as children, the 'sex cops' of parental–societal dominations forbid women the wild delight of an active, masturbatory desire; medico-psycho-analytic science denies the 'naturalness' of a free and independent sexuality: 'Who, feeling a funny desire stirring inside her ... hasn't thought she was sick?'[14] Taught to identify herself within the patriarchy, the girl learns the vicarious horror of untamed sexual feeling. She is socialized into an education which is imbued with the myths of witches and Medusas who claim the night, riding on the winds of desire and sisterhood, revelling in the self-lust whose impressive beauty the 'masculine' point of view calls a terrible abomination. Women's huge wealth of desire is named a frightful and ugly depravity, a corruption the fear of which women have been forced to internalize: 'Men have committed the greatest crime against women. Insidiously, violently, they have led them to hate women, to be their own enemies, to mobilize their immense strength against themselves. ... They have made for women an antinarcissism!'[15] By reclaiming the desires which are labelled monstrous, denying the civilization and institutions which stand in suffocating walls around the breathless female body and dancing again the unleashed witches' dance on the heath beyond the patriarchal walls, the 'economy that works against us and off our backs' cannot fail to collapse. It will be the resurgent oral culture of the body's rhythms, the songs and laughter of the Medusan beauty – recognized by a refocusing of the masculine gaze to the feminine: 'You only have to look at the Medusa straight on to see her. And she's not deadly. She's beautiful and she's laughing'[16] – which will bring about the ultimate destruction of the old order: 'she cannot fail, in seizing the occasion to transform directly and indirectly *all* systems of exchange based on masculine thrift. Her libido will produce more radical effects of political and social change than some might like to think.'[17]

The significance of the link between language, sexuality and the social construction of gender is drawn beautifully and painfully in Sylvia Plath's *The Bell Jar*. Esther, confronting at every turn the negative position of women in socio-sexual discourse is thrown into a depressing struggle to position herself within it. She is unable to accept the discourses which prescribe the nature of female identity, from the laws designed to swallow women into the transparent holes of a 'pure' asexualism to the misogyny which is born from an imbibed fear and hatred of female eroticism. In Lacanian terms, the 'subject is not an entity with an identity, but a being created in the fissure of a radical split. The identity that seems to be that of the subject is in fact a mirage arising when the subject forms an image of itself by identifying with an other's perception of it.'[18] Rejecting the phallic idea that man is 'an arrow into the future and ... woman is ... the place the arrow shoots off from', Esther listens to a yearning deep within her to transgress such codes with her own irrepressible desire: 'I wanted change and excitement and to shoot off in all directions myself, like the coloured arrows from a Fourth of July rocket.'[19]

It is at this point that Esther becomes conscious of her own alienation from society's perception of her; she is something other than the image which is pinned and hedged into her mother's 'breezeway' and her mind begins to fly free from the things which tie her to the world's greatest con-trick: the authority of the phallus is, after all, merely the 'turkey neck and turkey gizzard' of a flat non-desire. As she pulls away from a fixed identity – 'A wan reflection of myself ... ghosted over the landscape'[20] – and the certainty of a connection between the mirror-image and the self is steadily revealed as a deception – 'The face in the mirror looked like a sick Indian. ... It wasn't a mirror at all, but a picture'[21] – so Esther's link to language slips its chains: 'Words, dimly familiar, but twisted all awry, like faces in a funhouse mirror, fled past, leaving no impression on the glassy surface of my brain.'[22] Read using an analysis similar to that of Cixous or Irigaray, Esther's breakdown follows the patterns of a growing and agonizing awareness of her alienation from the self and the language which articulates her participation in society. The hard, dry conceptual mechanisms of male writing cannot be accommodated to her own sense of self, afloat in the ocean of her Unconscious and aware in her own representation of the slow, sweet flow of her body: 'Inertia oozed like molasses through Elaine's limbs.' Shored up on the hard sands of masculine writing, Esther is aware of her own lack of safety amid the potential violences of these logical sentences. 'I turned the words over suspiciously, like round, sea-polished pebbles that might suddenly put out a claw and change into something else.' The life and liquid sensation of her own body, moving like 'slow insects' in 'drops of sweat ... down her back' finds itself thrown against the mainland of a frozen, hard and immovable masculine language.

The blend of 'new' French feminisms which are embodied by Cixous and Irigaray are at odds, in particular ways, with Lacanian psychoanalysis, and

Jacqueline Rose mounts a critique of their approach from this theoretical position. Rose's account of the Unconscious also relies upon Lacan's concept that it is 'structured like a language', reading this statement, however, in terms which are more faithful to the original. In her introduction to *Feminine Sexuality* Rose outlines Lacan's use of the symbolic as the framework of the Unconscious. Language is, effectively, symbolization, and any sense of self, any self-articulation, relies upon a subjectivity which is created within a meaning system lodged in the outer social order. Language is the hum that fills the aching hollow of loss at which a primordial childhood need strives to replace missing objects. Words are calls to fill the moments of silence left by the flux and shift of the world, just as the naming and creation of a self-identity is merely a hallucination born from a vanishing-point: 'Symbolization starts, therefore, when the child gets its first sense that something could be missing; words stand in for objects, because they only have to be spoken at the moment when the first object is lost.'[23]

However, even this 'first sense' of loss is not a leap from a private, essential self-hood but is an inexorable part of a 'pre-existing hierarchy of values', an 'already assigned meaning' which is the first cell in the splitting, multiplying world of the Unconscious. From this point, Rose can challenge the Utopianism of the particular brand of French feminism which points towards a future imagination along the fabric of unconsciousness: 'For Lacan ... there is no pre-discursive reality ... no place prior to the law which is available and can be retrieved. And there is no feminine outside language.'[24] If the Unconscious is precisely language and femininity belongs to the symbolic, any direct link to the biological drives of the body is called into question. In fact the Unconscious 'severs the subject from any unmediated relation to the body as such ... the "feminine" is constituted as a division in language, a division which produces the feminine as its negative term'.[25]

It is here that Irigaray breaks with Lacan, arguing, as Rose herself puts it, that 'Lacan's use of the symbolic ... presupposes the subordination which it is intended to explain'. Irigaray's concentration is on a femininity which can challenge phallic lack, returning to an autonomous political space which will blow the symbolic sky-high and leave a vast landscape for women to run free in a magnificent linguistic subversion. Lacan merely claims that the only femininity is the femininity which comes into being as lack and not the 'real' or 'essential' body, the body towards which Cixous directs her plaintive and joyous incantation: 'Touch me, caress me, you the living no-name, give me myself as myself' ('The Laugh of the Medusa').[26] Jacqueline Rose negotiates a way out of the impasse in which Lacan seems to place women as the powerless in an immutable equation by highlighting Lacan's concept of a subjectivity which is constantly 'at odds with itself', of a 'femininity which is neither simply achieved nor ... ever complete' (the introduction to *Sexuality in the Field of Vision*).[27] If bisexuality is seen as the basis of the symbolic and not rooted in the body, women and men are envisaged on shifting ground which, due to the sliding of language away from fixity and against any metaphysical notion of a classic Western binarism, opens up a new path to play. This is the Derridean idea of *différance*, which is the 'sliding of language which only arbitrarily and repressively fixes onto identity and reference alike' and in which Rose glimpses the possibilities of a use for feminism: 'Feminists have been attracted to Derrida's reading precisely because of the possibility it seems to engender for a wholly other discursive and, by implication, political space.'[28] This is what Cixous would call 'this self-effacing, merger-type bisexuality', to which she would oppose 'the *other bisexuality* on which every subject not enclosed in the false theatre of phallocentric repre-sentationalism has founded his/her erotic universe' ('The Laugh of the Medusa').[29] Her insistence is upon the resurrection of a new body from outside the Freudian/Lacanian symbolic, a femininity which is not exclusive to either the male or the female, but of which the female, due to her mar-ginalization, is more aware and towards which she is more willing to move: 'In a certain way, "woman is bisexual"; man – it's a secret to no one – being poised to keep glorious phallic mono-sexuality in view.' This resonates Lacan's statement which is quoted by Rose in the introduction to *Feminine Sexuality*: 'the *jouissance* of the woman does not go without saying, that is, without the saying of "truth", whereas for the man, "his *jouissance* suffices which is precisely why he understands nothing"'.[30]

Here lies the power of the new writing, the text which will emerge from the dissolution of the old antagonisms when women and men will move towards a new feminine articulation, centred in the Unconscious. In the 'heightened' language of poetry which, according to Cixous ('The Laugh of the Medusa'), 'involves gaining strength through the Unconscious', the new 'text' will emerge: 'my body shot through with streams of song'. Once the phallus is deposed, the feminine text will inscribe the self and the other within itself in a play of *différance*: it will be a language formed from the multiple muttering of delight, a dappled scattering of sunlight on the awakened, unbound body:

> What is inscribed in the movement of a text which divides itself . . . is an abundant, maternal, pederastic femininity. A phantasmatical mingling of men, of males, of messieurs, of monarchs, princes, orphans, flowers, mothers, breasts, gravitates around a marvellous 'sun of energy' love, which bombards and disintegrates these ephemeral amorous singularities so that they may recompose themselves in other bodies for new passions.[31]

FROM THE THORNS AT THE FOOT OF THE IVORY TOWER: A BLACK FEMINIST RESPONSE

The privileging of the body in the writing of Cixous and Irigaray as the focal point for a radical subversion is in many ways, however, a dangerous political move. It is undeniably crucial to revalorize the female body, to rescue it from the vilification which, for centuries, has been practised against it through oppressive codes and institutions. When men are degrading women sexually, hating them carnally and violently, it is positive to reclaim and revalue the female body. To see the body as a source of potential power and intense pleasure is a needed reaction to the kind of anti-female sadism which is explored by Benoîte Groult in 'Night Porters',[32] and is the sad fate of the heroine in *The Story of O*. It is highly important, however, to determine which aspects of this femininity should be held up for celebration, and to sort out just what would be the political ramifications of such a move.

Lacan's insistence that there is no feminine outside language is useful here in that it marks out the difficulties into which Cixous and Irigaray fall. Cixous's description in 'The Laugh of the Medusa' of the painful moment of a woman speaking in public is an example of the dubious valorizations upon which she relies. The description concentrates upon the interplay of language and body which is the peculiarly feminine mode of discourse: 'She doesn't "speak", she throws her trembling body forward; she lets go of herself, she flies; all of her passes into her voice, and it's with her body that she vitally supports the "logic" of her speech.'[33] Here the woman is seen bursting from the 'snare of silence' and flying free in the *jouissance* of her own natural self-expression, a form of expression which spills out of the definite structures of 'masculine' discourse: 'Her speech, even when "theoretical" or political is never simple or linear or "objectified", generalized.' There is another way of reading this moment, however, which would be to examine the causes for such a manner of public address from a social viewpoint. Surely, this tremor which seizes the woman from the depths of her lungs, this irresistible use of the body to complement the unmanageable ripple of her voice, is an accurate account not of an inherent feminine essence but of the direct results of social marginalization and intolerable sexual visibility. Not conditioned to wear mastery in a public scene or to forget the role of her body in a voyeuristic male society, the female public speaker acts, in this prototypical case, with a shivering uncertainty, handling the language of politico-theoretical discourse with stumbling skill. Celebrating this part of feminine activity and so following the rallying cry of Marguerite Duras, 'We must move on to the rhetoric of women, one that is anchored in the organism, in the body',[34] Cixous runs on the same tracks as the 'Wages for Housework' campaign which, finding women incarcerated in the kitchen, rushes to sing the kitchen's praise.

This same danger recurs throughout 'The Laugh of the Medusa', where women's supposed empathy with nature, their removal from the construction of civilizations and their innate maternal instinct – 'In women there is always more or less of the mother who makes everything all right, who nourishes' – are merely valorizations of spaces into which women have been coerced by dint of a social world which will not tolerate women as law-givers. This quotation from *Questions Feministes*, which Deborah Cameron includes in her *Feminism and Linguistic Theory*, adequately pinpoints the risk that women run by celebrating an area of 'femininity' which is merely the very point of ineffectiveness outside and beneath social control to which they have been driven: 'To advocate a direct relation to the body is therefore not subversive because it is equivalent to denying the reality and the strength of social mediations, the very same ones that oppress us in our bodies.'[35]

Determinism through body language – the self at the centre of the orgasm and its roots in the unconscious – relies upon a belief in a pre-linguistic reality, a way of experiencing and understanding the self which is prior to the symbolic. The falsity of this search and its prescription for a Utopian future is evident in Simone de Beauvoir's *Memoirs of a Dutiful Daughter*, in which she recalls the bliss of a childhood perception uninitiated into words:

> White was only rarely totally white, and the blackness of evil was relieved by lighter touches; I saw greys and half-tones everywhere. Only as soon as I tried to define their muted shapes, I had to use words, and found myself in a world of bony-structured concepts.[36]

The memory here is of an understanding which is wholly informed by the senses, which runs intuitively with a flow of sensation that needs no translation into a socially conceptual language. Simone de Beauvoir imagines a period where her body articulated lights and shadows, safety and fear, joy and pain through a dreamtime in tune with the flooding nuances of life. Language arrives as a dam against the flow, where meaning comes up against more concrete definitions. However, this passage upon a mode of experience which is born with the body has a neutrality to the social world and history which has already placed white in direct opposition to black and qualified each according to the scale which is lodged in Western ideology: white as a purity far superior to 'the blackness of evil'. This recalls Jacqueline Rose's intimation (*Sexuality in the Field of Vision*) that 'the effects of the unconscious are tied to the key fantasies operating at the heart of institutions'. Seeping into de Beauvoir's 'pre-linguistic' experience and already forming her conceptions are the institutionalized values appraised by Sista Roots in her poem 'Dictionary Black', which apprehends the loaded metaphors of a deeply racist Western culture:

> A Darky is a Negro
> Not fair – atrocious – evil
> And the Prince of Darkness
> Is the Devil ...
> ... So I turn to 'white'
> All sweetness and light[37]

The spine of white culture also supports Hélène Cixous's 'The Laugh of the Medusa', the work being animated from within the nerve centre of a Western post-colonial backbone. Cixous consistently upholds her argument that women inhabit a pre-civilizational world which is closer to the pulse of nature and the rhythms of sensuality, a world which can be found in the germinating moments of childhood sexuality, by drawing a sustained analogy with black Africa. She stakes a claim for a true female identity by linking women's position with that of people outside Western culture, people whose land and bodies have suffered systematic vilification, thrown under a cloak of fear and mystery: 'they can be taught that their territory is black: because you are Africa, you are black. Your continent is dark. Dark is dangerous.' The principle for revaluing such a space is to celebrate its apparent 'natural' qualities: 'We the precocious, we the repressed of culture, our lovely mouths gagged with pollen, our wind knocked out of us, we the labyrinths, the ladders, the trampled spaces, the bevies ... we are black and we are beautiful.'[38]

This reference to African peoples in order to underline the position of women outside history and culture, beyond the self-conscious, adult world of reason and politics, is in indirect collusion with the deliberate policies of the Western colonial countries which aim to wipe out the achievements and the intricate pasts of the colonized. Ngũgĩ Wa Thiong'o (in *Decolonizing the Mind*) attacks just this Eurocentric myopia in Western philosophy, for instance 'Hegel with his Africa comparable to a land of childhood still enveloped in the dark mantle of the night as far as the development of self-conscious history was concerned'.[39]

If we apply this approach to the white feminist practice of hoarding accounts of black subjectivity in order to mark out a common linguistic ground we face a tricky political situation which pivots itself on questions of language, experience and identity. The fusion of metaphor and body, identity and experience is both a political choice and a historical coercion which, I believe, cannot be either swept aside by poetic licence or blindly embraced as immutable. Cixous legitimizes her use of black historical metaphors, based on references to colonialism, slavery and racism, by claiming that, 'In woman, personal history blends together with the history of all women, as well as national and world history.' The call for a feminine culture which sees itself as separate from the history of wars and colonialisms is validated by the assertion that women had nothing to do with all of this: 'This is known by the colonised people of yesterday, the workers, the nations, the species off whose backs the history of *men* has made its gold' (my emphasis).[40]

Liberating the female body from language creates flesh out of words. Desire explodes the social, sex subverses and recreates the political. Upholding a female experience which cannot – biologically/psychically – slide into the male and yet can slide racially and class-wise, Cixous and Irigaray legitimize a flagrant fluidity of metaphor. The question of who owns which metaphor is tied closely into an ongoing struggle over the past, over history, which will inevitably be a matter of eclectic analogy and constructions of fantasy. However, this eclecticism has definite political meaning in that the oppressions of the present are very often fixed in ways of perceiving the body – through race – as a personification of the past. The unconscious use of geography and time in understanding identity through the body is made conscious by Cixous's defiant attempts to disengage the specificity of historical metaphor, releasing women from the grip of time and placing a radical feminine identity beyond the tyrannies of race and class, 'so as to prevent the class struggle, or any other struggle for the liberation of a class or people, from operating as a form of repression, pretext for postponing the inevitable'. The joyous fervour with which Cixous cries for the blowing up of the past, of history and of political struggles outside the unconscious and the body relies on her understanding of difference as variations of sensual pleasure between women. Her drive to unlock women from a history she labels as exclusively male manages to lock all women into a history free-floating between images of black subjection and imperialist domination. Sensuality and the body suck in figurations of power drawn from colonial ideas of land and nature. Female masturbation is a 'unique empire', the unconscious is 'that other limitless country', and 'the Dark Continent' of the female psyche 'is neither dark nor unexplorable'.

The idea that women should ignore the divisions between themselves and sweep together across class, race and national boundaries to create a post-historical Utopian home, bypasses the knowledge that racial oppression has always created the body from obsessive fantasies of biology and environment. The power of Cixous's metaphors comes precisely from their continuing life in present ideologies of race. Black women are not in a position to bypass the histories and divisions, both of class and race, which block the development of a unified feminist movement.

For black feminists there can be no easy separation between blackness and womanhood, just as there cannot be a simple slicing apart of white racial identity and womanhood. This reality informs a black feminist approach to the body, sensual pleasure and political language. Chrystos, for example (in *This Bridge Called My Back*), writes in her poem 'I Walk in the History of My People', that her body and her relationship to it is also a communion with the culture and history of which she is a part. Like Cixous's celebration of white witchery, Chrystos becomes the living embodiment of centuries of anger:

> There are women locked in my joints
> for refusing to speak to the police
> my red blood full of those
> arrested, in flight, shot
> My tendons stretched brittle with anger.[41]

Sensual pleasure has as much to do with cultural identity as it has to do with physical sensation, and the articulation of the erotic for black women is the marker of a certain socio-historical belonging as much as it is for white women. From Sonia Sanchez's 'you and i exploding in/our blue black skins'

('Haiku'),[42] to Grace Nichols' 'Even Tho', the environment and the social sense of self is an indissoluble part of the erotic:

> I'm all watermelon
> and star-apple and plum
> when you touch me . . .
> . . . You be banana
> I be avocado[43]

The experiences entailed in being black or white are both cultural and psychological, and any thoughtless separation by white feminists of the powerlessness which is engendered by a socially constructed racial 'inferiority' or victimization seriously denies black women's sense of reality. Merle Collins's poem 'Same But Different' (in *Watchers and Seekers*) expresses the double sense of fear which is invested in black women by a racist society. Comparing her experience to a white friend who has reciprocal nightmares of 'rapists and robbers' at every lonely step of the night, Collins's persona must also contend with the terror of racial violence: 'Each sudden shadow/ was a threat of the National Front'.[44]

Toni Morrison's *The Bluest Eye* traces the extent to which racism affects the identity, the fantasies and the sexuality of black women (and men). The development of desire and understanding, of self-articulation and its source is expressed in Pecola Breedlove's childhood and adolescent encounters. Living in a world which is run by white domination, which informs the discourses of 'normality' of beauty and of worth, Pecola is continually slammed up against an image of herself which is sharply at odds with the white 'norm'. The novel opens with the script of a child's story-book: 'Here is the house. It is green and white. It has a red door. It is very pretty. Here is the family. Mother, Father, Dick, and Jane live in the green and white house. They are very happy.'[45] This is the doorway through which black and white children will enter into the social discourse, a discourse which will run into the mind of a childish imagination, forming the shape of a child's contact with the world around her. The script is repeated three times, each time letting the words seep closer together until a tightly woven fabric is created, a fabric which will run threads through the unconscious too deep to eradicate: 'othermotherisverynicemotherwillyouplaywithJanemotherlaughslaughmotherseefatherheisbigandstrongfather'. If this is the 'normality' with which a black child must identify, the result can only be a deep sense of alienation, a low, encrusted sense of worthlessness, a dizzying cellophane barrier between the self and the world, created by the standard literary discourse. Ngũgĩ Wa Thiong'o, in *Decolonizing the Mind*, writes that:

> the second aspect of language as culture is as an image-forming agent in the mind of the child. . . . But our capacity to confront the world creatively

is dependent on how those images correspond or not to that reality, how they distort or clarify the reality of our struggles. . . . Language is mediating in my very being.[46]

Looking around her, Pecola sees only images that are disjointed from the language of her reading. She sees a black father enraged with the impotence which burned in his body when white men enacted a vicious visual rape, a black mother whose fancied identity with the white film stars of the dark cinemas smashed along with her front tooth, and a grey and ugly home.

One of the effects of a discourse which makes blackness a concept of excruciating visibility is the suffocation of all other differentiation beneath it. If there is no place at which to position the self within this discourse, the result is a form of self-annihilation which, beginning in the mirror of white society, becomes a conscious and then an internalized unconscious activity. Pecola's visit to the sweet shop, owned by a white shopkeeper, is an episode which reveals the role of blackness in the formation of identity:

> But she has seen interest, disgust, even anger in grown male eyes. Yet this vacuum is not new to her. It has an edge; somewhere in the bottom lid is the distaste. She has seen it lurking in the eyes of all white people. So the distaste must be for her, her Blackness. All things in her are flux and anticipation. But her blackness is static and dread. And it is the blackness that accounts for, that creates, the vacuum edged with distaste in white eyes.[47]

At this point Pecola is aware of the white gaze as an outside force, translating who she is by virtue of her skin and features. Within her, another awareness ebbs and flows, the same awareness which appraised the dandelions on the edge of cultivation as 'pretty' and which gave her an immeasurable joy in her own reality. She knows the language her mind speaks, the 'codes and touchstones' which are available to her, the beauty upon which she relies and understands as her own: 'And owning them made her part of the world and the world part of her.' The part of the world she is able to articulate, however, has no corresponding moment in white consciousness and before the white shopkeeper she finds herself robbed of language and dumb in the loneliness of her perceptions: 'He cannot see her view – the angle of his vision, the slant of her finger, makes it incomprehensible to him.'

Such is the power of white discourse that it forces its values deeper than the surface, making Pecola internalize the scales of worth which are held before her. As her shame heats up the surface of her skin, the 'dread' blackness melts down through her pores, filling up the cracks of her imagination with the 'vacuum-edged distaste' that 'white eyes' attached to it: 'The shame wells up again, its muddy rivulets seeping into her eyes.' Believing in the ugliness in her mirror, just as she is coerced into believing that the dandelions after-all 'are ugly. They are weeds', Pecola's first move is self-extermination.

Praying to the same God which Cholly conceptualizes as 'a nice old white man, with long white hair, flowing white beard, and little blue eyes', there is only one plea at the centre of her mind, to blank out the ugliness in the only way possible. ' "Please, God", she whispered into the palm of her hand, "Please make me disappear" ... little parts of her body faded away.' In the gap, slotting into place at the centre of her dreams and at the tender core of her erotic fantasies, is the persona of a white girl, the epitome of that which a white-dominated society sanctifies as beauty:

> A picture of little Mary Jane, for whom a candy is named. Smiling white face. Blonde hair in gentle disarray, blue eyes.... To eat the candy was somehow to eat the eyes, eat Mary Jane. Love Mary Jane. Three pennies had bought her nine lovely orgasms with Mary Jane.[48]

This is the language of a little black girl's consciousness. Trickling through the membranes of her life, her Utopian fantasy splits her in two and she creates another mirror in which to view her new, blue eyes, another dialogue within which to articulate herself in relation to the world: 'Oh yes. My eyes. My blue eyes. Let me look again. SEE HOW PRETTY THEY ARE.... Prettier than Alice-and-Jerry storybook eyes? OH YES. MUCH PRETTIER THAN ALICE-AND-JERRY STORYBOOK EYES.'[49]

Cixous's writing is charged by an energy of love for the feminine, a joy in female eroticism and the experience of a woman's body. However, love itself is always that wild and bitter region where violences and fantasies obscure and pervert the meeting and recognition between individuals and groups. A world fissured on a fantastical plane between the images of white and black cracks and mutilates love into a method of violence. Deracialization of love cannot simply depend upon avoiding or redeploying the metaphors of black difference. Disinvesting value from colour involves the rehabilitation of blackness as a positive configuration as well as a critical stripping of power and absoluteness from the unbroken white body. Cixous's Utopian wishing, her love-wishing for the future, slips dangerously and prematurely into the realm of collapsed and dissolved differences. Her concept of a femininity unfettered by conflict and united solely under the concept of Woman involves an impossible confusion of political terms and is ignorant of the fact that a nightmare of the black, dead body is a term of the black psyche. Forgetting and forgiving seem alien to the fantasies of desire and biology.

The female body which emerges from the water in *Beloved*, for example, is one which is formed by death, violence and mourning, which has rocked the foundations of home, which forms and channels desire, disturbs the unities of love and revisits dead rages upon the living. Her name a metaphor for the gathering at the grave, her death a necessity of love, her resurgence reconstitutes the past as incarnation and female experience as an embodiment of histories within the present. It is suffering which lives on, which forces itself into physical reality, inhabiting tangible places through the agonizing creativity and destructiveness of love. *Beloved* theorizes a black conception of the body and of home as realities formed in the shape of past experiences which insist upon their place in the present through the exigencies of grief and anger.

The category of experience as a guarantee of ownership, of 'owning' a range of metaphors and power through a knowledge of mourning is not an answer to Cixous's redeployment of specifically 'black' historical images for the *jouissance* of all women. The racial diseases of language do not exclusively infect a 'white' or a 'black' consciousness. Esther's feeling of slipping away from words in *The Bell Jar* involves a sliding of self-perception along lines of racial panic which is visualized by the 'sick Indian' in the mirror, while Cixous's directive for liberation through language demands a tearing up of racial specificities to allow the female body to glitter in its play of metaphor. In both writings there is a recognition of the barriers which a racialized language erects between women.

The territories of fantasy and language, of history and political strategy are mapped on to each other and I would insist upon a commitment to, not disowning their workings, but to working through the responsibilities they entail. Dale Spender's early and unsophisticated battle to root out sexist terms in social discourses on a conscious level, points to the problematic notion of experience and ownership which remains insistent in black feminist responses to racial amnesia. The prevalent black feminist idea that black women must fight for expression in a language that will inscribe the particularity of their own collective cultural as well as feminine identity runs alongside the notion that forced invisibility results in acute and widened vision. The various racial, class as well as gendered margins which black women inhabit, being on the edge of systems which push them always to the sidelines, can be turned into positive and privileged positions as regards working out a coherent and enlightened theory of language. Bell Hooks, in *Feminist Theory: From Margin to Centre*, writes of the experience that the black people with whom she identified had to face on the peripheries of white society:

> Living as we did – on the edge – we developed a particular way of seeing reality. We looked from the outside in and the inside out. We focussed our attention on the centre as well as on the margin. We understood both.[50]

The devaluation of black culture is synonymous with the lack of societal status given to black languages. If, as Ngũgĩ claims when he refers to language: 'It is the final triumph of a system of domination when the dominated start singing its virtues',[51] there needs to be a determined move towards promoting the worth of, for instance, African, Caribbean and black British languages and dialects. This drive towards rejoicing in a way of speaking and writing which is part of a specifically black identity is not the same kind of message as Cixous or Irigaray would proclaim. Whereas they lust for a future feminine language which lies in a curiously ahistorical and apolitical unconscious, many black women writers search to assert the significance of their own speech and literature which is directly in tune with the socio-political histories of black culture. Merle Collins's 'No Dialects Please' stakes a claim for a Caribbean English dialect against an informed historical background. Against James Walvin's observation that 'the English in many respects have an acute sense of their own history',[52] Collins mocks the idea of a 'language elect' which is based on a narrow and blurred idea of English nationalism that does not, for one moment, take into account the role of the colonized people in creating such an identity. The poem ends on a surge of laughter which reveals that, when it comes to linguistic theory, black women have a broader understanding than do white women of the issues involved. By virtue of their endurance of white imposition, black women and men know two languages and cultures intimately, and knowledge is a route to power:

> To tink how still dey so dunce
> an so frighten o we power
> dat dey have to hide behind a language
> that we could wrap roun we little finger
> in addition to we own![53]

One (not the first) step for black feminism is to increase awareness among white feminists of the state of affairs which black women can never sweep from their minds – to focus on the colour which stains such texts as those written by Cixous and Irigaray and which give the lie to any supposed neutrality they claim to represent. While Salman Rushdie reveals the 'ease with which the English language allows the terms of racial abuse to be coined' ('The New Empire Within Britain')[54] white feminists, when they are not habitually swamping black feminists out of view, suddenly pick them up in the headlights of their discussions as oddities on the horizon, then sweep them away again, rarely bothering to notice their own white skin (for example, why does Deborah Cameron's book not bear the title *White Feminism and Linguistic Theory*, and how about *New White French Feminisms*?). Writers such as Amryl Johnson, in her poem 'Like Dogs' (*Watchers and Seekers*), cry out in anguish at the impossibility of wiping out the atrocities which have been committed against black people in history and which still burn reminders in the memories of black women:

> Black flesh
> like me
>   Forget??
> Believe me
> If I could
> I damn well would[55]

Maya Angelou's poem 'Family Affairs' explores the power/powerless equation between white and black women and the depth to which the humiliation, the anger and the sorrow go in the black psyche:

Tired now of pedestal existence
For fear of flying
And vertigo, you descend
And step lightly over
My centuries of horror
And take my hand,
   Smiling call me
     Sister[56]

In her subsequent words, 'Sister, accept/ That I must wait a/ While', Angelou points toward the need for a certain autonomy between women in the feminist movement if black women are going to avoid the dispersal of their cultural identity in the wastes of some 'objective' feminist discourse. This is a strategy for which Alice Walker signals her participation when she moves to the new title of 'womanist' for a 'black feminist or feminist of colour' (*In Search of Our Mothers' Gardens*),[57] the importance of which can be outlined in the quotation which the white feminist Deborah Cameron includes in her book, taken from the Dalston Study Group's report: 'Immigrants and working class people too have a negative point of entry into our culture, something no one has yet explained with reference to the penis/phallus.'[58]

Any feminist approach to language will commit serious errors of judgement unless there is a full appreciation of the position of *all* women as regards language. To state vapidly that women across national, racial, geographic and class boundaries have the same access to and alienation from the language of social discourse, and to leap from here into the belief in a common feminine identity, reveals a sad lack of awareness as to how language operates and how deeply all women are implicated in colonial history and present-day racism. The minefield of emotions, histories and identifications which arise from the battle over metaphors points, I believe, not to a theory of impossible ownerships but to a heightened awareness of the relationship between body and word, the past and the racial politics of the present. Meiling Jin's poem 'Strangers in a Hostile Landscape' (in *Watchers and Seekers*) outlines the bitterness and anger which burns deep beneath the 'Invisible-Ness' brought about by white culture. With a resistance that will linger beyond death, Jin's persona stores up the intense concentration of her identity, born beyond the Occident, and her gaze will redirect the scorching, alienating and maddening gaze of a Western racist world back upon the Occident through the continuing of herself in her people. This is nearer the Utopia envisaged by black women, this is the sweet concentration of delight which lies waiting at the closest throb of a long bruised collective consciousness:

and when I die
I shall return

to a place I call my own
Only my eyes will remain
to watch and to haunt,
and to turn your dreams to chaos[59]

NOTES

1 Dale Spender, *Man Made Language* (Routledge & Kegan Paul, London, 1985), p. 3.
2 ibid.
3 ibid., p. 1.
4 Luce Irigaray, 'This Sex Which Is Not One', in *New French Feminisms*, ed. Elaine Marks and Isabelle de Courtivron (Harvester Press, Sussex, 1985), pp. 99–106, esp. 101.
5 ibid.
6 Irigaray, op. cit., p. 99.
7 ibid., p. 100.
8 Hélène Cixous, 'The Laugh of the Medusa', in Marks and de Courtivron, op. cit., pp. 245–64, especially p. 246.
9 Jacques Lacan, 'God and the Jouissance of Woman. A Love Letter', in *Feminine Sexuality*, ed. Juliet Mitchell and Jacqueline Rose (Macmillan, London, 1985), pp. 138–60, especially p. 139.
10 Cixous, op. cit., p. 249.
11 Irigaray, op. cit., p. 103.
12 ibid.
13 Cixous, op. cit., p. 246.
14 ibid.
15 ibid., p. 248.
16 ibid., p. 255.
17 ibid., p. 252.
18 Juliet Mitchell, introduction to Mitchell and Rose (eds), op. cit., p. 5.
19 Sylvia Plath, *The Bell Jar* (Faber & Faber, London, 1985), p. 87.
20 ibid., p. 118.
21 ibid., p. 185.
22 ibid., p. 131.
23 Mitchell and Rose (eds), op. cit., p. 31.
24 ibid., p. 55.
25 ibid.
26 Cixous, op. cit., p. 252.
27 Jacqueline Rose, *Sexuality in the Field of Vision* (Verso, London, 1986), p. 7.
28 ibid., p. 19.
29 Cixous, op. cit., p. 254.
30 Rose, op. cit., p. 53.
31 Cixous, 'Sorties' in Marks and de Courtivron (eds), op. cit., p. 98.
32 Marks and de Courtivron (eds), op. cit., pp. 68–75.
33 Cixous, 'The Laugh of the Medusa', p. 251.
34 From an interview with Marguerite Duras by Susan Husserl-Kapit in *Signs*, Winter 1975, in Marks and de Courtivron (eds), op. cit., p. 238.
35 Quoted by Deborah Cameron (ed.), *Feminism and Linguistic Theory* (Macmillan, London, 1985), p. 130.
36 Quoted in Cameron (ed.), op. cit., p. 138.

37 Rhonda Cobham and Merle Collins, eds, *Watchers and Seekers* (The Women's Press Ltd, London, 1987), pp. 109–11.
38 Cixous, 'The Laugh of the Medusa', p. 248.
39 Ngũgĩ Wa Thiong'o, *Decolonizing the Mind* (James Currey and Heinemann, London, 1987), p. 16.
40 Cixous, 'The Laugh of the Medusa', p. 258.
41 Chrystos, quoted in Cherrié and Moraga and Gloria Anzaldúa (eds), *This Bridge Called My Back* (Kitchen Table: Women of Colour Press, New York, 1981) p. 57.
42 Sonia Sanchez, *Homegirls and Handgrenades* (Thunder's Mouth Press, NYC, 1984), p. 9.
43 Grace Nichols, in Cobham and Collins (eds), op. cit., p. 65.
44 Merle Collins, in Cobham and Collins (eds), op. cit., p. 32.
45 Toni Morrison, *The Bluest Eye* (Triad Grafton Books, London, 1981), p. 1.
46 Ngũgĩ, op. cit., p. 15.
47 Morrison, op. cit., p. 48.
48 ibid., p. 49.
49 ibid., p. 185.
50 Bell Hooks, preface to *Feminist Theory: From Margin to Centre* (South End Press, Boston, 1984).
51 Ngũgĩ, op. cit., p. 20.
52 James Walvin in *Passage to Britain* (Harmondsworth: Penguin in association with Belitha Press, 1984), p. 19.
53 Collins, in Cobham and Collins (eds), op. cit., pp. 118–19.
54 Salman Rushdie in *New Society*, 9 December 1982.
55 Amryl Johnson, in Cobham and Collins (eds), op. cit., pp. 134–5.
56 Maya Angelou, *And Still I Rise* (Virago, London, 1986), pp. 92–3.
57 Alice Walker, *In Search of Our Mothers' Gardens* (The Women's Press, London, 1984), p. xi.
58 Cameron, op. cit., p. 161.
59 Meiling Jin, in Cobham and Collins (eds), op. cit., pp. 123–6, especially p. 126.

Chapter 10

Why the Lady's eyes are nothing like the sun

Lorna Hutson

Everybody who knows anything about Aemilia Lanyer, author of the first
original poem by a woman to be published in the seventeenth century, knows
that she had black eyes, black hair and a dark past. Her poems are only
available to modern readers in complete form in A. L. Rowse's edition which
advertises them as *The Poems of Shakespeare's Dark Lady* and prefaces them
with pages of repetitive prose, the gist of which is to insist on reading the
text, 'rampant feminism' and all, as the Dark Lady's revenge:

> It is obvious that something personal had aroused her anger. Shakespeare's
> Sonnets had been published, though not by him, in 1609, with their
> unforgettable portrait of the woman who had driven him 'frantic-mad',
> dark and musical, tyrannical and temperamental, promiscuous and false.
> ... The portrait was defamatory enough. The very next year, 1610, her
> book was announced and in 1611 published.[1]

For all that he values the text as enabling us to 'read the character of
Shakespeare's Dark Lady at last', however, Rowse proves susceptible to
the charms of Lanyer's verse. The bits he likes best are, tellingly enough,
reminiscent of Shakespeare. He quotes, for example, from Lanyer's exhor-
tation to Anne Clifford to internalize the knowledge of Christ disclosed in
the text of her poem: 'yet lodge him in the closet of your heart,/whose worth
is more than can be shew'd by Art.'[2] In these lines, Rowse contends, we hear
the unmistakable accents and recall the *Sonnets*, where the Bard writes of
locking the image of his beloved in his chest.[3] I mention this not so much to
argue with the implication of Shakespeare's influence, as to instance the ex-
to which our understanding of the discursive medium in which sixteenth-
and seventeenth-century writers worked is filtered through our familiarity with
Shakespeare's deployment of its most fundamental metaphors. It will be one
purpose of this paper to suggest that this sense of familiarity obscures
from us the implication of these very metaphors in the humanist project of
relocating masculine virtue and honour in the power to authorize meaning.
Read in this context, Lanyer's attempt to produce, from a medium so heavily
invested in the articulation of masculine virtue, a poem which celebrates

woman as an effective reader and agent rather than offering her as a dark secret to be disclosed, becomes the subject of *Salve Deus, Rex Judeorum*.

First, however, to grapple with the issue of Lanyer's credibility as a poet. Refutations of Rowse's theory mostly turn on the paucity of evidence for positing Lanyer as Shakespeare's mistress; no-one denies that she was promiscuous but, as Samuel Schoenbaum has reminded us, there were no end of promiscuous women about in Elizabethan London. Besides, Schoenbaum argued, we must remember that the *Sonnets* are not an autobiography but a system of moral and poetic meaning: 'the opposition between Fair Youth and Dark Lady' needs no reference to a particular woman to explicate it, he concluded, for it is 'perfectly comprehensible in terms of moral and poetic symbolism'.[4]

Now, a 'moral and poetic symbolism' that is 'perfectly comprehensible' is one which is still *working*, still creating an evaluative language in which to articulate experience and authorize desire. Yet why should the antithesis between Fair Youth and Dark Lady recommend itself thus as a 'natural' symbolism? Critics of the *Sonnets* make us ashamed to ask such a naive question. They either read the moral evaluation of the antithesis as referring to the conduct of particular individuals known to Shakespeare, or exploit its signifying potential to consider larger issues, such as the possibility of integrity in poetic representation. This latter position is represented by John Kerrigan's sophisticated introduction to the Penguin edition of the *Sonnets*. For Kerrigan, the *Sonnets* are largely concerned with the unattainable goal of a poetic reproduction that would remain faithful to its object. This involves the apparent rejection of metaphor and comparison, principal devices of sonnet rhetoric. 'Shakespeare', he claims, intriguingly, 'exposes the competitive roots of similitude'.[5] He goes on to explain that similitude is an inherently competitive figure of speech because, in making a topic known to us by analogy with things conceded to be of value (as hair is likened to gold or lips to rubies) similitude implies that value itself is merely a discursive effect, a 'painted beauty'. What is more, similitude transforms its topic into the site of an implied rivalry between author and reader over the concession of value and credibility. Shakespeare, concludes Kerrigan, refuses to embroil his beloved in this invidious market-place of ingenuity, and aims at a text that is stripped of metaphor, a faithful reproduction of his beloved. However, one point which this attractive thesis overlooks should help us to understand why, in spite of Schoenbaum's easy dismissal of Rowse's identification of Lanyer as the 'original' Dark Lady, there can be no such easy dismissal of the implications of the 'Dark Lady' symbolism for our reading of Lanyer's text. The point is this: Shakespeare's text achieves the effect Kerrigan identifies – the effect of rising above a sordid dependence on hyberbolic comparison – by figuring the ethical bankruptcy of similitude (its transformation of 'worth' into a beautiful surface, or a site of contest between two men) as the dark space (a space traversed, not occupied, by value) signified by the use of the female gender. We comply in our willingness to understand the symbolism of 'fair' youth and 'dark' lady, a symbolism which equates the danger posed to the integrity of a poetic representation (the danger of being seduced from the 'truth' by the distracting beauty of metaphor) with the danger posed to the integrity of a masculine 'marriage of true minds' by the distractingly available female body. By overlooking the extent to which Shakespeare's dismantling of the usual strategies of sonnet rhetoric directs sceptical attention towards its own strategic uses of *gender*, Kerrigan tends to endorse the notion that there is an intrinsic beauty in masculinity to which the poetry is bound to remain true. Of sonnet 105, where Shakespeare rejects comparison ('leaves out difference') for identity, with the repetition of the refrain 'Fair, kind and true', Kerrigan writes, 'The text is stripped of metaphor, there are no false comparisons. ... The friend is co-extensive with the text; he really is "all" its "argument".'[6] This ignores a sly sub-text of sexual difference; if the usual female friend were to be praised for being 'kind', then she would certainly need a lot of false painting if she were to continue 'fair', let alone 'true'. So the scrupulous rejection of comparison that Kerrigan reads as a quest for integrity is actually an exposition of the extent to which the evaluative power of comparison depends on the mobilization and concealment of a single hierarchical opposition – in this case, that of gender.

The association of the impure motives of a comparative rhetoric, a rhetoric of praise, with the inherent 'falsehood' of woman is so germane to our making sense of Renaissance texts that we should not be surprised to find it informing critical assessment of a real woman poet of the Renaissance. Thus we find that when women scholars cease to celebrate Lanyer simply for managing to *be* a woman and a poet all at once, their comments on her text display a tendency to account for its embarrassing length, inappropriateness and apparent sycophancy by referring to the lady's notorious past. Thus, Muriel Bradbrook sums Lanyer up scathingly:

> To choose the subject of the Crucifixion and then surround it with several times its own bulk in carefully graded verses of adulation to various ladies, beginning with the Queen – and even interrupting the sacred narrative to bob a curtsy to the Countess of Cumberland, one of the richest women in England, seems to me very practical politics for an ex-mistress of the Lord Hunsden ... I doubt if 'feminism' or the defence of women was disinterested here.[7]

Barbara Lewalski, by contrast, is persuaded of the sincerity of Lanyer's feminism, but has doubts about her religious conviction:

> Given Lanyer's questionable past, her evident concern to find patronage, and her continuing focus on women, contemporary and biblical, we might be tempted to suppose that the ostensible religious subject of the title

poem, Christ's Passion, simply provides a thin veneer for a subversive feminist statement.[8]

The assumption is that a 'true' poem should not be making use of patronage relations, or of a rhetoric of praise; to do so is to betray a dark want of 'disinterestedness' which is in turn associated with a want of moral integrity, or chastity. Actually, Renaissance literary theory assumes the opposite: poetic discourse is never disinterested, but rather seeks to authenticate itself through the devices of rhetoric and the relations of patronage. Yet, as we have seen, our familiarity with a text like Shakespeare's *Sonnets*, which makes a theme of disavowing both these for a more inward source of authenticity, tempts us into easy swipes against the sycophancy of poets who rely on 'rhetoric'. Take sonnet 82, for example, where Shakespeare laments that his true friend should prefer the impurely motivated hyperbole of rival poets to his own plain-speaking sincerity:

I grant thou were not married to my Muse
And therefore maiest without attaint ore-looke
The dedicated words which writers vse
Of their faire subiect, blessing euery booke.
Thou art as faire in knowledge as in hew,
Finding thy worth a limmit past my praise,
And therefore art inforc't to seeke anew,
Some fresher stampe of the time bettering dayes.
And do so loue, yet when they haue deuisde,
What strained touches Rhethoricke can lend,
Thou truly faire, wert truly simpathizde,
In true plaine words, by thy true telling friend.
    And their grosse painting might be better vs'd
    Where cheeks need blood, in thee it is abus'd.[9]

I suggested that the naturalness of Shakespeare's *Sonnets* (the comprehensibility of their moral symbolism) depended on the fact that, by rejecting as 'false' and 'superficial' the analogical techniques normally used in sonnets, they managed to persuade us of the possibility of a love and a poetry that might remain true to its subject. The possibility is so congenial to our way of thinking that we scarcely feel the need to gloss it, but how is it constructed? Here, in sonnet 82, the subject is described as being 'as faire in knowledge as in hew', so that his inward beauty is identified as a kind of connoisseurship, a capacity to value and to validate the text as a cultural artefact. And this is typical of the beauty ascribed to him. For though we tend to read the *Sonnets* as if they were explorative of an emotional relation between the poet and his masculine subject, an equally prominent feature is the text's exploration of an *interpretative* and *mutually authenticating* relation between the *text* and its *subject*.

Indeed, the *Sonnets* enable us to experience the inward beauty of intellectual discrimination which enables the friend – 'as faire in knowledge as in hew' – to judge the text, as itself an effect of the text. In the play of antitheses we glimpse this authenticating, discriminating subject, the 'friend', in the process of being made up out of a comparative rhetoric which ambiguously privileges the contingencies of gender, of noble birth and a peculiarly 'economic' attitude to the text which is foreign to our assumptions about the purpose of reading. For example, the phrase, 'thou art as faire in knowledge as in hew' refers us back to Shakespeare's introduction of this unusual archaism in sonnet 20, where it disturbingly establishes the worth of a masculine as opposed to feminine poetic subject. The colours in the face of the 'Master-Mistres' are apparently authentic because he is 'a man in hew all *Hews* in his controwling'. Here 'hews' means colours in the sense of complexion, but it also bears reading in a rhetorical sense as well, with colours being the equivalent of discursive 'proofs', 'reasons' or 'arguments' for action.[10] 'All *Hews* in his controwling' thus indicates the reader's specifically masculine relation to the text, in which, as he reads, he discovers or 'invents' a store of resources for his own future uses in improvisation, thereby increasing his power to produce emotionally compelling discourse and to control its colours.

The relation between masculine author and masculine patron/reader emerges as inherently 'virtuous' (in the Renaissance sense of conducive to good action, rather than to theoretical speculation on the nature of good) by implicit comparison with the relation between masculine author and feminine pretext/reader, since the usual pretext of Petrarchan discourse – love for a woman – can only generate a 'face' or textual surface of rhetorical colours to be exploited by men. For, of course, it was only for men that Renaissance humanism identified the interpretative practices of reading with the prudence, or practical reason, which enables deliberation about action in political life. Only for men could the activity of reading be expected to increase the power to act and speak in emergency, to discover in the emergent moment an argument, a 'colour' for one's own uses.[11] So, as only a man can effectively reproduce from a discourse which celebrates beauty, this power of discursive reproduction becomes his intrinsic beauty, and only a man can therefore be 'truly' beautiful. The sonnet puts this in a cleverly 'moronic' or oxymoronic fashion: only a man can have 'a Womans face with natures owne hand painted'. The oxymoron is developed in the following sonnet, where the ambition to write 'truly' of a masculine beloved is defined against the market-place comparisons of the poet 'Stird by a painted beauty to his verse' (21.2). All this, of course, is highly ambivalent, since the location of his 'truth' in a capacity to reproduce colours implies (perhaps through a pun on 'hues' and 'use') that the masculine 'truth' which distinguishes itself from feminine 'paintedness' is that eloquence which 'heauen it selfe for ornament doth vse' (21.3).

However, the ascription of authenticity to the friend as a reader engaged in producing an inner self through the rhetorical 'finding out' or 'invention' of the text's colours for his own future hews/uses competes with his ascription of authenticating power as a patron. In sonnet 82, the suggestion of altitude in 'ore-looke' positions him less a reader engaged in inventing discourse than as a nobleman, who, in the words of Sir Thomas Elyot, should be 'set in a more highe place' where he may 'se and also be sene' by 'the beames of his excellent witte, shewed through the glasse of auctorite' [the 'authority' or 'authorship' of policy-making through patronage].[12] Again, in sonnet 20, the authority of the reader-as-patron to irradiate his image in the text is figured as exclusively masculine; the friend has a brighter, truer eye than any woman, an eye that is like the sun, 'Gilding the object where-vpon it gazeth'. Thus, the friend's ability to authenticate and enlarge the text's sphere of influence, figured in his gilding eye and validating hue, sceptically reveals the notion of man's 'truth' or his authentic inner nature, to consist in the privileging of a certain kind of discursive economy.

Throughout the *Sonnets* 'truth' and 'inward worth' are articulated as the generative capacity of the text's subject to forestall the dissipation of his own loveliness. What begins as a discourse of natural economy or husbandry – for the first seventeen sonnets the friend is playfully urged to convert his fading beauty to generative 'store' by begetting a son – is apparently superseded by the reproductive economy of the sonnet form itself, which enacts the conversion of beauty into discursive 'store'. This latter is an *economy* precisely because it articulates the pleasurable encounter with the text, the moment of interpretation, as the assimilation of potential for the production of discourse which will stimulate others to take similar pleasure in understanding. If we think of reading in humanist terms as an exercise of the interpretative potential of the text, preparing for the discovery of interpretative potential in practical situations requiring decisive action, then the economy celebrated by the *Sonnets* could be referred to as an economy of 'interpretative power' or 'interpretative virtue'. In his imaging of this economy, Shakespeare conflates a celebration of the friend as inspiration, a storehouse of *copia* or figurative potential for future readers, with a celebration of the friend as exclusive reader, whose invention of colours in the text will furnish him inwardly. Both these concepts derive from humanist ideals about the capacity of published discourse to bring about social change by fostering the political and discursive skills of the nobility, but Shakespeare's comparative rhetoric subverts the humanist fiction of author and patron as authenticating one another in a relation of pure interpretative increase, a pure reproduction of each other's inward worth. The inward worth which did not need painting is revealed to inhere not in the interpretative relation, the encounter with the text, but in the husbandry which appeared to have been superseded, the lines of life which produce noble blood: 'And their grosse painting might be better v'sd,/ Where cheeks need blood' (82.13–14).

From this rather protracted reading of the *Sonnets* we can begin, I think, to see why it is misleading to come to Lanyer's text with the preconception that a poet's sincerity towards his or her subject demands a 'disinterested' rejection of epideictic rhetoric, or a disavowal of dependency on the patron-as-reader. The *Sonnets* play out the moral implications of the assumption, built into humanist claims for the interpretative virtue of analogical rhetoric,[13] that things can only be made known in discourse by being displayed and praised (the very word 'epideictic' means 'adapted for display') so that 'patron' and 'compare' necessarily evaluate or 'authorize' one another. For the humanists, knowledge was not thought of as certain or objective; knowledge was only what was 'probable', what might be 'proved' in the quasi-forensic and epideictic disclosure of a topic through comparison, simile or analogy, a process which often destabilized itself in an oscillation between hyperbolic and ironic effects. This process of authentication was spoken of a disclosure or a 'discovery' or 'invention' of what had been hidden; a topic was 'unfolded' to be 'beheld' by the interpreting eye.[14] The beholder thus exercised virtue as a medium of knowledge, and the patron, in his exalted position as potential governor of society, exercised more than most, having eyes like the sun, to bring knowledge to the inferior sight of others.[15]

But could a woman patron, on these terms, have eyes like the sun? Could she gild the discourse that claimed to be a mirror of her virtue by inventing its colours for her own occasions, occasions on which she might speak or act to effect? Shakespeare's text would seem to imply not. Yet Lanyer makes extensive use of this trope in nearly all of her nine dedicatory poems,[16] beginning with a request that the Queen should 'Looke in this Mirrour of a worthy Mind' (p. 42). If, she goes on, the Princess Elizabeth should also deign to lend the text the credibility of an appreciative reading, 'Then shall I thinke my Glasse a glorious Skie,/When two such glittring Suns at once appeare' (p. 44). This is perhaps the moment to point out that Lanyer's poetic project is much more rigorously conceived than it has been represented as being. For it is not that she wrote a narrative of Christ and absent-mindedly kept apostrophizing the Countess of Cumberland because she could not keep her mind off the richest woman in England. Her subject, like that of Shakespeare in the *Sonnets*, is reflexive; it is the reading subject, the encounter of the patron's mind with the text, which is celebrated as a textual resource. Lanyer's poem sets itself out to 'unfold' or 'prove' the interpretative virtue of Margaret Clifford's mind through a dramatizing of the female recognition of Christ in the historical moment of his Passion. Hence it is that the narrative of the Passion acquires the status of a rhetorical 'proof', and the argument of the whole is the 'Mirrour of a worthy Mind'. But there are difficulties with the metaphor. For a female author cannot mirror the virtue of a female patron if the space of the gilding, mutually authenticating gaze (the space in which the virtue of the encounter between text and mind is tried and proved) is actually a *homosocial* space – a space of discursive and political opportunity conceivable only between men.[17]

I am not trying to say that there were no women patrons in Protestant-humanist England; of course there were, and it has been convincingly argued that Protestant-humanism, with its emphasis on the reformation of society through the education of its princes and the dissemination of texts on rhetoric, marriage and the reformed religion, actually depended on the intellectual participation of women patrons.[18] But the crucial issue here, I think, is the way in which such intellectual participation was assimilated to a masculine monopoly of interpretative increase. Lewalski observes that Lanyer's dedications to women linked through kinship or marriage to the Protestant Dudley faction celebrate 'the descent of virtue in the female line, from virtuous mothers to daughters'.[19] But if the author/text/patron relation, which I have been outlining, had any cultural significance, then the trouble with Protestant-humanist lines – whether of lineage reproduction or of textual production – is that the female virtue they articulate is assimilable to the masculine economy of interpretative virtue only in terms of chastity – the very virtue that would exclude and discredit Lanyer's text, 'given', as Lewalski says, 'her questionable past'.

Lanyer's poem seems to acknowledge some reservation about its own procedures in its opening, for having announced that her task will be to pen the praise of her patron, Margaret Clifford, the author immediately asks pardon for deferring a poem in praise of the estate of Cookham, which she apparently promised the Countess. Lewalski reads this as an excuse to force a much more substantial poem on the unwilling and unsuspecting Countess,[20] but what is intriguing is the care Lanyer takes, in her apology, to represent the suitability of the absent poem to the rhetorical task she has in hand:

And pardon (Madame) though I do not write
Those praisefull lines of that delightfull place
As you commaunded me in that faire night,
When shining *Phoebe* gave so great a grace,
Presenting *Paradice* to your sweet sight,
Unfolding all the beauty of her face
   With pleasant groves, hills, walks, and stately trees,
   Which pleasures with retired minds agrees.

Whose Eagles eyes behold the glorious Sunne
Of th'all-creating Providence, reflecting
His blessed beames on all by him begunne;
Increasing, strengthening, guiding and directing
All worldly creatures their due course to runne,
Unto his powrefull pleasure all subjecting:
   And thou (deere Ladie) by his speciall grace,
   In these his creatures dost behold his face.

(pp. 79–80)

As it happens this is not at all like the country house poem which Lanyer eventually offers; but what we have here is a deliberate and careful sketch of a rhetorical mode of proceeding which will not be followed. For if the process of making known in language involves the finding out of things by analogy, then the virtue of Margaret Clifford's mind, her capacity to know God, might well have been set forth as a progress of analogical discovery through the estate, which figures the natural economy of Providence as visible beauty. Lanyer expresses the Countess's power to know both as the ability to sustain the utter radiance of full, timeless disclosure (the 'Eagles eye' of the retired mind which is able to behold the 'glorious Sunne' of Providence) while at the same time rendering the temporal process of mediation, the work of interpretation, as the unfolding of an analogical discourse. What makes the incomprehensible radiance of the 'all-creating Providence' a *face* that can be beheld are 'these his creatures', disclosed, in the moment of the poem's inception, before the eyes of the Countess by the light of the moon, 'Presenting *Paradice* to your sweet sight/ Unfolding all the beauty of her face'. The operation of the moonlight thus establishes a model for the 'praisefull lines' which, by disclosing the estate's loveliness, would reflect the Countess's interpretative virtue or 'inward worth', admirably combining a fulfilment of her patron's request with Lanyer's prescription of the poem as the 'Mirrour of a worthy Mind'. But such a method would tend to the articulation of Clifford's interpretative virtue as an effect of her position within the estate and, in unfolding the estate as a topic of praise, might compromise that virtue by discovering it as a form of 'beauty'.

Lanyer's poem repeatedly impedes its own forward movement with hesitations of this kind. These may be read, I suggest, as attempts to avoid being caught up in a discursive economy that has an interest in gendering 'female' certain weak points in its projection of an ideally productive political community.

The ideal of altruistic productivity, directed towards the profit of the political community, is implicit in humanist methods of education, and in the prominence of 'intelligence gathering' or 'facilitating' as a form taken by patron-client relations in the sixteenth century.[21] The discourse in which this ideal is articulated enjoins men to form relations of interpretative increase for the good of the commonweal. Through these relations, masculine minds become 'treasure houses' or exchanges for the profit of the commonweal. However, as such patron-client relations cannot be forged without the competitive self-advertising that an open market of intellectual ability demands, the altruistic ideal accommodates itself uneasily to an older conceptual model of patronage as 'love' due to lord and kin, and accordingly articulates meritocratic competition as an unspecified 'betrayal' by a 'friend'.

But how does this betrayal come to be figured as transgression of the female body? A full answer would have to go beyond the scope of this paper. However, something can be achieved by interrogating, once again, the assumptions behind the humanist metaphor of the text as a mirror for princes. Underlying the metaphor is the classical conception (deriving from Seneca among others) of knowledge as the imitation and mastery of *auctores*.[22] This notion was adapted to the humanist enterprise of social reformation through print culture by approximating the idea of the text's circulation to the classical notion of the governor's charismatic and exemplary power. Thus, as we saw, reforming discourse tends to blur the distinction between the author and the authorizer of social change, allowing the author to claim the power to fashion the nobleman by creating in him interpretative resources which he could not previously command, while the nobleman, being visible and effective in office, could claim the capacity to realize the effects of his reading by conducting affairs with a foresight and eloquence that would move others to imitate him.

The theory, then, was that as the patron was modelled on the text, so society modelled itself on the patron or 'pattern' of behaviour. In Elizabethan England it was a peculiar feature of this discourse that the virtue of 'pattern-age' might be ascribed to gentlemen rather than to the prince, since she, after all, was a woman. So Lawrence Humphrey in his reforming book *Of Nobilitye* (1563) after acknowledging God's Providence in restoring religion through so weak a vehicle as Her Majesty, explains that he is addressing his text to the gentlemen of the Inner Temple because they are more sun-like by virtue of having more contact with more people. Princes 'haue small trafficke with the common people', writes Humphrey, but gentlemen, like licensed texts which 'frely roame and wander eche where' are 'cleare and bryghte, on whom all mens eyes and countenances gaze'; at the other extreme, the common people themselves, 'styll lurke in darkenes, nor almost se anye, nor are seene of others'.[23] So gentlemen, the ideal media of imitation, go about, mirroring one another in their 'traffic', as if their encounters took place in a purely interpretative economy, something like the one Jonson describes in the *Epigrams*, where virtuous men bond by 'understanding' and 'knowing' one another like texts:

> When I would know thee, Goodyere, my thought looks
>   Upon thy well-made choice of friends and books;
> Then I do love thee, and behold thy ends
>   In making thy friends books, and thy books, friends.[24]

But of what nature are these social encounters, these mutual mediations of knowledge, that make them so productive? The demonised other of this discourse, as we know from Jonson's *Epigrams*, is the unproductive circulator, the plagiarist, the gamester, the poet-ape or the inactive lord buried in flesh.[25] The space in which masculine virtue is proved, then, would seem to be at the nexus of sociability and textual encounter – the truly virtuous man is he who has internalized the power to organize and produce a convincing discourse and can, as Jonson says, 'know' his 'ends', that is, recognize and exploit a social encounter as the occasion of discourse (the 'colour' or the beauty of an opportunity recognized in the discursive moment), or as the space in which to assimilate resources, to 'look with thought' upon the discourse and behaviour of another man. However, in a society where privilege and preferment were theoretically obtained by the demonstration of this virtue, the space of its proof (for example, the published text with its 'dedicated words') was traversed by a gaze not only of cognition and authentication, but also of emulative rivalry and competition. Giles Fletcher the Elder dedicated his sonnet sequence *Licia* to the Lady Mollineux, but prefaced it with an apologia which justifies the publication of such an idle proof of wit on the grounds that such exercises distinguish gentlemen. Accordingly, gentlemen readers are at liberty to construe 'Licia' herself as Lady Mollineux, or as the 'discipline' of learning essential to composition. The crucial process of reflection here, then, is not the textual mirroring of the lover in his lady's eyes, but the mirroring of the published text – proof of the discriminating, interpretative power that distinguishes Fletcher as a gentleman – in the evaluating eyes of gentlemen readers. This has unfortunate consequences for 'Licia', who, in sonnet 6, discovers that an image of her naked body is currently circulating among men, since Fletcher has discovered his heart, 'wherein you printed were,/You, naked you'.[26]

The poet George Gascoigne dramatized this compromising interpretative 'gaze' of masculine minds across a coveted female body many years before, in his fictional account of the *Adventures of Master F.J.* (1573). Here F.J. finds his 'gazing eyes' drawn to admire not his lady's features but the mind of his rival, delineated in a witty rebuff to his conceited exposition of desire. Thus rapt in his rival's authenticating appreciation of his own wit, F.J.'s response replicates the orientation of the published narrative as a whole, which the narrator offers to gentlemen readers as a context from which to appreciate the advantages in amorous and social encounter to be gained by F.J.'s *extempore* compositions. Minds, of course, cannot gaze admiringly at one another across a vacuum; they require a discursive medium in which to disclose their loveliness. For this purpose, the most common analogical proof of a man's cognitive virtue comes to be the epideixis of the female body. So F.J.'s rival is a *secretary*, whose writing discloses the secret knowledge of his mistress which that virtue has occasioned. His riding to London, however, offers F.J. an 'occasion' to 'lend his mistress such a pen in her secretary's absence as he should never at his return be able to amend the well-writing thereof'.[27]

The mistress's eyes, then, were never like the sun in the discriminating, evaluating sense; they never 'looked with thought'. They merely shared in the play of bright bodily surfaces, the 'blondeness, whiteness, sparkle',[28] which in Petrarchan discourse entangled the male subject, thereby acknowledging the 'superficial' nature of a poetic exercise, the object of which was to practise and display virtuosity at the level of analogical and antithetical invention. 'Of thine eyes I made my mirror,/From thy beautie came mine error', as Lodge put it in his rather lovely sequence, *Phillis*.[29] Serving as the 'occasion' or pretext for such a text, woman is associated with what Kerrigan called the 'competitive roots' of similitude. This is plain from the very earliest English texts advocating eloquence as essential to the mediation of knowledge; thus, for example, William Baldwin's *Morrall Phylosophie* (1548) demonstrates by analogy the power of analogical eloquence in stimulating the exercise of interpretation and therefore the *activity* of knowledge:

> Lyke as a louer delyted in the goodly bewtie of his loue, can neuer be satisfyed in beholdyng her, neyther can take any rest until he haue by praysing, enflamed other to delyte in the same, labouryng to the uttermost to set forth hys beloued; euen so the phylosophers rauyshed in the loue of wisdome, haue not only labored to knowe it to the uttermost, but haue also deuysed al maner meanes ... to set out wisdome in sondry kyndes of wrytyng, that euery man might find wherein to delyte, and so to be caught in his owne pleasure.[30]

But if the humanist ideal of eloquence as a productive exchange of knowledge could be thus disturbingly figured as the analogical unfolding of a female body to arouse forbidden desire, the homosocial rivalry involved could equally be masked in the related metaphor of the female body as the internal organization of the masculine mind, a kind of self-sufficient estate. This metaphor derives from what I call the 'discourse of husbandry', which pervades the entire Protestant-humanist literature of reform, from marriage doctrine to the education of the orator. The function of this discourse in the early reforming texts was to articulate, in an unspecific way, the humanist sense that the reformation of the nobility through classical paradigms would make for an increase in society's productivity. In Humphrey's *Of Nobilitye*, the idle nobleman, 'coasting the stretes' with his 'wauering plumes' and his wasteful 'rout of seruaunts' is a foil to the new style of nobleman who can be productive and organize discourse, but Humphrey can express this productive potential only by way of a discourse in praise of farming (husbandry) among the ancient nobility of Greece and Rome.[31] This *topos* of the virtuous governor as 'good husband' in the commonwealth involves woman as a vital principle of elision, for 'husbandry' articulates the notion of the bourgeois household as a domain which, internally organized and guarded by woman, releases man into the spaces of social encounter which enable him to make productive contacts. The internal organization of the household then becomes analogous to the principle of reading to increase one's *copia* or store of discursive resources 'ready for production'.[32] Thus, as the intimate encounter with the text actually enables men to produce the occasions of competitive social encounter, so the apparent integrity and self-sufficiency of the well-organized household actually demands a mercantile site of contingency and competition to prove the virtue of its well-preparedness. Woman as the cultural product of a husband and a figure of chaste reproduction may be invoked to mask this required space of contingency either in the plot of the outrageous violation of the household's integrity (the rape of Lucrece), or as a fiction of the bountiful independence of its economy. Either way, the female virtue of chastity is subsumed by the masculine virtue of good husbandry.

While Shakespeare's *Sonnets* make suspect the fiction of a 'husbandry' of signifying power, shared between the patron and the text, Jonson's *Epigrams* and *The Forest* seem to endorse it, moving as they do from the literary market-place to the great estate. The *Epigrams* marks out an urban space of social and textual encounter which distinguishes idle haunters and incompetent readers from those who circulate more productively, like well-organized discourses, commanding credit and friends. The second part of the volume, divided off by a kind of waste-disposal section in the voyage down London's sewers, is devoted to the Pembrokes and two of its poems celebrate the husbandry of great estates. In *To Penshurst* the lady, 'noble, fruitful, chaste withal',[33] is metaphorically elided with the self-replenishing fruitfulness of the estate, which resists any acknowledgement of an exchange relation, even that implicit in the gift-giving of hospitality. The vital contact with the court is thus expressed as the estate's capacity to provide. King James's fortuitous discovery of and entry into the house may be read (through the rhetorical associations of 'forest' and 'found') as a discovery of the contingent *extempore* space, the 'occasion' for which the masculine virtues of productive reading and good husbandry are always prepared. So the estate's chastity with regard to economic advantage is expressed in its readiness to receive contingency as the guest of a wife who could

> Have her linen, plate, and all things nigh
> When she was far, and not a room but dressed,
> As if she had expected such a guest![34]

The other country house poem, *To Sir Robert Wroth*, uses woman rather differently to mask the dependence of the estate on political and economic contact with the court. Lady Mary Wroth transgresses, as it were, the conceptual boundaries of the book, being praised in the *Epigrams* as a dancer at court masques; specifically, as an index of the language of mythological representation that commands credit at court. Thus she, as David Norbrook has pointed out, implicitly belies Jonson's praise of Wroth's estate as austerely self-sufficient, and of Wroth himself as eschewing participation in the race for favour and economic preferment that contact with the Jacobean court implied.[35]

It is in the context of this discourse of husbandry, I think, that we have to read Lanyer's decision to defer the praise of Cookham. Samuel Daniel had, some years earlier, dedicated to Margaret Clifford *A Letter from Octavia to Marcus Antonius* which implicitly referred to the Countess's own marital situation, George Clifford being a known philanderer and adventurer.[36]

Daniel prefaced the poem with an expression of his hope that he might one day be 'secretary' to the Countess, to 'spread' her 'own faire vertues' as he had those of Octavia. But the chief virtues he discloses on Octavia's behalf are those of invisibility and chastity, arguments to redeem Antony as a good husband. 'These walles that here doe keepe me out of sight', she writes, 'Shall keepe me all vnspotted vnto thee'.[37] Lanyer's poem betrays an awareness of the difficulties of negotiating these complex masculine investments in the articulation of female virtue. She too hopes to be the secretary of a woman's virtue, but without disclosing it as a secret kept by men. Having deferred the setting forth of Cookham's loveliness, she prefaces the narrative of Christ with a highly problematic 'Invective against outward beauty unaccompanied with virtue' (p. 85) which in our terms appears to be indifferent to the virtue of the women involved, since Lucrece, whom all authorities allow to have been violated as a consequence of her exemplary chastity and huswifry rather than her beauty, is nevertheless incriminated along with the more obvious *exempla* of the evils of seduction, such as Rosamond and Cleopatra. But the beauty and violability of Lucrece's body is a figure for the competitive re-alignment of homosocial relations in the aspiration to good husbandry. So Vives, in *The Office and duetie of an husband* (trans. 1550) offers Lucrece as an example of how 'strangers and gestes' in a man's house become enemies and how 'the secrets of matrimony' should be kept from other men, to reduce the risk of a wife's 'giftes and vertues' inciting the cupidity of rivals.[38] Rosamond, too, offers an example of how the 'proof' of masculine virtue (i.e. the capacity to disclose the rhetorical potential of an encounter) is displaced and expressed as the transgressive visibility or 'beauty' of a female body. In his influential sonnet sequence *Delia*, Daniel had the ghost of Rosamond request that he try his skills at narrative, since by telling Rosamond's story he might move the stony-hearted Delia to the yielding that all his praises of her have been unable to effect. In Daniel's telling, the 'setting forth' of Rosamond's body from 'Countrey ... to Court', from obscurity to visibility, 'armed ... With rarest proofe of beauty euer seene',[39] is the cause of her fall; but of course his setting out of Delia's beauty, the proof of his rhetorical skill, is ostensibly motivated by a desire to bring about a similar fall. The ghost of Rosamond ascribes both happy and unhappy consequences to the same cause: beauty. If Daniel's rhetoric succeeds, with her as topic, in moving Delia to show kindness, then 'I (through beauty) made the wofull'st wight/By beauty may have comfort after death'.[40]

Distinguishing 'outward beauty' from inward virtue, then, has its problems, since beauty is a (gendered) way of speaking about the effect of disclosure as a form of textual pleasure and potential for the future; a form of what I have been calling 'interpretative virtue'. Lewalski, referring Lanyer's invective back to the stanzas on the Countess's retirement, reads them as a conventional foil to the 'inward virtue' therein proved.[41] But this would leave no poem to write, for the Countess's virtue would then be taken to have been signified by the enclosure of itself in her estate. What Lanyer is trying to do with the virtue/beauty antithesis is, I think, more complicated. She explicitly refers her invective forward: 'That outward Beautie which the world commends/Is not the subject I will write upon' (p. 85).

So what she will write upon is beauty, and beauty as the expression of her patron's interpretative virtue. But she will avoid the articulation of this virtue as the incriminating display of the female body by avoiding the analogical rhetoric through which such a display is produced, the rhetoric which implicitly strives to match 'those matchlesse colours Red and White' and celebrate its ingenuity in the 'perfit features of a fading face' (p. 85). She returns to this mode of proving knowledge only in the final stanzas of the poem, where a discourse in praise of the Christian martyrs is expressed in terms of disclosing their beautiful features to the sight of the Countess: 'Their freshest beauties would I faine disclose'; 'The purest colours both of White and Red' (p. 136). Having achieved the object of the poem, and dramatized woman as a cognisant subject, Lanyer can afford at this point the gesture of 'Folding up' the beauty of these histories in the breast of her patron, the implication being that they will suffer no discredit, though undisclosed, since their habitation is so radiant. A similar sort of gesture concludes the narrative of Christ's Passion. The Saviour as beloved, made known through a series of comparisons deriving from the Song of Songs, and extravagant as any sonnet,

> This is the Bridegroome that appeares so faire,
> So sweet, so lovely in his Spouse's sight,
> That unto Snowe we may his face compare,
> His cheekes like scarlet, and his eyes so bright
> As purest doves that in the rivers are,
> Washed with milke,
>
> (p. 120)

is the climax on which Lanyer abandons her topic to the heart of her patron, begging permission to leave 'This taske of Beauty which I tooke in hand' (p. 120).

But how has she fulfilled the task (a technical term for a dialectical 'trial' or 'proof') of beauty? How has her narrative proved the position of women as the subjects of interpretative experience rather than the analogues and occasions of discursive virtue between men? She organizes the narrative of the Passion so as to give maximum scope to the relation of these problematic metaphors of knowledge as the beholding of beauty. The trial and prosecution of Christ becomes a series of trials in which men's capacity to 'see and know' or to interpret the text of sacred history offered to them by the face of God in persecuted man fails by comparison with the capacity of politically disadvantaged women, whose interpretative virtue is proved by a literalization of the humanist metaphor of textual power as a mutually authenticating reflection when Christ lifts his face to the tears of the daughters of Jerusalem. Lanyer stylizes the movements of Christ throughout the narrative, so as to emphasize her allegorization of the historical moments of his appearance as moments in the experience of rhetorical disclosure as interpretative potential. So the appearances of Christ are treated as interpretative exercises. In Christ lies hidden the meaning of the historical moment; he is the object of the interpreting gaze, the matter to be heard and evaluated, the space in which to 'prove' the colours of argument. Adapting sacred history thus uncompromisingly to the humanist discourse of knowledge as a form of encounter with and trial of discursive potential, Lanyer's work reveals a troubling contradiction in the premisses of 'Christian humanism'. For Christian humanism, distinguishing itself from scholasticism on the basis that eloquence is required to set out wisdom, tends towards a definition of knowledge which has the logic of an economy; knowledge is the power to assimilate the resources or exploit the occasions which lie latent in the (sur)face of the text, or in the *extempore* moment of encounter.[42] So men in Lanyer's narrative apparently mistake the encounter with Christ as a discursive occasion in which to discover potential advantage. But there can be no encounter of God in man under such conditions. God remains obscure to the gaze trained to disclose contingency as the power to determine historical events, revealing his face only to the gaze which comprehends eschatological history in the form of compassionate response to human suffering.

Lanyer's narrative is thus overarched by two moments of suffering which call for compassionate response, one ignored and the other realized. It begins in Gethsemane, where the obscurity of night figures human ignorance of the events to be unfolded. The metaphor of a failure to see articulates both the irony of the disciples' assertions that they will never forsake Christ, and their inability to respond to him in the present hour of need. The contrast is significant: though the foreseeing eyes of Christ ('Wisdom's eyes') might 'looke and checke' Peter's misplaced confidence in his own 'cleare ... sight' of events to come, we as readers are only invited to judge the disciples' failure to realize the knowledge to which any human being has access, the present and immediate knowledge of suffering which is realized in compassionate response. A failure in compassion is registered as a crucial failure in interpretation, 'Yet shut those Eies that should their Maker see' (p. 92). At this stage, however, Lanyer articulates the failure as human rather than specifically masculine. God, in that moment is 'farre ... of Man from beeing pittied' (p. 93). As the narrative goes on, however, this representative use of 'man' is modulated. When events move into the light of the political centre stage and the disciples 'see' Christ on the brink of death, then, 'Though they protest they never will forsake him,/They do like men, when dangers overtake them' (p. 98). The unspoken antithesis of 'men' here signals the absence of women from the official spaces of interpretative encounter, the judicial sphere which produces events as discourses to be interpreted towards the making of history.

Christ's emergence into these official spaces is treated as a comedy of redundant labour; his arresters, armed with all the paraphernalia of detection, repeatedly fail to seek out and find the name and face which he repeatedly discloses to them: 'Nay, though he said unto them, I am he,/They could not know him whom their eyes did see' (p. 94). From the arrest as an attempt to discover what needed no special interpretative virtue to disclose, Lanyer stages the trial before Caiaphas as an exercise in the ingenious misconstruction of Christ as text, an attempt to 'heare the answere, which he will not make' (p. 100). At this point, when *'Pontius Pilate* must the matter heare' (p. 101), the absence of woman from the privileged spaces of interpretative virtue now intervenes in the unheard request brought from Pilate's wife (who remains at home) that proceedings should be stopped on the strength of her knowledge of Christ in a dream. This intervention operates as a sceptical frame for recalling the authoritative account of woman's position in the original trial of interpretative virtue, where Eve, credited with no special 'powre to see', 'simply good' and easily persuaded by the calculated discourse of a serpent, is contrasted with Adam, persuaded by the sight of a fruit:

> If *Eve* did erre, it was for knowledge sake,
> The fruit being faire perswaded him to fall

> (p. 104)

Lanyer's conclusion,

> Yet men will boast of Knowledge, which he tooke
> From *Eves* faire hand, as from a learned Booke.

> (p. 104)

turns the paradigm of woman's beauty as analogical proof of man's interpretative virtue, his quality of being 'faire in knowledge as in hew', inside out. Through the adjective 'fair', with its connotations of light and disclosure, Eve is metonymically figured as fruit; knowledge, defined by men as the capacity to disclose the 'fair fruits' of a textual or social encounter, here becomes indistinguishable from ignorant appetite. As a gloss on Jonson's ideal of virtuous encounter as 'looking with thought' and 'knowing one's ends' in the text or person before one, Lanyer's rewriting of the Fall defers and ironizes Pilate's decision to overlook his conviction of Christ's innocence in view of the political imperative to remain a friend to Caesar.

Lanyer figures the climax of the narrative as a drama of interpretation, in which women elicit radiance and meaning from the event which had remained mute and indecipherable to masculine exegesis. The Christ who could not be brought, by all the forensic techniques of society's governors, 'To speake one word, nor once to lift his eyes' (this is obviously not naturalistic, since the earlier failure in interpretation is located in Christ's forthcomingness) is accessible to women, whose interpretative power at this decisive moment of human history is brought about by compassion, figured in the suggestion

that their reflective knowledge is enhanced by the refraction of light in their
tears:

> Most blessed daughters of Jerusalem
> Who found such favour in your Saviors sight,
> To turne his face when you did pitie him;
> Your tearefull eyes, beheld his eyes more bright;
> Your Faith and Love unto such grace did clime,
> To have reflection from this Heav'nly Light:
>   Your Eagles eyes did gaze against this Sunne,

(p. 110)

Lanyer here picks up the metaphor of full disclosure – the eagle looking
directly at the sun – from her earlier refusal to develop the *topos* of Margaret
Clifford's retirement as a means to prove it. In the wake of this long-deferred
and carefully prepared-for dramatic moment, it becomes possible for the
poem to return to a comparative rhetoric, and to express female knowledge
of Christ in the blason of a lover's beauty without solipsism. Here, the text
takes its departure from the question in the Song of Songs framed by the
daughters of Jerusalem in response to a request for help in finding the absent
beloved:

> What is thy beloved more than another beloved, O thou fairest among
> women? What is thy beloved more than another beloved that thou dost
> so charge us?

(Song of Songs, 5:9)

The textual 'finding out' of the beloved in the comparisons that follow thus
works as a shared rather than competitive discourse, taking its origin in a
request to women for help in discovery rather than a display of secret
knowledge designed to arouse rivalrous desire (as, for example, in Baldwin's
model of analogical rhetoric as the lover enflaming another man to take
delight in his love). The transition to blason, moreover, enables Lanyer to
return to the interpretative virtue which it has been the object of the narrative
to delineate, to its source in the 'knowing by heart' of Margaret Clifford.
Here it is proved as an internal spectacle and a daily influence on the
Countess's conduct; her heart is the stage on which knowledge of God
sometimes appears in the figures of protection and power, sometimes in those
of men in need, 'in miserable case', demanding response in compassionate
action (p. 120). The representation of the exercise of female interpretative
virtue thus breaks out of its enclosure in the discourse of husbandry
and becomes something more than the protection of its own violable
boundaries.

Searching for analogues for Margaret Clifford's interpretative virtue,
Lanyer finds an approximation in the Queen of Sheba. The 'Ethyopian

Queen' affords an image of woman actively motivated by desire to interpret, proving the worthiness of King Solomon's mind with her discourse:

> Yea many strange hard questions did shee frame,
> All which were answer'd by this famous King:
> Nothing was hid that in her heart did rest,
> And all to proove this king so highly blest

(p. 128)

Once again, interpretative encounter is figured as mutual reflection, 'Beauty sometime is pleased to feed her eyes,/ With viewing Beautie in anothers face', but here the experience so figured is active, stimulated by desire:

> And this Desire did work a strange effect,
> To draw a Queene forth of her native Land,
> Not yeelding to the niceness and respect
> Of Woman-kind; she past both sea and land
> All feare of dangers shee did quite neglect,
> Onely to see, to heare, and understand
>   That beauty, wisdome, majestie and glorie,
>   That in her heart imprest his perfect storie

(p. 129)

The Queen of Sheba's going forth to 'prove' in dialectical encounter the qualities which she had 'imprest' as a 'perfect storie' in her own heart proves herself an image of the ideal reader, exercising and storing up, in the pleasure of interpreting a text or 'storie', the potential for argument and decisive action. It is a measure of the poem's achievement that the cognisant going forth of beauty here should risk no misconstruction as that casualty of masculine ideals of intellectual productivity, 'outward beauty unaccompanied with virtue' which seemed so inescapable in the early stages of Lanyer's articulation of female agency. Lanyer's poem appears not to have been received and circulated by the women whose influential countenances would have made its subject 'fair' with the reflection of their credibility. But in whose eyes would it have been fair? One is tempted to say, vaguely echoing the idiom of the *Sonnets*, 'fair … in the eyes of men'. But that is precisely the difficulty. The description of Cookham which Lanyer eventually wrote emphasizes the ephemeral and contiguous (rather than metaphorical) relation of the estate to its mistress, in the form of a valedictory elegy, where just for a moment 'all things … did hold like similes' (p. 137), not asking to be taken for the truth at the expense of the sun.

NOTES

1 A. L. Rowse, *The Poems of Shakespeare's Dark Lady: Salve Deus, Rex Judeorum by Emilia Lanyer*, London: Jonathan Cape, 1976, p. 20; on the issue of responsibility for the publication of the 1609 *Sonnets*, see Katherine Duncan-Jones's

account of scholarly attempts to exonerate Shakespeare and blame his publisher in 'Was the 1609 *Shakespeare's Sonnets* really unauthorized?', *Review of English Studies*, new series, 34, 1983, 151–71. The recent feminist scholarship on Lanyer includes Barbara Lewalski's valuable 'Of God and Good Women: the Poems of Aemilia Lanyer' in *Silent But for the Word: Tudor Women as Patrons, Translators and Writers of Religious Works*, ed. Margaret Patterson Hannay (Kent, Ohio: Kent State University Press, 1985), and Elaine Beilin, 'The Feminization of Praise: Aemilia Lanyer' in *Redeeming Eve: Women Writing in the English Renaissance* (Princeton NJ: Princeton University Press, 1987).

2 Rowse, op. cit., p. 28. Hereafter references to Lanyer's poetry will be cited from this edition by page number in the text.

3 A. L. Rowse, *Simon Forman: Sex and Society in Shakespeare's Age* (London: Weidenfeld & Nicolson, 1974), p. 111.

4 Samuel Schoenbaum, 'Shakespeare, Dr. Forman and Dr. Rowse', in *Shakespeare and Others* (London: Scholar Press, 1985), p. 76.

5 John Kerrigan, introduction to *The Sonnets and a Lover's Complaint* (Harmondsworth: Penguin, 1988), p. 23.

6 ibid., p. 29.

7 Muriel Bradbrook, reviewing *The Paradise of Women: Writings by Englishwomen of the Renaissance*, ed. Betty Travitsky, in *Tulsa Studies in Women's Literature* 1, 1982, p. 92.

8 Lewalski, op. cit., p. 207. Though I take issue throughout this paper with Lewalski's reading, I am greatly indebted to her fine article.

9 I quote from *Shakespeare's Sonnets*, ed. Stephen Booth, New Haven: Yale University Press, 1977, p. 73. Further references to the *Sonnets* will follow the quarto as transcribed in this edition and will be indicated simply by sonnet and line number in the text.

10 Booth does not include a rhetorical sense in his gloss of 'hues' but as the rhetorical sense of 'colour' itself could not escape a reader with a humanist education, I suggest a synonym such as 'hue' might bear this metaphorical sense without undue difficulty, giving added point to the pun Booth detects in 'hues'/'use', p. 164.

11 See Victoria Kahn, *Rhetoric, Prudence and Scepticism in the Renaissance* (Ithaca: Cornell University Press, 1985), pp. 39–45; Quintilian, *Institutio Oratoria*, X.vi.5–6. On reading as inventing a store of resources, see Erasmus, *On Copia of Words and Ideas*, ed. and trans. D. B. King and H. D. Rix (Milwaukee, Wis.: Marquette University Press, 1963), pp. 87–9; Terence Cave, *The Cornucopian Text* (Oxford: Clarendon Press, 1979, p. 133); Lorna Hutson, *Thomas Nashe in Context* (Oxford: Clarendon Press, 1989), pp. 38–54.

12 Sir Thomas Elyot, *The Boke named the Gouernor* (London: Dent, 1907), p. 5.

13 See, for example, the section on the analogical 'opening out' of adages and proverbs in William Baldwin, *A treatise of morrall phylosophie* (London: 1547), bk. 3, cap. 1, sig. M7^r.

14 See Erasmus, *De Copia*, pp. 67–89; Quintilian, op. cit., V.ix–xi; Cave, op. cit., p. 30, p. 122; Thomas Wilson, *The Arte of Rhetorique* (1560), ed. G. H. Mair (Oxford: Clarendon Press, 1909), pp. 6–12.

15 Hutson, op. cit., pp. 56–7.

16 Rowse's edition prints all the dedications, but see Lewalski's notes on the omission of certain dedications in extant copies, in Lewalski, op. cit., p. 264n.

17 My use of the word 'homosocial' follows Eve Kosofsky Sedgwick, *Between Men: English Literature and Male Homosocial Desire* (New York: Columbia University Press, 1985). My debts to Sedgwick and to Nancy Vickers, especially ' "The blazon of sweet beauty's best": Shakespeare's *Lucrece*' in Patricia Parker and Geoffrey

Hartman, eds, *Shakespeare and the Question of Theory* (London: Methuen, 1985) pp. 95–115, are apparent throughout this paper.

18 See John King, 'Patronage and Piety: The Influence of Catherine Parr' in Patterson Hannay (ed.), op. cit., pp. 43–60. King does not discuss the relation between the patronage of women and the representation of their agency in the reforming works in question; Catherine Brandon's support of Thomas Wilson does not prevent 'woman' from being either a figure of dispraise or part of a discourse in praise of husbandry in a treatise on rhetoric designed to give access to the production of effective discourse exclusively to men (Wilson, op. cit., p. 13).

19 Lewalski, op. cit., p. 214.

20 From a discussion following her paper, 'Rewriting Patriarchy and Patronage: Margaret Clifford, Anne Clifford, and Aemilia Lanyer', delivered at Reading, July 1989.

21 William Sherman, '"Official Scholars" and "Action Officers": Research Intelligence and the Making of Tudor Policy in Early Modern England', unpublished research paper delivered at the London Renaissance Seminar, 1990. See also Lisa Jardine and Anthony Grafton, '"Studied for Action": How Gabriel Harvey Read His Livy', *Past and Present* 129 (1990), pp. 30–78.

22 See Richard Peterson, *Imitation and Praise in the Poems of Ben Jonson* (New Haven: Yale University Press, 1981), pp. 3–34; Cave, op. cit., pp. 39–53.

23 Lawrence Humphrey, *Of Nobilitye* (London: Thomas Marshe, 1563, sigs a4^r–a5^r). Humphrey imagines a nobility fashioning themselves through their mastery of paradigms of similarly fashioned classical governors, so 'the auncient Nobilitye, shaped by the Monumentes of auncient writers and drawen from the pattern of Kinges, princes and other auncient nobles, maye be raysed as a mirrour in a hyghe and playne mount to shine and glister to the men of our dayes' to revive 'the auncient discipline and true prayse of their auncestors', sig. b3^r.

24 Ben Jonson, *Poems*, ed. Ian Donaldson (Oxford: Oxford University Press, 1975), p. 44.

25 See epigrams 11, 12, 56, 58, 81, 100 in Jonson, *Poems*, pp. 11–55.

26 Giles Fletcher, *Licia: or Poemes of Love, in Honour of the admirable and singular vertues of his Lady, to the imitation of the best Latin Poets and others* (London: 1593, sigs A2^r–B1, sig. C3^r).

27 George Gascoigne, *The Adventures of Master F.J.* in *An Anthology of Elizabethan Prose Fiction*, ed. Paul Salzman (Oxford: Oxford University Press, 1987), p. 10, pp. 15–16.

28 Nancy Vickers, 'Diana Described: Scattered Woman and Scattered Rhyme', in *Writing and Sexual Difference*, ed. Elizabeth Abel (Brighton, Sussex: Harvester, 1982), p. 96.

29 See Thomas Lodge, *Phillis* (London: John Busbie, 1593, sig. H3^v). On the importance of Petrarchism as an exercise in technical virtuosity to extend the flexibility of the vernaculars, see Leonard Forster, *The Icy Fire* (Cambridge: Cambridge University Press, 1969), p. 73.

30 Kerrigan, op. cit., p. 23; Baldwin, op. cit., sig. M7^r.

31 Humphrey, op. cit., sigs h8^v–i8^v. Humphrey's discourse derives, by way of Cicero's *De Senectute*, from Xenophon's *Oeconomicus*, a text also at the heart of humanist marriage doctrine.

32 Compare Cave's discussion of Quintilian on improvisation (Cave, op. cit., pp. 126–7) with Xenophon on the productive potential of the wife-governed household as an efficient retrieval system (*Oeconomicus*, viii.2–23).

33 Jonson, op. cit., p. 91.

34 ibid.

35 David Norbrook, *Poetry and Politics in the English Renaissance* (London: Routledge & Kegan Paul, 1984), pp. 190–1.

36 Joan Rees, *Samuel Daniel* (Liverpool: Liverpool University Press, 1964), pp. 76–7.

37 Samuel Daniel, *The Complete Works in Verse and Prose*, ed. A. B. Grosart (London: Spenser Society, 1885, i.124).

38 Juan Lodovicus Vives, *The Office and duetie of an husband*, trans. Thomas Paynell (London: John Cawood, 1550, sigs U4^r–x4^r). On the significance of Lucrece in the humanist mystification of the dependence of republican *virtus* on commercial contact and secrecy, see Stephanie H. Jed, *Chaste Thinking: The Rape of Lucretia and the Birth of Humanism* (Bloomington, Indiana: Indiana University Press), 1989.

39 Daniel, op. cit., vol. i, p. 85.

40 ibid., vol. i, p. 83. In interpreting this text, Kerrigan makes the classic move of translating Daniel's attribution of agency to the 'beauty' of Delia and Rosamond into a form of guilt: 'In *Delia*, Daniel had shown chastity at two extremes: coldly unyielding in his mistress's case; all too weak in Rosamond's' (p. 17). It is difficult to imagine what kind of conduct could be defined as 'chaste' on these terms!

41 Lewalski, op. cit., p. 214.

42 Kahn, op. cit., p. 51: 'The problem for a Christian humanist is that in a Judeo-Christian world ... there is, in theory, no contingency.'

Chapter 11

Unsilent instruments and the devil's cushions: authority in seventeenth-century women's prophetic discourse

Sue Wiseman

> To speak the word of exhortation, and information, to the conforming of Saints in the truth, is to prophesie. ... Another passage to this purpose is Revel.19.10. *For the testimony of Jesus Christ is the spirit of prophesie*. This passage gives a most clear answer to the question, What is it to prophesie?[1]

Where, if anywhere, is the authority, or the voice of authority, in seventeenth-century prophetic discourse by women? This was the question which I began this article hoping to answer. Where does the voice of the female prophet 'come from' – the Bible? God? A fixed subject position? These are not clear questions, and the prophetic texts do not supply clear answers, but the problematic of what authorizes the voice or writing in women's prophetic discourse is central to an analysis of the relationship of women to the genres of Puritan polemic and sacred writing. It brings together the issue of women's identity in radical sectarian writing and the Pauline interdictions against women's speech. In prophecy by women these two intersect at the place where women's speech is most visibly gendered and therefore prohibited – the public sphere of the written or spoken word – and the place where women, if they are accepted as prophets, are most *not* themselves in that they are speaking 'for' (in favour of, but also more literally on behalf of) God. For this reason writing which presents itself as prophecy (and which was or was not accepted as such) provides a limit case in any discussion of the relationship between women and the radical Protestant discourses which emerged in the mid-1640s. This in turn has more general implications for the way in which we think about political/religious authority in the seventeenth century. Furthermore, it has a sequence of implications for the contemporary feminist drive to 'recover' texts by seventeenth-century women and see them as 'feminist'.

Although this essay does examine conversion narratives, preaching and justifications of women's speaking, the focus is an analysis of the relationship between an 'I' inevitably gendered as female (in the eyes of God?) and prophetic language. The word 'language' here points towards the frequent ambiguities and irresoluble questions around prophetic discourse by women, one of which is how far they are to be considered printed texts and how far transcribed speech. For instance, Hester Biddle's tracts, such as *A Warning From the Lord God of Life and Power Unto the City of London and to the Suburbs Round about thee*, use address and the techniques of dramatic monologue although they are printed texts which were not, unlike Trapnel's *The Cry of A Stone*, or Sara Wight's prophecy or the 'dumb woman' Elinor Channel's *A Message From God By a Dumb Woman*, a transcribed record of speech mediated by an amanuensis who might interfere.[2] (Arise Evans did interfere in Channel's prophecy, attempting to use his own spiritual authority and literacy to give it a royalist interpretation.)[3]

Sometimes it is difficult to decide whether to consider a text as fully written, or as fully spoken – Biddle's written text reads like a monologue or rant, and Trapnel's recorded spoken text reads, with some interjections from the transcriber, like a polished and finished piece of poetry. This in turn pinpoints the problematic of women's prophecy; where does the voice we hear (the text we read) come 'from'? Is it written or spoken? Is the voice that of the woman, the gathered church she belongs to, or God? What seems to generate this rhetorical doubleness? How does the question of projected voice (ventriloquism?) relate to the issue of whence a text, written/spoken by a woman and dealing with the Logos derives its authority.

There are several different kinds of prophecy in the mid-seventeenth-century period, from Lady Eleanor Douglas's literal predictions based on voices that she heard, through visionary communion with God (as in the case of Jane Lead), mediated and multiple relationships to God (Anna Trapnel) and the intricate intellectual fusion of typological and historical calculation found in the writing of the Fifth Monarchist prophet Mary Cary. In each case God is the central authority of the prophecy, though of course the texts have to negotiate a path between the speaker's femininity, prophetic authority and any body of readers. In each case the reader is invited to understand not an eruption of the semiotic into the symbolic but a combination of spiritual inspiration and generic horizon of expectation. Interwoven in these texts are invitations to the reader to respond to the 'experience' of the prophet (which we might think of as coded in the aspects of the texts which call attention both to the prophet's interior experiences, bodily manifestations and, in the text, the use of the idea of the speaking voice) and the explanation of Biblical precedents which work as a structuring rhetoric for prophecy and which signal its 'readerly' status (in Barthes's terms) by calling attention to its rich intertextuality.[4]

The way authority is conceptualized in such texts, with constant recourse to Biblical discourse, is sharply distinguished from the texts by seventeenth-century women which have drawn most critical attention hitherto. These texts have been in the dominant *literary* genres – poetry, fiction, drama – and surprisingly often have followed the pattern of royalist writers set out so long ago by Virginia Woolf in *A Room of One's Own*.[5] For instance, the much-anthologized royalist writer Margaret Cavendish, sometimes claimed by critics as feminist, slides from positions which are recognizable as 'feminist' to a twentieth-century critic to positions which are equally recognizable as anti-feminist. But, either way, any conception of authority in Cavendish's writing calls up the figure of a man like a genie from a bottle.[6]

It seems that generic unfamiliarity combined with a radical Protestant and even implicitly republican/millenarian conception of authority has kept the wide range of women's prophetic writing off the agenda of twentieth-century feminist criticism, yet it is here, I shall argue, that we can see not only an attempt to manipulate what might generally be called patriarchal codes, but to use the space of religious writing to reinvent models of authority, language and control. Of course, radical Protestant theology and the revival of the new age of prophecy never quite delivered the potential it had to actually de-gender speaking, and even as they claim the 'free space' offered by speaking with the grace of God female prophets negotiate the material and ideological constraints of their circumstances.

Texts by fairly well-known women prophets (the Fifth Monarchists Anna Trapnel and Mary Cary) as well as Eleanor Douglas, Ann Wentworth and Jane Lead give me a chance to explore these questions in relation to both dominant kinds of radical prophecy (and preaching) and to outline the beginnings of a theory of the relationship between prophetic utter-ances/writing and the material circumstances of women 'speakers' within the gathered churches of the mid- and post-Restoration period. But first, what was the relationship of sectarian women to the Pauline interdiction? The most readily available response is that of the Quaker Margaret Fell (later Fox). Although it has been said that she was carrying on the ideas of her husband George Fox, to whom she was married by the time the tract was published, Margaret Fell's *Women's Speaking Justified* is a free-standing polemic.[7] Fell's text does what Ann-Rosalind Jones has perceptively called manipulating the codes which exclude women and making forwardness appear to be virtue.[8]

Jones is discussing women and poetry, but Fell's commentary is not on secular discourse but on the key texts interdicting women's speech – the last part of Paul's First Epistle to the Corinthians (1 Corinthians 14:34 and 35). Importantly, this interdiction follows the rest of the chapter on the nature of prophecy and the ordering of meetings at which Christians are prophesying and speaking in tongues; Paul has been giving advice on the ordering of prophetic oratory in gatherings – 'For ye may all prophesy one by one' – to prevent confusion (14:31), and therefore his strictures apply to women in particular relationship to sacred language.

Fell's rhetoric is that of the polemic Protestant tradition of revision, exe-geses of Biblical texts based on the insight afforded by truth. Therefore *Women's Speaking Justified* demonstrates her rhetorical competence (the rhetoric concerned being that of Protestant debate) and the insights she draws from exegesis at the same time as offering a re-reading of the texts which denied that such things were possible.[9] This makes the text doubly a meta-commentary, first in that it is a commentary upon the interdiction of women's speech, and second in its deployment of tropes and structures by a woman in the very mode of the Protestant discourse which is denied. However, by weaving a seamless web of commentary upon and by deployment of the discourses forbidding women's speech, the piece participates in the discourse it is justifying as available to it – a complex rhetorical sleight of hand. The sophistication of the tract's entry into the rhetoric proper to the discourse does not mean that *Women's Speaking Justified* is weak in the re-explication of Corinthians that Fell proposes. All forms of speech are assumed to be available to women and the Pauline interdictions apply only to gathered churches in 'confusion' (1 Cor.14:33); in this way she turns Paul's words against himself, and makes them actually authorize women's preaching. The Bible is reinterpreted from Genesis:

> Let this Word of the Lord, which was from the beginning, stop the mouths of all that oppose *Womens* Speaking in the Power of the Lord; for he hath put an enmity between the Woman and the Serpent; and if the Seed of the Woman speak not, the Seed of the Serpent speaks.

(p. 4)

Fell uses the ungendered 'seed' of woman to put in place an opposition between women's speaking and the voice of the Devil (important, as I shall suggest later, in terms of very real possibilities of the accusation of witchcraft). She also uses the woman clothed with the sun from Revelations 22. But centrally, the way Fell justifies women's speaking is by invoking 'the Power of the Lord'. As we will see in a moment, this emendation serves to cover all eventualities in which women might be forbidden speech, for the Lord may speak through anyone, including Anna the prophetess (Luke 2: 36–8). The interdiction is, she suggests, for those without grace and interweaves 1 Corinthians 14 and Eve's sin to explain that it is circumstances and spiritual state, not gender, which authorize or forbid women's preaching. Corinthians,

> speaks of women that were under the law, and in the transgression as *Eve* was, and such as were to hear and not speak publicly, but they must first ask their husbands at home. . . . And what is all this to Women's Speaking? that have the Everlasting Gospel to preach, and upon whom the promise of the *Lord* is fulfilled, and his spirit poured upon them according to his word *Acts 2, 16, 17, 18.*

The scriptural exegesis and echoing of Biblical language situates the writing as a document of sectarian polemic. However, 'the Power of the Lord' (p. 4) as the quality which lets Fell off the Corinthian hook also foregrounds the dialogism of the preaching text, and therefore reintroduces the question of authority in a different place. Who is to say whether or not anyone is speaking with God's blessing; 'by their fruits ye shall know them' but what are the proper, decorous, fruits of women's prophecy?[10] The power of the Lord is something which can be contested between the speaker and the hearer, and historically during the seventeenth-century prophetic revival (as in the cases of Anna Trapnel, Ann Wentworth and Katherine Evans and Sarah Cheevers locked up by the Inquisition in Malta) this was exactly the site of struggle.[11]

Fell's justification of women's speaking relies on her re-reading of Paul which, in turn, relies on him addressing situations in which people were 'confused' (and therefore should not speak) or enlightened (and therefore might). Such a justification relies on a community of recognition which sees grace in a speaker's words. This relationship between the female 'I' that at least appears to speak (though it may also be the voice of God) and the authority or 'Power of the Lord' of that voice is a problem in play in different ways in the prophetic utterances of each of the three prophets discussed below, displayed most evidently in prophecy because of the potentially high sacred status of that discourse (and the correspondingly high possibility of demonization for the female speaker).

In her *A Word in Season to the Kingdom of England* Mary Cary demonstrates her awareness that the decision about who has the power of the Lord is in the hands of the reader by pointing to the reader's own spiritual state: 'Whoever thou art that readest the insuing discourse, know, that if thou art one that art active in helping on of that which I call the positive part; then thou dost what lies in thee to bring happiness and tranquility of thy native Kingdom' (A2v) – implying that those who do not believe her words are sowers of discord.[12] The coercive power of words like 'tranquility' in the years after the first civil war (1647 was also the year of the Putney debates between the army leaders and the agitators) cannot be underestimated, and are used here to situate the 'Power of the Lord' in the accepting and agreeing reader (see also p. 9 of the same tract). In this tract Mary Cary negotiates the borders between the politics of preaching, testimony and prophecy (with the material implications of demonization) and the imperative for truth to be spread. She argues in favour of an accommodation between earthly and heavenly powers whereby the former endorse only speakers with the blessing of the latter – another attempt to structure the bestowal of the 'Power of the Lord', phallogocentric authority and permission to be within the symbolic.

In *The Resurrection of the Witness* Cary also locates the authority of her prophetic voice in the overriding 'Power of the Lord', but in this case it is in signs external to the prophet rather than visionary experience, which causes her to prophesy:[13]

> Amos 3.8. '*The Lion hath roared, who will not fear? The Lord hath spoken, who can but prophesie? ... Acts 4.20. For we cannot but speak the things which we have seen and heard.* In both these places it appears, that it is not

possible for instruments to be silent, nor to sit still, when God hath spoken to them, and given them commission to doe his work.'

(Preamble p. 19)

Again the text attempts to annex the judgement of the reader through Biblical analogy and by the exteriorization of inspiration which is made to seem empirically measurable.

The non-sectarians constantly mocked the relationship between women and sacred discourse in the sects; such ridicule is present for example in the parodic and satiric pamphlet literature such as *The Ranters Monster* (discussed below), *The Mistris Parliament* (1648), playlets, and in *A Brief Dialogue Between a Zelotopist one of the Daughters of a Zealous Round-head, and Superstition* (1642). The sexual relationships of the government leaders were also satirized – see Hugh Peter as characterized in *The Famous Tragedy of Charles I* (1649) and elsewhere.[14] Within the sects though, leaving aside questions of the Ranters (as at least their enemies identified them, and there are several arguments for seeing them as a group of some sort), where a religious community may also have been a sexual community the position was unstable and variable.[15] For example their 'literal interpretation of the Bible' led Baptists to be much less willing to hear women preachers than Quakers or Fifth Monarchists and both Quakers and Baptists policed women's behaviour after the Restoration and the imposition of the Clarendon Code (1661–5).[16] During the 1640s and 1650s attitudes to women's speaking also varied from church to church and congregation to congregation.

An example of negotiation of boundaries, and a particularly clear case of the erasure of a gendered 'I' from the main part of the text can be found in Mary Cary's double publication *The Little Horn's Doom and Downfall*. Cary has been described as one of the clearest expositors of Fifth Monarchist doctrine.[17] However, in this dual text one of her writings is suggested as acceptable and the other is presented as dubious – *The Little Horn's Doom*. It is a case of the gender erased (or repressed) from the speaking voice returning in the extra-prophetic situating material. This return takes the form of an introduction to the text written by the army chaplain, Hugh Peter. It can be seen as both constituting the return of the repressed of Cary's text and demonstrating, in its language, the return of its own repressed – which could in turn be read as the anxiety of castration and/or the overproductivity of the female body as structured in a repressed fantasy of sexual rapaciousness returning in language.

The Little Horn's Doom[18] was printed in 1651 (Thomason dates his copy April), during the Commonwealth, when for republicans and millennial Puritan sects it must have seemed that the events of history and Biblical typologies were finally weaving themselves together in the last age. The death of Charles I in 1649 seemed like a world-historical event, and did indeed play a part in transforming European political relationships and political theory.

Accordingly, Cary writes that her prophecy reveals the way in which history and Biblical typology are enabling prophets to interpret the new and coming age and revealing the meaning of 'the late tragedies which have bin acted upon the Scene of these three Nations: and particularly the late King's doom and death, [which] was so long ago as Daniel pre-echoed' (A1v).

The organization of the text itself amounts to a complex rhetorical negotiation of where the authority of the text lies, whether prophetic discourse is to be taken seriously, and it exposes the lineaments of the contradiction of women (forbidden to speak) prophesying (with the grace of God). The first thing a reader encounters in this book is the dedication, not to Cromwell and Ireton (later reviled by Trapnel during the Protectorate), but to their wives, 'the Vertuous, Heroicall and Honourable' ladies Cromwell, Ireton and Role. This suggests both the invocation of a community (of some sort) of independent women and an appeal to some sort of female readership to endorse the text's authority as prophecy. Moreover, it repeats Cary's ploy of attempting to appropriate the 'Power of the Lord' for her text and coerce the reader into granting her text to be inspired by grace. She continues, 'being pressed in spirit to divulge this insuing discourse',

> And observing, how that among the many pious, precious and sage Matrons with which this Commonwealth is endowed; as with so many precious jewels, and choice gemmes ... God hath selected your Ladyships and placed you in some of the highest places of honour (according to your present capacities) in these Nations;

> (A4r–v)

Thus the wives of the army leaders are both decorations to the Commonwealth and exemplify the high authority the new age invests in women, while at the same time the highest honour of prophecy is withheld from them ('according to your present capacities'). Cunningly, Cary both points to other culturally important women (significantly wives rather than maids), weaving together the religious and political significance of her dedicatees.

Cary follows this with an address to the reader which is also a careful placing of the reader as one who recognizes truth, understands scripture and can discern true typology. Distancing and dignifying *The Little Horn's Doom* with the claim that it was written 'above 7 years ago' (A7r) but not published, we are invited to attend to the text as knowing and acquiescent readers.[19] The prophecy was not published when it was first written because 'men would then generally have been more incapable of receiving such things, then now they are, because now these things are fulfilled; and prophesis are then best understood when they are fulfilled' (A7v). Once again the truth status of the text is put into play, here using several different kinds of time and prophecy. First there is Daniel's prophecy, and then Cary's exegesis of the prophecy and its annexation for a Fifth Monarchist reading of history. Obviously Cary here seizes upon historical events to factify a text which would otherwise be wholly prophetic, and we are asked to read the text as prophesying events which have already happened, and which underwrite its truth.

Finally, Cary points to the truth value of her words as inspired by God, suggesting that her own agency in their production was as non-existent as if she had been a pen or pencil:

> If any shall hereby receive any light, or any refreshment, let them blesse the Lord for it, from whom alone it came: for I am a very weake and unworthy instrument, and have not done this work by any strength of my owne, but have been often made sensible, that I could doe no more herein, (wherein any light or truth could appeare) of my selfe, then a pencill or pen can do.

(A8r)

This rhetorical doubling of the status of the text works alongside the earlier dedication in the text's attempt to use the rhetorical positioning of the reader to establish as much as possible the typological, historical, spiritual and factual veracity of the coming narrative. The text does this very thoroughly and I have tried to suggest the ways in which it attempts to manipulate the reader to acquiesce to the text as truth, rather than question the sex of the author. I have dealt with these manoeuvres at length not because of their relationship to the extraordinary (though ordinary) introduction which follows. This is by Hugh Peter, famously zealous in the cause of the army and like Cary in favour of the use of violence to establish the reign of the Saints. It appears to be an introduction endorsing the tracts though in fact it sits like a little bomb or Pandora's box filled with all the assumptions, demons, stereotypes and interdictions of the feminine which Cary's introductory material has so carefully positioned. The first thing Peter's piece does is to question the truth value Cary has so carefully established by saying that he agrees with the tract only in part.

Peter's introduction reads like a classic demonstration of the Freudian commonplace that there is no negative term, coupled with the impossibility of the woman's 'no' in her desire to be desired. The other, undifferentiated, is desired and this text projects its own desire on to the object of that discourse, at the same time that it purports to be cancelling, contradicting, the idea that the other desires to be desired. Or, to put it more simply, it uses its articulation of the cancellation of sexuality in Cary's text to reimport it; the female prophet is reinscribed as sexual in a public place (writing) by the way in which Peter denies the potentially demonizing link between prophetic discourse and femininity which I outlined in the introduction. He writes,

> She hath taught her sexe that there are more ways than one to avoid idleness (the devils cushion) on which so many sit and sleep their last. They that will not use the Distaff may improve a Pen.
> Secondly, a holy, modest and painfull spirit runs through her endeav-

ours; which I desire may not be slighted by any, nor thrown by: for good
wine may be found in this Cluster: in this dress you shall see neither naked
Breasts, black Patches, nor long Trains; but an heart breathing after the
coming of Christ and the comfort of saints.

(A2r)

Printed without Cary's own prefatory material this looks suspiciously like
the parodic discourse of anti-sectarian journalism which, though at its most
extreme when addressing Familists and Ranters, consistently links the language used by sectaries to describe spiritual experience with the desire (indeed
to be desired – to have 'congress' with the 'spirit', etc.) of the female Puritan
sectary represented as unpoliced, rampant and endless. This extract returns
the female prophet to the domestic sphere and invokes the language of
conduct books, the dominant discourse which delineates the borders of that
sphere in its opening reference to idle femininity. The cushion directs our
attention to the female body (lower parts) and the wilfulness of the female
prophet is pointed out by the phrase 'they that will not use the Distaff', as
though, after all, that is what the woman should use. Peter continues:

More I would say; but my feeble thoughts or words will adde but little to
her labours. Doubtless she had good help from above in her traval for this
birth: but I will bequeath her Solomons last words of his good housewife.
Favour is deceitful, and beauty is vain; but a woman that feareth the Lord,
she shall be praised.

(Prov.31: 30)

Alongside Peter's self-marginalizing rhetoric is a turn from the texts to Cary
as a woman. He has already compared her to other clever women, but this,
as the conclusion of the introduction, gives Peter the opportunity to both
domesticate Cary's text using the comparison of her and a housewife and to
end by using Proverbs to praise her, rather than her text.

Two movements are detectable in Hugh Peter's introduction; first the
return of the repressed in the way that the female body, sexuality, the
conduct of women reappear (each of these was excluded from Cary's own
introduction), second, there is a parallel movement from attention to text
and argument to the person of Mary Cary and her relationship with God.
We can see the contradictory ways in which the text is producing the authority
of the prophetic voice. Peter's intervention mediates reception of the prophecy
by acting as a doubting reader who reads the prophecy sceptically, but who
also refuses Cary the benefit of the 'Power of the Lord' in redirecting the
reader's thoughts to a pre-textual source which is a woman (and we are
carefully reminded of the place of women) rather than a prophet – the
conjunction of femininity and prophecy are posed by Peter in terms of the
proper role of the Christian woman. By contrast a second mediating document, 'Touching this Treatise' by Henry Jessey, returns our attention to the

prophetic text, albeit sceptically, commenting 'for the *application* here of the *Little Horn* to the *late King*. . . . Time will make the truth evident' (A4v). The presence of yet a third introduction, by Christopher Feake compounds the text's anxious prevarications, but it also actually addresses the question of the authority of the female prophet: 'Indeed, many wise men after the flesh have been (and now are) much offended, that a company of illiterate men, and silly women, should pretend any skill in dark prophesies, and to have foresight of future events' (A5r).

Although Feake goes on to affirm the importance of prophecy he has articulated the problems about mid-century prophecy. 'Wise men after the flesh' (Anglicans of sorts?) might well question the authority of sectarian churches to take up the prophetic tradition which was abandoned after Malachi, and this must in Cary's case be exacerbated by the vehicle or vessel of the prophecy being female.

At times millenarian and prophetic rhetoric sat at the centre of government; for example, when Cromwell opened the short-lived Barebones Parliament of 1653, with a speech which ended with him revealing the instrument of government – as Wilbur Cortez Abbot notes, proof of his acceptance of his own 'ascendancy in civil as in military affairs' – he spoke of the rule of Saints in prophetic terms.[20] Referring to Psalm 68 he regards it as 'a glorious prophecy, I am persuaded, of the Gospel churches – it may be, of the Jews also'.[21] So in 1653 Cromwell was anticipating, possibly, the conversion of the Jews which was considered to herald the millennium. Such thinking is central to the millennial hopes of both Mary Cary and Margaret Fell. But although millenarian thinking was, for a time, part of the religio-political centre the place of a woman inspired by God to speak in public was fraught with cultural perils. As Nigel Smith notes, women prophets 'needed to be part of godly communities in order to have the authority to prophesy', but although such a community might ensure them an audience (in Cary's case for a written rather than an oral prophecy), the context of the gathered church might import problems which undermine the authority of female prophets.[22] Sarah Wight, the female prophet on whom Trapnel seems to have modelled herself, plays on the issue of the authority of the word in her signature to *A Wonderful Pleasant and Profitable Letter Written by Mrs Sarah Wight*.[23]

The letter, which outlines her affliction and rebirth in God's love, was published (we are told) without her consent for '*the many* bewildered ones *to whom it might serve as a* Witness' (A3²). The way the text is organized as a private (feminine) document brought without the author's agency into the public sphere points once again to the question of the authority of a woman's religious text, which here seems to rely on a collective decision to publish it (A3²r). Even more interesting is Sarah Wight's signature as 'Sarah Wight,/an empty nothing, whose fulness is all in that Fountain that filleth all in all' (p. 80). The play on 'empty vessels', and feminine identity as a cipher, points towards the authority of Wight's text as derived from God, which fills her voice. Indeed, *A Wonderful ... Letter* involves God's voice as it spoke in Biblical phrases to Wight – reproduced in italics. So Wight uses her femininity, or status as cipher, nothing, to underwrite her text as filled with God's meaning. The intricacy and careful 'placing' of the authority to speak by both Fell and Wight underscore that we cannot see prophetic texts by women as wholly 'highly personalized'; if they point 'out' of the text towards a self it is to a self that is instrumental, both gendered and not gendered, a 'vessel' for God's purpose, a channel for God's signals, a multiple self having agency only in the grace of God.[24]

The cases of Cary and Wight are instances of the mediation of prophetic discourse produced by women, and so far I have examined the way in which women prophets (in the seventeenth-century sense of visionaries and, in the case of Cary, typographical predictors) manipulate the codes of prophecy and Biblical exegesis to underwrite their status as prophets. A more specific question of authority remains: what is the voice to be heard in the prophecy itself, and what relationship does this bear to the feminine 'I'? It must be evident already that the conceptualization of authority in sectarian texts is radically different from that in many royalist texts. I shall return to this later on, but first I want to examine the way in which authority inhabits many voices (and none) in the prophetic writings and testaments of Anna Trapnel.

Anna Trapnel, as her autobiography for her gathered church tells us, was born and bred in Stepney. She became a Fifth Monarchist and a prophet. As she relates in her autobiography, she had visions and direct communications of various sorts with God, who explained the situation of the nation to her in quasi-typological terms, and she then explained it to the nation in language drawn from the scriptures. As long as she was in London the nation was relatively receptive, but her *Report and Plea* published in 1654 tells of her prophetic mission to the South-west, which ended with her in jail in Plymouth and then in Bridewell. She was tried and accused of drunkenness, madness, witchcraft and – importantly, she suggests – she was accused of sedition. Her best-known prophecy, *The Cry of A Stone* draws on Esdras in which it is said that even voiceless stones will prophesy. Like a stone Trapnel, voiceless in her femininity and social status, prophesies. It is now well known that she became famous for her prophecy at Whitehall, transcribed in *The Cry of A Stone*, when she fell into a trance on 11 January 1654 while waiting outside the trial of Vavasour Powell after the dissolution of the Barebones Parliament in the previous December. The beginning of Cromwell's Protectorate was marked by the arrest of Fifth Monarchists and provoked Trapnel's first public trance, at which many came to see the spectacle of the fasting, singing, prophet and Trapnel's status was confirmed after her examination by John Simpson.[25]

Characteristic of her writing is the emphasis on voice and the connection between that and political circumstances and God. The title itself gives voice to an altogether voiceless aspect of the Creation, and is evidently a commentary on the question of who society allows to speak, and what they are allowed to say. And in the summary of her best visions to date, given in the spiritual autobiography that precedes the prophecies in *The Cry of A Stone*, we find politics as scripture (and vice versa) – Cromwell becomes a bull from Daniel, England the New Jerusalem and so on – all transpositions familiar from the radical sectarian writing of the Civil War. With the radical writers of the Civil War Trapnel also shared an emphasis on the word, the word of God mediated through the Saints who spoke His word and did His work, enacting the building of the New Jerusalem. By 1654, when *The Cry of A Stone* was published, the Saints were becoming visibly excluded from any say in Government.[26]

Trapnel's prophecies were delivered when she was 'siezed upon by the Lord ... carried forth in a spirit of prayer and singing from noon till night' (p. 1), a performance lasting twelve days. What she said in the trance was set down by a 'relator', sometimes in a garbled and incoherent way. This means that the written texts of Trapnel's visions, prayers and prophecies are a written record of an abnormal event, very possibly not 'truthful' or absolute renderings of what was spoken, nor, necessarily, pure vessels containing the 'meaning' of the spoken prophecies. At points the relator comments that he just transcribed as much as he could. We might say that Trapnel's *Cry of A Stone* is not attributable to a single subject or voice. The issue of authorship however is not only between Trapnel and the 'relator'; in her introductory remarks she suggests that it is the Lord Himself speaking through her.

The overriding concern of Trapnel's text is the speaking and writing of God's word. The tract is initiated by a passage linking the coming day of wonders and Trapnel's own voice, not explicitly defined as female. We read:

> It is hoped in this day, a day of the Power of God, a day of Wonders, of shaking the heavens and the earth, and of general expectations of the approaching of the Lord to his Temple, that any thing that pretends to be a Witness, a Voice, or a Message from God to this Nation, shall not be held unworthy the hearing and consideration of any, because it is administered by a simple and unlikely hand.
>
> *(Cry of A Stone*, sig.a2)

Her voice expresses a message from God. Authority for speech here is returned to the ultimate source and origin of all things; like those of her male contemporaries Trapnel's prophecies use Biblical language extensively. The text allies itself linguistically to that of the canonical prophecies.

The only part of *The Cry of A Stone* which is written from a gendered subject-position is the conventional autobiographical conversion narrative inserted between a description of the trance-like state in which Trapnel delivered her songs and prayers and the songs themselves. The emphasis on self here and in the *Report and Plea* contrasts with her prophetic mode, but even here the two voices of Trapnel and the relator are interwoven. The autobiography begins by placing Trapnel in the context of the usual nexus of family authority, whereas the ensuing songs and prayers present a speaking voice, or voices, in direct communication with God. The autobiography tells us her identity – 'I am Anna Trapnel', followed by her family status – 'the daughter of William Trapnel', followed by his occupation, 'shipwright', also implying a class position, and ends by pointing out that her parents died 'in the profession of the Lord Jesus'. This mode, acknowledging as it does all the social axes of authority which bring an individual into being in society, appears in sharp contradistinction to the discourse of politicized prophecy which ensues. Within a paragraph of this statement Trapnel is talking directly with God, and soon he is advising her to pursue her visions and vocations. In this way the discourses of political prophecy and civil society cut across one another. At the end of the autobiographical fragment the narrator suddenly intervenes to ask Trapnel how she felt when speaking, and she replies, 'I neither saw, nor heard, nor percieved the noise and distractions of the people, but was as one that heard only the voice of God sounding forth unto me.' The relator confirms that she looked like one in 'the Visions of God'. When asked why she fell silent she replies, 'It was as if the Clouds did open and recieve me into them: and I was swallowed up of the glory of the Lord and could speak no more.' This emphasizes that God's authority inheres in the visionary speech and silence of Trapnel – for both come directly from God.

Trapnel's prophecies are clearly concerned with contemporary political issues of national importance, and are replete with religious and class con-notations. For example she characterizes Cromwell as a bull from Daniel (13–14), yet as they are also the words of God spoken by one in a trance Trapnel is removed as the source or author of the utterance. At the same time the interventions of the relator call attention to the fact that the text is incomplete, heightening the distance between the text and the 'author' who utters the speech it records. There is a continuous ambiguity about *who* is speaking. Is the subject-position that of the narrator (Trapnel?) as mediated through the words of the relator, or is it God who is speaking, or an entangled mixture of the two? The aporia between recorded speech and absent subject tends to blur any question of gender-subjectivity, since this is in any case a filtered discourse; while the text cannot be read as by 'a woman', or anyone at all, as long as its prophetic status is accepted. The fact that the text may represent the word of God problematizes any critique of the issue of the right of a 'woman' to speak, at least for those who accept the validity of prophetic discourse.

The issue of what a 'genuine' prophetic discourse might be probably affords no answer (except in terms of generic conventions and what Habermas would call the 'speech communities' of seventeenth-century England; and Trapnel seems, as I have suggested, to have been accepted by her London sect). But of more general interest is the way in which these texts disrupt the authority of any anterior 'author', in a way analogous to the practice of the group of British writers using the 'multiple name' Karen Elliot – a name which anyone can use. In some ways God is the ultimate multiple or composite name which gives the text simultaneously no authorial authority and the ultimate authority. In her record of the journey into Cornwall, *Anna Trapnel's Report and Plea*, she writes of her defence before the court which accused her:

> In all that was said by me, I was nothing, the Lord put all in my mouth, and told me what I should say, and that from the written word, he put it in my memory and mouth: so that I will have nothing ascribed to me, but all honour and praise given to him whose right it is, even to Jehovah, who is the King that lives for ever.[27]

To put it crudely one could say that Anna Trapnel's work is not recognizable to a humanist feminist critical approach as having anything to do with feminist practice or ideas because texts by her present us with no unified and gendered subject-position and no masculine representation of authority short of God. God is the transcendental significant and the guarantor of meaning and authority which, in these texts, reside inseparably in the Word with all its many meanings. The word of God, as spoken to, by or through Trapnel is an intervention at a super-linguistic level in the symbolic order. To represent oneself as speaking God's word is theoretically to dissolve the unified subject-position of the speaker – for when is the speaker an 'I' and when God's agent?

Thus the language of 'prophecy' as constituted in these texts permits them to encode in Biblical language a criticism of the present which is offered as underwritten by God. Meaning does not rest in a patriarchal order but with the great patriarch in the sky: there are no intermediate steps. God is the law, word, father. The authority of the text is not located in any subject with attendant socio-economic conditions: access to the logos liberates it from this. Authority rests in the word, and the power to speak it. Trapnel in a narrative passage presents temptation as a 'hoarseness' which mars speaking: it is the Devil, rather than human agencies, which might threaten to silence her.

Finally, what are the sexual politics of Trapnel's writings? These texts, as I have suggested, comment on politico/spiritual issues from a multiple subject-position – trance voice/God/Trapnel – in a way which attempts to subvert gender distinctions, and the problems of a woman writing. The prophetic voice is never an 'I', a unified subject, and therefore is never directly addressing the symbolic order from a marginal (feminine) position. To a humanist/feminist criticism they are not readily recognizable as 'feminist'; there is no obvious *woman* standing behind the text to guarantee it as 'women's writing', nor do the texts consistently or explicitly pursue the notion of the oppression of women.

If Cromwell was using millenarian language in 1653, by 1654 he was one of the culprits in Trapnel's visionary texts. After 1654 and the fall of the Barebones Parliament the Fifth Monarchists were in opposition; in her vision of the bulls Anna Trapnel reread the Bible in order to read Cromwell in relation to the new situation in which he was the enemy. The millennial sects were marginalized for the rest of the 1650s, and after the restoration of Charles II in 1660 their situation worsened once more. I want to use the example of Jane Lead, who joined John Pordage's group at Bradfield when her husband died and who published prophetic writings in the last two decades of the seventeenth century, to examine the relationship between disenfranchised Puritan polemic and religious rhetoric. Jane Lead claimed to have 'communed with good and evil spirits' and certainly claimed to be able to distinguish between them.[28]

From this it is possible to map out briefly a connection between marginalized prophetic writing, gender and rhetoric. Recently rhetoricians have been attempting to articulate the connections between magic and rhetoric, starting from the assumption that rhetoric is a sanctioned form of persuasion and making something out of the multiple nothings that are words, and magic an unsanctioned discourse which also makes something out of nothing. Lead's endless visions, dreams and contemplations demonstrate a different appeal to authority – one based on marginalization in both genre and discourse (a marginalization which has been re-enacted by literary history, feminist or otherwise, which has seen prophetic writing as peripheral, doomed, uninteresting for those without faith). As John O. Ward argued recently, 'the conjunction of magic and rhetoric ... promises interesting insights into both *authorised* social and intellectual power structures ... and *unauthorised* ones'.[29]

It has been my contention that both before and after the Restoration the conjunction of radical religious discourse and rhetoric would serve to illuminate authorized and unauthorized power structures in terms of gender. Ward goes on to point to the distinction between control (which he associates with legitimate rhetoric, ultimately the sanctioned exegesis of the state church in the case of Protestantism) and a less satisfactory category 'emotional power' which attends unsanctioned rhetoric, such as prophecy (pp. 66, 72). In terms of historical circumstances we might draw broad parallels between the punishment of nonconformists in post-Restoration England and other religious deviants, but more circumstantial evidence is available in the characterization of the worship of Ranters and Brownists as secret rites and rituals and the accusations of witchcraft levelled against women prophets such as Trapnel. A poignant example is that of Mary Adams who features in *The Ranters Monster* (1652). A Baptist, then Familist and finally Ranter, Mary Adams's sad story is told by way of an awful warning in the introduction to the pamphlet:

The Ranters Monster: Being a True Relation of one Mary Adams living at

Tillingham in Essex, who named herself the Virgin Mary, blasphemously affirming that she was conceived with child by the Holy Ghost; that from her should spring forth the saviour of the world; and that those who did not believe in him were damned; with the manner how she was delivered of the ugliest ill-shapen *Monster* that ever eyes beheld, and afterwards rotted away in prison.[30]

This suggests clearly enough the associations made by the dominant church between antinomianism and its wild exegesis and rhetoric, diabolism (evidenced in the monster) and femininity. In another article on witchcraft Peter Brown uses Mary Douglas's insight that the practitioner of sorcery is likely to be interstitial, inhabiting the borderland between systems of power. Such a position seems to me strongly to recall the social organization in which women prophets operated, excluded from the centres of political power and speech on the grounds of gender, sometimes demonized and hunted as witches (as in Trapnel's *Report and Plea*), as prophets fostered but also perhaps policed by their religious peers (as is clear in the mediation of Mary Cary's *Little Horns Doom and Downfall*) and inhabiting a Protestant rhetoric 'by the Power of the Lord' which might use the Pauline injunction against them (as I have suggested in relation to Margaret Fell's *Women's Speaking Justified* and as the Baptists did through their literal use of the Bible).

Thus women prophets and their claims to authority exist between two (at least two) social contexts, one religious rhetoric as expounded by those in control and the other the shifting perceptions of gender in the sects – Quakers, Fifth Monarchists, Baptists. The apparent mysticism (even occultism) of the visions of Jane Lead seems to me to signal the role of gender in a culture of nonconformity which, in the period following the Restoration found itself marginalized. Lead's increasingly millenarian thought and her isolation in a community suggest the transformation of the role of the female prophetic voice after the Restoration from the interstitial position between dominant and alternative cultures to a new border between the marginalized silenced sects, and mainly silenced women prophets, and the occult. Lead describes her visions including the meaning of beasts seen and their Biblical and millennial implications (see her *Signs of the Times*).[31] The interstitial status of the woman prophet in the 1640s and early 1650s is suggested by the way in which in 1649 Eleanor Douglas reprinted the judgement of the court against her when she prophesied the death of Charles I. Under the new order she reprints her condemnation by the old (her judges recommended 'Excommunication', 'Bedlam') as vindication of her status and absolute authority as a prophet of the 1640s.

Indeed, read in the light of events up to 1649, Douglas's pre-war condemnation does suggest a corresponding change in status is due to her, but in each case it is her position between (and subject to) both sanctioned (monarchical/legal) and unsanctioned (religious, prophetic, millenarian) discourses. What changed is the power relations between the two discourses. The first had denied her authority in the 1630s when she predicted the death of Charles I, and this may have strengthend her authority when the millenarian discourse moved towards the centres of power in the 1640s; after all, her judges had accused her as follows:

> touching those matters of high nature, which concerned his Majesty [i.e. her prediction of his death] the Court did not anyways proceed against her, as holding them of too high a nature for this *Court* to meddle withal, but forasmuch as she took upon her (which much unbeseemed her Sex) not only to interpret the Scriptures, and withal the most intricate and hard places of the Prophet *Daniel*, but also to be a Prophetess, falsely pretending to have received certain Revelations from God, and had compiled certain Books of such her fictions and false Prophesies and Revelations.[32]

She was imprisoned and the keeper told not to supply 'pen, ink or paper to write anything in respect that she hath so much abused her liberty in that kind already'.[33] The nature of her punishment reminds us that for a woman access to written words depended on a relationship not only to God but to a whole socio-cultural system beginning with the family (which Lady Eleanor, like several other prophets, evaded).

If Eleanor Douglas's pre-war persecutions lent her some credibility in an age of prophecy, but one where women might also be driven out of their churches for speaking, the situation was more extreme after the Restoration. Lead's mystic and even occult visions, like Ann Wentworth's individual project for New Jerusalem, suggest that after the Restoration, prophecy, and women's prophecy in particular, was placed on an outer border of consciousness, overlapping with madness and the occult. The way in which these texts attempt to manipulate the codes which authorize prophetic speaking, and how such textual assertions alongside various mediations suggest both a concept of authority and a social context operates to police prophets in a way quite distinct from the free spiritual speech and access to truth which their prophecies assert.

Women's prophecy of the seventeenth century can be seen as drawing on a range of contradictory codes and meanings to emphasize and underwrite their prophetic status. I began this essay by calling attention to the way prophetic utterance, or writing, endeavours to mediate between writing (and rhetoric) and speaking (and experience); as the essay progressed I hope it became clearer that this was not the only contradiction. The women present themselves as lacking agency, yet the texts I have examined negotiate a special position for women prophets in relation to God. Both Trapnel and Cary are at pains to establish the high status of prophecy in relation to the ministry of the gathered churches. The female body was also a theatrical signifier in the way the women refused food, had visions, fell into trances – again Trapnel is probably the most theatrical of these. As Diane Purkiss says, 'the staging of the divine voice emanating from a female body' meant that women were constantly negotiating 'their bodily and spiritual identities'.[34]

Most important, however, for a reader of printed texts, is the multiplication of subject-positions found in prophetic writing, and which I have elucidated in the writing of Fell, Cary, Trapnel and Lead. Cary presents her prophecy as reading the typological and historical signs of the times, registering her position as free of agency, an instrument who, nevertheless, is filled with the authority to 'read' the signs. Trapnel talks to God, sees visions, and like Wentworth she constantly draws on Biblical intertexts. But the question of who, exactly, speaks shifts: the authority of her text is in the relationship between her and God. Wentworth's Biblical intertexts and denials of madness work to voice the scripture intertextually through her own voice, and Lead offers her own spiritual methodology as a guarantee of her visions. Thus, although the prophetic 'experience' and 'understanding' are central to women's prophecy, such claims are very carefully validated by the rhetoric of the texts. I would suggest, by way of a generalization, that these texts seek to evade the dangerous charge of not having the 'Power of the Lord' (Margaret Fell's phrase again) by putting the authorizing voice of their text into perpetual motion in between – between speech and writing, between an agent and an instrument. The prophet herself and her voice is the 'vessel' between God and the people, between the Bible and the present (Trapnel, Wentworth), at the interstices of typology, history and contemporary politics (Cary), between gender and un-gender.

Perhaps these textual manoeuvres themselves suggest a social context; certainly, the mediation, policing, validation and rejection of women's prophecy can be seen to be central to their texts, as I have shown; we can see the shifting authority of women's prophecy as between opening up and structuring new potentially anti-patriarchal conceptualizations of political and religious authority, at the same time as attempting to negotiate the material dangers which attend upon a woman claiming the highest privileges of a spiritual elite in a culture which was predicated on 'women' being what men were not, but also on the subordination of women to men (we remember the charges against Trapnel, Douglas, Elizabeth Poole).

Finally, it is this implicit but continuous rejection of the patriarchal model of authority which has made the prophets invisible to feminist scholars searching, in Francis Barker's phrase, for similarity deployed along a continuum.[35] Monarchist and literary texts from the same period are available to an a-historicized humanist definition of feminism, or women, because, in both their feminist and anti-feminist modes they ascribe all authority to *men*. They emerge from a set of political ideas which perceive the king and father as absolute ruler: the recognizability of Margaret Cavendish's texts as feminist rests on their emergence from a conservative politics which sought to reinforce the supremacy of king and father. The multiple positions of authority available to a republican text, or a millenarian one such as Cary's or Trapnel's prophecy, or Fell's polemic, or Lead's visions, both bypass earthly powers and negotiate with them: authority is in speaking, but also in manipulating an audience that was material rather than heavenly. But the texts do not invoke a king or father.

The marginalization of seventeenth-century prophetic discourse in relation to the literary canon, and the repeated movement of marginalization in the work of male and feminist scholars, means that the power structures of the seventeenth century appear to be patriarchal, organicist or Hobbesian. But perhaps prophetic discourse offers us a gap in those moments of the grand narrative of the history of political thought. It also enables us to consider the relationship between gender, religio-political theory and specific circumstances in relation to women's entry into discourse. As Philippe Sollers notes,

> the historical field is *discontinuous*; it discloses, first, the exclusion by means of which 'literary history' has made and continues to make its ideological profit, exclusion in the sense of 'repression' or 'negation' (Freud). Its strategic points, its *borders*, are designated by the words 'mysticism', 'eroticism', 'madness'.[36]

Sollers here places the texts excluded by literary history as ensuring the value of those it includes: women's prophecy undercuts literary history, and some emergent feminist literary histories, by disclosing a concept of authority which is double, treble, multiple and perpetually shifting, disappearing and negotiating.

NOTES

1 Mary Cary, *The Resurrection of the Witness* (London, 1648 version), p. 67.
2 Hester Biddle, *A Warning From the Lord God of Life and Power Unto the City of London and to the Suburbs Round about thee* (London, 1660).
3 See Elaine Hobby, *Virtue of Necessity: English Women's Writing 1649–88* (London, 1988), p. 29.
4 Christine Berg and Philippa Berry, 'Spiritual Whoredom: An Essay on Female Prophets in the Seventeenth Century', in *Literature and Power in the Seventeenth Century*, ed. Francis Barker (Essex, University of Essex), 1981: 'prophecy in its most exaggerated form – that is, in the form in which it most clearly distinguishes itself from a rational discourse – has much in common with that phenomenon described by Luce Irigaray as "the language of the feminine", and by Julia Kristeva as the semiotic' (p. 39).
5 *Kissing the Rod: An Anthology of Seventeenth-Century Women's Verse*, ed. G.Greer (London, Virago), 1988. Exceptions include *Her Own Life* and *Virtue of Necessity*.
6 See, for example, *Youth's Glory and Death's Banquet, Playes*, London, 1662, Part 1, Act 3, sc. 5, p. 131; *The Worlds Olio* (London, 1653), p. 41.
7 The editor of the Augustan reprint sees Fell as only continuing the work of Fox, page v. As Elaine Hobby notes, other earlier defences of women's right to prophesy included Richard Farnworth's *A Woman Forbidden to Speak* (1654), Priscilla Cotton and Mary Cole, *To the Priests and People of England* (1655). See Hobby, op. cit., pp. 43–4.

8 Ann-Rosalind Jones, 'Surprising Fame: Renaissance Gender Ideologies and Women's Lyric', in Nancy K. Miller, *Poetics of Gender* (Columbia, 1986), p. 80.

9 Margaret Fell, *Women's Speaking Justified* (London, 1666), reprinted Augustan Reprints no. 194, 1979. Subsequent references are in the text.

10 See, for example, Nigel Smith on the ambiguous status of dreams, *Perfection Proclaimed: Language and Literature in English Radical Religion 1640–1660* (Oxford, 1989), pp. 73–103.

11 See Elspeth Graham, Hilary Hinds, Elaine Hobby, Helen Wilcox, eds, *Her Own Life: Autobiographical Writings by Seventeenth-Century Englishwomen* (London, 1989), esp. p. 123.

12 Mary Cary, *A Word in Season to the Kingdom of England* (London, 1647). Subsequent references are in the text.

13 Mary Cary, *The Resurrection of the Witness* (London, 1648). Subsequent references are in the text. This tract was reprinted in ?1653 with corrections probably drawn from *The Account Audited* (London, 1649), which responded to *The Resurrection of the Witness*.

14 *A Brief Dialogue Between a Zelotopist, one of the daughters of a Zealous Roundhead, and Superstition* (London, 1642), *The Mistris Parliament Plays* (London, 1648), ed. Lois Potter, *Analytical and Enumerative Bibliography*, NS vol. 1, no. 3, 1987, pp. 100–71, *The Famous Tragedy of Charles I* (London, 1648). See also *The Life and Death of Mistris Mary Frith* (London, 1662), A2v–A3v.

15 For the debate on the Ranters and Marxist versus revisionist versus 'oppositionist' historiography, see Christopher Hill, *The World Turned Upside Down* (Middlesex, 1975); J. C. Davies, *Fear, Myth and History* (Cambridge, 1986). A recent article is an important analysis of different ways of thinking about history: James Holstun's 'Ranting at the New Historicism', in *English Literary Renaissance*, nV, 19, no. 2, 1989, pp. 189–226.

16 Graham *et al.* (eds), op. cit., p. 181.

17 Alfred Cohen, 'The Fifth Monarchy Mind', *Social Research* vol. 31, no. 2, 1964, pp. 195–213, p. 200. There are problems with Cohen's argument about totalitarian thinking and he gives a perhaps rather misleading idea of the aim of Cary's prophecy.

18 *The Little Horn's Doom and Downfall* (London, 1651). Subsequent references are in the text.

19 Cary's claim is challenged by Alfred Cohen who compares it to the tract *The Glorious Exercise of the Spirit*, 1645, which he finds theologically very different: Alfred Cohen, *A Biographical Dictionary of British Radicals in the Seventeenth Century*, ed. Richard L. Greaves and Robert Zaller (Brighton, 1983), 3 vols, vol. 1, p. 128.

20 *The Writings and Speeches of Oliver Cromwell*, ed. Wilbur Cortez Abbot (Cambridge, 1937), vol. 3, p. 67.

21 ibid., p. 65, 'Speech to the Nominated Parliament July 4 1653'. Elizabeth Poole, the Baptist prophet, spoke to the government; her message was against the regicide.

22 Nigel Smith, *Perfection Proclaimed*, p. 51.

23 Sarah Wight, *A Wonderful Pleasant and Profitable Letter Written by Mrs Sarah Wight* (London, 1656). Nigel Smith, ibid., p. 51.

24 Berg and Berry, op. cit., p. 38.

25 See also Hobby, *Virtue of Necessity*, op. cit., pp. 31–2; Nigel Smith, pp. 46–51. Smith notes that 'At Whitehall she was visited by many people, members of government and respectable society as well as Fifth Monarchists' (p. 51).

26 Anna Trapnel, *The Cry of A Stone* (London, 1654). Subsequent references are in the text.

27 Anna Trapnel, *Anna Trapnel's Report and Plea* (London, 1654).

28 Jane Lead, *The Enochian Walks With God* (London, 1694), p. 19.

29 John O. Ward, 'Magic and Rhetoric From Antiquity to the Renaissance: Some Ruminations', *Rhetorica* vol. VI, no. 1, Winter 1988, pp. 57–118, p. 57. See also Mary Douglas's influential analysis of sorcery as interstitial which I draw on here: *Purity and Danger* (London, 1966), new edition 1984, pp. 171–9.

30 *The Ranters Monster* (London, 1652), Reprints of English Books 1475–1700, ed. Joseph Arnold-Foster, 1940, p. 1.

31 Jane Lead, *Signs of the Times* (London, 1699), pp. 1–2.

32 Eleanor Douglas, *The Blasphemous Charge Against Her* (London, 1649), p. 10.

33 ibid., p. 13.

34 Diane Purkiss, 'Producing the voice, consuming the body', forthcoming.

35 Francis Barker, *The Tremulous Private Body* (London, 1984), pp. 15–41.

36 Philippe Sollers, *Writing and the Experience of Limits* (New York, Columbia University Press, 1983), p. 6.

Part IV

Representations

Chapter 12

Getting down to basics: art, obscenity and the female nude

Lynda Nead

Avoid 'glamour' poses that exaggerate the model's charms like a publicity photograph of a star. Such paintings tend to look like caricatures. For the same reason, don't exaggerate details like eyelashes, ruby lips, pink cheeks, painted fingernails or toenails. In fact, it's usually best for the model to wear a minimum of makeup. In general, avoid *all* kinds of exaggeration. A nude figure in a natural, relaxed, harmonious pose is inherently beautiful.[1]

I don't know much about ART – but I like looking at NUDE ladies (plate 1).[2]

This essay is concerned with the ways in which the categories of 'art' and 'obscenity' are defined and differentiated and the critical place of representations of the female nude within this cultural process. The first extract takes the form of a piece of friendly advice from a painter and critic to his readers. Potential painters of the female nude are guided away from any signs which connote the popular or the vulgar (publicity shots and glamour photography) and are steered instead towards the apparently natural and inherently beautiful forms of the female nude. Artifice must be eschewed and above all the constructions and manipulations which go into the representation of the female nude must be obscured; the female nude must appear natural and unadorned. Distinctions are what are important here. The exaggerations and commercialization of non-art are set against the honesty and harmony of the high art tradition.

And then there is the caption from a 'new wave' comic postcard, sold in the Cartoon Gallery in Bloomsbury, London. The joke is not very original or particularly funny but it does present some important and popular conceptions of the female nude. Its humour rests on our perhaps awkward *recognition* of the attitude expressed by the cartoon character and the identification of a paradox centred on the female nude.

More than any other subject, the female nude connotes 'Art'; it is the most important icon of Western culture, a kind of hieroglyph which expresses civilization and accomplishment. And yet there is something awkward about the nude. At the centre of art but also at the very edge of the category, it

Plate 12.1 Mel Calman, 'I don't know much about art, but . . .', Artist's Cards, London, no. 17. Reproduced by kind permission of The Cartoon Gallery, London

involves a risk. The female nude pushes to the edge, presses to the very limit and can spill over into something which is not art at all but a cliché, a poor joke, smut, even obscenity. The cartoon plays, gently, on this issue of transgression. It illustrates the dual nature of the female nude: easel painting, subject of high art, but also always consumable as 'body'. In the cartoon the insistent black pencil line 'framing' the nude attempts to contain the 'subject' – colour, form, 'Art' itself – from merger with the earthly desires which lie outside the frame.

The cartoon and the art manual are part of a process of cultural categorization which defines acceptable and unacceptable forms of representation and differentiates the elevated and elevating from the vulgar and degrading. But to understand the ways in which this process works and how art is defined we will have to focus on the edges or limits of the category, where judgements of what is *in*trinsic or *ex*trinsic to the proper concerns of art are made. It will involve what Jacques Derrida, in *The Truth of Painting*, has called 'a discourse on the frame'.[3]

But let's begin with a text which is located firmly within art historical discourse, Kenneth Clark's *The Nude*, first published in 1956 and currently sold in the eighth edition of a Penguin paperback. Clark's book has become the classic survey of the nude and there have been curiously few scholarly attempts to revise or rework it.[4] The text stands as a monument to official culture. In his lifetime Lord Clark held almost every influential, public position within British culture: Director of the National Gallery, Surveyor of the Royal Collection, Chairman of the Arts Council, Chairman of the Independent Television Authority and so on. Publicly, his reputation was largely established by his television series *Civilization* which was broadcast in Britain in 1969–70. And although his contribution to art history may now seem rather outmoded, the continuing healthy sales of his books should prevent us from dismissing his work too precipitously. The significance of *The Nude* now partly lies in the fact that it has remained one of the only serious major surveys of the most central subject within Western visual culture.

The Nude traces the history of the male and female nude from Greek antiquity to European modernism. Throughout this narrative Clark wrestles with the competing impulses of sensory and contemplative pleasures, trying to hold them together in a balanced combination without allowing either element to dominate judgement. Again and again, when assessing a female nude, he expresses the need to balance the appreciation of pure artistic form and the response to the content concerned: the body. It is this combination of abstraction and representation which, according to Clark, makes the nude unique.

Perhaps the best known passage of the book is where Clark differentiates the naked and the nude. It is a distinction between bodies deprived of clothes, 'huddled and defenceless', and the body 'clothed' in art: the nude, the body re-formed rather than de-formed – 'balanced, prosperous and confident'.[5] The transformation from the naked to the nude is thus the shift from the actual to the ideal; the move from a perception of unformed, corporeal matter to the recognition of unity and control, the controlled economy of art. It is this process of transfiguration which renders the nude the perfect subject for the work of art. As Clark states early on in the book, 'The nude remains the most complete example of the transmutation of matter into form' (p. 23).

Predictably enough Clark begins with classical antiquity and the Greek ideal of the nude based on mathematics, proportion and harmony. This regulation of sensory and organic perceptions through order and geometry reaches its apotheosis in Leonardo's 'Vitruvian man' (plate 2). Here the matter/form dichotomy is brought to a temporary resolution, with the male nude perfectly articulated through mathematical relations – the body as pure form.

But the resolution of matter and form cannot be accomplished in the same way in the representation of the *female* nude. Historically, the female body – woman – has occupied a secondary or supplementary role in Western religion and philosophy. As Eve, formed from one of Adam's ribs, woman was created to assuage Adam's own sense of loneliness. The Adam and Eve pairing is a founding opposition within Western thought. The two terms share a structural link (i.e. Adam's rib) but they are not equal. The primary subject is Adam; Eve has a supplementary function, secondary but threatening since her existence always testifies to the basic lack in Adam, the primary term. Many other value oppositions map on to this man/woman relationship including the culture/nature pairing: if the male signifies culture, order, geometry (perfectly visualized in Vitruvian man), the female stands for nature, physicality – biologically determined and potentially wayward. Now, if art is defined as the conversion of matter into form, then imagine how much greater the triumph for art if it is the *female* body that is thus transformed. Pure nature transmuted, through the forms of art, into pure culture. The female nude, then, is not simply one subject among others, one form among many, it is *the* subject, *the* form.

These sets of values and beliefs can be seen working in Clark's chapters on the female nude. Initially, he attempts to keep the sensual and the spiritual apart by dividing the female nude into distinct types: Venus (1) and Venus (2) or the Celestial Venus and the Earthly Venus. But his entire assessment of the Western tradition is based on the assumption that artists have made vulgar objects celestial through the controlling discipline of artistic form. He compares two early representations of the female nude: a prehistoric figure of a woman (plate 3) and a Cycladic doll (plate 4), which he designates respectively Vegetable and Crystalline Venus. In the first example, the body is lumpy and protruding but in the second image, 'the unruly human body has undergone a geometrical discipline' (p. 64). This is the important point; the female body has undergone a process of containment, of holding in and

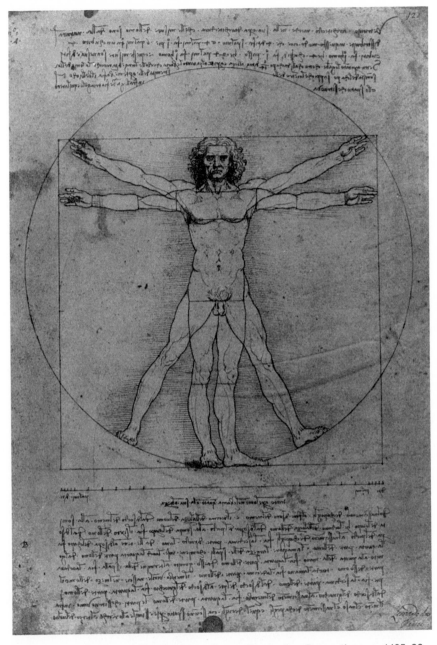

Plate 12.2 Leonardo da Vinci, *Human Figure Illustrating Proportions*, c. 1485–90.
Venice Accademia

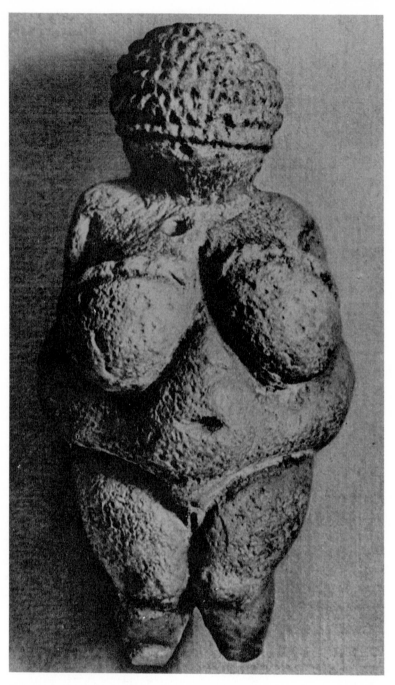

Plate 12.3 Prehistoric figure of a woman (the Willendorf Venus), 21,000 BC.
Vienna Natural History Museum

Plate 12.4 Cycladic marble doll, 2,500–1,100 BC. Reproduced by courtesy of the Trustees of the British Museum

keeping out. The contour, the frame of the body has been sharpened, thus hardening the distinction between inside and outside, between figure and ground. The female body has become art by containing and controlling the limits of the form, precisely by framing it. So the female nude is more than a picture with a nude inside it; rather, by giving a frame to the body, the female nude symbolizes the transforming effects of art generally; it is complete, it is its own picture, with inside, outside and frame.

Clark attempts to make the relationship of the female figure and artistic form a natural one; he argues that the conventions of art are particularly suited to the natural contours of the female body. For example, he takes the classical pose of the weight resting on the right leg with the left leg bent as if to move (plate 5). The pose, he writes, was invented for the male figure but had a greater and more lasting impact on the representation of the female body (plate 6). He explains:

> this disposition of balance has automatically created a contrast between the arc of one hip, sweeping up till it approaches the sphere of the breast, and the long, gentle undulation of the side which is relaxed; and it is to this beautiful balance of form that the female nude owes its plastic authority to the present day.

(p. 71)

According to this rationalization, the female body is naturally predisposed to the contours of art; it seems simply to await the act of artistic regulation.

Things, however, are not quite as under control as might first appear, and signs of the physical, sensory world regularly interrupt the smooth contours of the female nude. The most significant cause of these breaks appears to be the personal desires of individual artists. Clark reads brush marks and lines as though they are part of a symbolic language of sensual impulses, telling traces of sexual desire. For example, his critical eye detects that: 'behind the severe economy of Botticelli's drawing we can feel how his hand quickens or hesitates with his eye those inflections of the body which awaken desire' (plate 7, p. 99). But although desire can be awakened it needs to be kept under control; the armour of artistic form can be relaxed but it cannot easily be removed entirely. Clark goes to considerable lengths to try and specify the degree of physicality which can be integrated within the nude without upsetting the unity and integrity of art. Thus Correggio's figure of Antiope in *Jupiter and Antiope* (plate 8) is described as being 'as seductive as possible' but 'the reverse of obscene' (p. 127). Seductive but *not* obscene. Now we might ask *why* Clark needs to make this point, why he needs to make this careful manoeuvre between a seductiveness that is permissible within the limits of art and a category of obscenity which goes beyond art, which is outside of art. Art is being defined in terms of the containing of form within limits; obscenity, on the other hand, is defined in terms of excess, as form beyond limit, beyond the frame.

Plate 12.5 After Polyclitus, *Doryphoros*, *c.* 450 BC. Museo Archeologico
Nazionale, Naples

Plate 12.6 Bronze figure of a girl, *c.* 400 BC. Staatliche Antikensammlungen und Glyptothek, Munich

Plate 12.7 Sandro Botticelli, *The Birth of Venus*, c. 1485. Uffizi, Florence

Plate 12.8 Antonio Correggio, *Jupiter and Antiope*, 1524–5. Musée du Louvre

As might be anticipated, Rubens provides Clark with a particularly demanding case for appraisal but the critic again uses the form/matter opposition to affirm the artist's status (plate 9).

> [Rubens] learnt what a severe formal discipline the naked body must undergo if it is to survive as art. Rubens' nudes seem at first sight to have been tumbled out of a cornucopia of abundance; the more we study them the more we discover them to be under control.
>
> (p. 133)

So all is well: form triumphs over matter, and style is privileged over substance. There is an interesting economic dimension to Clark's language too. If, as we have already seen in his description of the nude, the ideal figure is balanced and prosperous, then this model of artistic practice as a kind of controlled economy is developed in his assessment of Rubens. The image of excess, presented by a 'cornucopia of abundance' is brought under control; the female bodies are not tumbling out and beyond the procedures of art and parsimony but are regulated through the discipline of form and thus are able to survive as art.

So we can begin to see the sets of values which Clark is working with; a category of *art* which is concerned with stylistic procedure and form, and a category of *obscenity* which seems to do with excess and lack of boundaries. Furthermore, the two categories are not held apart, away from each other, but are abutting, touching, exerting a pressure at their defining edges. Too close for comfort.

Clark's procedure can be fully exposed by looking at the examples he selects to demonstrate failure to assert control, where the image goes beyond the edge, beyond art. The first is the work of Jan Gossart which, for reasons which will become clear, Clark does not illustrate in his book (plate 10). Clark describes Gossart's work as an unhappy mixture of Italian style and Flemish realism; he continues:

> This unresolved mixture of conventions has the result of making Gossart's nudes curiously indecent. They seem to push their way forward till they are embarrassingly near to us, and we recognise how necessary it is for the naked body to be clothed by a consistent style.
>
> (p. 322)

Here the artistic process seems to be working in the opposite direction; form has devolved back into matter, pure form has been turned into something impure, and Clark's language suggests that the figures threaten to break away from the edge of the picture surface. The figures become lifelike, physical, they 'push their way forward' so that faced with this violation of artistic procedure we become embarrassed rather than elevated. It is the overlapping, the unstructured blending of conventions in Gossart's art which produces this disorder; coherent style is necessary to encase and enclose the nude.

Plate 12.9 Peter Paul Rubens, *The Three Graces*, *c.* 1639. Museo del Prado

Plate 12.10 Jan Gossart, *Neptune and Amphitrite*, 1516. Staatliche Museen zu Berlin Gemaldegalerie, Bode-Museum. Foto: Staatliche Museen zu Berlin

Another example of failure to assert formal control over the matter of the female body is provided by Georges Rouault, but in this case Clark's conclusion is significantly different. Considering Rouault's series of prostitutes, he writes (plate 11):

> All those delicate feelings which flow together in our joy at the sight of an idealised human body ... are shattered and profaned ... from the point of view of form, all that was realised in the nude in its first creation, the sense of healthy structure, the clear geometric shapes and their harmonious disposition has been rejected in favour of lumps of matter, swollen and inert.
>
> (p. 333)

What exactly has happened here? The ideals of the nude: structure, geometry, harmony, have given way to unhealthy, unformed lumps of matter. More specifically, Clark refers to both the image of the body and the feelings of the viewer as having been profaned, that is, desecrated, violated. Profane means literally 'outside the temple' and once again we have an image of the body that connotes an inside and an outside, a distinction, here, between the sacred and the defiled. Rouault's female nude has been broken up (shattered) and has broken out of its framing contours. The body is swollen, it is in excess of art. But Clark goes on to state that the image was conceived in a spirit of religion and that it inspires us with awe and fear; it is apparently sublime. Now this notion of sublimity would seem to contradict the earlier perception of the image as shattered and beyond the temple, the framing limits of art. But I want to suggest that the image is being defined precisely in terms of the sublime. If the ideal nude in art, the beautiful, is conceived of in terms of the perception of unity and harmonious completeness, then the image created by Rouault belongs to a different category, a category which invokes awe and fear through the recognition of something beyond human limitation and control.

So far, I have identified a set of value oppositions (art/obscenity, intrinsic/extrinsic, form/matter, etc.) which form the basis of Clark's critical language and judgement; to this set of pairings I have also now added the beautiful and the sublime. In using these categories Clark is not inventing a new set of aesthetic criteria, but is adopting and working within a system which has dominated the philosophy of art before and since Kant. So, in order to understand what may be at stake in this system, it is necessary to go beyond the particularities of Clark's text and to consider, more generally, the history of aesthetics.

Modern European aesthetics is generally held to have its origins in the eighteenth century and the attempt by writers such as Winckelmann, Lessing, Burke and Baumgarten to provide universal principles for the classification, judgement and experience of beauty, and especially of works of art. But the question of taste and aesthetic judgement can be traced back further to the

Plate 12.11 Georges Rouault, *A Prostitute*, *c*. 1904. Bakwin Collection, New York

roots of the Western philosophical tradition in the Platonic concept of ideal forms. Plato argued that objects which we encounter in sensory experience are mere tokens or echoes of absolute forms which lie beyond the reach of our senses and beyond physical experience. The basic set of distinctions which was established through the Platonic system – between the ideal and the actual, between mind and body, between form and matter – also formed the framework of Enlightenment aesthetics. Again, as in the Adam/Eve pairing, it is wrong to see both terms in these pairs as equal. In each case, one term occupies a primary position whilst the other functions as an accessory or supplement. And as the French feminist Hélène Cixous has shown, the dichotomies of Western metaphysics have never been sexually neutral but are gendered according to the classic heterosexual coupling of male and female.[6] Thus, in Western religion and philosophy, form (the male) is preferred over matter (the female); mind and spirit are privileged over body and substance and throughout the history of metaphysics the only way to give meaning and order to matter in nature has been through the imposition of technique and rhetoric, or style, if you prefer. This powerful tradition has been systematically adopted within modern aesthetics and Kenneth Clark is simply one element in this history.

Immanuel Kant's *Critique of Aesthetic Judgement* (1790) was fundamental in the formation of European aesthetics and its influence is still easily discernible in art history and criticism today although usually in a somewhat 'hand-me-down' and popularized way.

The form/matter opposition governs the whole of the *Critique*.[7] Kant sought to distinguish sensory from contemplative pleasures. According to Kant, although the pleasure experienced in the beautiful is immediate, it involves a reflection on the object and this sets it apart from the merely sensuous pleasures which may be derived, for example, from eating or drinking. Aesthetic pleasure is thus more refined than physical forms of pleasure since it necessarily involves the 'higher' faculty of contemplation. Perhaps one of the most influential of Kant's ideas was the axiom that the individual object is detached in aesthetic judgement and considered simply for 'its own sake'. The art object should serve no ulterior purpose and aesthetic judgement itself should be disinterested; the observer's desires and ambitions should be held in abeyance in the act of pure contemplation. Kant also distinguished 'free' from 'dependent' beauty; the first derived without the aid of conceptualization, the second requiring an interest in the material existence of the object. For Kant the judgement of 'dependent' beauty is necessarily less pure or open to abstraction than the contemplation of 'free' beauty. Whereas examples of free beauty are found in nature they are rarely seen in art; art usually requires some conceptualization of the subject expressed. This system establishes a hierarchy of aesthetic experience. As far as possible, judgement should be free of interest both in relation to the material condition of the individual object and the aims and desires of the viewer, for it is only through this act of liberation from individual preference that a judgement may be claimed as universally valid for all rational beings.

This set of distinctions may seem clear enough but it has been devastatingly analysed and dismantled by Derrida in his essay entitled 'Parergon' included in the collection *The Truth in Painting*. Derrida makes an apparently simple observation: in order to make a 'pure' judgement you have to be able to judge what is intrinsic to the object and thus the proper concern of aesthetic judgement and what is extrinsic to the object and thus irrelevant. This permanent requirement, Derrida writes, structures all philosophical discourses on art and, most importantly, it 'presupposes a discourse on the limit between the inside and the outside of the art object, here a discourse on the frame' (p. 45).

So Kant's whole analytic of aesthetic judgement presupposes that you *can* distinguish rigorously between the intrinsic and the extrinsic. Judgement should properly bear upon intrinsic beauty (which is within the proper limits of art) and not upon mere decoration or sensuous appeal (which are outside the limits). According to Kant (and we have seen the same values operating in Clark's book) what is bad, what is outside or goes beyond aesthetic taste and judgement is matter, that which is motivated, sensory matter which seduces, which embarrasses or leads the viewer astray, away from the proper consideration of intrinsic form.

But how, or where, are these distinctions between form and matter, between intrinsic and extrinsic made? Derrida suggests that the critical place of judgement is not at the centre of the category where differences are most clear, but at the very limit, at the framing edge of the category where the surplus or secondary term most nearly belongs to the main subject. It is at these crucial edges where the distinction between inside and outside, inclusion and exclusion, acceptability and unacceptability, is most exquisite.

I have been taking this detour via Kant and Derrida because I believe that together they offer a way of understanding the critical importance of the female nude in the tradition of Western art. If we go back to the basic opposition of art and obscenity which I discussed earlier, we can now begin to place the female nude not only at the centre of the definition of art but also on the edge of the category, pushing against the limit, brushing against obscenity. The female nude is the border, the *parergon* as Derrida also calls it, between art and obscenity. The female body – natural, *un*structured – represents something which is outside the proper field of art and aesthetic judgement but artistic style – pictorial form – contains and regulates the body and renders it an object of beauty, suitable for art.

The frame, then, is a metaphor for the 'staging' of art, both in terms of surrounding the body with style and of marking the limit between art and not-art, that is, obscenity. Here, etymology seems to confirm the metaphor. The etymology of 'obscene' is disputed but it may be a modification of the Latin '*scena*', so meaning literally what is off, or to one side of the stage, beyond presentation. Within this context, the art/obscenity pairing represents the distinction between that which *can* be seen and that which is just beyond presentation. The female nude marks both the internal limit of art and the external limit of obscenity. This is why the representation of the female nude is critical. It is the internal structural link which holds art and obscenity and an entire system of meaning together. And whilst the female nude can behave well, it involves a risk and threatens to destabilize the very foundations of our sense of order.

There is just one more relationship which can be introduced to this system. The art/obscenity opposition can also be mapped on to Kant's distinction between the beautiful and the sublime. Following Edmund Burke, Kant differentiated between the experience of the sublime and the experience of the beautiful. He wrote in the *Critique*:

> The beautiful in nature is a question of the form of the object, and this consists in limitation, whereas the sublime is to be found in an object even devoid of form, so far as it immediately involves, or else by its presence provokes, a representation of limitlessness.[8]

So whereas the form of the beautiful is seen to lie in limitation (e.g. in the contemplation of a framed picture), the sublime challenges this act of judgement by suggesting the possibility of form beyond limit. Whereas the sentiment of beauty is predicated on a sense of the harmony between man and nature and the rationality and intelligibility of the world, the sublime is conceived of as a mixture of pleasure, pain and terror which forces us to recognize the limits of rationality.[9] Kant specifies this relationship in terms of framing: the beautiful is characterized by the finitude of its formal contours, as a unity contained, limited, by its borders. The sublime, on the contrary, is presented in terms of excess, of the infinite; *it cannot be framed* and is therefore almost beyond presentation (in a quite literal sense, then, *ob*scene). For Kant the sublime is encountered more readily in nature than in art. If art is defined as the limiting or framing of formed matter, then the sublime must necessarily be beyond or outside the parameters of art.

It is also significant that Kant expresses the distinction between the beautiful and the sublime in relation to the *viewer's experience* of the object. Whereas the pleasure provoked by the beautiful is one of life enhancement which may be united with the play of the imagination, the pleasure (Lüst) which is excited by the sublime is of a different and negative order. According to Kant, the feeling of the sublime arises indirectly; it is characterized by an inhibition of the vital forces and, as a result of this momentary retention, is followed by a 'discharge all the more powerful' (1911, p. 91). It is a violent, explosive experience; serious rather than playful, it goes beyond simple charms and attraction and is caught up in an alternating rhythm of attraction and repulsion.

We can find the echo of this Kantian differentiation of the beautiful and the sublime in Kenneth Clark's attempts to define art and obscenity. Clark describes the experience of beauty as a bringing together of delicate feelings but refers to the figure of the prostitute by Rouault as 'shattered and profaned' – broken up, out of shape; beyond art and yet conceived in a spirit of awe and inspiring fear. For Clark, the figure is sublime and almost beyond representation (obscene).

Of course, for Kant and other eighteenth-century writers on aesthetics, the sublime and the beautiful are clearly gendered. In a gesture towards fairness and balance, Kant observed:

> It is not to be understood ... that woman lacks noble qualities, or that the male sex must do without beauty completely. On the contrary, one expects that a person of either sex brings both together, in such a way that all the other merits of a woman should unite solely to enhance the character of the beautiful, which is the proper reference point; and on the other hand, among the masculine qualities the sublime clearly stands as the criterion of his kind.[10]

Whereas the beautiful is associated with feminine attributes, the sublime is seen characterized by masculine traits. But in the light of this relationship between the sublime and the obscene we arrive at a new and more subtly nuanced understanding of the gendering of aesthetics. The sublime is not simply the site for the definition of masculinity but is also where a certain deviant or transgressive form of femininity is played out. It is where woman goes beyond her proper boundaries and gets out of place.

But in the final instance the beautiful and the sublime are primarily defined in terms of their effects upon the viewer. Whereas the experience of the sublime is seen to be kinetic, the pleasure of the beautiful is always contemplative. Kant writes: 'The mind feels itself *set in motion* in the representation of the sublime in nature; whereas in the aesthetic judgement upon what is beautiful therein it is in *restful* contemplation' (1911, p. 107).

This opposition of a quiet, contemplative pleasure and a form of excited arousal can be related back to the art/obscenity opposition. The axiom that the experience of high art should be static and reflective and that this differentiates it from the experience of non-artistic forms such as pornography recurs again and again in nineteenth- and twentieth-century European aesthetics. There is an interesting example in James Joyce's *A Portrait of the Artist as a Young Man* (published 1916). The novel presents a dramatized version of Joyce's own early aesthetic. In one passage Stephen Dedalus discusses the function of art with Lynch, a fellow undergraduate. The discussion is provoked by the fact that Lynch has scrawled graffiti on the bottom of the Venus of Praxiteles. Lynch argues that his action was stimulated by desire; Stephen replies:

> The feelings excited by improper art are kinetic, desire or loathing. Desire

urges us to possess, to go *to* something; loathing urges us to abandon, to go *from* something. The arts which excite them, pornographical or didactic, are therefore improper arts. The aesthetic emotion ... is therefore static. The mind is arrested and raised above desire and loathing.[11]

And so we are back with the Greeks and the female nude as an icon of high art but also precariously at the edge of art and able to excite desire – graffiti scrawled on the bottom of the Venus of Praxiteles as the gesture which denies the aesthetic emotion.

There is a set of value oppositions which has dominated the philosophy of art before and since Kant and which organizes the way in which we conceive of the meaning of art and of meaning as such. And yet, as Derrida has shown, categories, or frames, are: 'essentially constructed and therefore fragile'.[12] You cannot be certain of what is intrinsic and extrinsic, you can only engage in a ceaseless definition of contours and edges, limitations and frames. This is what is happening in Kenneth Clark's work; he takes the subject which is right on the edge – the nude – and embarks on a process of definition. We can agree or disagree with his judgements and opinions but this hardly seems the point. Unless we move beyond the traditional terms of the debate we can only engage in a meaningless tug-of-war concerning whether images are more or less obscene, beautiful, sensual, erotic and so on.

And so it is a question of 'getting down to basics' because an investigation of the female nude raises some of the most fundamental values which shape our attitudes to and judgements of art. I have argued that within the Western tradition, art is defined as the transmutation of matter into form and that, within this account, the female body – as nature, pure matter – becomes a most critical subject for art. The female nude stands as the perfect aesthetic achievement and yet also threatens to undo the very principles which structure and sustain the cultural values of art. In the meantime, however, mainstream art will never turn away from the female nude. It cannot afford to. The recent return to the life class is hardly surprising; it is a perpetual question (and I use the word knowingly) of *mastery* over matter.

NOTES

1 W. Blake, *Figures in Oil* (London, 1980), p. 65.
2 Mel Calman, *'I don't know much about art, but ... '*, Artists' Cards (London, no. 17).
3 Jacques Derrida, *The Truth in Painting*, trans. G. Bennington and I. McLeod (Chicago and London), 1987, p. 45.
4 There is of course John Berger's revision of Clark's argument in *Ways of Seeing* (Harmondsworth, 1972). I have discussed this text in 'The Female Nude: Pornography, Art and Sexuality', *Signs*, vol. 15, no. 2, Winter 1990.
5 Kenneth Clark, *The Nude: A Study of Ideal Art* (London, 1956), p. 1.
6 For a fuller discussion of the gendering of metaphysical dichotomies see A. Jardine, *Gynesis: Configurations of Woman and Modernity* (Ithaca and London, 1985), pp. 71–3.

7 For a useful summary of Kant's *Critique of Aesthetic Judgement* see Roger Scruton, *Kant* (Oxford, 1982) on which the following discussion is based.

8 Immanuel Kant, *Critique of Aesthetic Judgement*, trans. J. C. Meredith (Oxford, 1911), p. 90.

9 Kant goes on to argue that it is through this experience of the sublime that we are made aware of divinity. He thus sets up an uneasy tension within the category of the sublime – the site of the divine but also, at the same time, beyond control and fearful. The aesthetic of the sublime and its reworking within post-modernist philosophy is considered by Dick Hebdidge in his fascinating article 'The Impossible Object: Towards a Sociology of the Sublime', *New Formations*, no. 1, Spring 1987, pp. 47–76.

10 Immanuel Kant, *Observations on the Feeling of the Beautiful and Sublime* (1764), trans. J. H. Goldthwait (Berkeley and Los Angeles, 1960), pp. 76–7.

11 James Joyce, *A Portrait of the Artist as a Young Man* (Harmondsworth, 1960), pp. 204–5.

12 Derrida, op. cit., p. 73.

Chapter 13

Do or die:
problems of agency and gender
in the aesthetics of murder

Josephine McDonagh

On a railway journey to Paris and Belgium, D. G. Rossetti is held up in Paris by French bureaucracy. As he waits, he sees the rotting body of a murdered man and imagines the figure of the murderer standing in the crowd beside him, coolly observing his victim:

> You fancy him
> Smoking an early pipe, and watching, as
> An artist, the effect of his last work.[1]

The detached nonchalance of this aesthete-murderer becomes increasingly disturbing as the poet's identification with him deepens. Poet and murderer are finally drawn together, as both are subject to the restrictive practices of passport officialdom and the law.

The aesthete-murderer is something of a feature in nineteenth-century literature. The cult of the murderer as artist was popularized by Thomas De Quincey in a series of essays entitled 'On Murder Considered as One of the Fine Arts' published between 1827 and 1854. Murder and writing are identified as activities perpetrated in the interest of power and pleasure; both are acts of transcendence offering passage beyond the social institutions in which men feel themselves to be trapped, affording the agent the power to act freely, unhampered by the structures of social life. But if Rossetti's murderer is likely to be caught, so is the writer, whose quests for self-empowerment in writing meet with varying degrees of failure and frustration. De Quincey, the opium eater, is perhaps the least empowered and most frustrated of writers in the period, continually inscribing in his lengthy and digressive writings an inability to take control of his pen or his life. For De Quincey, writing is as difficult as murder in Paris when one cannot travel without a passport.

The association of murder and writing in an aesthetic that glorifies the transcendence of art and murder has been criticized recently by feminist critics who argue rightly that such an aesthetic is gendered: it is an inscription of male violence against a feminized object, whether that be a woman, a boy, or as in the case of De Quincey, the entire family. Thus the aesthetic that celebrates art as murder reinforces and legitimates a set of power relations and results in real instances of male violence – assault, rape, murder. However, such a phenomenon rests awkwardly with an aesthetic that has been constituted in relation to a pervading sense of lack of control, as writing inscribes loss of agency and an inability to act. At issue between the aesthetic of murder and this critique is the relationship between representation and power; while the critique asserts that both writer and murderer gain empowerment through their acts, producing and reproducing power and control, the aesthetic of murder is constructed with a sense that both acts lead only to disempowerment and loss of self in the ceaseless circulation of social institutions. The difficulty raises a number of significant questions concerning the nature of representation. We must ask, what is the relation between a representation and its effects? Is it necessary or possible to control representations, and what is to be gained or lost by doing so?

In their book *The Lust to Kill*, Deborah Cameron and Elizabeth Frazer posit a direct relation between physical violence against women, in particular sex murder, and various representations of gender relations in aesthetic, legal, sociological discourses.[2] In our society, cultural codes that exalt violence and celebrate the murderer as a transcendent being are dominant; such codes also work to eliminate society's responsibility for such violence, so that murderers are regarded as deviants, sex beasts and monsters rather than the inevitable products of our own society. They argue that sex murder is an extreme form of masculinity, existing on a continuum in which 'normal sexuality' (i.e. male heterosexuality) also takes its place. This masculinity is constructed and learned from dominant cultural codes through which we all unconsciously order our own experiences. Cameron and Frazer use the example of a pair of spectacles:

> when we contemplate our future acts we have to do it through the 'spectacles' of these concepts; when we attempt to interpret what other people are doing we only have these categories to use as a framework; when we look into our pasts we can only organize them into the patterns given by our culture.[3]

As they also point out, these categories are not fixed, for there is always the opportunity for the formation of new and possibly oppositional concepts such as those suggested by feminism.

Since cultural codes are instrumental in the structuring and understanding of our lives, their book focuses on these representations that work toward the construction of a violent masculinity. In the introduction, answering a possible criticism that they analyse only representations of murder and consequently fail to reach 'the heart of the matter', making the traditional Kantian point, they explain how representations are indeed 'the heart of the matter' and, in a sense, all we can know: there is no possibility of getting any closer to the original act itself, for sex murderers themselves understand and represent their acts through the same categories that are available to us all;

their acts are already represented, and one can only ever engage with those representations. Quoting from Alan Sheridan's discussion of Foucault's edition of the memoirs of the murderer Pierre Rivière, they show how discourses structure and legitimate Rivière's disturbing and transgressive behaviour as, in Sheridan's words, 'Desire, text and action were indissolubly linked, because they were shaped, made possible, therefore in a sense *produced* by a particular "discursive practice".'[4] Cameron and Frazer point out that the 'discursive practice' did not *cause* Rivière to commit the murders but that 'human culture crucially involves processes of representation, and the representations available to Rivière shaped the form of his killing and the way he understood it'.[5]

A significant point that is raised by Rivière's confessions is the way in which murderers have a compulsive need to represent themselves. *The Lust to Kill* is full of accounts of murderers' self-representations: for example, the diaries of the South African sex murderer Ronald Frank Cooper; the letters, diaries, poems and pictures of Dennis Nilsen, the necrophiliac killer of young boys; the photos of Ian Brady; Jack the Ripper's letters to the police; and so on. The interesting point about these examples is the way in which the murderers constantly express the feeling that their accounts are inadequate to represent their actions, their desires, their guilt. For instance, Nilsen's vast body of writings display his frustration at not being able to represent himself accurately; each rationalization of his act gives way to another: he is at once the possessor of a compulsion to kill, a generosity of spirit to comfort his lonely victims, and a schizophrenic personality; finally, he is a 'cold mad killer'. Commenting on this struggle for self-representation, Cameron and Frazer write, 'In his dilemma, finding that the language cannot adequately describe what he is and utterly failing to make up what the language lacks, Nilsen graphically illustrates the extent to which our reality is bound by our discourse.'[6] However, rather than stopping writing in the wake of his frustration, the impossibility of his endeavour seems to make it all the more alluring, and he keeps on trying to find the right words with which to represent himself.

When Nilsen meets this failure to represent his experience with a vast body of aesthetic representations, he is not the first, nor will he be the last, to do so. His response is best understood in terms of the Romantic sublime. For the Romantics after Kant, the sublime experience, in which the subject was confronted and overwhelmed by an unrepresentable experience, such as the infinite magnitude of nature, was followed by a checking or, in Neil Hertz's words, a blockage, in which the subject had consciousness of his inability to comprehend.[7] Wordsworth's celebration of the power of the imagination in *The Prelude* after his strangely unrepresented and unrepresentable experience on the Simplon Pass is clearly conceived in these terms; the imagination, impelled by 'a flash that has revealed / The invisible world', enables him to speak, and he says, 'I recognise Thy glory.'[8] The realm of the aesthetic can thus be seen in terms of a celebration of the mind's consciousness of its inability to comprehend or represent what Kant would call the noumenal world. For Nilsen, the unrepresentable experiences are his acts of murder; his compulsive writings, which moreover consciously aestheticize his murders, can be seen as vain attempts to comprehend his acts.

In fact, Cameron and Frazer characterize Nilsen as 'the Incurable Romantic'. They refer to his aestheticization of the dead body, which they link to the Gothic and an aesthetic of the 'horrid', and his sense of self-affirmation that occurs through the obliteration of the object of his desire. However, this act of self-affirmation is rather odd in Nilsen's account, for it comes from an identification with his victim and the staging of his own death.[9] Thus, he dresses up as a dead body and fantasizes about being the object of another necrophiliac's desire and sees his own murders as acts of self-destruction. Cameron and Frazer quote Nilsen: 'I was engaged primarily in self-destruction. . . . I was killing myself only but it was always the bystander who died.' 'I killed them as I would like to be killed myself. . . . If I did it to others I could experience the death act over and over again.'[10] It is a strange and troubled self-affirmation that comes through the repeated staging of self-destruction. For him murder is an act of will that enables him to take control over his own life through having consciousness of the limits of his own being. Strangely like the anorexic, the murderer attempts to control his own life through the regulation of his own death. However, unlike the female anorexic, the male murderer externalizes this desire and represents his own death through the death of another. Nilsen recognizes that to produce his own death would be self-defeating: it could only happen once, and he would be denied that vital moment of self-consciousness for which he strives. However, a representation is only ever a representation; his need to repeat the experience time and again points to the flawed nature of his attempt. Just as he is unable accurately to represent himself in discourse and thus achieve self-affirmation, the representation of his own death through the murder of another comes up against the same problems. His persistent aestheticizing of the murders shows that the moment of self-consciousness, the point at which he has knowledge of his own limits, can only ever be represented in language, in discourse.

Throughout *The Lust to Kill* Cameron and Frazer discuss the dominant notion of murder as transcendence in Romantic and post-Romantic literature. Through murder, flouting the law, and imposing one's will so that it has direct and unmediated effect, one has the possibility of becoming a totally free individual, existing outside and unhindered by the realm of culture. In the context of a book that explores the way in which our 'reality is bound by discourse', a discussion of the cultural meanings of murder seems all the more significant, for aesthetic representations of murder have constituted it in response to the sense of disempowerment that is experienced in culture, discourse, or language; for them, murder is that 'reality' that at least attempts to exceed the bounds of discourse. However, that murder is the most unrepresentable and yet one of the most represented of acts in our culture points to the fact that rather than take one out of discourse, murder ironically leads one back into it, with a vengeance, to which the vast and ever-expanding plethora of murder literature bears witness: horror stories, detective stories, criminological literature, video nasties, and so on. *The Lust to Kill* could be seen as another addition to this monstrous body, and, indeed, this essay yet one more.

Thomas De Quincey, who was obsessed with the idea of murder, is, however, not mentioned in *The Lust to Kill*. Cameron and Frazer would justify this omission on the grounds that they address the specific phenomenon of sex murder, which occurs in the 1880s as a response to increasing urbanization and the growing independence and militancy of women.[11] However, they do, rightly, locate the beginning of a developing trend of conceptualizations of murder at around the time of the French Revolution, and they refer rather vaguely to the Gothic and more specifically to the works of Sade. De Quincey's writings are clearly set in this tradition,[12] and I would argue that they are relevant here on a number of counts: first, they formulate a sociology of murder that is not dissimilar to that in *The Lust to Kill*; second, De Quincey is interested in domestic murder, that is, the annihilation of complete family units, a phenomenon which is linked to the further oppression of women, as the home is defined as the woman's proper sphere. The significant point to be gained from reading De Quincey's texts is that murder is constituted not as an act of transcendence, as Cameron and Frazer claim, but rather as a desperate bid for empowerment in the face of the impossibility of transcendence. Rather than a movement out of culture, I would suggest that it is a retrogressive act of control, in the midst of rapid social and political change. All in all, De Quincey's account of murder shows that it is an act of frustration rather than of triumph. Of course, none of this makes it less reprehensible, but it does, I think, shift its cultural meanings.

In 1818, as a young man, De Quincey took over the editorship of the *Westmorland Gazette*, a country newspaper, which he filled with lurid accounts of assize proceedings at the expense of local domestic and agricultural news. De Quincey argued that such accounts were necessary for two reasons: first, reports of murders educated the working class, for they learned by example the punishment that was the inevitable result of transgressive behaviour; and second, such accounts represented the state of the nation's morals to the ruling class, so that any significant decline could somehow be checked.[13] At this stage, then, murder constitutes an untroubled site of representation which works to sustain a particular class structure.

Nine years later, in 1827, however, after extensive readings in German philosophy and in particular Kant, De Quincey published the first of his essays 'On Murder Considered as One of the Fine Arts', which was followed by a second essay of the same title in 1839 and a 'Postscript' in 1854.[14] Kant suggested for De Quincey a different and difficult relation between the subject, representation and the world. The subject experiences a strong sense of disempowerment in representation: caught in the phenomenal realm of representation, any glimpse of the noumenal to be experienced can only be represented in terms of a consciousness of the unrepresentability of this experience. It is thus no longer possible for the representation of murder easily to convey a particular set of social values, for the very processes of representation engage one in a hopeless pursuit of this untroubled, transparent representation. Indeed, as has been suggested, murder itself seems to be offering a way of moving beyond the strictures of representation, itself a way of reaching the noumenal, a sublime experience. However, this bid for transcendence and self-affirmation beyond representation always fails. De Quincey's essays show the way in which this bid for power always incurs the movement back into representation. Put simply, De Quincey's essays display the impossibility of murder as transcendence.

For De Quincey, as for Nilsen, murder is a bid for control in the midst of loss of agency in representation. In the first essay De Quincey writes about the positive advantages of being murdered over not being murdered. 'To hear people talk, you would suppose that all the disadvantages and inconveniences were on the side of being murdered, and that there were none at all in *not* being murdered' (13: 42). The advantage of being murdered is that you have consciousness of your own death. The problem of course is that such knowledge is not much good to you once you are murdered. That this notion is deeply embedded in philosophical thought is made clear in De Quincey's preposterous claim that all philosophers since Descartes have been the victims, not the perpetrators, of an attempted murder. As Descartes thinks in order to be, gaining self-affirmation through self-consciousness, the greatest self-affirmation is reached through the consciousness of the limits of his own existence. De Quincey's fetishizing of the throat as the site of the murderous attack indicates the connection between mind and body, where the death of the mind will always incur the death of the body.

De Quincey is not the only writer to recognize that an intellectual shift concomitant with the work of Descartes is manifested in representations of murder. As Francis Barker points out, the shift occurs at the same time as significant political and social changes which announce the construction of the new, bourgeois subject. Barker reads *Hamlet* to show the beginnings of an interiorizing of the subject in a movement away from 'the corporeal order of the spectacle' of Jacobean drama.[15] In *Hamlet* the all-important first murder, the death of the king and the death of the father, preempts the drama, but within the course of the play it is represented many times: once by the ghost, once by the dumb show preceding the play in Act 3, and again in the play. There is perhaps no better example of the burgeoning mass of aesthetic representations that come to supplement the unrepresented murder, the primal death.[16]

In De Quincey's comedy of philosophical murders a second significant shift occurs with Kant. Unlike his Cartesian forefathers, Kant does not experience his own murder; instead, the murderer chooses to kill a small child. The attainment of self-consciousness is thus never achieved, and Kant remains oblivious to the whole affair. The explanation is curious; ironizing Kant's scrupulous morality, De Quincey claims that the murderer's motives are moral, for he considers that an old philosopher 'might be laden with sins' and concludes that it is less damaging morally to condemn to death a child who is blameless than a man who has yet to atone for his many sins. De Quincey, however, is dissatisfied with this version and substitutes an aesthetic motive: to murder old Kant would provide no satisfaction, he claims, for 'there was no room for display, as the man could not look more like a mummy when dead than he had done alive' (13: 35). This disturbing and anarchic moment, which precipitates the murder of a child, is the moment of the aesthetic; the aesthetic is inscribed at the point at which self-knowledge is rendered unobtainable. At this point of transgression he is able to move beyond morality, culture and representation itself. For all its disturbing implications, this is a potentially radical and liberating moment, the point which provides an escape from culture and the strictures of discourse; this is the moment of transcendence.

To pause for a moment on the brink of this transcendence in a grand De Quinceyesque gesture of anticipation, we see that we have arrived at a particularly important point for contemporary feminist debate, for the implications of this potentially radical moment have been explored by two very different strands of feminist thought. When Cameron and Frazer trace a history of such troubling notions of murder as transcendence through major literary and philosophical texts of the last two centuries, they concentrate in particular on the works of the Marquis de Sade, in which sexual transgression and violence provide a similar sense of freedom, and later existential texts, in which murder is celebrated as the supreme act of liberation. As they show that these accounts are generally gender specific, cases of male violence against women, they demonstrate that such literary glorifications of violence and murder are all too easily transferred on to real cases of violence against women. Other feminist writers, such as Angela Carter, have re-read Sade to reclaim for women the potential liberation of his transgressive moment, thereby laying themselves open to the claims of radical feminists that they glory in and thus perpetuate patriarchal violence. However, for Angela Carter, Sade's work encapsulates a radical transgression of values which suggests the possibilities for women to transcend the oppression that is deeply embedded in patriarchal social and cultural practices.[17] At stake in these wildly oppositional readings, which nonetheless are both engaged with integrity in the same pursuit of women's liberation, is the relationship between representation and experience; at the centre of both readings is an acknowledgement of the dynamic capacity of representations to interact in and construct the 'real world', but while the former see a direct link between the two, for the latter the connection is more devious, less controllable and more dangerous. Carter is interested in the ways in which representations can transform consciousness at the level of fantasy. For her, the indeterminacy of his meanings enables a recuperation of Sade's sadism for the liberation of the objects of his oppression.

De Quincey may not be the most pertinent contributor to feminist debate (indeed he is no feminist); however, to return at this point to his essay on murder is not to sidestep these issues. I would suggest that the nervous laughter inspired by De Quincey's ghoulish moment of liberation suggests that it is one about which he too is deeply troubled. But his anxiety is not that of feminist writers who are troubled by the effects of the dramatic glorification or the comic trivializing of such moments of violence. Rather, his anxiety responds to the political and social chaos that is implied in the breakdown of culture suggested by his reading of Kant's aesthetics. Perhaps it is necessary to stress that De Quincey is writing in the wake of the French Revolution and, more particularly, in the context of increasingly militant radical activity leading up to the Reform Bill of 1832. The fear of social and political chaos has substantial grounds in the realities of his environment. If Carter is able to reclaim the radical indeterminacy of Sade's writing for the liberation of women from patriarchal society, De Quincey is equally able to use his radical moment for the deeper inscription of conservative values, the values of the family that add substantial pressure to the already weighty burden of women's oppression. For him murder comes to represent no more and no less than the powerful display of violence and force that it is, an exhibition of male agency, a flash which he uses to reinforce existing social relations.

The major anxiety faced by De Quincey and his contemporaries was that of alienation resulting from mechanization and the all-consuming circulation of capital that stopped for no man, rich or poor. The most astute critique of alienation experienced under such conditions is given by Marx, but comparable critiques are formulated by writers of quite different political interests, such as Arthur Hallam, Carlyle and De Quincey. Significantly, De Quincey structures his response to capital in terms of the sublime, in which the unstoppable flow of money is the incomprehensible infinite event in the face of which subjectivity dissolves. De Quincey's particular interest in economic theory is an attempt to rationalize this, and significantly he alights on Ricardo as his ideal political economist, regarding him as a Kantian economist.[18]

Amid the flow of capital there is nevertheless one place in which a man can still possess and exercise agency; this, of course, is the family. As Marx and Engels write in the *German Ideology*, in the family a man can possess and command his wife and children as his slaves.[19] If his own labour and his own will are alienated in the work-place and the market-place, the gendered economy of domestic relations provides a context in which a man can still make a particular effect and in which his desires and wishes might be gratified. Indeed, the very furnishings of the Victorian home demonstrate a man's power within his own private space. As Walter Benjamin writes in *Charles Baudelaire*, the thick, lush fabrics that draped the interiors of the bourgeois home provided surfaces on which the inhabitants could make a lasting impression, so that their agency might be displayed and confirmed on every surface of every room. He writes: 'Living means leaving traces. In the interior, these were stressed. Coverings and antimacassars, boxes and casings, were devised in abundance, in which the traces of everyday objects were moulded. The resident's own traces were also moulded in the interior.'[20] It is significant that people desire to leave traces, so that their very act of living might be represented at the moment of its happening. There is thus a vital relation between representation and agency, for the home, the domain of private property, affords a man direct control over the circumstances of his environment. His life assumes a particular meaning because every action has a direct, material consequence; that is, its inscription in his furnishings. If the products of his labour are put into circulation, his own work altered and dispersed in the flow of exchange, in the home his very being makes an effect that is always visible, for his agency is represented and constantly on display.

It seems apparent that the need for these direct displays of presence points to the precarious nature of the control that is to be gained in the home, for the family is always under threat from the public sphere, the world outside. In fact, the imminent breakdown of the family and of domestic contentment is the subject of one of De Quincey's little-read Gothic stories, entitled *The Household Wreck, or the Juggernaut of Social Life*.[21] Published in 1838, the year before the second of the murder essays, this little melodrama depicts the major anxieties of the age. In it the domestic idyll of the narrator and his family is dramatically foreshortened when the man's wife is wrongly implicated in the theft of some lace. As the plot unfolds, it is clear that the woman has been duped by a lascivious shopkeeper who plans to blackmail her into submission to his lecherous desires through a brush with the law. The case, however, exceeds his control, and an incident that was meant merely to scare and humiliate a respectable wife results in her long-term imprisonment, during which time the narrator suffers a long illness, his baby son dies and, after her escape from prison, the wife also dies.

This is a story of sexual harassment, but more particularly it is a story of misrepresentation; that is, the systematic and varied misrepresentations of a woman who never corresponds to these definitions of her. Grevel Lindop notes De Quincey's fascination with big women, but Agnes in this story is one big woman whose power is consistently withdrawn.[22] Referring to her large stature, he writes that 'though in the first order of tall women, yet ... she seemed to the random sight a little above ordinary height'. If to strangers she appears 'commanding', to her husband she possesses a 'childlike innocence' and 'feminine timidity'. She is the perfect wife, the beautiful, desexualized child-woman, who '[in] perfect womanhood ... retained a most childlike expression of countenance, so even then in absolute childhood she put forward the blossoms and the dignity of a woman' (12: 165). Neither child nor woman but a mixture of both, Agnes's powerful but undeveloped body has a curious modernity; but in De Quincey's context, her most striking feature is her unstable and constantly slipping identity, which gives the sense that she is always transgressive and disruptive. As he constantly refers to her as his Eve, once even his Pandora, he ominously misses the implications of her less than perfect mythic sisters.

In the power relations of the family, the man's inability to represent his wife becomes his inability to control her; this power is lost entirely when she enters the market-place. If her sexuality is effaced in the home, in the outside world she is attributed a rampant and uncontrollable sexuality that is desired by all men and possessed by none. The shopkeeper's trick to harness this seductive commodity that she flaunts so unwittingly fails as his misrepresentation is circulated publicly. As the woman is taken into circulation and is misrepresented by the husband, the shopkeeper and the law, the family breakdown is complete and the man loses all semblance of agency. The last resort is her physical incarceration. One has a sense that she is imprisoned as much for her transgressive nature as for her part in the alleged crime. When her husband visits Agnes in prison, he finds

> her beautiful long auburn hair had escaped from its confinement, and was floating over the table and her own person. She took no notice of the disturbance made by our entrance, did not turn, did not raise her head, nor make an effort to do so, nor by any sign whatever intimate that she was conscious of our presence.... Her breathing, which had been like that of sinless infancy, was now frightfully short and quick; she seemed not properly to breathe, but to gasp.
>
> (12: 209–10)

Sexuality and madness combine as her unbound hair is a sign that marks her unbridled passion, released as she escapes the confines of her socialization. Like Bertha Mason in *Jane Eyre*, Agnes's madness is the visible and only permissible sign of her active sexuality; having lost her state of childlike innocence, Agnes must gasp and pant like an aroused woman. Although guilty of no indiscretion, Agnes has become a fallen woman, for her sexuality has been acknowledged and publicly circulated. If in the family the husband's control was gained only through the effacement of her sexuality, describing a child-woman with no sexual power or desires, the public acknowledgement of her sexuality suggests the possibility of a sexual promiscuity, the fundamental threat to the family. The only remaining control is her imprisonment, a physical incarceration that is more effective than the family. In this, the text is one of many to prefigure the actual confinement of a particular group of sexualized women, that is, prostitutes, instituted in response to the Contagious Diseases Acts of the 1860s.[23]

There are thus two significant points to be drawn from this story: first, the man loses agency when representations of his wife are removed from the private sphere and brought into public circulation, when he no longer enjoys the control that is afforded by the marks of presence available in the home; and second, it is the woman, whom he is never able to define or represent accurately, who implicitly causes this breakdown of family life. Agnes is certainly not the only literary lady to exceed patriarchal definitions and thereby constitute a major threat to male agency; from Salomé to Alexis Colby, literature is overflowing with dangerous, transgressive and castrating women. What is significant about De Quincey's own castration anxiety is the way in which representation and control are so closely allied. The family, and with it the subjection of women, is to be sustained in order to protect the context in which a man can make his mark; but the point of *The Household Wreck* is to enact the precariousness of that very institution. It is in this context, I would suggest, that murder is formulated as a display of force that is more powerful, more permanent than, for instance, the marks of agency displayed in Walter Benjamin's flimsy piece of velveteen. Significantly, in his essay Benjamin suggests that these traces of domestic life are nevertheless the basis of the detective story: '[the] detective story appeared, which investigated these traces. [Poe's] *Philosophy of Furniture*, as much as his detective stories, shows Poe to have been the first physiognomist of the interior.'[24] As the detective retraces the traces of the murderer to discover the primal scene of the crime, the first trace is the wound, the deathly mark of the murder. Like the marks of the interiors, the wound is the mark that displays the agency and power, the force of the murderer. Murder is the mark of power whose meaning for the perpetrator does not alter in circulation, a form of representation that makes an unmistakable bid for control.

Thus De Quincey writes that the perfect murder is one that obliterates an entire household: the murders with which he is most fascinated are those that involve the massacre of a family complete with servants. I wish to suggest that for De Quincey, whose writings constantly display anxieties concerning the imminent and inescapable collapse of the family, murder is an expression of power and agency in the face of this breakdown of social order.

The murderer to whom he returns obsessively is one John Williams, who 'during the winter of 1812 ... in one hour smote two houses with emptiness, exterminated all but two entire households, and asserted his own supremacy above all the children of Cain' (13: 74). Williams's own tangential position in relation to the family is always emphasized: he is a traveller, a sailor who has no family and no home of his own, but lives in a hostel with other sailors of mixed nationalities: his own birthplace, writes De Quincey, 'was certainly not known' (13: 116). His foppish appearance is often referred to, his unnatural and unmanly interest in clothing, and hair which was of the 'most extraordinary and vivid colour, – viz, bright yellow, something between an orange and a lemon colour'. His synaesthetic hair colouring is a legacy of trips to India, where 'it is notorious that in the Punjab horses of a high caste are often painted – crimson, blue, green, purple' (13: 77). Such curious details confirm his position in relation to the family, the home, and the nation, for he is tainted with all things that mark the boundary of the family. Nevertheless, the casual reference to Indian caste indicates an interest in the preservation of particular hierarchical values that might not always be protected in the family. In this case, India seems to imply not the undermining and threatening Orient, but the existence of a jealously preserved set of social relations, a precapitalist idyll, which is presently at risk in the 'democratic' West.

The families that he selects to murder significantly already show signs of being under threat from such a breakdown of social order. The first family, the Marrs, employ a maid who exists in sisterly relation to the wife, thus usefully inscribing relations of labour into the family. At the time, however, De Quincey tells us, '[a] great democratic change ... is passing over British society. Multitudes of persons are becoming ashamed of saying "my master" or "my mistress": the term now in the slow person of superseding it is "my employer"' (13: 82). Protection for the Marrs family from the democratic change that promises to revolutionize the power relations of society, we suspect, is only temporary, for De Quincey describes a tide that is sweeping over the entire nation; their only certain escape from this is death. The other family, the Williamsons, are the keepers of a hostelry 'on an old patriarchal footing', he writes, in which 'although people of considerable property resorted to the house in the evenings, no kind of anxious separation was maintained between them and the other visitors from the class of artisans or common labourers' (13: 97–8). Once again class relations are so deeply inscribed that they need not be acknowledged; in both cases relations of labour are naturalized and effaced. However, like the Marrs, the Williamsons cannot guarantee the continuation of this arrangement. By annihilating them, Williams protects them from a certain breakdown in social relations.

In his own iconoclastic way Williams is the ultimate guardian of the family. Like Peter Sutcliffe, the Yorkshire Ripper, who claimed 'I were just cleaning up streets', and Jack the Ripper's indignant plea that he was 'down on prostitutes',[25] Williams is the protector of family values, of moral respectability, a Mary Whitehouse with a knife, a murderous moral majority. In De Quincey's text, to protect the family is to maintain the context in which a man can possess agency and control, in which he can mean what he says and say what he means and is not at risk from the misrepresentations of circulation. Significantly, his second victims, the Williamsons, are in name his own family, the family of his son. If the family offers the conditions for control and the expression of agency, I would suggest that De Quincey, who recognizes the precarious nature of the family, presents murder as the one act of total and individual control. To kill his son is to kill the trajectory of his own actions, his own being; it is to control the circulation of his own representations.

It is therefore significant that Southey considered the Williams murders preeminent, for they 'ranked amongst the few domestic events which, by the depth and expansion of horror attending them, had risen to the dignity of a *national* interest' (13: 124, note). The murderer makes the private public; however, it is only through death, an ending that preempts any form of interference, that he is sure that his actions can be represented or displayed without fear of alteration. Alternatively, De Quincey remarks that to kill a public figure is self-defeating, for no-one would believe that you had done it: the representations of public figures are already in circulation and therefore cannot be controlled. He gives two examples: the pope, who 'has such ubiquity as the father of Christendom, and like the cuckoo, is so often heard but never seen', and Abraham Newland, the man whose name appeared on all banknotes (13: 47). One cannot stop the circulation of paper money by murdering the man whose name was 'a shorthand expression of paper money in its safest form' (13: 47, note). If existence in the public realm offers immunity from murder, it is only because agency and control have already been lost; murder has nothing to retrieve outside the home.

The issue of the murder of public figures, or assassination, is raised early in the first essay in a discussion of its significant difference from domestic murder. In this discussion it becomes clear that the difference is historical. Tracing the etymology of the word 'assassin', De Quincey links it to the Arabic *hashishin* or 'hashish-drinkers', the name of certain Muslim fanatics in the time of the Crusades who were sent by their sheikh, the 'Old Man of the Mountains', to murder Christian leaders. These assassins were 'nerved for their task by the intoxication of *hashish*' (13: 21–2, note 2). Perpetrated in this drug-induced stupor, then, assassination could never constitute the display of will or power that domestic murder came to later. In this history of murder the dates are significant; of De Quincey's list of famous assassinations, the most recent occurred in 1634 during the Thirty Years War, thirty-four years after *Hamlet*, three years before the publication of Descartes's *Discourse on Method*. Public murder gives way to private murder at around the time of the establishment of the family as the major social, moral and economic unit and the constitution of the free-thinking, self-determining Cartesian subject.

De Quincey's family murders, I would suggest, are not transcendent acts; rather, they are displays of violence and force strategically constructed in culture to halt a process of social democratization. His murderer is the guardian of a nostalgic world of hierarchical social relations, the keeper of a precapitalist idyll. Significantly De Quincey is always motivated by a desire to take control of the flow of capital and likewise to control the circulation of representations. Murder for him constitutes a blockage in this flow, and I would suggest it is no coincidence that this takes us back to the beginning of my essay, to the sublime. In Neil Hertz's conceptualization of the sublime, the checking that occurs in response to this overwhelming experience is a similar blockage, but one that takes the form of aesthetic representation. However, in the nineteenth century, aesthetic representation, like murder, often fulfils this role, bearing nostalgic values of organic communities and uncontested hierarchies of power; that is to say, aesthetic representation performs the same function as murder.

In terms of the feminist debate, De Quincey's attempt to check the flow of representations has yet more resonances, for this desire for control is not dissimilar to the radical feminist quest to halt the circulation of pornographic and oppressive representations of women. Indeed, radical feminist writings on censorship often repeat the model of representation that the Romantics could only dream of. For example, in *The Lust to Kill*, discussing the idea that Nilsen's murders were the result of an inability to distinguish fantasy from reality, Cameron and Frazer argue that, on the contrary, all representations are produced in the social world. Following Susanne Kappeler they write, 'Kappeler argues that far from being "nothing to do with reality" representations are *produced* and that production is a human activity which takes place in the social world, the realm of reality.'[26] Indeed they continue to assert that the power relations that are established in the production of an image are those that are necessarily transmitted in the circulation and consumption of an image. Kappeler takes this point to its logical conclusion and argues for the end of representation and a 'practice in the interest of communication'.[27] Ironically, Kappeler seems to be engaged in an endeavour to control the circulation of representations that is similar to the one embarked on by De Quincey in his murder project. Both arguments ultimately tend toward a Utopian version of language, a language which is unmediated and direct. This is all the more significant in a book such as Cameron and Frazer's, which deals with the impossibility of stepping beyond culture and discourse.

Reading De Quincey's murder writings thus shows that rather than a bid for transcendence beyond the structures of social relations, the aesthetic of murder is constructed with a view to its own social consequences and, specifically, to controlling those consequences; this is a censorship not of the production of representations but of their circulation and consumption. For De Quincey and writers of his political sympathies, certain kinds of representations such as poetry, that were not traditionally reproduced for the developing mass audience of an increasingly literate public, were indeed held to be the guardians and, ideally, the redeemers of an old, feudal social order. The violence of the aesthetic that attempts to protect this order demonstrates the desperation of this implausible proposition. Lacking this controlled context, people are subject to the instabilities of representations whose effects are unpredictable and uncontainable. This of course is the scenario of

De Quincey's writing, for, try as he might, he can never achieve the control he desires. But the life and writings of the opium eater are not all misery and alienation, and, despite himself, he constantly celebrates his disempowerment. When his comedy of murder appears distasteful, we might bear in mind that this is not a discourse of the empowered but a relinquishing of himself to disempowerment.

This essay was first published in *Genders*, Number 5 (Summer 1989), published by the University of Texas Press.

NOTES

1 D. G. Rossetti, 'The Paris Railway Station' (1849) ll. 14–16, in *Collected Works of Dante Gabriel Rossetti*, ed. William M. Rossetti, vol. 1 (London, 1887), p. 258. I wish to thank Linda R. Williams for drawing this poem to my attention.
2 Deborah Cameron and Elizabeth Frazer, *The Lust to Kill: A Feminist Investigation of Sexual Murder* (Cambridge, 1987). Jane Caputi in *The Age of Sex Crime* (London, 1988) engages with similar material in another comprehensive study of sex murder.
3 Cameron and Frazer, op. cit., pp. 151–2. Wittgenstein uses this analogy of a pair of spectacles in a discussion of the ways in which language determines the way in which we perceive: '[it] is like a pair of glasses on our nose through which we see whatever we look at. It never occurs to us to take them off.' See *Philosophical Investigations*, trans. G. E. M. Anscombe (Oxford, 1958), section 103.
4 Alan Sheridan, *Foucault, the Will to Truth* (London, 1980). Cited in Cameron and Frazer, op. cit., p. xiii.
5 ibid.
6 ibid., p. 151.
7 See Neil Hertz, 'The Notion of Blockage in the Literature of the Sublime', in *The End of the Line: Essays on Psychoanalysis and the Sublime* (New York, 1985), pp. 40–60.
8 *The Prelude: or Growth of a Poet's Mind*, ed. Ernest De Selincourt, revd Helen Darbishire, 2nd edn (Oxford, 1959), book 6, ll. 601–2.
9 For details of the case of Dennis Nilsen they cite Brian Masters, *Killing for Company* (London, 1986).
10 ibid., pp. 264, 277. Cited in Cameron and Frazer, op. cit., p. 153.
11 This point is also made by Caputi, who bases much of her discussion on the significance of Jack the Ripper's crimes of 1888. She deems him the 'central/father figure' (p. 13) in the social drama of sex crime.
12 Mario Praz suggests some connections between De Quincey and Sade and the darker side of Romanticism. See *The Romantic Agony*, trans. Angus Davidson, 2nd edn (Oxford, 1951). In particular he compares the secret society of murderers, the Society for the Encouragement of Murder, to which the lectures 'On Murder Considered as One of the Fine Arts' are addressed, with Sade's Société des Amis du Crime in *Juliette*. He also refers to certain societies that existed at the turn of the century whose members indulged in 'reckless sexual license' and criminal practices. See E. Beresford Chancellor, *The Hell-fire Club* (London, 1925).
13 See Charles Pollitt, *De Quincey's Editorship of 'The Westmorland Gazette', July, 1818 to November, 1819* (Kendal, 1890), pp. 11–12. Cited by David Masson in *Collected Writings of Thomas De Quincey*, ed. David Masson, vol. 13 (Edinburgh, 1889–90), p. 95, note.

14 Masson (ed.), op. cit., 13: 9–124. All subsequent references to De Quincey's *Collected Writings* are included in the text.

15 Francis Barker, *The Private Tremulous Body: Essays on Subjection* (London, 1984), p. 35.

16 Cf. Freud, *Totem and Taboo: Some Points of Agreement between the Mental Lives of Savages and Neurotics* (1912–13), Standard Edition of the Complete Psychological Works of Sigmund Freud, trans. James Strachey, 24 vols (London, 1953–74), 13: 1–161, in which the primal parricide is never known but endlessly represented in religious and unconscious ideation; for example, in the Oedipus complex.

17 Angela Carter, *Sadeian Woman: An Exercise in Cultural History* (London, 1979).

18 See Thomas De Quincey, *Confessions of an English Opium Eater*: 'Mr. Ricardo had deduced, *a priori*, from the understanding itself, laws which first shot arrowy light into the dark chaos of materials, and had thus constructed what hitherto was but a collection of tentative discussions into a science of regular proportions, now first standing upon an eternal basis' (3: 432).

19 See K. Marx, F. Engels, 'Private Property and Communism', *The German Ideology*, ed. C. J. Arthur (London, 1970), pp. 52–7.

20 Walter Benjamin, *Charles Baudelaire: A Lyric Poet in the Era of High Capitalism*, trans. Harry Zohn (London, 1973), p. 169.

21 Thomas De Quincey, *The Household Wreck* (1838), 12: 157–233. For a relevant discussion of De Quincey's Gothic, see Eve Kosofsky Sedgwick, *The Coherence of Gothic Conventions* (London, 1986).

22 See Grevel Lindop, *The Opium Eater: A Life of Thomas De Quincey* (London, 1981), pp. 207, 327. Lindop follows many other critics in reading Agnes as a portrait of De Quincey's own wife, who died shortly before he wrote this story. See also V. A. De Luca, *Thomas De Quincey: The Prose of Vision* (Toronto, 1980), pp. 52–4, A. S. Plumtree, 'The Artist as Murderer: De Quincey's Essay "On Murder Considered as One of the Fine Arts" ', pp. 144–5, in *Thomas De Quincey: Bicentenary Essays*, ed. Robert L. Snyder (Norman, Okla., 1985), pp. 140–63. To read Agnes as De Quincey's wife requires that we accept this to be an idealized version overlooking her humble social background. Another possible model for Agnes might be Mrs K—, who cares for De Quincey during a period of his childhood. She is noted for the love which she generates through her household and with which she is able to command the respect and duty of the servants. De Quincey also notes that the deaths of Mrs K— and her child are associated with some 'commercial embarrassment'. See the revised *Confessions* (1956), 3: 243–6.

23 See Judith Walkowitz, *Prostitution and Victorian Society* (Cambridge, 1982).

24 Benjamin, op. cit., p. 169.

25 Cited in Cameron and Frazer, op. cit., pp. 122–3 and Caputi, op. cit., p. 33.

26 Cameron and Frazer, op. cit., p. 154. See Susanne Kappeler, *The Pornography of Representation* (Cambridge, 1986).

27 Kappeler, *Pornography*, p. 222.

Chapter 14

The politics of focus:
feminism and photography theory

Lindsay Smith

PHOTOGRAPHY THEORY: HOW FAR HAVE WE COME?

'Focus' or its synonym 'depth of field' is a crucial term in photography history. For histories of photography have assumed as authoritative a link between the photograph and a fine art tradition, in part, through a conception of photographic focus as correlative with 'style' in painting. More particularly, in histories of documentary photography, 'focus' has been instrumental in confirming a belief in the sovereignty of geometral perspective as one of documentary photography's key enabling factors. Geometral perspective, the dominant Western system for articulating three-dimensional space as two-dimensional, assumes an established linear relationship between a vantage-point (the eye of a subject looking) and a vanishing-point (the culmination of the look upon an object) according to the eventual convergence of lines of geometral projection. Since the function of documentary as photographic genre has relied upon a translation of geometral perspective – originally used by the discourse of painting – into photographic depth of field, it has thereby seemed to confirm documentary photography as a similarly authoritative mapping of the visual. These appropriations of photographic 'focus', both to 'style' in painting and to the authority of a geometral model in documentary, are, however, highly problematic and, as I hope to demonstrate, crucial to any debate upon gender within photographic discourse.

As a consequence of these appropriations, depth of field has occupied a significant place in recent photography theory, especially that which has challenged the very mystificatory model upon which documentary photographic practice relies.[1] A deconstruction of the 'truth' of documentary and the self-sustaining rhetoric of its images has grown out of a recognition of the historical, material, ideological and psychic complexities implicit in Barthes's now familiar coinage, 'the evidential force of the photograph'. Yet attempts by photography theory to address, in these terms, the politics of the photograph, particularly documentary and how it relates to a politics of gender, have to some extent still required for their persuasiveness a construction of nineteenth-century photography theory and practice as unproblematic at its inception. This version, characteristically, represents nineteenth-century photography as that which is understood to 'confirm' a centred subjectivity prior to 'the militant avant-gardism of the post-World War I period'.[2] Such an extreme simplification of photography at its inception has made it possible for theorists to locate the first 'real' questioning of the ideological functioning of photography in the 1920s and to reiterate a stable nineteenth-century model in which gender politics are also elided. Even some of the most radical and important work in photography theory replicates a version of nineteenth-century photography as an unproblematic historical juncture against which to posit subsequent deviations. We find, as a result, wide acceptance of the position expressed in such phrases as 'photography does not so much confirm our experience of the world as it was understood to do in the mid-nineteenth century'.[3] Few seem impelled, however, to enquire by whom such confirmation was understood.

This appropriation of nineteenth-century photography to an enabling historical generalization has been written into photography's history by a variety of methods. I do not mean here to refer simply to a rhetorical habit or to develop a retrospective attribution of ignorance to a previous era – another version of that which the nineteenth century did to the eighteenth and the eighteenth to the seventeenth and so forth. For there is something much more troubling at stake in theoretical approaches that ultimately sanction the reproduction of a stable and essentially unproblematic nineteenth-century discourse of photography. Such approaches, in their proposition that the nineteenth century believed photographic reproduction to be unquestionably 'true', assume as *a priori* a nineteenth-century blind spot to the workings of photographic representation and fail therefore to allow for any contestation of dominant ideological modes. Furthermore, this misrepresentation of nineteenth-century photographic discourse elides those disruptions of the geometral monopoly on the visual field, those interventions which photography courts from its inception. In fact, since nineteenth-century discourses of vision and visuality conversely constitute highly contested domains that are themselves intrinsically disrupted by photography, an allegedly stable and totalizing model of nineteenth-century theory and practice occludes a complex politics of focus and gender as they come together and are played out in the early decades of photography. With these previous occlusions taken into account, nineteenth-century photographic practice can no longer comfortably provide a foil of stability against which to posit our own twentieth-century 'radical' practice.

In order to address further questions of precisely what is elided by an erroneously stable nineteenth-century model that, as I will go on to argue, ultimately refutes difference in vision – those contestatory debates in optics and visual theory – and simplifies simultaneously constructions of subjectivity and photographic representation, we can turn to important recent photography theory. Alan Sekula and John Tagg among others have re-read the history of nineteenth-century photography in terms of disciplinary institutions, engaging discourses of surveillance, the body and institutions of social control.[4] Foucault's two 'Birth' books, and especially his work on Bentham's conception of the panopticon (as an unprecedented means of surveillance and optical mastery) have provided one of the most significant and widely used paradigms in this area of debate. However, in many ways such attempts by materialist work on surveillance and the body to problematize those old linear histories, as characterized by the domino-like progression of optical invention, have reinscribed a unifying myth of a nineteenth-century photographic unity by ascribing an historical monopoly to surveillance. Surveillance, it seems, now threatens to become the new unifying agency in photography history that was previously occupied by geometral 'truth'. In other words, a reductive model of nineteenth-century photography may persist in part as a result of an overstatement of a thesis of social control that only transfers a version of photography's 'inherent coherence' to the operations of 'the social formation itself'. For in Tagg's thesis the 'nature of photographic practice' (its implicit unity) is displaced to the 'agents and institutions which set it to work'. But these institutions themselves are brought together under the umbrella term of surveillance, the unificatory project of which is subjection.[5] And even if we accept that his project is designed only to extend to particular nineteenth-century institutions, this does not account for the fact that he completely elides a politics of gender. In this sense Tagg does not fully allow for the production of counter-tendencies to the dominant; he underplays, in other words, spaces of contestation. The cameo's ability to resolve itself into an intaglio, to take a favourite nineteenth-century optical metaphor, goes unrecognized. The logic of Tagg's approach is therefore in many ways at odds with the existence of multiple scopic regimes, totalizing them all, as it does, ultimately to the panoptic stare. He may rightly preempt the possibility of such an overstatement in the introduction of *The Burden of Representation*, but he fails to predict the possible consequences of his own position for photography theory. We are left, consequently, to wonder why and how a division of gender, for example, demarcates, to quite an extent, a division between historical materialist work in photography theory and that work which situates its origins in psychoanalysis and film theory. And, in this respect, we are reminded of the way in which Victor Burgin rationalizes, in *Thinking Photography*, an absence of essays by women with the statement that women are working in another field, one more clearly aligned to developments in feminist film theory.[6]

It is important, then, that photography theory be conscious of the dilemma we find in Tagg. Difference in vision needs to be recognized as occurring at photography's inception, as we can detect, for example, in the nineteenth-century theorization and construction of multiple photographic practices – such as combination printing – as both endorsing and contesting various scopic regimes. But in fact such an inherently problematic nineteenth-century practice as combination printing (the construction of a photographic image from more than one negative) is still primarily regarded as an uncomplex stylistic gesture in the direction of a fine art tradition, in spite of the fact that combination printing foregrounds competing ideological positions and is a structural antecedent of radical photo-montage in the twentieth century. Perhaps most troubling, as dramatized by this example, is that the original appropriation by traditional photography histories of certain nineteenth-century practices as akin to fine art has thus consigned those nineteenth-century practices to a position of relatively minor interest as compared to the more overtly political status of nineteenth-century photography as an instrument of surveillance and social control. Thus, although recent photography theory has demystified certain aspects and functions of nineteenth-century practice, it has not been entirely resistant to one of the dominant strategies of those 'traditional' histories it has sought to subvert, namely the privileging, to the exclusion of many other discourses, of a kinship between photography and painting. In many ways theory has left the problematic of so-called nineteenth-century 'fine art' photography untouched.

Therefore, while, on the one hand, successfully undermining the authority and coherence of previous unproblematic photography histories and dramatically opening up critical debate, recent theory has retained, on the other, a ghost history, that of nineteenth-century photographic discourse as confirming a centred subject. The direction of future development for photography theory remains then a matter of history, involving questions of periodization and of renegotiating the relationship of theory to photography history. Exorcism of its residual ghost is only possible if theory engages more willingly and extensively the discourses of optics and visual theory that attend the invention of photography and out of which it is produced. But, I contend, we must not only not dismiss those early and apparently unproblematic instances of photographic practice, but we must actually re-read and re-utilize those photographic historians and collectors (such as Helmut Gernsheim) if we are to rethink the interplay between that which is historicized and that which is omitted.[7] For it is with such rethinking that areas of contestation in early nineteenth-century photographic practice emerge. It may be, in fact, the seemingly dispensable bathwater and not the baby that we need to retrieve in order to address those means by which difference in vision, gender difference and a politics of focus have been written out of seminal histories of photography to eclipse particular sites of contestation, sites already written out when photography was detached from discourses of optics and visual theory.

Just how productive such a retrieval of these seminal histories can be becomes apparent when we compare the work of Lewis Carroll with that of his contemporary, the Victorian woman photographer Julia Margaret Cameron, whose politics of focus inscribes a sexual politics in a critique and refusal of the brand of perceptual mastery that geometral perspective is designed to guarantee. But before examining Gernsheim's histories and charting a politics of focus as manifest in the photographs of Cameron and Carroll, I wish to contextualize further the agency of 'focus' in nineteenth-century discourses of photography and visual theory.

THE POLITICS OF FOCUS AS SEXUAL POLITICS

Focus, in the photographic sense, derives from the Latin focus, meaning 'hearth'. The etymology of the term incorporates the origins of photography in fire (light), as in the optical sense of a 'burning point of a lens or a mirror', and in the meaning of centredness, implied in the centring function of hearth, and by extension, in the centring function of photography. Moreover, as the centre of the home, the private domestic space with all its symbolic and much rehearsed iconographic import, focus thereby brings to the fore this other much contested Victorian domain. As Rosalind Krauss reminds us, 'it is not surprising that the camera and photography have been placed within the ritualised cult of domesticity', for the photographic record 'is an agent in the collective fantasy of family cohesion', while similarly the camera is 'part of the theater that the family constructs to convince itself that it is together and whole'.[8]

Interestingly, in a now obsolete sense 'focus' also connotes theatre in its meaning of 'the best illuminated part of the stage', and it is not much of a shift from this sense to that of 'the best articulated part of a photographic image'. Of a lens, then, focus is 'the power of giving a "sharp" image of objects not in the same plane, now usually expressed as a distance, and used as a synonym of "depth of field"'. Thus, 'focus' is that which confers intelligibility upon objects in spite of their planar disparity and further implies centredness in its signification of 'a centre of activity'.[9] The cultural and conceptual possibilities that are opened up by this generative connection of focus to literal and figurative hearths would be worthy of exploration in greater detail, but for the moment let us concentrate upon their relation to a politics of focus in specific nineteenth-century photographic practices, and particularly in those of Cameron and Carroll.

A concept of photographic 'focus' is politicized in nineteenth-century visual theory precisely in the sense that from the announcement of the invention of the daguerreotype in 1839, the professed superiority of photography in delineation of the visible is predicated upon the newly discovered ability to harness (chemically) the *focused* images in the camera obscura. Photographic meanings of the term 'focus' immediately imply therefore a new potentiality in visual representation since photography recreates a scale upon which are situated literal and metaphorical calibrations of being 'in' and 'out' of this state. The new 'sun pictures' revealed the variability of focus together with the fact that it was contingent upon particular conditions. Thus, Fox Talbot's

'Pencil of Nature' was from the first a sharp one in more than one sense of the word. By introducing as variable the focal lengths that could be (re)-produced in photographic representation, the sun pictures inevitably stressed or presupposed an absolute state of 'in focus' against which to measure deviations. By definition, a knowledge or demonstration of variables of focus functioned in relation to and thereby ratified an unwritten consensus upon an absolute state. From the beginning, the photographic definition of focus was made to serve existing systems of visual representation, and in particular to conspire with the dominance of geometral perspective, thus further confirming the sovereignty of the latter in various media. In one fundamental and immediate sense, photography could appear to guarantee the continued ubiquity of geometral accounts of space by seeming to represent geometral spatial mapping in the greatest degree of verisimilitude experienced in visual perception up to that time. For the function of a photographic lens in recording depth of field could be read as confirming the desired ubiquity of this particular system of representing space by further attributing to it that which was eclipsed by the geometral model, the sovereign agency of light.

Reactions to early photography as the independent work of the sun have been extensively recorded, and interpretations of photography as 'fairy' work suggest ways in which the new sun pictures could be thought to resolve or simplify agency. Talbot pinpoints a primary difference between the camera obscura and the camera lucida (as aids to drawing) and the new invention of photography. Whereas the former 'do not work for' the artist because 'the actual performance of the drawing must be his own', the latter negates the agency of the photographer since 'the picture', Talbot writes, 'makes ITSELF'.[10] Talbot thus raises the potentiality of photography as a technology for reducing human labour in modes of representation. In addition, however, his notion of auto-mimetic agency (the ability of representations to 'make' themselves), when set in relation to the ideology of mastery, links significantly with a newly defined photographic condition of focus. Indeed, the way in which the sun is thought to be able to 'naturalize' photographic representation, in early accounts of the medium, is analogous to the manner in which a photographic conception of absolute focus is able to sanction the continued sovereignty of geometral perspective by appearing to naturalize it further. Moreover, the application of photography to a visual representational realm dominated by geometral perspective may appear to give to geometral perspective the power to reproduce itself as seemingly available in reality, by conferring a sense that the image was 'out there' in reality, able to imprint itself as it was (geometrically mapped) by way of photography. Preserved in such a primarily scenic representational model is that crucial Cartesian duality of vantage-point and vanishing-point without which the authoritative geometral threads unravel.

However, from its very inception photography did not simply appear to ratify a geometral model but instead foregrounded the existence of multiple scopic regimes and enacted a critique of the ahistorical, 'disembodied' subject perpetuated by 'Cartesian Perspectivalism'.[11] Yet, this problematization by photography in the nineteenth century of the status and function of geometral perspective has, as I have implied, been repeatedly overlooked, in spite of the fact that the shared ubiquity of the geometral model in painting and of the photograph in mechanical reproduction invites interrogation of their interrelationship. By questioning the relationship of agency to focus, photography then actually problematizes and reinscribes, in the first decades, a critique of the ideology of perceptual mastery as that which geometral perspective appeared to ensure. In other words, it does not simply confirm the sanctity and centredness of hearth that its etymology seems to promise.

In fact, a twinning of photographic focus and geometral perspective as authoritative visual mapping was systematically subverted from photography's inception by radical manipulation of both the concept of focus and the concept of agency. Just as a demystification of geometral authority in painting has since the Renaissance been repeatedly performed in the oblique constructions of anamorphosis, as the frequent and continued recourse to the suspended skull of Holbein's *Ambassadors* bears witness, so too in photography attempts to fly the nets of geometral authority masquerading as retinal authority have been made continuously. Anamorphosis, the Renaissance fascination with the so-called 'right view' viewed 'awry', is the de-centring visual rupture in the seemingly snag-free net of geometral optics. In nineteenth-century photography a similar disruption that foregrounds multiple scopic regimes occurs in the mid-century technique of combination printing in which, as we shall see, there is a significant coming together of focus with questions of agency in an assault upon geometral authority.

In the 1850s and 1860s, combination printing (the production of a single photographic image from more than one negative) emerges as a new process that intervenes radically at the level of depth of field. A wilful manipulation of the photograph occurs initially as a means of controlling technical weakness. Early lenses had a relatively narrow depth of field and lengthy exposures necessary for recording objects occupying different spatial planes tended to bleach out areas such as the surrounding sky for example; photographic depth of field was at once determined by technical and aesthetic considerations. Combination printing aimed to resolve limitations in focal length by combining and arranging on different focal planes separate negatives of objects taken at the required focal lengths to guarantee 'sharpness' in an eventual composition. Thus, by extension, the technique aims to produce and confirm a consensus upon 'sharpness', upon that condition of being 'in' focus as an unhesitant and irrefutable signature of the photographic medium. But, in fact, the effect of the medium repeatedly frustrates this strategy as is evident in adverse contemporary reaction to what it regarded as the 'patchwork quilt school of photography'.[12] Significantly, a technique (thought to be instigated by Hippolyte Bayard in France and developed most substantially in Britain by Henry Peach Robinson) becomes highly polemical in its deployment, not only because it is understood to assault photographic 'naturalism' in terms of subject matter, but also because it is considered by some to violate the uniqueness of the claim of photography upon the mechanical reproduction of the visual.

Nineteenth-century critics read combination printing as an ostensible denial of that agency singularly intrinsic to photography, the chemical harnessing of solar conditions at particular moments in time. Crucially, however, a theoretical positioning of an early technique together with a rhetoric of its legitimation arises as inseparable from a complex and strategic inscription of gender. Robinson locates the legitimation of combination printing in classical ideals of the female body. There can, indeed, be little danger of overstating Robinson's links between the claim of photography to a status equal with that of painting and with constructions of femininity. Robinson cites a familiar classical anecdote, illustrative of the ideal, and popular in painting, by which to authorize the technique:

> Rather more than two thousand years ago Zeuxis, of Heraclea, painted his famous picture of Helena for the people of Crotona, in the composition of which he selected, from five of the most beautiful girls the town could produce, whatever he observed nature had formed most perfect in each, and united them all in one single figure. A reference to the dim traditions of antiquity might perhaps be considered out of date in treating of an art which was discovered only a few years since; but the purpose ... is to induce you to do in photography something similar to that which the old Greek did in painting, that is, to take the best and most beautiful parts you can obtain suitable for your picture, and join them together into one perfect whole.[13]

Rather than elucidating Greek methodology, Robinson locates justification for composite printing in a version of a dismembered female subject. The female body, as model of classical 'perfection', becomes a gauge by which to measure transgressions which photographers may legitimately perform. That is to say, he legitimates a cropping and realignment of photographic negatives by a parallel dismemberment and realignment of the female body, such that the feminine becomes synonymous here with both the subject matter of the photographer and the photographic process and with the fetishism of an absolute focus. More tellingly still, for Robinson the female body as composite of male gaze – a visual dismantling of the female subject in order to reconfigure it – works strategically to reconfirm a particular structuring of the male gaze as that which is rooted in geometral authority. Robinson's impetus to solve failures of vision entails this particular appropriation of femininity to his composite theory and establishes an initial problematic identification between photographic process and the feminine.

Clearly, Robinson implicates a politics of gender in relation to a politics of representation in order to argue access for photography into fine art at the highest point in the hierarchy. Paradoxically, however, the effect of combination printing is such that it subverts one of the main tenets of that fine art tradition, the authority of geometral laws of composition. For Robinson's technique works, in spite of his conscious claims to the contrary, as a critique of the geometral model, precisely that which the initial 'scissors and paste' were brought in to preserve. Recent theory has, however, overlooked this crucial aspect of combination printing, as expressed in its uncomfortable relationship to geometral perspective. It has therefore failed to recognize how nineteenth-century combination printing implicates geometral vision in two distinct ways. First, it reconfigures it, a fact which might initially appear to reconfirm geometral authority, with an irreconcilable unease. Second, the combination print harbours, structurally, a singular potential splitting apart – the means for its own dismantlement.

Nineteenth-century photographers, such as Robinson, regarded combination printing as the type of concession that photographic composition was obliged to make if photography were to be able to replicate the geometral perspective of Victorian genre and narrative painting. Paradoxically, however, it did not ensure this. The 'look' of combination photographs, the appearance of their readiness to 'fly apart' (together with their cultural positioning) indicates that they did not function simply to sanction the perceptual mastery that a replication of geometral perspective seemed to offer. Moreover, combination printing complicates, in structural and theoretical terms during the mid-nineteenth century, the ideology of visual mastery. The labour of photographers to conceal completely the seams of multiple negatives is crucial to the actual compositional effects because even in the most technically 'accomplished' photographs by Robinson wherein one cannot find actual seams, phantom seams appear to unsettle the eye, and precisely because their multiple compositional vanishing-points, as irrefutable signature of the technique, prohibit the eye from settling into the familiar spatial certainties of geometral perspective. Thus, in Robinson's 'Sleep' of 1867, for example, oddly apparent are those additional disjunctions that are caused by combination printing's uncanny assault on the visual (as geometrically represented) – and not through actual structural cuts but through what we might call 'referred' ones, those created in many composites by the mismatched directions and functions of the represented looks. In this context a later combination print such as Robinson's 'When the Day's Work is Done', 1877, that represents the happy domesticity of hearth becomes almost a parodic version of the origins of photographic focus itself. The photograph, made from six negatives, shows an old man and woman, engaged in the activities of reading the Bible and darning, sharing the hearth which, although not particularly prominent in the composition, is indicated by the kettle which hangs above it. More emphatically, 'Dawn and Sunset', 1885, combines, from three negatives, the figure of an old man with a mother and child seated at the hearth. Again, an uncanny perspective is created, especially around the crowded left-hand foreground, and the hearth, as focal point, is here centralized compositionally, as a semi-obscured glow.

Too often we dismiss combination printing as aesthetic whim or as an unreliable pretension of photographers towards painting, and fail to question just what it means to cut up a photograph in 1860, what it means, that is, to tamper with the newly articulated negative/positive process. We neglect to ask what it means, in other words, to deny the single take, the unitary image, and to manipulate its temporality. Indeed, in Robinson's combination prints and photographic collages one is struck by the numbers of prints in which a disparity between objects in terms of geometral perspective is so great and geometral relations so disrupted that one feels that something else is going on. For a controlling desire to preserve an even, and geometrically controlled, level of focus frequently creates uncannily mismatched gazes, lines of sight between subjects – a disjunction not only created by the composite physical distribution of figures (and combination prints nearly always contain figures) but in the look itself. Combination prints, it must be said, create a radical disjunction in the direction and the function of the look. And this rather than the 'joins' frequently 'gives them away', and troubled nineteenth-century critics.

But, the look of the viewer from vantage-point to vanishing-point is also that which geometral vision articulates as an uninterrupted and centring distance, a Cartesian relationship of exchange. And this uninterrupted linear relation, crucial to documentary, is what combination printing destabilizes. The disrupted look – eye contact in combination prints – disturbs the engendering relation, expressed as a look to a vanishing-point, of a viewer. Viewing the image becomes newly problematic. Focus – as centring 'hearth' – is no longer such a stable place to define. It is precisely then within the context of nineteenth-century debates on combination printing, that Cameron's and Carroll's photographs may provide a different theoretical and ideological functioning.

RETRIEVING THE BATHWATER NOT THE BABY: GERNSHEIM'S CAMERON/GERNSHEIM'S CARROLL

In his book *Julia Margaret Cameron. Her Life and Photographic Work*, Helmet Gernsheim cites a letter of 1864 from Cameron to Sir John Herschel in which she discusses her singular photographic style:

[I] believe in other than mere conventional topographic photography – map-making and skeleton rendering of feature and form without that roundness and fulness of force and feature, that modelling of flesh and limb, *which the focus I use only can give, tho' called and condemned as 'out of focus'. What is focus – and who has a right to say what focus is the legitimate focus?*[14]

Gernsheim cites part of the same quotation again later (p. 70) in an attempt to shed 'light' on what he believes to be Cameron's haphazard technical methods:

> Mrs Cameron was so obsessed by the spiritual quality of her pictures that she paid too little attention to whether the image was sharp or not, whether the sitter had moved, or whether the plate was covered in blemishes. ... Lacking training, she had a complete disregard for technical perfection. Exactly one year after taking up photography she asked Sir John Herschel in a letter: *'What is focus – and who has a right to say what focus is the legitimate focus?'*[15]

In the shift from Gernsheim's first to his second usage of the quote we witness here a particular and now familiar positioning of Cameron, the Victorian woman photographer as technically inept. In fact, in the interplay between these two quotations Gernsheim reverses the motivation for and the tone of Cameron's discourse with Herschel. Instead of a contestation of a photographic 'law' of focus (in an optical hierarchy), Cameron's communication with Herschel is made by Gernsheim into one in which she is primarily situated as enquiring incompetent regarding technical details. This creation occurs in a transference from the first to the second quotation in which Gernsheim observes the rhetorical nature of Cameron's question, 'What is focus?' For Gernsheim chooses to render Cameron's remark as if it were a literal enquiry when it is clear from the original context, from the dash and the deferral of the question mark in her use of the compound interrogative, that the remark is a rhetorical statement and one that does not correlate with an inability to understand the relatively simple procedure of stopping down a lens to achieve variables of focus. For Cameron is raising with Herschel, a scientist well-versed in optics and visual theory and her long-term friend and coiner of several photographic terms, including the word 'photography' itself, the issue of a politics of focus by contesting the authority of focus as law in the discourse of photography. In so doing, she is questioning the very roots of that chief tenet of photography's authority on the visual.

To support his contention, however, Gernsheim strategically slices Cameron's syntax, effectively inverting its meaning and silencing the rhetorical move that articulates 'focus' as a potential site of nineteenth-century debate, as a contested domain in the fields of vision and visuality, and, by implication, the Victorian hearth and home. Focus becomes gendered territory.

That Gernsheim is charging a woman with the inability to grasp no more than how to stop down a lens appears to him to have sufficient credibility. For when the case of gender on one particular side of the camera is at issue then a mystification of technical knowledge serves conveniently to contain a potentially disruptive questioning of photographic authority, and by extension, as I have shown, a questioning of the ideology of perceptual mastery along geometral lines. Thus, while Gernsheim maintains that Cameron 'paid too little attention to whether the image was *sharp or not*', it is conversely evident that that is what she in fact paid a great deal of attention to – a refutation of 'sharpness' by means of a photographic method which is, as she writes, 'called and condemned as out of focus'. Moreover, by taking a stand upon an already established commonplace, Cameron implicitly undermines the sovereignty of geometral perspective in Western systems of visual representation, in the sense that the ubiquity of geometral perspective in the nineteenth century is that which (as discussed above) would appear to be further guaranteed by photographic reproduction, and she even more implicitly shakes, as I will show, the foundations of the nineteenth-century hearth.[16]

Influential photo-historians such as Gernsheim have forged as 'natural' and inevitable a relationship between Cameron's photographs and a fine art tradition, in part through an approximation of photographic focus to style in painting, and thus there has occurred a simplistic mediation of the one discourse through the other together with the dehistoricization of focus into the bargain. Gernsheim typifies a dominant strategy to appropriate Victorian photographers to an art history predicated upon matters of 'style' in which gender is deeply implicated. In such a scheme Cameron's photographs are said to display a style, roughly categorizable as 'soft' focus, which comes to stand for a type of optimum aesthetic value in photography owing to a supposed contiguity of 'focus' to 'style' in painting. But this construction is a dehistoricized version of Cameron's theory and practice, and it succeeds essentially in detaching Victorian photography from the multiple discourses that attend and participate in its invention in order to leave a single discourse as *the* naturalized discourse for correlation and comparison. More crucially still, it repeatedly eclipses precisely those dehistoricizing stages required to arrive at a neat equation whereby 'soft' focus equals a greater aesthetic value than does 'sharp' focus in Cameron's portrait photography. It forgets, however, that 'soft' focus is a relatively new construction, for the term refers, in fact, to the aestheticization of focus. Such a construction also obscures the fact that focus or its synonym depth of field operates primarily in nineteenth-century photography as a mark of, or signature for, the mechanics of the medium whose meanings are invariably different from its pre-photographic ones. In one important sense, then, a concept of focus, deriving from the discourses of geometry and optics, becomes that which is singularly intrinsic to photographic reproduction. In this sense, instead of aligning photography with painting, 'focus' is that which elicits a conception of photography at its farthest remove from painting.

Thus, what has occurred in photography history to make us read

Cameron's unfocused images as 'soft' focus images (notice what a considerable shift in signification is implicit here) is an aestheticization of focus, as popularized by Gernsheim's history. To continue to read as 'style' the problematic concept of focus in nineteenth-century photography theory and practice is to continue to privilege the relationship of photography to painting to the exclusion of all other discourses. Furthermore, it is to write out of history, as does Gernsheim in his omission of the counter-tendency from Cameron's syntax, primarily on the grounds of gender, contestation and critique of the ideology of perceptual mastery. Most importantly, as I will go on to demonstrate, when read contextually, Cameron's decision not to approximate a focused image, together with her questioning of focus as photographic law, constitutes a critique of the ideology of perceptual mastery as that which is continually affirmed in the notion of a stable relationship of subject to visual field along the lines of a geometral grid. Contextually, Cameron's photographs have to be read as problematizing photographic discourse, by employing it to challenge one of the most dominant (and phallocentric) paradigms in Western modes of visual representation. By subverting a photographic law of focus close to photography's inception, Cameron destabilizes the assurance of hearth, both in its technical and its social senses.

A second reference to Gernsheim and his highly influential book *Lewis Carroll, Photographer* allows us to examine, even more explicitly, the problematic of a relationship between nineteenth-century visual theory and gender difference as enacted in a politics of focus.[17] As with his work on Cameron, Gernsheim was the first critic to devote a book-length study to Carroll as photographer, and in particular to Carroll's portraits of children. As Gernsheim notes, Carroll, like Cameron, was a self-taught amateur. However, while the myth of Cameron as technical incompetent has to some extent endured, variously translated as a condition of chronic myopia, Carroll is mythologized, beginning with Gernsheim, as a master of composition. As part of his strategy of mythologization, Gernsheim, writing on Carroll, compares the two contemporaneous photographers in a way that genders their photographic styles according to an inversion of their gendered positions:

> Mrs Cameron was urged on by great ambition, and her work is the expression of an ardent temperament. Lewis Carroll had no ambition; *his art springs from delight in the beautiful; he is feminine and light-hearted in his approach to photography, whereas she is masculine and intellectual.*[18]

The conscious sexual inversion here operates to indicate ultimately a preference for the 'feminine and light-hearted' in a man with 'no ambition' over the 'masculine and intellectual' in a woman 'urged on by great ambition'. In this sense the gender disruption that each photographer suggests does not involve a strict motility between these two positions. That is to say, it is more admirable to be a nineteenth-century male photographer with no ambition than a female photographer with a great deal of it. Ambition for a woman is invariably equivalent to a surfeit of it. Such interrelations of gender and focus become more acute when Gernsheim brings into his comparison of the two photographers questions of composition. But, as we shall see, there is a problem with reading in Gernsheim the two photographers as straight-forwardly gendered 'masculine' and 'feminine', for he disrupts the opposition as he finds it expedient to do so. Gernsheim cites a comment by Carroll on the relationship of his photographic 'style' to that of Cameron which further dramatizes ways in which a complex politics of focus and gender are here each implicated in the other. In referring to an evening in August 1864, spent in looking at photographs at Cameron's house, Freshwater, Isle of Wight, Carroll writes of Cameron's photographs: 'some are very picturesque, some merely hideous. *She* wished she could have some of *my* subjects to do *out* of focus – and I expressed an analogous wish with regard to some of *her* subjects', a statement that Gernsheim annotates then as implying that Carroll wished to do some of her subjects 'in focus'.[19]

We have here a fantasy hinged upon substitution in which the photographic 'subjects' of each photographer are articulated as a theoretical visual antithesis, that of being 'in' or 'out' of focus. But what then is the status of this type of fetishism of focus – and by extension a fetishization of its absence – in nineteenth-century photographic discourse and those discourses with which it intersects? What is articulated at this stage in Victorian photography in the passage or potential slippage between these two newly photographically inscribed extremes of being 'in' and 'out'?

IN/OUT, IN/OUT, SHAKE IT ALL ABOUT

We have, then, a hokey-cokey situation; to be alternately 'in' and 'out' is the legacy of photographic focus, as becomes evident in comparisons of photographs by Cameron and Carroll in which we find difference articulated at the level of depth of field. Quite simply, the comparison shows that where Cameron largely refuses to approximate a highly focused picture-plane, Carroll in his portraits of 'child friends' preserves above all else a centrally focused object. Indeed, in Carroll *all* represented space leads ultimately to a focused region, that of a child's body. The ramifications of Carroll's obsession with focus is demonstrated by the extraordinary portraits in the Gernsheim Collection of one of his favourite models, Alexandra Kitchin, nicknamed Xie. The photographs represent a repetition of the 'set-up', highly staged portrait. In them we find Xie in Greek dress, 1873, wearing a crown, 1874, sleeping in ragged dress, 1875, as a Chinaman, in white hat and coat, playing the violin, and as Reynolds's Penelope Boothby, 1876 among others. Not only in these photographs do we repeatedly encounter the same persistently makeshift studio interior, the same properties (Chinese boxes and crown for example) but we find that the articulation of space surrounding the subject remains the same. However, what becomes most troubling is the articulation of the centrally focused and elaborately clothed body of the child. For the look is repeatedly stopped upon the child's body. But this literal and abrupt stopping is created as such by the inclusion of the photographer/viewer's route to it. In other words, it is created by the depth of field that intervenes between vantage-point and vanishing-point and secures their interdependent relation.

Rather tellingly, Gernsheim dismisses wholesale Carroll's 'costume portraits' by condemning them as artistically inferior and as 'errors of taste'. But in fact more than any other of his photographs these 'set-ups' of Xie enact the obsessional repetitive methods of the photographic entries in Carroll's diaries, those elaborately circuitous schemes for securing an infinite supply of child subjects for the lens, those processes by which Carroll's literary authority precedes and sanctions his photographic identity and practices.[20] Nevertheless, Gernsheim makes the following distinction:

> Whereas Lewis Carroll's other photographic work shows a remarkable independence of contemporary photography, the sentiment of these pictures is a lamentable concession to Victorian taste. As a producer of costume pictures Lewis Carroll is almost always banal; as a photographer of children he achieves an excellence which in its way can find no peer.[21]

There is a striking paradox here, an imbalance in this perfectly parallel sentence. For surely the point is that Carroll's 'costume pictures' are *always children* in costume. Yet when is a child portrait not a child portrait? Gernsheim seems to imply – When it's in costume! His attempt to make a distinction here unwittingly further problematizes Carroll's portraits of children – children standing in here of course for girls ('I am fond of children', Carroll once wrote, 'except boys'). If we extend this point to the controversial case of the lost but now retrieved though tampered-with images of naked children, together with those negatives that Carroll is known to have destroyed himself, we are reminded of how questions of sexuality in Carroll always hinge upon these images. Perhaps not surprisingly, we discover here then that the clothed ones are, always, the most troubling, especially those that enact various cultural and national fantasies – the Indian, the Greek, the Turk, the directly theatrical guises, or Carroll's unrealized lifelong desire to create a 'gypsy'.[22] In other words the most problematic of Carroll's photographs are those which Gernsheim directs us away from – those of children repeatedly clothed and set-up against a blank studio wall, undressed, that is, to be reclothed in the garb of various cultural fantasies. The manner in which these portraits articulate gender in terms of a politics of focus therefore makes them central to a comparison with Cameron.

The intrusiveness of photographer/viewer, in these portraits of Xie Kitchin, is dramatized by the repeated inscription of wide expanses of floor area in front of the subject which creates an odd effect rendered all the more oddly pervasive by the inclusion of tatty sections of carpet that cover or uncover the floorboards. In many of these portraits of Xie particularly there is a missing piece to the left foreground. Carroll's missing carpet square, in the end, becomes a haunting aspect of these photographs. The presence of the absent piece is emphasized by the fact that the piece behind the exposed boards is kinked up slightly to give the further impression of our viewing the scene from a low point of view. We might even suggest that this missing square of carpet in Carroll's photographs of Xie serves as a tawdry inscription of the ideology of perceptual mastery. Yet no one has ever, as far as I know, remarked upon its blatant presence, nor (not wishing to expose emperors) has anyone chosen to see its persistence in the work of a 'master' of composition.

The photographs 'Playing the Violin' and 'Penelope Boothby' may demonstrate my point. Xie Kitchin playing the violin shows the model posed in the balletic third position to appear as if playing the instrument. But it would be impossible for her to do so from where she is standing, since the bow is pressed right up against the wall. Xie stands, off-centre to the right, with her heels up against the skirting-board, her back against the wall with a large expanse of foreground space and the ever-present, though here somewhat obscured by damage to the negative, signatory carpet. She is dressed in a heavy velvet dress with white sash and sleeves, and she looks out to the camera with a slight smile. Dressed as Penelope Boothby (the standing rather than recumbent pose) Xie is posed in the same interior, centrally located up against the wall with the same absent piece of carpet to the left foreground. She wears striped stockings, transparent fingerless gloves, and around her neck hangs a black choker with heavy metal cross. This time her look is directed slightly off to the left. Again, what is disturbing here is the foreground space which precisely suggests the encroachment of the point of view, of the photographer's vantage-point. In other words, the location of the figure beyond empty foreground space itself signals that she has been set up to view in geometral terms. The vantage-point of the photographer/viewer is extremely uncanny in both of these and various other portraits by Carroll. Carroll appears, in effect, to be toying with geometral mastery in more ways than one. The object of the look/lens is literally mastered here optically, displayed for view before a blank ground, somewhat in the manner of a projection, located at the vanishing-point of our look. This is why the inclusion of the foreground space is so crucial here, and the persistently absent carpet square so troubling. The set-up in terms of depth of field, as much as the child portrayed, inscribes, with the agency of invisible ink, Carroll's irrefutable forge-proof signature.

In this context, Gernsheim's reading of Carroll as a master of composition might be rephrased as a 'master' of successfully replicating the type of visual mastery articulated or exercised by geometral perspective. Significantly, nothing like this mastery is present in Cameron, and therefore it should not surprise us that Gernsheim labels her 'weak' at composition. This point of

Plate 14.1 Lewis Carroll (C. L. Dodgson) *Xie Kitchin Playing the Violin*, *c.* 1876.
Photo: with kind permission of the Gernsheim Collection, Harry Ransom
Humanities Research Center, University of Texas, Austin

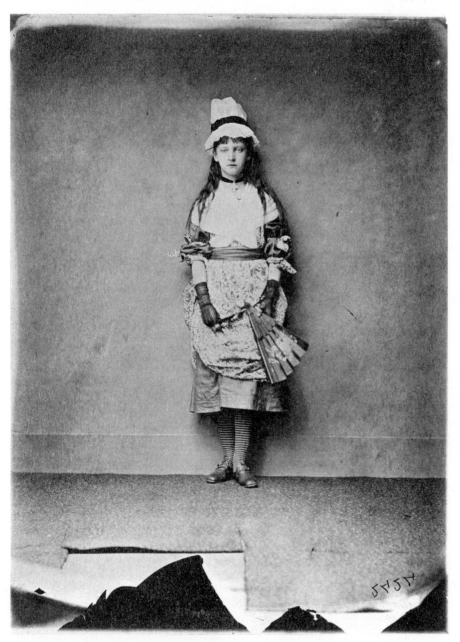

Plate 14.2 Lewis Carroll (C. L. Dodgson) *Xie Kitchin as 'Penelope Boothby'*, *c.* 1875. Photo: with kind permission of the Gernsheim Collection, Harry Ransom Humanities Research Center, University of Texas, Austin

comparison does not of course make Cameron, for Gernsheim, a less successful photographer, but it keeps her in her gendered place in a fine art tradition, as more interested in representing the 'souls' of her sitters as opposed to Carroll's more pragmatic interest in laws of composition.

Thus we can ascertain more clearly the relationship between a politics of gender in photographs and photographic histories of Cameron and Carroll with a politics of focus. The oddly repetitive depth of field in Carroll, culminating in a captive displayed literally up against a wall, represents a space assumed necessary to mobilize that geometral binary relation, which is also the space of male fantasy. In Carroll this intervening space is in focus indicating the sovereignty of hearth. And he is called a master of composition in Gernsheim's history because his photographs more nearly approximate the colonizing gaze of documentary practice, that which as we have seen requires geometral mapping for its intelligibility.

But such so-called mastery also has direct implications for the roles of gender as they are established in and by the relationship of focus to hearth and home, that bastion of patriarchal power. And, as Christian Metz reminds us, the intrinsic link between photography and the fetish occurs with the home, the 'birthplace of the Freudian fetish'.[23] While Metz addresses the fetish in order to determine some of 'the basic differences between photography and film' I am here concerned with the way in which photographic focus in Carroll mobilizes processes of fetishism. Freud in his essay 'Fetishism', 1927, defines the fetish as 'a substitute for the woman's (the mother's) penis that the little boy once believed in and – for reasons familiar to us – does not want to give up'.[24] Thus, fetishism occurs in the boy's disavowal of the woman's lack of penis as a means of displacing his own fear of castration. Carroll, in these portraits of Xie Kitchin seeks to 'stop' the look 'half-way' as it were, to arrest it with fetishized articles of clothing (upon those 'India shawls' for example).[25] Focus as photographic state may thus in a sense be read as fetishized with its antithesis 'out of focus' thereby becoming commensurate with a fear of castration (or with 'the unwelcome fact of woman's castration') symbolized, we might say, in the loss of patriarchal power in the home. We can further rewrite this formation as the fetishism that *is* focus in the sense that focus in photographic representation newly mobilizes the fetish. Moreover, returning to the substitutive relationship of 'in' to 'out' of focus, for a subject to be 'out' of focus for Carroll becomes an issue because of the relationship of photographic focus to the institution of the fetish, because to deny focus is to deny the institution of the fetish as a displacement of loss. Carroll approximates this position when articulating his lack of aesthetic interest in the bodies of young boys, for he maintains they always give the impression of needing to be covered up. Yet, to put it simply, for Carroll the bodies of boys are still not worth dressing up to be photographed. To dress up boys would not constitute an attempt to ward off this loss, for they are always already redundant with regard to fetishism since it is not the sight of the phallus that the voyeur seeks to ward off but rather the sight of its absence.

Cameron, however, unlike Carroll, does not stop the look, and, with an absence of 'sharp' focus, her photography cannot therefore in the same way serve fetishism. In subverting photography's authoritative self-defining law of absolute focus Cameron effectively denies the phallocentricism of geometral perspective and rewrites the contingency of depth as her subject. Consequently, Cameron typically situates the subjects of her portraits, including those of children, close up to the picture-plane. She does not invite the eye into the recessional certainties of geometral perspective; she removes the intervening distance between vantage-point and vanishing-point. Her portrait, of the child Annie Philpot, 'Annie, "My First Success"', 1864, shows the subject, without sharp focus, in a three-quarter left profile. Her clothing is detectable only as a dark coat with large buttons. The image is devoid of props and since the subject occupies virtually the whole space of the picture-plane, the small proportion of background works against a recessional register; the female subject is here newly realized. This portrait has been described as 'unusually modern by virtue of its informality';[26] in fact its effect of 'informality' derives as much from a denial of Cartesian perspectivalism as from an absence of the staging characteristic of Carroll. Similarly, 'Daisy', 1864, portrait of Daisy Bradley, shows the subject, again without sharp focus, close up to the picture-plane, occupying virtually the entire image. The child looks directly out, with hand held to her collar and the representation disrupts conventional modes of identification (voyeurism and narcissism) for the viewer through its reformulation of the agency of focus.

By definition, then, Cameron's politics of focus also denies the fetish. Since a condition of 'in' focus becomes fetishized (as a displacement of loss) then her denial of focus conversely prevents the look from being blocked or displaced, by the 'pre-eminence of certain forms as the objects of its search',[27] and thus condemns it to perpetual unease, to the relative 'blur' of its mobilization. Constructed in such a way, Cameron's contestation of focus contains clearly wider historical and cultural ramifications. In other words, Cameron threatens more than merely an aesthetic principle. She represents the possibility of demobilizing the whole mechanism of fetishism in the field of vision, and all that demobilization clearly implies for the Victorian patriarchal sanctity of home and hearth. As we are reminded by Lacan, Freud singles out the scopic drive as 'not homologous with the others' precisely because it is 'this drive that most completely eludes the term castration'.[28]

Thus, to read nineteenth-century debates upon photographic focus is to confront a primary identification of contestatory photographic practice with problematic constructions of gender; it is to see the ideology of perceptual mastery (as exemplified by geometral perspective) laid bare in a simultaneous problematization of photographic agency and a politics of gender. Furthermore, Cameron specifically then may be seen to threaten the most reliable means by which for the male the castration complex may be disavowed: the

Plate 14.3   Julia Margaret Cameron, *Annie, 'My First Success'*, *c*. 1864. Photo: with kind permission of the National Museum of Photography, Film and Television (National Museum of Science and Industry), Bradford, West Yorkshire

Plate 14.4 Julia Margaret Cameron, *'Daisy' (Margaret Bradley)*, *c.* 1864. Photo: with kind permission of the National Museum of Photography, Film and Television (National Museum of Science and Industry), Bradford, West Yorkshire

scopic realm. Moreover, since psychoanalytic theory has appropriated, from visual culture, most specifically the geometral as a model for the psychic apparatus, the potential displacement of such a model in nineteenth-century photography also suggests new ways in which to think about the relationship of sexual difference to photographic representation. In this way, Cameron's politics of focus should be read as undermining dominant scopic regimes, and theories of representation that underpin the whole patriarchal structure of Victorian society.

NOTES

1 See in particular Andrea Fisher, *Let Us Now Praise Famous Women* (London: Pandora), 1987.
2 John Tagg, *The Burden of Representation. Essays on Photographies and Histories* (London: Macmillan), 1988; Alan Sekula, 'The Body and the Archive', *October* 39, Winter 1986, pp. 4–64.
3 Abigail Solomon Godeau, 'Reconstructing Documentary: Connie Hatch's Representational Resistance', *Camera Obscura* 13/14, 1985, p. 116: 'Not before, however, the militant avant-gardism of the post-World War I period was it possible to at least partially address some of the underpinnings of photography's ideological functioning.'
4 ibid., p. 116.
5 Tagg, op. cit., p. 118.
6 Victor Burgin, ed., *Thinking Photography* (London: Macmillan), 1982, p. 114. Burgin writes: 'There are no essays by women in this anthology. This is a matter neither of oversight nor prejudice, it is the contingent effect of conjecture. Much of the work by women occupies different theoretical registers, and/or engages different practical projects from those of this present collection.'
7 Helmut Gernsheim together with his wife Alison Eames Gernsheim amassed numerous holdings of photo-historical images and literature and began, in London in 1945, the Gernsheim Collection. Over the next two decades they published twenty books and over two hundred journal articles on photography and photography history. When the University of Texas acquired the Gernsheim Collection in 1964, it was the largest photo-historical archive in private hands.
8 Rosalind Krauss, 'Photography and the Simulacral', *October* 31, Winter 1984, p. 57.
9 The Latin *focus* was first used in plane geometry by Johannes Kepler in 1604 to signify 'one of the points from which the distances to any point of a given curve are connected by a linear relation'. In optical discourse, 'focus' describes 'the position at which an object must be situated in order that the image produced by the lens may be clear and well-defined'.
10 William Henry Fox Talbot, *Literary Gazette* 1150 (2 February 1839), p. 73.
11 The demystification of geometral or Cartesian perspective, together with a critique of mastery inherent in its disruption, has been addressed recently – in relation to painting – by Norman Bryson and Martin Jay in one of a series of talks at the Dia Art Foundation; see *Vision and Visuality*, ed. Hal Foster, Dia Art Foundation Discussions in Contemporary Culture, no. 2 (Seattle: Bay Press, 1988). Whereas Bryson locates a critique of geometral perspective in the work of Erwin Panofsky, Jay argues that although geometral perspective has been 'the target of a widespread philosophical critique', owing to its dependency upon an ahistorical 'disembodied' subject, this does not mean that as a representational system, 'it was quite as

uniformly coercive as it is sometimes assumed'. And Jay cites the position of Michael Kubovy (*The Psychology of Perspective and Renaissance Art*, Cambridge: Cambridge University Press, 1986) to argue that we cannot identify the theoretical rules of perspective 'with the actual practice of the artists themselves'. However, absent from the Dia lectures is a recognition of the problematization by photography in the nineteenth century of the status and functioning of geometral perspective.

12 *The British Journal of Photography* contained an ongoing debate upon combination printing during 1860. See in particular: 2 April, 15 June, 2 July. Of course nineteenth-century combination printing is itself a massive subject, and I can only begin here to suggest for what reasons it has remained an 'unhomely' technique in photography theory and practice.

13 Henry Peach Robinson, *The British Journal of Photography*, 2 April 1860, p. 94. Robinson is in many ways unabashedly disrespectful of 'naturalism'; moreover he is not very good at foreseeing the logical extensions of his theoretical strategies, thus opening himself to the accusations of second-rate 'patchwork'. It is further significant that in the debates, in this journal, upon combination printing, the critic A. H. Wall opposes Robinson to Oscar Rejlander, allegedly to demonstrate Rejlander's greater respect for 'composition' as evidenced in his never overlooking 'the superiority of painting over photography' (A. H. Wall, *The British Journal of Photography*, 2 July 1860).

However, in fact, Rejlander turned to combination printing for a reason that systematically brings together a politics of focus and gender: in order to reproduce a gendered spatial ordering. Rejlander describes his first use of the technique as a means of reconfirming a particular structuring of the male gaze. As William Crawford remarks, 'vexed and despairing, he found that, after arranging three figures in a portrait group, his lens would not give sufficient sharpness to the male subject who stood behind a couch, on which two ladies were seated' (*The Keepers of Light*, p. 53). Thus, in order not to disrupt traditionally gendered relations in portrait photography, nor to allow the man to drift out of focus, Rejlander adopted combination printing.

14 Helmut Gernsheim, *Julia Margaret Cameron. Her Life and Photographic Work* (London: Aperture, 1948), rev. edn (London: Aperture, 1975), p. 14 (my emphasis).

15 ibid., p. 70.

16 The claim that Cameron's photographs may be read as engaging a critique of dominant nineteenth-century representational theories and practices might initially seem incompatible with her claim of part of her project as an attempt to secure for photography 'the character and uses of High Art'. Cameron's above claim is not so unquestionably at odds with a politics of focus if we read her phrase as more commensurate with pre-Renaissance art, or at least with the versions of medievalism that she explores in her Tennysonian subjects. Nor is it so if we take into account her recognition of the inherent problematic of a desire to position her own discourse in relationship to that of painting.

17 Helmut Gernsheim, *Lewis Carroll, Photographer* (New York: Dover, 1969). In the preface to the first edition, 1949, Gernsheim explains how, while collecting material for his biography of Cameron, his attention was first drawn to an album by Carroll.

18 ibid., p. 29 (my emphasis).

19 Quoted in Gernsheim, *Lewis Carroll*, p. 30.

20 Gernsheim chooses to refer to Carroll by his literary name, even though Carroll used C. L. Dodgson for his photographic identity. This point would be in itself

interesting even if it did not relate to Gernsheim's dismissal of Carroll's costume pieces. While I do not wish to join the Jekyll and Hyde debate, I would like to point out the manner in which, in practice, Carroll's literary identity fronted the photographic one. The author of *Alice in Wonderland* usually procured photographic 'victims' by first sending them a copy of his book. The book as gift was generally followed by a letter to the parents asking permission to 'borrow' their child.

21 Gernsheim, *Lewis Carroll*, pp. 20–1.
22 For plates of the four surviving 'nude' studies, see Morton N. Cohen, *Lewis Carroll, Photographer of Children: Four Nude Studies* (New York: Potter, 1979).
23 Christian Metz, 'Photography and Fetish', *October* 34, Fall 1985, pp. 81–90, p. 82: 'Photography enjoys a high degree of social recognition in another domain: that of the presumed real, of life, mostly private and family life, birthplace of the Freudian fetish.'
24 Sigmund Freud, 'Fetishism', 1927, *The Standard Edition of the Complete Psycho-analytical Works of Sigmund Freud*, ed. James Strachey and Anna Freud, 24 vols (London: Hogarth Press, 1953–66), vol. 21, pp. 147–57, pp. 152–3. Freud also writes:

> In the situation we are considering ... we see that the perception has persisted, and that a very energetic action has been undertaken to maintain the disavowal.... But this interest suffers an extraordinary increase as well, because the horror of castration has set up a memorial to itself in the creation of the substitute.
>
> (p. 154)

But later he further adds: 'In very subtle instances both the disavowal and the affirmation of the castration have found their way into the construction of the fetish' (p. 156).
25 On the question of the relationship of fetishism to Orientalism see David Simpson, *Fetishism and Imagination* (Baltimore: Johns Hopkins University Press, 1982), p. iv. There is not space here to discuss at length, in the work of Carroll, the question of fetishism as 'anthropological concept', but Simpson discusses Melville and Conrad as demonstrating the 'exporting of the fetishised imagination from one's own society to distant places: the very places from which, ironically enough, the first accounts of fetishistic practices had originally been taken'.
26 Amanda Hopkinson, *Julia Margaret Cameron* (London: Virago, 1986), p. 106.
27 Jacques Lacan, *The Four Fundamental Concepts of Psychoanalysis*, trans. Alan Sheridan (London: Penguin, 1977), p. 182.
28 ibid., p. 78.

Chapter 15

The hand of the huntress: repetition and Malory's Morte Darthur

Catherine LaFarge

'So sir Launcelot and sir Lavayne departed, that no creature wyste where he was becom but the noble men of hys blood. And whan he was com to the ermytayge, wyte you well he had grete chyre. And so dayly sir Launcelot used to go to a welle by the ermytage, and there he wolde ly downe and se the well sprynge and burble, and somtyme he slepte there.

So at that tyme there was a lady that dwelled in that foreyste, and she was a grete hunteresse, and dayly she used to hunte. And ever she bare her bowghe with her, and no men wente never with her, but allwayes women, and they were all shooters and cowde well kylle a dere at the stalke and at the treste. And they dayly beare bowys, arowis, hornys and wood-knyves, and many good doggis they had, bothe for the strenge and for a bate.

So hit happed the lady, the huntresse, had abated her dogge for the bowghe at a barayne hynde, and so this barayne hynde toke the flyght over hethys and woodis. And ever thys lady and parte of her women costed the hynde, and checked hit by the noyse of the hounde to have mette with the hynde at som watir. And so hit happened that that hynde cam to the same welle thereas sir Launcelot was by that welle slepynge and slumberynge.

And so the hynde, whan he cam to the welle, for heete she wente to soyle, and there she lay a grete whyle. And the dogge cam aftir and unbecaste aboute, for she had lost the verray parfyte fewte of the hynde. Ryght so cam that lady, the hunteres, that knew by her dogge that the hynde was at the soyle by that welle, and thyder she cam streyte and founde the hynde. And anone as she had spyed hym she put a brode arow in her bowe and shot at the hynde, and so she overshotte the hynde, and so by myssefortune the arow smote sir Launcelot in the thyke of the buttok over the barbys.

Whan sir Launcelot felte hym so hurte he whorled up woodly, and saw the lady that had smytten hym. And whan he knew she was a woman he sayde thus:

'Lady, or damesell, whatsomever ye be, in an evyll tyme bare ye thys bowe. The devyll made you a shoter!'

'Now, mercy, fayre sir!' seyde the lady, 'I am a jantillwoman that usyth here in thys foreyste huntynge, and God knowyth I saw you nat but as here was a barayne hynde at the soyle in thys welle. And I wente I had done welle, but my hande swarved.'

'Alas', seyde sir Launcelot, 'ye have myscheved me'.

And so the lady departed. And sir Launcelot, as he myght, pulled oute the arow and leffte the hede stylle in hys buttok, and so he wente waykely unto the ermytayge, evermore bledynge as he wente. And whan sir Lavayne and the errmyte aspyed that sir Launcelot was so sore hurte, wyte you well they were passyng hevy. But sir Lavayne wyst nat how that he was hurte nothir by whom. And than were they wrothe oute of mesure. And so wyth grete payne the ermyte gate oute the arow-hede oute of sir Launcelottis buttoke, and muche of hys bloode he shed; and the wounde was passynge sore and unhappyly smytten, for hit was on such a place that he myght nat sytte in no saddyll.

'A, mercy Jesu!' seyde sir Launcelot, 'I may calle myselff the moste unhappy man that lyvyth, for ever whan I wolde have faynyst worshyp there befallyth me ever som unhappy thynge.'

(*The Works of Sir Thomas Malory*, ed. E. Vinaver, 2nd edn (Oxford, 1963), vol. III, p. 1103/31–1106/9)

In the latter part of the medieval period narrative was moving inward from the masculine arena of epic combat to what was progressively being delineated as at once the inner, the feminine and the proper matter of story. Paradoxically this arena, despite its new status and articulation in story, remained alien and frighteningly other. The Age of Romance, as it has been named,[1] constructed much of what modern Western civilization would call the feminine and the masculine. At the same time medieval culture retained a conception of gender which permitted the two discrete positions to remain, in imaginative use, remarkably free from the strictures of biological gender. Nor did the misogyny of the age stabilize these categories, firmly matching one with the positive and the other with the negative.

Malory's *Morte Darthur*, however, largely seems to be determined to prevent such liberties. There the feminine is located as both the inner and the utterly outside, that which lies beyond the known and the social – in short, the wild (a geographical region notably unromanticized in medieval culture). But the rise of penance as an annual duty and a psychological skill and the Abelardian shift of guilt from deed to intention[2] had made new claims for the priority of the inner, at the same time as narrative was designating that as the territory of the feminine. Even in Malory, this positive rendering of the inner places the masculine and the feminine, the public and private, in a new and uneasy tension.

These configurations have a special relevance to what Malory does with plot and cause. From the syntactical level to the episodic, *Le Morte Darthur* is notable for its general ignoring of what makes things happen. The great unspeakable cause in the plot is, of course, adultery, that narratorially denied encroachment of the private upon the corporate in a text which conflates the masculine with the public and explicitly plays down the value of the feminine: 'Quenys I myght have inow, but such a felyship of good knyghtes shall never be togydirs in no company' (1184/3–5). Arthur's often-quoted statement should not, however, disguise the fact that in Malory difference of gender is largely overlooked. As Mark Lambert points out, Sir Lavayne's infatu- ation with Lancelot is strikingly undifferentiated from that of his sister, Elayne of Astolat.[3] But the disregarded problem of gender, particularly the role of the feminine, comes back to haunt the progress of the narrative, as Elayne's own corpse floats back down the Thames within view of Arthur's window.

The huntress who makes her appearance immediately after this embar- rassing incident raises questions not only about the role of the feminine but also about the roles of repetition and repression. In a way which belies the blind spots of the text, she is extravagantly gendered. The wound she inflicts reiterates the preceding episode sufficiently for Lancelot, in a particularly unintrospective episode, to remark upon it himself. At the same time, other features of the story seem set upon neutralizing these forces of recognition or at least using them as a kind of inoculation against further symptoms of the kind.

The huntress combines the features of feminine and masculine in an alarm- ing fashion. Eschewing the company of men, she has the arms and proficiency of a man supported by men's exclusive corporate fellowship transposed to members of her own sex. She is surrounded by a superabundance of the feminine: she frequents the forest, that secret region which is structurally equated with disguise and disappearance and peopled by hermits and women. Men in Malory yearn for contact with their peers and betters; she shows no interest in even the best of men when she happens upon him, and only does so because her hand slips. Her transgression of the female estate is foregrounded by repetitious gender markings tailing off into verbal fumblings: she is the 'lady hunteras',[4] 'lady, or damesell, whatsomever ye be'; Lancelot, having 'whorled up woodly', blurts out that idiom most expressive of conservative estates theory: 'The devyll made you a shoter!' (1104/30–4).[5]

Lancelot, meanwhile, has been feminized. Like Gawain in *Sir Gawain and the Green Knight* he has been caught off guard, snoozing in an arena outside his field of competence. His wound, 'on such a place that he myght nat sytte in no sadyll' (1106/2–3; cf. 1085/30), is, precisely, an endangerment to his role as man and knight. For Malory, as for Caxton, to be unhorsed is to be unknighted; to be unknighted is to be unmanned.

The easy reading of these reversals is that the huntress's is unnaturally ambitious, Lancelot's humiliating, and each comic in its impropriety. This, minus the humour, which understandably is lost on him, is Lancelot's own view, and Malory's narrative line is known for its symbiotic relationship with its hero.[6] But this standard signalling of the derogatory by way of the feminine is not the whole picture. In the Middle Ages the feminine and the masculine are figures for two positions, each with its particular value and potential, and each, although in romance often with some accompanying levity, to a certain extent open to occupancy by members of either sex. Read in its cultural context and in its immediate narrative setting, the feminization of Lancelot brings into play a complex of meanings which includes but exceeds the familiar hierarchical pattern. Lancelot becomes not just less than himself, but, more importantly, different from himself.

Recognition, in short, is at once an organizing and an unsettling principle of this and surrounding episodes. This is an unrecognition scene. The naming and identification of Lancelot (Where is Lancelot? Who is the Knight with the white shield, the red sleeve, the gold sleeve?) amount to a thematic refrain elsewhere in 'The Tale of Lancelot and Guinevere', but this lady does not recognize Lancelot nor he her. More peculiarly, criticism has been loath to speak about her, as if subject to the same repressions as *Le Morte Darthur* itself.

What is unmistakable, with that discomforting force which Freud associated with the uncanny confirmation of primitive beliefs,[7] is the huntress's likeness to the Dianas of classical and medieval stories, and the suitability of the circumstances for the occurrence of something strange. Perhaps this discomfort accounts for the text's insistence, through the mouth of the lady herself, that she is just a 'jantillwoman that usyth here in thys foreyste huntynge'. The crucial details are, of course, the proficiency and relentlessness of her hunting and that of her companions, and her constant carrying of her bow and equally constant exclusion of men; her appearance near a refreshing well facilitates the association. In Boccaccio's *Caccia di Diana* the goddess's troupe listen to her admonitions while sitting round 'un gran monte' of quarry.[8] The linking in Malory of 'ever' present bow and 'never' present men recalls the traditional signification of Diana's weapon; it is 'in dispyte of Diane the chaste' that the servants of Venus in *The Parlement of Foules* have hung up their broken bows.[9] In Boccaccio, in Ovid's tale of Actaeon, indeed in the earliest recorded cult of Diana and in countless folk-tales of transformation and other marvels, water plays a crucial role.[10]

But we do not need to look beyond French Arthurian romance to find a Diana who was a great huntress and lived in the forest. The prose *Lancelot* says that she was considered a goddess by the pagans but that we now call her a fairy.[11] This fairy Diana is closely associated with the Lady of the Lake who, due in part to her admiring imitation, has many of Diana's attributes. Marvelling by Diana's lake, to which Lancelot will owe his name, the Lady says that Diana 'ama toute sa vie la deduit del bois autant que je faic ou plus'.[12] In this way the French romances often acknowledge both the doublings of romance and the transformations of myth in a rationalized manner, and uncanniness is forestalled.

The classical Diana, the Arthurian Diana and the latter's disciple share a relation to men in which aversion forms a continuum with passionate abductions, occasionally coming full circle in violent murders which recall the dismemberment of Actaeon and the unmanning of Ancaeus.[13] The chaste goddess whose wrath was thus expressed was in the ancient world often merged with the fickle moon goddess who desired and controlled the sleeping mortal Endymion.[14] The Arthurian Diana, likewise fickle, becomes obsessed with Faunus to whom she promises a healing herbal bath but instead drowns in boiling lead.[15] Here woundedness assumes the role of sleep as a token of vulnerability and an access point for control. The Lady of the Lake, herself sometimes called a fairy, who is said to live chastely in the forest and to laugh at the idea of lovers, abducts Lancelot in the *Merlin* and the prose *Lancelot* and plunges with him into Diana's lake.[16] While benevolent, she is a 'taker' with a family resemblance to the fairies of *Sir Orfeo*[17] and Froissart's *Meliador*; in the latter the hero is carried off to the bottom of a lake in the forest of Archinai, a known abode of fairies, where he dreams of his beloved and where it is revealed that it is 'nimphes et pucelles / A Dyane ... qui ravirent le chevalier'; later he is said to have been 'des fées pris'.[18] The conception of Diana as an underworld fairy must have been encouraged by the fact that possibly her most frequent epithet aside from virgin and huntress is 'three-form': goddess of heaven, earth and underworld. Emely in *The Knight's Tale* uses this name, and in the narrator's unpropitious portrayal 'Hir eyen caste she ful low adoon / Ther Pluto hath his derke regioun.'[19] L. A. Paton points out that Diana was feared as the noonday demon in German literary tradition and cites Burchard of Worms' and the fifteenth-century Johannes Herolt's casting of her as leader of the Wild Hunt.[20] Contemporary audiences would have recognized a repertoire of motifs as virtual invitations to such beings who sometimes seem to be spontaneously generated by the heat of the hour or season and daytime slumber. The tales in which they appear do not always make it clear why a particular mortal was selected, but suggestions of involuntary surrender or even violence often overlap in function with seduction or the erotic.[21]

The existence of the Lady of the Lake and the fairy Diana of Arthurian romance in Malory's own literary tradition and direct sources can only lend support to a reading of Lancelot's wounding as having a particular relevance to his gender, his knighthood and his relation with women, and to gender and wholeness in Malory generally. The attention to Lancelot's 'slepynge and slumberynge' and the mention of 'heete', literally referring to the animal's exertions but contributing to one's impression of warm weather, lead the reader to expect something more than a bit of ordinary bad luck. The reiterated 'dayly' is a marker of the imminence of Lancelot's capture with the queen in the last two tales.[22] Malory in any case rarely finds room for local colour in the form of unnamed inhabitants of the vicinity. The other 'accidents' of the last part of the book – the poisoned apple, the snake in the bush – lay claim to vast mythic affinities. In short, the situation is ominous.

In the case of the huntress, *Le Morte Darthur*'s refusal to face up to its literary shades may confirm rather than throw doubt upon their presence, given the nexus of special features involved. Freud writes that 'an uncanny experience occurs either when infantile complexes which have been repressed are once more revived by some impression, or when primitive beliefs which have been surmounted seem once more to be confirmed'.[23] He sees the two eruptions as linked, the latter based upon the former, and difficult to distinguish from it. Elsewhere he stresses the particular energy of the returning repressed 'when a person's erotic feelings are attached to the repressed impressions – when his erotic life has been attacked by repression'. He goes on to quote '*Naturam expelles furca, tamen usque recurret* (You may drive out Nature with a pitchfork, but she will always return) – It is precisely what was chosen as the instrument of repression – like the *furca* of the Latin saying – that becomes the vehicle for the return.' Among the examples he provides is Rops's etching of an ascetic attempting to banish sexual thoughts by meditating upon the image of the crucified Christ only to have it reassemble in his mind as that of a naked woman. The formal properties of the instrument of the repression become the conveyance of the return.[24]

What has happened to Lancelot contains the blur Freud notes: in the context of the episode's insistent gendering of action and Malory's equation of man and knight, the wound approximates a castration, and Lancelot recognizes it as part of a series he is afraid will never stop. At the same time, the spectacle of a Diana-like being exploiting, however unintentionally, the vulnerability of a sleeping human repeats and confirms a well-known primitive belief which was very much at home in medieval romance. Both readings involve the erotic; both contribute to the event's intimation of inevitability, of the reappearance of the long-known and dauntingly familiar.

Lancelot is eminently suited to be the site of *Le Morte Darthur*'s repression and partial recognition of the private and the erotic. Privately he 'holdith' his lord's wife; his public self holds neither with marriage nor paramours. As in Hoffmann's Nathanael, his recurrent terrors are linked to the presence of a woman.[25] While sleeping earlier in the story, that time under an apple tree,[26] he is the victim of the enamoured but hostile fairy, Morgan, whose abductions are symmetrical to the patronage of the Lady of the Lake. The necrophiliac Hallowes, who asks for his sword and his kiss, fantasizes of having him in a tomb to kiss and hug (280/35–281/27) – a scenario which recalls both the sleep of Endymion and the tomb into which the fairy Diana ushers Faunus for his fatal bath. Lancelot's dealings with women, preeminently and most recently Elayne of Astolat, are so unfortunate that the huntress episode, among other things, functions as a caricature of such mishaps: even when he and a female passerby have not seen each other, things go wrong.[27]

The ambiguous goddess whom the huntress resembles displays the turncoat quality of Freud's 'vehicle of repression'. Diana, represser of desire, by her formal likeness cannot avoid in certain circumstances at once suggesting her twin and equal in archery, Venus. What brings forth dubious visitants – violent or otherwise – overlaps generously with what produces, often in sleep, a revelation of love. It has been pointed out that the opening of Boccaccio's *Caccia di Diana*, with its spring setting, love-struck narrator and list of ladies, makes Venus rather than Diana the expected convenor, the latter coming as something of a surprise. But the title means not only 'the hunt of Diana' but equally 'the chasing out of Diana' – by Venus.[28] The two provide a superlative illustration of the convergence of X and not-X, a merging recognized in art and literature of the European Renaissance which gave rise to a hybrid Venus-Virgo. Edgar Wind stresses the extent to which the 'dei ambigui' offset but also share in the temperament of other gods, and none more so, it seems, than 'the chaste Diana [who], despite her coldness, is a mad huntress and changeable as the moon'.[29]

Troilus's jeering at 'ye loveres' released the punitive arrows of the God of Love. It is less clear whose arrows Lancelot has earned. His clumsy rejection of Elayne and rehearsal of his policy (1089/9–1090/7) may be felt to deserve the anger of Venus, but his secret meetings with Guinevere, with whom he has even more recently had a reconciliation and whose sleeve he has promised to wear (1103/14–24), might be expected to rouse the wrath of the goddess who never counts men among her companions. Far from the paradoxical invitations and verbal teasings of Boccaccio, Malory's episode raises our expectations only to answer them blankly: 'I am a jantillwoman that usyth here in thys foreyste huntynge, and God knowyth I saw you nat.' The insistence, against the grain of her own iconography, is typical of Malory's narrative in which not seeing, not hearing, not knowing are the last refuge from an inexorable plot.[30]

In love hunt allegories Diana and Venus are the rival patrons of action who may, respectively, forestall the desired effects of the male suitor's archery or step in and do it for him. From their weapons come the motive forces of such tales: passion and denial. In the chase of the beloved lady, figuration traditionally reverses gender, choosing to depict her not as a female deer but as a male, a stag. While secular texts of the Middle Ages do not display the same degree of fluidity in their use of gender as religious works do, this habitual reversal is a good example of the unembarrassed freedom of signification in this area from the constraints of the literal. There is no concomitant sense of indecorum; on the contrary, as Marcelle Thiébaux points out, German poems such as the *Jagd der Minne* go so far as to theorize the use of gender: the stag is the noble, lofty, hard-to-capture lady; mere hinds, female deer, are the more amenable, even fallen women whom the lover scorns. They are 'game that can be captured'; ready to be taken, their status is frequently emphasized by a wound.[31]

On the face of it, the love hunt traditions, however freely positional in their assignment of gender, refer us back to a moral hierarchy of the sexes. Lancelot suffers not only the humiliation of becoming the hunted, as after all Troilus did, but he is only a stand-in for a mere hind, and one that has gone to soil. While thus proclaiming her accessibility, the hind turns out to be more elusive and of more interest to the huntress than Lancelot. His situation would be more dignified if Malory had retained the 'gran cerf', the large stag, which the king's hunters are trying to shoot in the matching passage of the source, the animal which, as the noblest of all, was traditionally associated with Diana and considered to be her consecrated prey.[32] Given both the huntress's skill and intentions and the literary history of the hind, it is the animal which ought to be wounded, but her hand swerves.

Stories of Diana abound with substitutions and metamorphoses of human and animal. The goddess saves Iphigenia by exchanging her with a stag; the narrator of the *Caccia*, playfully reversing Actaeon's transformation, wonders at Venus's ability to turn Diana's prey into men.[33] By placing Lancelot alongside the hind, without actual metamorphosis the knight acquires the nuances which properly belong to the animal: not so noble, not so elusive after all, ready to be taken.

More central, however, to the pattern of wounding in the surrounding episodes of *Le Morte Darthur* is a second incalculably influential trope of the wound whose effect is of a very different kind: the *compunctio* (etymology *compungere*, to prick severely, to sting) or 'knowledge'. Exceeding the love hunt in this regard, the *compunctio* is structured upon a whole series of gender reversals. This multiple piercing arises from Longinus's spear in Christ's flesh which brings forth life-giving blood and water: a sacramental outpouring which in the mystical tradition becomes the milk of his nurturing motherhood.[34] In turn this piercing of the feminized Christ becomes the sword of grief in Mary's soul and then the longed-for, stigmata-like penetration of the penitent by the pain of his or her own sin. The wound is then redeemed, like the *felix culpa* of Adam's fault, by the outpouring of grace, and is validated as self-knowledge. The series is often concluded symmetrically by a final effluence in the form of tears.[35] Significantly it is Mary Magdalen who is the paradigm of compunction.[36] The choice of a woman as the ultimate sinner sits comfortably with the gender patterning of the love hunt, but the system of valuation is reversed when the greatest sinner is lauded as the greatest lover and most beloved by God.

The important wounds of 'Lancelot and Guinevere' actively trace aspects of the *compunctio*. The hermit to whom Lancelot is brought after his wounding by Bors 'thought that he sholde know hym; but he coude nat brynge hym to knowlech bycause he was so pale for bledynge' (1075/27–30). After the refrain ('What knyght ar ye?') the hermit 'saw by a wounde on hys chyeke that he was sir Launcelot' (1075/31, 36–7). Here recognition and consciousness are punningly merged by the wound: 'than anone the ermyte staunched hys blode and made hym to drynke good wyne, that he was well refygowred and knew hymselff' (1076/12–13). Consciousness blends with conscience, 'knowlech' with acknowledgement or confession (both in circulation as meanings of the word at the time); the awakening, conscience-struck Lancelot claims, against the drift of the source, that it was his pride which caused the wound, and gives out for Bors's sake 'by what tokyns he scholde know hym' – not the shield by which he has been said to have been known fourteen lines earlier, but 'by a wounde in hys forehede' (1082/33–4). Unwholeness, not defending armour, is now his sign.

In the later episode, awakened by the huntress's arrow, Lancelot is quick to place it in the series, to call it a repetition, but the inward orientation of the preceding story has dissolved, leaving in its place an oddly mechanical repetition. As woundedness is now part of Lancelot's status, it no longer matters where he gets it from. Abandoning motivation, a narrative inertia will simply keep producing wounds, whether by crystallizing a huntress out of thin air or by ironically requiring him to search the wounds of a mortally 'unwhole' knight. He will get wounded now even if all he does is lie still. In the preceding episode, Lancelot went to the tournament and was wounded; this time, like the White Queen, he is wounded and then goes to the tournament. The previous episode had described a course of insistent motivation; the huntress's arrow is pulled into this orbit as if unawares.

When Lancelot, two episodes later, encounters with terror his double, Sir Urry, the compunction suggested in 'The Maid of Astolat' is further adumbrated, but in a less logical and less explicit manner. Terence Cave writes of the 'fascination and fear of a "doubled" self – a mirror-image, a Doppelgänger, a ghost'; Freud called the repetition of self a 'harbinger of death'.[37] The narrative converts fascination into public compulsion: a royally commanded searching. The weeping which ensues, while suggesting the authenticating gift of tears, is also a more embarrassing epiphany, not only a recognition of self but also of *in*authenticity. Perhaps the fear of fraudulence which Cave associates with *anagnorisis* always underlies the gift of tears, in which grace gratuitously and overbearingly supplements the self. Lancelot cries because he is Urry and not Urry, massively unwhole and yet, for no good 'reason' (in the sense of the word played upon in *Pearl*[38]), able to heal. Like Gawain in *Sir Gawain and the Green Knight* he is uncomfortable with the public acclaim which, inside, he knows he does not match. Wholeness, a state verbally linked with the desired unity and completeness of the male fellowship, 'all wholly togydirs', is the conceit in Malory around which revolves all sense of self and of the possibility for effective human action. Personal integrity is revealed, rather than achieved, through the 'body', a word frequently repeated in the text; the body (and it is the male body which is meant) is the site where through physical combat one might at least fleetingly touch mysterious truths.[39] Elayne's brother, Lavayne, exemplifies the norm of personal wholeness and social incorporation, his passion seamlessly leading to union in the fellowship. *Sir Urry* continues this designation of the body as the residence and testing-ground of the unknown, but it does so with new trepidation and a new acknowledgement of incompleteness. This pageant of unwholeness searches out the much sought Lancelot, discovers him to be what he called himself, the knight with the wound, and then validates his unwholeness with success and with tears, the emblem of grace. A verbal struggle took place at the very beginning of 'Lancelot and Guinevere' between 'inward' and 'outward', 'prievy' and 'opyn', between the competing claims of the outer and the inner to be aligned with the good. It is the public realm of the whole, of the male, of fellowship, upon which *Le Morte Darthur* generally places its bets, but the unease with which it does so has been underestimated. 'The Maid of Astolat' and 'The Healing of Sir Urry' are, to use William James's terms, 'twice-born' episodes in an almost aggressively 'healthy-minded' text.[40] *Pearl*, again, parallels 'Sir Urry' when in the vision of the Lamb, the ultimate pearl is revealed to be not whole, not 'wemless' after all, but horrifyingly and redemptively rent.[41]

Wholeness, oneness of the self, thus has as its feared antagonist repetition. Identity is revealed as fractured not only by the confrontation of Lancelot with Sir Urry, not only by wounds, but also by their multiplying *per se*. What is of interest about this plenitude of piercings is not just that Lancelot is well and truly wounded, and knows it, or that he has gone beyond this to think of himself as positively accident-prone, but that more than one kind of repetition is at work. The wound on the cheek which the hermit recognizes cannot logically be the new one wrought by Bors; it is not even certain that the one Lancelot points to on his forehead is the new one, although he treats it as if it were. It is rather that, in both cases and in the huntress scene, 'wounded' manifests itself as the appropriate way of naming Lancelot, and precisely what wound came first, or which is which, fails to cohere. The reader is left with a vague sense that an old wound, original in the sense of the word in 'original sin' and with a force not unlike that, is being indicated as the ultimate explanation, a fatal unwholeness which will assert itself. (This will be the pattern of Gawain's explanation of his own death (1230/22).) Such a reading is encouraged by a genuine example of this simpler kind of repetition: the bursting 'both within and withoute' of the 'bottom' of the wound received from Bors and not quite healed (1086/3–4). But the series of wounds cannot be fully subjected to this model, and we are faced instead with something of the same ghostly, dream-logical, 'ungrounded doubling' which J. Hillis Miller notes in nineteenth-century novels.[42] There is not so much a secure source of meaning to be traced, an original of which the repetitions are renewals, as a haunting sense of ineluctability, of the uncontrollable breeding of wounds in both directions in time, not least in the mind of the wounded. Lancelot's faints and sleeps interpret and recharge repetition, both for him personally and for the narrative; they are the appropriate arena not only for incubi, fairies and Diana but also for what Benjamin calls 'a Penelope work of forgetting' which reveals not the order of events nor the distinction of original and copy or cause and result but rather an uncanny sense of discovering something already familiar and a concomitant sense of guilt.[43]

The huntress episode, or for that matter the whole of 'The Great Tournament' tale, in shedding cause also shuns the explicit insistence on guilt of 'The Fair Maid of Astolat' or the dramatic embarrassment with excess of 'Sir Urry'. It is odd in the face of the claim by the huntress to ordinariness and lack of intention that, as if to cap the repetition lest it go on, Lancelot at first represses the source of the wound despite its evident severity. Perhaps this silence in itself belies the inconsequence of the incident, revealing the reductiveness of its own mode of telling. More peculiar still is the delayed recital by Lancelot of the story to the king and queen, and the exhibition and measuring of his wound at a moment which would be more appropriate if it had been received in battle. Here it substitutes for his own disguise and paratactically keeps company with the dangerously unwieldy complex of assumed identities and covert identifications which in the Great Tournament have jeopardized the wholeness of the fellowship. But the repetition of the wounding itself, recognized by Lancelot only as repetition of 'som unhappy thyng', and his eventual telling of the tale suggest Freud's diagnosis of repetitions which attempt to master.[44] It is as if by this mimicry of the motifs of the foregoing episode, without their unpalatable patterns of cause and result – notably Lancelot's pride, the division of the fellowship and the death of Elayne – the Great Tournament episode seeks to exorcise the narrative of the unthinkable. The repetition works on the Scheherazade principle, putting off the end having perceived that to be a dreadful eventuality, and interposing its own excessively positive conclusion (1114/16–32). The comic impulse which in drama breeds copies of the plot, as if to fill the space available with its significant shape, may in some cases share this desire to control the story and make it safe.

But the jumbling of sequence goes beyond the looking-glass reversal in time of battle and wounding; the attempt at mastery fails. In 'The Maid of Astolat', Lancelot, wearing Elayne's sleeve, goes to battle, gets wounded, loses consciousness, and then wakes up and tells the story, pointing to the wound as the sign of his identity and guilt. In 'The Great Tournament', equipped with Guinevere's sleeve as if determined to get it right this time, he loses consciousness (in sleep), gets wounded, wakes up and analyses the situation (as unhappy repetition), goes to the battle, and then tells the story, pointing to the wound. The paring down of analysis to mere recital and to consciousness of repetition borders on belief in a controlling daemonic force (the very opposite of mastery): every time I set out to do something important something bad happens to me. The purity of the repetition, unburdened of motive, content and established sequence, shares the 'gratuitously rhetorical' nature of those most feared manifestations of the compulsion to repeat. The precedence granted to the unconscious in the rearrangement of events gives the huntress scene a peculiar foundation. It lacks the conflicting reports in *Sir Orfeo* in which the narrative says that Heurodis went to sleep but she herself claims she has been taken away by the fairy king and that moreover it is going to happen again. But the familiar ingredients of such scenes and above all the helplessness of the sleeping state suggest the release of forces which, while felt as external, lend themselves to being located within the unconscious mind.

Since his return from the Quest, Lancelot increasingly slips into the arena of the other: disguise, disappearance, woundedness. His feminization in the huntress scene is another way of mapping this state: the probing of the self by arrows, introspection and sick surrogate are its investigations in story. Repetition itself is a close cousin to the feminine, both threatening oneness and wholeness by facing it with an other.[45] But perhaps it would be more accurate to say that a red or gold sleeve, a white shield, a wound, a disappearance, the feminine are all ways of giving colour to the feared compulsion to repeat and thereby making it visible. Neil Hertz suggests that what is uncanny may be repetition itself rather than the thing repeated, although the former cannot manifest itself without the latter. Acknowledging Deleuze's *Différence et répetition*, he writes of 'the irreducible figurativeness of one's language [which] is indistinguishable from the ungrounded and apparently inexplicable notion of the compulsion itself'.[46] While 'pure repetition' may theoretically exist on a different plane from figurations such as the feminine, the figurative cannot truthfully be banished from the discussion like the dyes used by doctors to make traceable the inner state of the body.

In the tale between 'The Great Tournament' and 'Sir Urry' the persistence of gender as a language for Lancelot's status confirms that that figuration is not arbitrary and roots the exploration in the realm of the political. In 'The Knight of the Cart' Lancelot is not just unseated; his horse, symbol of knighthood, is destroyed, reducing him to the vehicle of the oxymoronic title. Rather than displaying his precarious position through the medium of a wound, he insists upon his traditional centrality in the proceedings, calling out for a military solution, befuddled and offended by the alternative, private peace which Guinevere has established before his arrival. If Elayne's body floating down the river figured the redundancy of women in the public sphere, this anti-climactic attempt to rescue Guinevere turns the tables: Guinevere has rescued herself and Lancelot's military services are comically superfluous.

When one looks back at the century before Malory it becomes clear that the second arena, the arena of the other, inner, feminine is more confidently explored in earlier secular as well as religious literature, and that Malory's text may represent something of a rearguard action in defence of the first: wholeness, the public, the masculine, a desire for wholeness which Felicity

Riddy links to Malory's generation.[47] In Chaucer's *Troilus* the war is repeatedly mentioned as the expected motive for action and emotion, and a more promising topic for a book, only to be repeatedly dropped when the inner world instead asserts itself as the reason why things happen. *Sir Gawain and the Green Knight*, structured on a series of tropes similar to those in *Lancelot and Guinevere*, places its major contest in the bedchamber when only the ladies are still at home and it would seem that the men are all out engaging in the manly pastime of hunting.[48] Once again, the public arena loses out to the sphere of scruple. Gawain engages in the hunt, but he does so as its prey, his identity is doubted and he receives a wound as token of his already unwhole condition, a flaw which the Green Knight seems to consider more or less inevitable or at least par for the course, and to which, like Lancelot's wound, it is hard to assign a source in time.

But *Le Morte Darthur* is interesting in this regard precisely because in repressing the second arena but failing to repress it immaculately it produces eloquent apparitions such as the lady huntress whose shape reveals both the forgotten matter and the process by which it was buried. For all her chastity, Diana is a 'transitional object'[49] and an icon of both the repression of the erotic and of the erotic itself. In romance she and her like are associated with the return of the dead and with their remorseless taking of the living, abetted by the free play of dreaming minds. The desired refutation of all of this adds a second tier to the defence, a second iridescence of strange and familiar: the huntress is nothing to do with Diana and her kind; she is homely, a local, eccentric but well-meaning. And yet the only thing that is familiar about her is that she looks and hunts like Diana. The joke is that she only achieves her Diana-like accuracy in hitting Lancelot, whose appropriateness for this plight is so overdetermined, by a most unDiana-like swerving of the hand – to use the popular term, by a Freudian slip.

Peter Haidu, elucidating 'what seems to us a most extraordinary patience with repetition in medieval art', argues that there repetition is valued because of its membership in the chain of being and its consequent revelation, each time around, of the abstract form to which it owes its shape and meaning. According to this view of recurrence as Platonically motivated, inconsequential doubling cannot exist; indeed, given the propensities of medieval exegetic practice, it is likely to be excessively magnetic where meaning is concerned: 'The entire world consists of traces of divine intent, and intentionality is lodged throughout the created world.'[50] The implication of this theory for a reading of the episode at hand might be felt to go so far that the playing again of Lancelot's incapacitation has to have meaning. The invisibility of motivation serves to authenticate the supernatural status of ultimate agency. Such an agent might make both the author of a book and a huntress within it its reluctant or unknowing accomplices. Chance is only the flawed, human assessment of the plottings of Providence.

Dumézil distinguishes between the 'sins of the warrior', each of which has to be committed for its discrete, matching punishment to fall, and the single 'suprafunctional' 'sin of the sovereign', always reducible to the sin of pride, which triggers for once and for all the demise of the guilty in every sphere of his activity.[51] What is of interest here is not so much the typology of sin but rather of narrative motivation. For Lancelot as for the ancient Iranian Yima, it is no longer necessary to provoke the arrows because the process is already in train. This credence in underlying design gives medieval literature an unexpectedly modern feel; for medieval aesthetics, as for modern psychoanalysis, there are no accidents.

A complete distinction between repetition and recognition is no more satisfactory than a collapsing together of the two. In the last part of *Le Morte Darthur*, Lancelot – and he is not alone in this – becomes Foucault's confessing animal, a compulsive fiction-about-himself-telling animal;[52] the sense of a true basis in reality for his analyses in 'The Maid of Astolat' or his 'drama of recognition' in 'Sir Urry' recedes as wounds begin to spread like a rash. If one can situate historically a fall of recognition from grace, the end of allegiance to 'a sacred system of things' which rendered it partial and problematic, it must have taken place in time for English romances of the fourteenth and fifteenth centuries to share in its fruits – or, rather, its losses. Peter Brooks sees melodrama as a response to such an event, but much of what he associates with that genre, which he calls 'the genre of recognition', could equally be said of that earlier 'scandalous' and devalued genre, romance. If romance, like melodrama, resembles psychoanalysis, it does so allowing for the fact that 'modern psychoanalysis emerg[ed] as a symptom of the very insecurity it was supposed to cure'.[53] Some romances are, admittedly, more curative than others. 'Lancelot and Guinevere' is a kind of anti-*Gareth*, the work of the text's ravelling left hand.

NOTES

1　See R. W. Southern, 'From Epic to Romance', in *The Making of the Middle Ages* (Oxford, 1952).
2　In addition to Southern, see Michel Foucault, *The History of Sexuality, vol. I: An Introduction*, trans. R. Hurley (Harmondsworth, 1976), esp. pp. 58–9.
3　Mark Lambert, *Malory: Style and Vision in Le Morte Darthur* (New Haven and London, 1975), p. 104 n. 48.
4　Here the double feminine, likely to have been suggested by 'damoisele chaceresse' which describes the Lady of the Lake in the French *Merlin*, marks class as well as gender, the latter perhaps emphasized because hunting was unusual for women; see R. Hands, ed., *English Hawking and Hunting in the Boke of St Albans* (Oxford, 1976), p. lviii n. 1.
5　Cf. Geoffrey Chaucer, *The Canterbury Tales*, in *The Riverside Chaucer*, ed. L. D. Benson (Oxford, 1988), A.3903. See this edition for all further references to Chaucer.
6　See in particular Lambert, op. cit., chs 2 and 3.
7　Sigmund Freud, 'The Uncanny', *The Standard Edition of the Complete Psycho-*

logical Works, trans. and ed. J. Strachey, vol. XVII (London, 1919), p. 249. See this edition for all further references to Freud.

8 V. Branca (ed.), in *Tutte le opere di Giovanni Boccaccio*, vol. I (Verona, 1967), xvi, p. 32.

9 *The Parliament of Fowls*, in Benson (ed.), op. cit., pp. 281–2.

10 See for instance Boccaccio, *Caccia* in Branca (ed.), op. cit., bk. ii, ll. 229–39; Boccaccio, *Filocolo*, ed. A. E. Quaglio in *Tutte le opere*, op. cit., bk. ii, ll. 3; Ovid, *Metamorphoses*, trans. M. M. Innes (London, 1955), pp. 78–80; C. B. Lewis, *Classical Mythology and Arthurian Romance, A Study of the Sources of Chrestien de Troyes' 'Yvain' and Other Arthurian Romances* (Oxford, 1932). For other depictions of Diana see *Metamorphoses*, pp. 41–2, 61–2, 175–6, 193–4, 254, 269; *Fasti*, ed. J. G. Frazer, rev. G. P. Goold (Cambridge, Mass. and London, 1989), I, 387; III, 155; IV, 761ff; *Amores*, I, xiii, 44; II, v, 27; III, ii, 31; and *Heroides*, IV, 87, xx, 191, both ed. G. Showerman, rev. edn G. P. Goold (Cambridge, Mass., 1977). See also W. C. Curry, *Chaucer and the Medieval Sciences*, rev. edn (New York, 1960); *Chaucer* ed. W. W. Skeat (Oxford, 1926), V, 82; R. Klibansky, E. Panofsky, F. Saxl, *Saturn and Melancholy* (London, 1964), p. 388 n.42; E. Panofsky, *Studies in Iconology* (New York and London, 1972), p. 149; J. Seznec, *The Survival of the Pagan Gods* (New York, 1953).

11 *Lancelot do Lac, The Non-Cyclic Old French Prose Romance*, ed. E. Kennedy (Oxford, 1980), p. 7/1.

12 *Merlin, roman en prose du XIIIe siècle*, ed. G. Paris and J. Ulrich (Paris, 1883), vol. II, p. 145. Interestingly, one of Malory's own Ladies of the Lake is the agent of other disruptive episodes: the young Arthur is glad when she leaves the court 'for she made such a noyse' (103/12), the word which will be used for the enunciation of adultery (see Lambert, op. cit., p. 183). Soon after, fearful of him and weary of his sexual interest, she buries alive the besotted Merlin, embodiment of plot (125–6). His burial, that most precise figuration of repression, is in the text a counter-repression. The Lady is dependent upon the powers of her suitor but appropriates them by erotic delay, manipulating her role as the object of desire, that force which the text elsewhere sedulously eclipses.

13 Ovid, *Metamorphoses*, pp. 78–80, 186–90.

14 For summaries of her roles, see 'Diana', 'Hecate', 'Artemis' in *The Oxford Companion to Classical Literature*, 2nd edn, ed. M. C. Howatson (Oxford and New York), 1989.

15 Paris and Ulrich (eds), op. cit., II, pp. 145–8.

16 See discussion in L. A. Paton, *Studies in the Fairy Mythology of Arthurian Romance* (New York, 1960), chs XII–XIV.

17 A. J. Bliss (ed.), *Sir Orfeo* (Oxford, 1966); see introduction, pp. xxxii–xxxix.

18 Jean Froissart, *Meliador*, ed. A. Longnon, vol. III (Paris, 1899), 28824–26, 30343.

19 Benson (ed.), op. cit., A 2313; 2081–2.

20 Paton, op. cit., p. 277. See discussions of the noonday demon, other noon-related misfortunes and their overlap with the reputation of fairies in P. B. R. Doob, *Nebuchadnezzar's Children, Conventions of Madness in Middle English Literature* (New Haven and London, 1974), pp. 29–39, 197; 165 n47, 178–9, 198.

21 It is telling that the issue of which is involved is often the subject of critical debate; see, for instance, analyses of *Sir Orfeo* in Doob, op. cit., pp. 178–9 and in J. B. Friedman, *Orpheus in the Middle Ages* (Cambridge, Mass., 1970), pp. 186–9.

22 Almost half of the occurrences of the word in Vinaver's 1,260-page edition belong to the final 115 pages. See esp. 1045/23, 25, 32; 1164/24.

23 Freud, op. cit., p. 249.

24 Sigmund Freud, 'Delusions and Dreams in Jensen's "Gradiva" ', in Strachey (ed.), op. cit., vol. IX (1906–8), pp. 34–5.

25 In addition to Freud, 'The Uncanny', see E. Wright, *Psychoanalytic Criticism, Theory in Practice* (London and New York, 1984), p. 144.

26 Yet another motif of mysterious visitations, coinciding at 253 with heat, noon and a 'grete luste to slepe'; cf. the 'ympe-tre' in A. J. Bliss (ed.), *Sir Orfeo*, 70, 166, 186, 407, 456, and introduction p. xxxv.

27 On Lancelot's relations with women earlier in his career, see J. Jesmok, ' "A Knyght Wyveles": The Young Lancelot in Malory's *Morte Darthur*', *MLQ* 42 (1981), pp. 315–30.

28 R. Hollander, *Boccaccio's Two Venuses* (New York, 1977), p. 13. Examples of the dream vision of love include *Le Roman de la rose*, *The Parliament of Fowls* and *The Book of the Duchess*.

29 Edgar Wind, *Pagan Mysteries in the Renaissance*, rev. edn (Harmondsworth, 1967), pp. 77, 196. For the symmetry of Diana and Venus see, too, Hollander, op. cit., p. 62; J. L. Smarr, *Boccaccio and Fiametta: The Narrator as Lover* (Urbana and Chicago, 1986), p. 10; Martianus Capella, *Seven Liberal Arts, The Marriage of Philology and Mercury*, trans. W. H. Stahl (New York, 1971), p. 29; Alanus de Insulis, *Anticlaudianus or the Godd and Perfect Man*, trans. J. J. Sheridan (Toronto, 1973), p. 176.

30 For this pattern in dialogue see C. LaFarge, 'Conversation in Malory's *Morte Darthur*', *Medium Ævum* LVI, 2 (1987), pp. 225–78.

31 Marcelle Thiébaux, *The Stag of Love, The Chase in Medieval Literature* (New York, 1974), esp. pp. 215–33.

32 *La Mort le roi Artu*, ed. J. Frappier (Paris, 1936), p. 64, l.8. The reflection in Malory's episode of details of his source, down to some details of sentence structure, suggests that the displacement of Arthur's hunters by the lady and the stag by the hind is particularly deliberate. For Diana and the stag see Martianus Capella, op. cit., p. 29; Pierre Bersuire, 'The Moral Reduction', book XV: 'Ovid Moralized', trans. and ed. A. J. Minnis and A. B. Scott, in *Medieval Literary Theory and Criticism, c. 1100–c. 1375* (Oxford, 1987), p. 371.

33 Ovid, *Metamorphoses*, p. 269; Boccaccio, *Caccia*, in Branca (ed.), op. cit., pp. xviii, 11–12 (whether this is an improvement has been the subject of disagreement: see Hollander, op. cit., pp. 18–19; Smarr, op. cit., p. 11).

34 The feminization of Christ, present in the sermons of Bernard of Clairvaux, is strong in the women mystics, e.g. Julian of Norwich and Margery Kempe. See C. W. Bynum, *Jesus as Mother, Studies in the Spirituality of the High Middle Ages* (Berkeley, Calif., 1978), pp. 110–69.

35 For a poetic extension, see the persistent images of gushing in *Pearl*, ed. M. Andrew and R. Waldron, in *The Poems of the Pearl Manuscript* (London, 1978): for God's gifts, grace, the blood of the Lamb, the river of life. On the freedom of gender in a religious lyric, see T. D. Hill, 'Androgyny and Conversion in the Middle English Lyric "The Vale of Restless Mynd" ', *ELH* LIII (1986), p. 459.

36 See, for instance, *The Cloud of Unknowing*, ed. P. Hodgson (Oxford, 1944), pp. 44ff., where she is, as often, conflated with the sister of Martha.

37 T. Cave, *Recognitions* (Oxford, 1988), p. 171; Freud, 'The Uncanny', p. 235.

38 See Andrew and Waldron (eds), op. cit., esp. ll. 580–720.

39 See Lambert, op. cit., pp. 63–4; J. Mann, 'Malory: Knightly Combat in *Le Morte Darthur*' in *The New Pelican Guide to English Literature*, ed. B. Ford, part 1, pp. 331–9.

40 William James, *The Varieties of Religious Experience* (New York, 1902), pp. 78ff.

41 Andrew and Waldron (eds), op. cit., ll. 1135–40; see also 'Blood in *Pearl*', *Review of English Studies* XXXVIII (1988), pp. 1–13.

42 J. Hillis Miller, *Fiction and Repetition: Seven English Novels* (Oxford, 1982), p. 6.

43 W. Benjamin, *Illuminations*, trans. H. Zohn (New York, 1969), p. 202, quoted and discussed by Miller, op. cit., p. 7; see also pp. 69–70.

44 See Freud, 'Beyond the Pleasure Principle', in Strachey (ed.), op. cit., vol. XVIII (1929–), pp. 7–64, and Peter Brooks, *Reading for the Plot* (Oxford, 1984), pp. 97–8.

45 For a useful study of wholeness, gender and language see J. Swan, 'Difference and Silence: John Milton and the Question of Gender', in *The (M)Other Tongue: Essays in Feminist Psychoanalytic Interpretation*, ed. S. N. Garner, C. Kahane, M. Sprengnether (Ithaca, NY, 1986), pp. 142–68.

46 Neil Hertz, 'Freud and the Sandman', in *Textual Strategies: Perspectives in Post-Structuralist Criticism*, ed. J. V. Harari (Cornell, 1979), p. 320.

47 Felicity Riddy, *Sir Thomas Malory* (Leiden, 1987), esp. pp. 142, 145, 153–4.

48 Ovid's *Remedia Amoris* and manuals on hunting recommend hunting as a defence against failings associated with idleness; see Thiébaux, p. 77.

49 For discussion and bibliography see E. Wright, *Psychoanalytic Criticism, Theory in Practice* (London and New York, 1984), pp. 92ff; particularly relevant are the linking of object relations theory with fear and relief (p. 97) and misrecognition (pp. 100–1).

50 Peter Haidu, 'Repetition: Modern Reflections on Medieval Aesthetics', *Modern Language Notes* XCII (1977), p. 880.

51 G. Dumézil, *The Destiny of a King*, trans. A. Hiltebeitel (Chicago and London, 1973), pp. 109–12. I am grateful to Maire Herbert for drawing this to my attention.

52 Foucault, op. cit., p. 59; Brooks, op. cit., p. 277; Cave, op. cit., p. 218.

53 Cave, op. cit., p. 218; see too p. 212. Peter Brooks, *The Melodramatic Imagination: Balzac, H. James, Melodrama, and the Mode of Excess* (New Haven and London, 1976), pp. 200–2; and *Reading for the Plot*, pp. 40, 42ff.

Part V

Others

Chapter 16

New hystericism:
Aphra Behn's *Oroonoko*: the body,
the text and the feminist critic

Ros Ballaster

Historicism gives the 'eternal' image of the past; historical materialism supplies a unique experience with the past. The historical materialist leaves it to others to be drained by the whore called 'Once upon a time' in historicism's bordello. He remains in control of his powers, man enough to blast open the continuum of history.[1]

Since the second half of the nineteenth century, history has become increasingly the refuge of all those 'sane' men who excel at finding the simple in the complex and familiar in the strange. This was all very well for an earlier age, but if the present generation needs anything at all it is a willingness to confront heroically the dynamic and disruptive forces in contemporary life. The historian serves no one well by constructing a specious continuity between the present world and that which preceded it. On the contrary, we require a history that will educate us to discontinuity more than ever before; for discontinuity, disruption, and chaos is our lot.[2]

In recent years, literary criticism and theory has turned to a reassessment of the epistemological role of history in our understanding of the nature of the literary text. What bearing, if any, does the radical reworking of our conceptualization of history in literature have upon feminist literary criticism? History has, of late, through the work of American 'new historicism' and British 'cultural materialism' come to figure as a locus of conflict, an arena of 'discontinuity, disruption, and chaos' as Hayden White puts it, rather than the source of meaning and 'the real' in the enterprise of literary criticism. 'Tradition', so to speak, has become a thing of the past. This article sets about an assessment of the recent history of feminist criticism and of historical criticism, employing Aphra Behn's early colonial narrative, *Oroonoko; or, the Royal Slave* (1688), as just such a stage of conflict for literary critical reading. In so doing, it touches upon some of the most urgent questions for contemporary feminist theory, in particular the role and uses of historical analysis in the reading of women's texts and the place and function of race in the constitution of ideologies of gender.

If the signposts of feminist criticism in the late 1970s were Kate Millett's polemical archaeology of masculinist counter-revolution in her *Sexual Politics* (1969), Gilbert and Gubar's piecing together of the sybilline leaves of women's nineteenth-century novelistic imagination in their *Madwoman in the Attic* (1979) and Elaine Showalter's plotting of a 'more reliable map' for negotiating the female authored novel in *A Literature of their Own* (1977), then the late 1980s were marked by a significant turn to the deconstructive 'reading' of individual texts and genres.[3] Symptomatic of this shift is the increasing popularity of the published essay or conference paper collection amongst feminist critics. See, for example, Mary Jacobus's startling 'correspondences' between disparate historical and literary texts in her *Reading Woman* (1986), Gayatri Chakravorty Spivak's strategic deployment of the question of racial difference to undo white feminist and masculinist critical theory alike in her *In Other Worlds* (1987) and Patricia Parker's tropological dilations of the figure of Renaissance woman in her *Literary Fat Ladies* (1987).[4] In feminist criticism, then, as elsewhere, textual 'difference' has come to supplant literary history.

This problematization of the category of 'History' in feminist criticism was, of course, long overdue, if only made possible by the clearing of a space for more sophisticated reading by the strategic claims for the validity of women's writing as an object of study in the 1970s. However, as others have pointed out, the erasure of the historical subject, woman, under the discursive categories of 'sexual difference', may be, if not theoretically, then at least politically, premature.[5]

This same criticism has been levelled at recent manifestations of historical analysis in literary study at large. My primary aim here is to assess the significance of new historicism for the practice of feminist reading in so far as it can be seen as an attempt to reconcile the exigencies of formalism and historicism in literary criticism. Since, for British readers and critics, the term 'new historicism' is still a relatively obscure and recent one in literary critical discourse, I will first produce a working definition of this critical practice and then briefly consider the reasons why feminist critics might be interested or threatened by its increasing hegemony in literary studies. Having outlined some of the plots and perils of new historicism, I will turn to look at my own 'exemplary' text for a newly historical and feminist reading, Aphra Behn's *Oroonoko*. *Oroonoko*, as my own reading of the text and recent interpretations of it by other feminist critics will demonstrate, sets into motion a certain drama of conflict and repression between the white feminist reader, author or critic and the black female subject.

New historicism, then, takes its theoretical premises from the work of such founding fathers of twentieth-century historiography as Michel Foucault and Walter Benjamin with some debts to the Marxist and psychoanalytic theory of Louis Althusser and Pierre Macherey. In the United States, critics such as Stephen Greenblatt, Louis Montrose and Jonathan Goldberg have been most commonly associated with the school, while in the United Kingdom it supposedly finds its theoretical counterpart in the 'cultural materialism' of Jonathan Dollimore and Alan Sinfield, who, in turn, find their theoretical origins in the historico-cultural analysis identified with the Marxist criticism of Raymond Williams. Nearly all of the critics named would doubtless resent many, if not all, of these labels, but the terms have stuck and it does seem that there is a distinctive attitude toward the theorization of history and power in their work that justifies the otherwise somewhat empty appellation 'new historicism'.

Recent essays by Edward Pechter, Louis Montrose, Jean Howard, Laura Brown and Felicity Nussbaum have all attempted to give an account of the premisses behind new historicist approaches.[6] The first of these premisses is summarized by Montrose as the assumption that 'the freely self-creating and world-creating subject of bourgeois humanism is now (at least in theory) defunct' (p. 9). Equally, new historicism abandons the 'vulgar' Marxist framework of determining base and reflective superstructure as an alternative to this bourgeois concept of the subject. Michel Foucault's now well-known theorization of the nature of power in the first volume of his *The History of Sexuality* might be seen as the generating premiss of all new historicist work:

> Power's condition of possibility, or in any case the viewpoint which permits one to understand its exercise, even in its most 'peripheral' effects, and which also makes it possible to use its mechanisms as a grid of intelligibility of the social order, must not be sought in the primary existence of a central point ... in a unique source of sovereignty from which secondary and descendent forms would emanate; it is the moving substrate of force relations which, by virtue of their inequality, constantly engender states of power, but the latter are always local and unstable.[7]

History, within this theoretical model, cannot be understood as having a single determining or originating cause whether in the humanist conception of the 'mind of man' or the simplified Marxist model of the ultimate determining power of the economic base. It is rather a text understood only from readerly perspectives that are themselves historically contingent, partial and 'interested'.

New historicism seeks to produce what Stephen Greenblatt has called a 'poetics of culture', that is, a rhetorical analysis of the production of different subject-positions in relation to diffuse centres of power within specific historical formations, through the synchronic reading of literary and non-literary texts alike.[8] History is thus always already historiography. As Jean Howard notes, the recognition that 'man is a construct, not an essence' must also admit that the 'historical investigator is likewise a product of his history' (p. 23). In conclusion, then, new historicism as a critical practice has been characterized by a rejection of progressive, continuist and essentialist theories of history, in favour of a study of difference, discontinuity, conflict and contradiction across a variety of historical 'texts', literary and non-literary alike. History is no longer deployed as 'background' to the literary text, nor is the literary text to be used as evidence of historical 'experience' in any transparent or mediatory way.

Why, we might ask, should the feminist critic be interested in any of this, particularly in the light of the fact that the insistent vocabulary and metaphorization of new historicism has been that of a challenge to the notion of an essence of 'man' with little or no concomitant interest in the place of 'woman' in his undoing? There are certain obvious sites at which new historicist concerns intersect with feminist interests. The first lies precisely in the abandonment of a grand narrative of history and the subsequent turn to those 'local and unstable' 'states of power' to which Foucault points.[9] The 'female traditions' of the 1970s to which I referred earlier were inclined to replace the conventional masterplots of literary history elaborated by F. R. Leavis and T. S. Eliot in the 1930s in Britain and America with a subterranean counter 'mistressplot' of women's writing, rather than with the synchronic or local analyses that might better have revealed the specific 'powers' that lay in women's textual production at different historical moments. In other words, the feminist challenge to masculinist literary history manifested itself in the making of alternative progressive and continuist traditions of women's writing rather than a wholesale onslaught on the theorization of history itself.

Second, new historicism, in the wake of the post-structuralist 'undoing' of authorial intention, appears to succeed in resituating the author as a category of investigation in literary criticism, without positing him or her as the sole and originary source of the text's meaning. Stephen Greenblatt reads both authors and 'characters' of the Renaissance period as 'self-fashioners', presenting both as the sites for the intersection and articulation of multiple social codes. At least theoretically, then, the gender of an author within new historicist critical practice is a relevant determining factor, where theories of 'écriture feminine', to the consternation of many historically-minded feminist critics, may appear to have done away with gendered signature as in any way significant in feminist textual analysis.

However, the practitioners of new historicist criticism have for the most part not displayed any specific interest in questions of gender difference in their understanding of the 'poetics of culture'.[10] Indeed, in a recent article in *Diacritics*, Marguerite Waller notes that Greenblatt's self-conscious 'positioning' of himself as critic in relation to his textual object slides into a claim to representivity that is wilfully blind to the viewing position of the 'other' (woman). Waller makes an analogy between Greenblatt's strategy and the use of camera angles in the film *Tootsie* to endorse the perspective of its cross-dressing male protagonist's viewing of woman and viewing of himself as woman at the expense of the female protagonists in the film.[11] Greenblatt's *Renaissance Self-Fashioning* claims to 'lay bare' the text's relations to power through the mimetic repetition of its own logic. This endeavour carries with it, however, certain risks, not least in the fact that it can become an exercise in the *critic's* self-fashioning against his own mysterious other, the monolithic category of history, all too frequently figured as female (as in the Benjamin quotation with which this article opened). Greenblatt asserts that '[s]elf-fashioning is achieved in relation to something perceived as alien, strange or hostile. This threatening other – heretic, savage, witch, adulteress, traitor, Antichrist – must be discovered or invented in order to be attacked or destroyed' (p. 7). Like Benjamin's historical materialist, Greenblatt's self-fashioning critic asserts himself as subject, shoring up an abstract authority (church, state, party, revolution) which serves to protect and legitimate his own agency, by constructing an 'other' from which he is radically different and with which he is perpetually at odds. The 'new historicist' critic, in contrast with the self-fashioning subjects he studies and mimics, always proves 'man' enough to prevent his wastage at the hands of the whore in historicism's bordello.

As with Foucault, it is hard to locate the specificity of the woman in these new historicist texts; she appears largely as the object of the discursive formations under analysis, the 'talked about' other rather than the self-fashioner. Moreover, as in Foucault, 'woman' appears as only one among many representatives of social bodies (the savage, the traitor, the heretic) represented as marginal by the self-fashioner in order to confirm (his) social power. New historicism in its present form thus consistently fails to address the role of the woman as historical agent, and in particular the place of the woman writer in relation to the ideologies of sexual difference to which the study of masculinist self-fashioning gestures. Janet Todd's comments in her *Feminist Literary Histories* accurately register the anxiety that some feminist critics have felt about this reduction of the study of 'woman' common to most forms of post-structuralist analysis to a purely discursive function:

> Feminist literary history finds signature important. The woman who wrote is no doubt in the end unknowable, but at some level or in some gap, trope or choice, she was working to be known. In her, history does become herstory, and not simply hysteria, a generalized feminine predicament which can variously be expressed in men or women.[12]

If we simply turned the techniques of new historicism upon women's texts, would our problems be solved, as this line of argument might suggest? Surely not, since the same need for a recognition of critical 'interest' and a certain 'blindness of insight' would obtain in feminist as in historical analysis. If contemporary masculinist critics are inclined to characterize themselves as mastering and governing literary history, blasting open its continuum, and refashioning it into a new and startling if artificially created topography, feminist critics have been too willing to portray themselves as handmaids to an already given 'female literary history', facilitating its re-emergence, in order to restore its 'natural' shape, without acknowledging their own responsibility and agency in the shape and meaning of the texts they supposedly 'serve'. Aphra Behn's *Oroonoko* is a peculiarly appropriate text to employ as a test-case in this regard since in the course of its own narrative it dramatizes the problematization of the mimetic activities of the 'historian' in relation to his or her object. Behn's tale of a black West African prince tricked into slavery, his insurrections in the British colony of Surinam in the early 1660s and eventual execution at the hands of the brutal white colonists, is, as the few critics who have paid it serious attention have pointed out, a highly self-conscious and self-reflexive piece of literary art.[13] While it purports to be simple 'unadorn'd' biography, it meditates obsessively upon the seductive power and the unstable status of fictional writing in relation to the simple dichotomy of truth and lie.

There are a number of reasons beyond the meta-historical nature of the narrative of *Oroonoko* why it should be of interest to new historicists and feminists alike. First, and most obviously, because it is a text of early British colonialism and colonialist discourses have proved of considerable interest to new historicist scholars in that they almost inevitably inscribe an attempt to discursively contain a (racial) other on the part of a dominant culture.[14] Second, it is a text by a woman in which the femaleness of the narrating subject is a vital source of its authority in the action of the text and as writer and interpreter of that action. It is, then, a text which opens up a series of questions that are crucial to contemporary criticism to do with the means by which gender, race and class differences are historically generated, articulated and put into conflict in the literary text. *Oroonoko* as an allegory of racial and sexual conflict enacts a drama familiar to contemporary readers, at the same time as its interlacing of political history, Tory ideology and late seventeenth-century theories of race and monarchy makes it radically 'other' to our own understanding of these categories.

I will look first at two influential and ground-breaking readings of *Oroonoko* of the 1980s, the first by Jane Spencer in her *The Rise of the Woman Novelist* (1986) and the second by Laura Brown in a recent collection entitled *The New Eighteenth Century* (1987). These two readings might be roughly characterized as feminist historicist and feminist new historicist, in that the former places *Oroonoko* within a diachronic history of the development of the woman's novel within the tradition of Showalter, Gilbert and Gubar, and the latter in synchronic relationship to non-literary ideologies of colonialism and gender difference in the late 1680s in Britain. Both, I would argue, are symptomatic of a general tendency in studies of *Oroonoko*, and in white bourgeois feminist criticism in general, to suppress the problem of a conflictual relationship between the white and black woman in favour of exploring the relationship between the black man and white woman as a mutual interchange of marginalities that wilfully produces a myth of intersexual and interracial harmony. Within this myth, the black man comes to represent 'race' and the white woman 'gender' in a mini-allegory of strategic political alliance. Behn's own conclusion to the story might cause us to resist such an easy equation in that she makes it clear her aim is to immortalize a heroic *couple* rather than a single man. Behn writes: 'I hope the reputation of my pen is considerable enough to make [Oroonoko's] glorious name to survive to all ages, with that of the brave, the beautiful, and the constant Imoinda.'[15] The decline of Imoinda's 'name' next to that of her husband and her elision with the personality of the white female narrator set in only seven years after the novella's publication. In Thomas Southerne's dramatic redaction of the novel, first performed at Drury Lane in 1695, it was considered improper for a white actress to 'black up' along with her male counterpart, so the role of Imoinda was scripted and played as white.[16]

Imoinda has her place in both Spencer's and Brown's interpretations, but neither, I would argue, pay full attention to her figurative importance within the novel as a difference that cannot be appropriated by the operations of Behn's otherwise comprehensive textual strategies that repeatedly convert racial otherness into familiar political allegory. For Spencer, *Oroonoko* 'marks an important stage in the history of women's quest for literary authority'.[17] Behn's gender, Spencer notes, acts as her alibi at every stage for her lack of activity with regard to the abuse that Oroonoko receives at the hands of the leading white colonists. Although Behn tells us that, as the daughter of the man who was to have been Lieutenant-General of Surinam but unfortunately died on the sea passage to take up his post, she 'had none above [her] in that country' (p. 25), she fails to save him from death and is crucially absent due to feminine fear or illness at those points when he needs her protection. Yet it is this very (explicitly feminine) powerlessness which, Behn argues, enables her to sympathize with Oroonoko's position as victim and differentiates her from the tyrannical male white colonists.

Spencer goes on to note that whilst Behn encourages an identification between herself and her hero, she insists on her difference from her heroine, Imoinda. It is Behn's uneasiness with woman's place in the conventions of the heroic romance, Spencer concludes, that is the source of this explicit differentiation. If Imoinda figures as the idealized heroine of the romance, the still object of the (masculine) erotic gaze and passive spur to heroic action, Behn takes up the role of the 'great mistress' (p. 69), manipulating and controlling the heroic action from behind the scenes. Thus, Spencer notes, 'at a time when heroine and woman writer were coming to seem almost synonymous, Behn insisted on making a sharp distinction between them' (p. 52). However, in making her own distinction between Behn's attitude to her male and female protagonists, a distinction of sexual difference, Spencer virtually erases the distinction of race between the two women in the narrative. For Spencer, the only significant difference between Imoinda and the female narrator is that of romance heroine and romance writer.

Laura Brown, in contrast, is inclined to view Imoinda as purely an extension of the function of the female narrator in *Oroonoko*. Claiming that '[t]his narrative must have women; it generates female figures at every turn', Brown sees women as fulfilling the role of 'incentives or witnesses' to Oroonoko's heroic exploits.[18] Imoinda joins the female narrator's mother, sister and maid as mere 'proxies' for Behn in the course of the plot. Brown's complex and powerful reading of *Oroonoko* persuasively argues that Behn's text critiques the traditional colonialist practice of demonizing the black slave as disruptive and dangerous other to the white colonial subject by representing the slave within the familiar framework of the aristocratic romance. The story of Oroonoko, presented as that of the civilized man amongst barbarians, inverts the opposition in dominant colonial ideology of the slave as barbarian and the Christian colonist as civilized culture.[19] Startlingly, Oroonoko's history and execution become a means of renarrating the English revolution in which Oroonoko finds his allegorical correlative in the figure of the heroic martyr (for a Tory Royalist like Behn), Charles I. In this process of allegorization, Brown points out, women function as the intermediaries between two radically disjunct worlds, the ideal order or mythoi of aristocratic romance and the new 'bourgeois' world of mercantile trade. Women are both the ultimate arbiters and consumers of romance and the supposed recipients of the benefits of mercantile expansionism. They consume the silks, furs, jewels won from the latter as well as the imaginative excesses produced by the former.

Brown asserts that the 'mediatory role' of women in this text:

> make[s] possible the superimpositions of aristocratic and bourgeois systems – the ideological contradiction that dominates the novella. And in that contradiction we can locate a site beyond alterity, a point of critique and sympathy produced by the radical contemporaneity of issues of gender with those of race.

(pp. 54–5)

Here too, then, a feminist analysis comes to rest upon the argument that a sympathetic identification with the black slave and critical perspective on white colonialism is made possible by the recognition of similarities between racial and gender oppression. However, Brown's formulation, like Spencer's, still operates only by ignoring the question of racial difference *within* gender.

In contemporary feminist debate it is Gayatri Spivak who has produced the most sustained critique of white feminist critics' tendency to ignore the disruptive effect of the figure of the black women within their project of the 'tropological deconstruction of masculism': the price of learning that 'not only the power but even the self-undermining of man may be operated by the troping of the woman' is, Spivak claims, 'the performance of a blindness to the other woman in the text'.[20] It is this attention to the 'objectified' subject-position of the non-white woman in Behn's text that will trouble any straightforward interpretation of the tale as an allegory of race and gender similitude within an analysis of oppressive power. If, as Brown has cogently suggested, the figure of the white woman succeeds in mediating between contradictory worlds in *Oroonoko*, it appears to me that the figure of the black woman is 'framed' into setting up division and conflict, or restoring alterity.

Aphra Behn provides us with a full paragraph description of her hero as a model of European beauty. 'His nose was rising and Roman, instead of African and flat; His mouth the finest shaped that could be seen; far from those great turn'd lips, which are so natural to the rest of the Negroes' (p. 33). Imoinda appears as 'female to his noble male; the beautiful black Venus to our young Mars' (p. 34). So far the heroic couple seem to be one in their distinctive difference from the 'rest of the Negroes' with whom they are enslaved and whom Oroonoko as a Coramantien prince had previously been involved in selling. Imoinda, however, serves as an enlarging mirror of her husband's properties and this magnifying propensity has the ultimate effect of separating her from his 'Europeanization'. One example of this disturbance of the absorption of the black royal slave into a white Western aesthetic by the presence of his female counterpart lies in Behn's brief discussion of body carving. Behn informs us that the Coramantien nobility 'are so delicately cut and rais'd all over the fore-part of the trunk of their bodies, that it looks as if it were japan'd, the works being raised like high-point around the edge of the flowers' (p. 68). The use of a simile of a Western female art of embroidery fails to naturalize the paradox of this phenomenon. Body carving signifies simultaneously a sophisticated aesthetic sensibility (particularly in contrast with the unadorned nakedness of the Indian natives of Surinam) and extreme barbarity. Yet Oroonoko is 'only carved with a little flower, or bird, at the side of the temples', whereas Imoinda is 'carved in fine flowers and birds all over her body' (p. 68). Imoinda's capacity to magnify her husband's symbolic function in the text here tips over into an excess that makes her alien rather than familiar to the white European reader's fascinated gaze.

The leitmotif of the embracing of pain in the service of an aesthetic ideal signified in the brief mention of body carving has its grotesque counterpart in the heroic ideals of the Indian tribes of Surinam. On a visit into the interior of Surinam, Oroonoko, his 'great mistress' and a small group of interested colonists encounter some Indian war-captains who, it transpires, win command through a trial of endurance in which two candidates calmly chop off their facial appendages and slash their cheeks until such point as one or other concedes. Behn, always fascinated by visual effect, writes: 'so frightful a vision it was to see 'em, no fancy can create; no sad dreams can represent so dreadful a spectacle. For my part I took 'em for hobgoblins or fiends, rather than men' (p. 80). Oroonoko, she reports, is equally shocked. '[I]t's by a passive valour they shew and prove their activity; a sort of courage too brutal to be applauded by our black hero' (p. 81). However, later in the story, it is precisely this form of passive valour that Oroonoko himself comes to embrace and enact, specifically through the influence and example of his wife.

After his attempt to lead a slave rebellion fails, Oroonoko falls into a vengeful despair and determines to murder the corrupt Deputy Governor of

Surinam, Byam, who has been the major cause of his sufferings. He leads his beloved Imoinda into the woods and informs her of his plans, urging her to allow him to take her life and that of their unborn child so that she may not be left to the mercies of the colonists after his inevitable execution. He finds his wife, however, 'faster pleading for death than he was to propose it' (p. 93). Behn explains Imoinda's willing self-sacrifice in terms of the traditions of Coramantien rather than Western Christian submission: 'wives have a respect for their husbands equal to what other people pay a deity; and when a man finds any occasion to quit his wife, if he love her, she dies by his hand' (pp. 93–4). Imoinda is decapitated by her husband who remains by her body for two days in a delirium. He is recaptured only after he ritually cuts out a piece of his own throat and disembowels himself in full view of his pursuers. This action and his subsequent stoic endurance of execution by dismemberment aligns Oroonoko with the 'passive valour' of the Indian war-captains and his wife, an ethic he had earlier eschewed.

It is thus, I would argue, in the willingness to undergo self-mutilation, to write suffering on to the body as a symbol of heroism, a practice associated from an early stage of the text with the black woman, that the white female narrator finds an alterity that she cannot, or rather will not, identify with nor appropriate. Oroonoko's decision to take his wife's life is vindicated by the narrator who tells us that once he has explained his reasons '(however horrid it first appear'd to us all) ... we thought it brave and just' (p. 93). Yet Imoinda's submission can only be explained by virtue of a social code explicitly identified as alien to Behn's own culture. Behn resists the obvious interpretation of Imoinda's behaviour within the Western allegory of Christian martyrdom. At an earlier stage in the novel, Behn describes herself seeking unsuccessfully to fit Imoinda into just such a Christian framework by 'telling her stories of nuns, and endeavouring to bring her to the knowledge of the true God' (p. 69). Although the white female narrator makes a concerted effort to 'interpret' or 'comprehend' her black hero from within Western classical myths of the heroic champion, she sidesteps the opportunity to perform a similar act of appropriation with regard to her black heroine by reading her through the lens of sentimental self-sacrifice as adumbrated in Christian ideology. This refusal to employ the black woman as anything other than inappropriable symbol of alterity and incomprehensible suffering is further registered on the level of naming in the text. Throughout the Surinam episodes in the novel, Behn refers to Oroonoko by the Western romance name, Caesar, conferred on him by his slave-masters, but she refers to her heroine only infrequently under her new 'slave' name of Clemene.

This process of differentiation between white female narrator and black female character is, I would argue, central to Behn's project of 'self-fashioning', or what Janet Todd terms the conversion of 'history' into 'herstory' by way of the avoidance of 'hysteria' in the making of the woman writer. In *Oroonoko*, Aphra Behn, always conscious of her singularity as a professional woman writer in the misogynist world of European art of the late 1680s, is precisely 'working to be known'. The telling of the royal slave's history is simultaneously an act of autobiography on the part of his white female 'biographer'. Behn's artful fiction-making, her love of specularization, rhetorical display and self-conscious performance of seduction through narrative art, is sharply contrasted throughout the text with the passive, feminine and 'other' mode of representation associated with the Indian native and the black slave through the figure of the black woman. As feminist and new historicist critics we cannot afford to ignore the fact that Behn's position as white 'herstorian' is only established through the simultaneous representation of her black heroine as inarticulate 'hysteric'. A Utopian picture of gender and race symbolically marrying in the shape of white female narrator and black male hero in order to 'deconstruct' colonial discursive power may be attractive, but it is, like Behn's own self-fashioning, only a consoling fiction.

The conflictual relation between black and white women to which *Oroonoko* draws our attention is not a single occurrence in Behn's texts. In another short fiction, written in the late 1680s, *The Unfortunate Bride; or, the Blind Lady a Beauty* (1700), in which Behn again figures as an agent in the drama of the narrative, she introduces the figure of Moorea, 'a blackamoor Lady' (*Oroonoko and Other Stories*, p. 236). Moorea, like Imoinda, stands for absolute alterity, contrasted with the white sentimental heroine, Belvira, but this time the black woman occupies the familiar stereotype of overpowering sexual desire. Moorea is variously described as 'the devil in the flesh' (p. 236), 'black in her mind, and dark, as well as in her body' (p. 237). Infatuated by the hero, Frankwit, she intercepts his letters to his mistress when he is sick and convinces the latter that he died having succumbed to her passion. Once again, the white female narrator, Behn, is powerless in the narrative. She obtains the intercepted letters and sends them on to Belvira but they arrive too late to prevent the latter's marriage to Frankwit's friend and a tragic denouement in which both men and Belvira herself are killed.

The example of Moorea should be enough to convince us that Behn's ambiguous and subtle responses to colonialism did not extend as far as a modern anti-racist sensibility. It does, however, reinforce my own suggestions that Behn's ingenious uses of racial and gender ideology have a peculiar contemporaneity for modern readers in that they challenge us to consider the ways in which a white 'feminist' impulse to win 'authority' for the female voice has historically been complicit in forms of racist misogyny. This article has offered another allegorical reading to accompany the many already inscribed into Behn's novel of *Oroonoko*. Behn's white female narrator has the twentieth-century white feminist critic's fascination with the black woman as embodying material otherness. She inspects and puts on show the black woman's suffering but ultimately refuses to 'comprehend' it. Here, then, the figure of the black woman becomes purely iconic, the mute bearer of female suffering on to whom the white female subject can project her own hysteria and be left at liberty to write. The recent fascination of white feminist critics with black women's writing, and particularly Afro-American narratives of black women's experience under slavery might, on one level, be interpreted as just such a move of objectification and displacement. In our own project of 'self-fashioning', those white feminist critics concerned to comprehend the mutual articulations of gender and race must beware of constructing their own 'other' in the black woman, suppressing the conflict between racial interests within the politics of gender. Aphra Behn's *Oroonoko* can serve, then, as a starting-point for the attempt to produce a politics of diversity that acknowledges disruption and discontinuity in our own 'history' of feminist theory and criticism.

NOTES

1 Walter Benjamin, 'Theses on the Philosophy of History', *Illuminations*, trans. Harry Zohn (London: Fontana, 1978), p. 264.
2 Hayden White, 'The Burden of History', *Tropics of Discourse: Essays in Cultural Criticism* (Baltimore and London: Johns Hopkins University Press, 1978), p. 50.
3 Kate Millett, *Sexual Politics* (London: Virago, 1977); Sandra Gilbert and Susan Gubar, *The Madwoman in the Attic: The Woman Writer and the Nineteenth-Century Literary Imagination* (New Haven: Yale University Press, 1979); Elaine Showalter, *A Literature of their Own: British Women Novelists from Brontë to Lessing* (London: Virago, 1978).
4 Mary Jacobus, *Reading Woman: Essays in Feminist Criticism* (London: Methuen, 1986); Gayatri Chakravorty Spivak, *In Other Worlds: Essays in Cultural Politics* (London: Methuen, 1987); Patricia Parker, *Literary Fat Ladies: Rhetoric, Gender, Property* (London: Methuen, 1987).
5 See in particular, the comments of Elaine Showalter in her 'Shooting the Rapids. Feminist Criticism in the Mainstream', *Sexual Difference*, special edition *Oxford Literary Review* 8 (1986), pp. 218–24 and those of Carol Thomas Neely in her 'Constructing the Subject: Feminist Practice and the New Renaissance Discourses', *English Literary Renaissance* 18 (1988), pp. 5–18.
6 Edward Pechter, 'The New Historicism and its Discontents: Politicizing Renaissance Drama', *Publications of the Modern Language Association* 102 (1987), pp. 292–303; Louis Montrose, 'Renaissance Literary Studies and the Subject of History', and Jean Howard, 'The New Historicism in Renaissance Studies', *English Literary Renaissance* 16 (1986), pp. 5–12, 13–43; Laura Brown and Felicity Nussbaum, 'Revising Critical Practices', in *The New Eighteenth Century: Theory, Politics, English Literature*, eds Laura Brown and Felicity Nussbaum (London: Methuen, 1987), pp. 1–22.
7 Michel Foucault, *The History of Sexuality*, vol. 1 (London: Penguin, 1981), p. 93.
8 See Stephen Greenblatt, *Renaissance Self-Fashioning: From More to Shakespeare* (Chicago: University of Chicago Press, 1980), p. 5. All further references are in the text.
9 For the argument that feminist criticism has always in fact been 'new historicist' in this respect, see Judith Newton, 'History as Usual? Feminism and the "New Historicism"', *Cultural Critique* no. 9 (Spring 1988), pp. 87–122. For the importance of Foucault to feminist criticism as a whole see the excellent collection of essays in *Feminism and Foucault: Reflections on Resistance*, ed. Irene Diamond and Lee Quinby (Boston: Northeastern University Press, 1988).

10 Louis Montrose's analysis of the role of ideologies of gender and sovereignty with relation to Queen Elizabeth is the honourable exception here. See Montrose, 'The Elizabethan Subject and the Spenserian Text', in *Literary Theory/Renaissance Texts*, eds Geoffrey Hartman and Patricia Parker (London: Methuen, 1986), pp. 303–40.

11 See Marguerite Waller, 'Academic Tootsie: The Denial of Difference and the Difference it Makes', *Diacritics* 17 (1987), pp. 2–20.

12 Janet Todd, *Feminist Literary Histories* (Oxford: Basil Blackwell, 1988), p. 136.

13 See Lennard J. Davis, *Factual Fictions: The Origins of the English Novel* (New York: Columbia University Press, 1983), pp. 108–10; Michael McKeon, *The Origins of the English Novel 1600–1740* (Baltimore and London: Johns Hopkins University Press, 1987), pp. 112–14.

14 See Hayden White, 'The Noble Savage Theme as Fetish', *Tropics of Discourse*, pp. 183–96.

15 Aphra Behn, *Oroonoko and Other Stories*, ed. Maureen Duffy (London: Methuen, 1986), p. 99. All subsequent references to Behn's works are to this edition and are included in the text.

16 Imoinda appears as the daughter of a Frenchman living in the Gold Coast region of Coramantien. Thomas Southerne, *Oroonoko: A Tragedy* (London: H. Playford, 1696).

17 Jane Spencer, *The Rise of the Woman Novelist: From Aphra Behn to Jane Austen* (Oxford: Basil Blackwell, 1986), p. 47. All further references are in the text.

18 Laura Brown, 'The Romance of Empire. *Oroonoko* and the Trade in Slaves', in *The New Eighteenth Century*, p. 50. All further references are in the text.

19 On this convention, see Abdul R. Johammed, 'The Economy of Manichean Allegory. The Function of Racial Difference in Colonialist Literature', in *'Race', Writing and Difference*, ed. Henry Louis Gates (Chicago and London: University of Chicago Press, 1985), pp. 78–106.

20 Gayatri Chakravorty Spivak, 'Imperialism and Sexual Difference', in *Sexual Difference*, p. 228.

Chapter 17

The great distinction:
figures of the exotic in the work of
William Hodges

Harriet Guest

I

In 1780, five years after his circumnavigation with Cook, William Hodges travelled to India. He had already made the representation of unfamiliar landscapes and foreign peoples his speciality, and was known and celebrated for his large canvases of scenes in the South Pacific, and he consolidated this reputation when he became the first European professional landscape painter to portray the interior of Northern India. In 1793 he published an account of his *Travels in India*, a journal of his observations and experiences that would, he wrote, 'enable me to explain to my friends a number of drawings which I had made during my residence in India'. There he described his first perception of the coast, the sight of the English town of Fort St George (Madras), and the climactic moment at which he felt the excitement of encounter with the foreign:

> Some time before the ship arrives at her anchoring ground, she is hailed by the boats of the country filled with people of business, who come in crowds on board. This is the moment in which an European feels the great distinction between Asia and his own country. The rustling of fine linen, and the general hum of unusual conversation, presents to his mind for a moment the idea of an assembly of females. When he ascends upon the deck, he is struck with the long muslin dresses, and black faces adorned with very large gold ear-rings and white turbans. The first salutation he receives from these strangers is by bending their bodies very low, touching the deck with the back of the hand, and the forehead three times.

The difference of this country, the great distinction that the European feels, is not predominantly for Hodges a matter of the colours and contours of the landscape, the strangeness or incongruity of the architecture, although he notes that these 'present a combination totally new' to the English eye. The novelty of this view, and the strangeness of the climate to one 'accustomed to the sight of rolling masses of clouds floating in a damp atmosphere',[1] are remarkable and pleasing. But 'the moment', the great distinction, is for him the encounter with people who rustle and hum, in alien and inarticulate conversation, people who are incomprehensible but evidently not alarming, curious but not threatening.[2] And their strangeness, the difference of dress, colour and language, seems to the spectator to present an essential and momentous distinction that he understands in terms of gender: for a moment he entertains not the *metaphor* but the *idea* of an assembly of females.

The primacy of gender in Hodges's account of his initial perception of the difference between Europe and Asia is, of course, hardly surprising. European travellers repeatedly employ what might be described as discourses of gender in this context in the seventeenth and eighteenth centuries, and these work to distinguish the spectacular unfamiliarity of dress, of physical build, and to homogenize, to colonialize and to conceal what might otherwise appear to be discrepancies or inconsistencies in European observations.[3] Hodges goes on, immediately after the passage I've just quoted, to unfold his apprehension of Asia into a sequence of sights and sounds, a description that is more particular to Madras, and to complexify his identification of the great distinction with that of gender. He writes:

> The natives first seen in India by an European voyager, are Hindoos, the original inhabitants of the Peninsula. In this part of India they are delicately framed, their hands in particular are more like those of tender females; and do not appear to be, what is considered a proper proportion to the rest of the person, which is usually above the middle size. Correspondent to this delicacy of appearance are their manners, mild, tranquil, and sedulously attentive: in this last respect they are indeed remarkable, as they never interrupt any person who is speaking, but wait patiently until he has concluded; and then answer with the most perfect respect and composure.[4]

It is in particular the hands of the Hindu people of business that seem to the European spectator to be '*like* those of tender females'. Their gender is no longer a matter of an idea, an identity, presented to his mind in an overall and startling apprehension of difference, but a simile, produced by his detailed powers of observation. But although these people are above middle size, the simile is implicitly appropriated to the description of their 'delicacy of appearance', and it is alluded to in the account of their mode of conversation. The Hindu merchants 'never interrupt', but listen sedulously, and answer with composure, and it is the implicit gendering of their presentation that makes it unnecessary for the narrator to explain why this is 'indeed remarkable' – their attention is remarkable, he implies, both because it marks the feminine docility of their manners, in contrast to the impatience of European men, and because it contrasts with the garrulous flow of unusual conversation that had first impressed him with the idea of an 'assembly of females'.

The importance of this idea, this synecdoche, in Hodges's narrative is apparent in a range of the issues his account raises – his perception of the differences between the Hindu and Muslim peoples, his conception of their religion, their 'stage' of civilization, his construction of them as a curious and cryptic spectacle passing before his knowing gaze.[5] But its immediate implications, in the opening chapter of the *Travels*, seem to have more to do with the position of the English in Madras in the early 1780s. It's worth noting that in the writings of Hodges's near-contemporaries, for example, in William Robertson's *Historical Disquisition Concerning Ancient India* (1791), or in the writings of Sir William Jones, the 'soft and voluptuous' nature of the Hindu people,[6] expressed in their poetry, or manifested in religious practices appropriate to 'the extreme sensibility both of their mental and corporeal frame',[7] is itself the focus of interest. But in Hodges's account of Madras, his allusions, both implicit and explicit, to their spectacular femininity do not take it to be symptomatic of their historical or national character, though later in his narrative it does acquire this significance. The femininity that is attributed to the Hindu people of Madras works, rather, to emphasize the immediate and striking 'first impression' that they make 'upon an entire stranger', an impression that precludes the possibility of significant depth. The gendered construction of the Hindu business people, and later of the indigenous population of Madras, indicates that they are passive, attentive, responsive in their relations with Europeans, and allows the spectator to elide or gloss over the question of what they are responsive to, what European activities demand their sedulous attention. In that first passage that I quoted, the transition from the perception of these people as merchants, engaged in business, to the description of their obeisances, is enabled, smoothed, by the account of their strange femaleness, a startling idea that makes it unnecessary to acknowledge, in the account of their behaviour, the problematic combination of military and commercial power wielded by the British in Madras. The spectacular strangeness of what he observes obscures the difficulties of the spectator's own position in relation to that British power – his dependence on the licence and patronage extended by the East India Company, and his repeated claims to independent impartiality of perception and judgement.[8]

The femininity of these 'original inhabitants', in this context, does not appear to be itself the object of the spectator's curious interest. It seems to indicate the lack of any historical or characteristic depth, to mark the great distinction that confronts him as essentially natural, and beyond change or investigation. He focuses on it perhaps in order not to look elsewhere, rather than because it gratifies his curiosity. Hodges writes:

The appearance of the natives is exceedingly varied, some are wholly naked, and others so clothed, that nothing but the face and neck is to be discovered; besides this, the European is struck at first with many other objects, such as women carried on men's shoulders on pallankeens, and men riding on horseback clothed in linen dresses like women: which, united with the very different face of the country from all he had ever seen or conceived of, excite the strongest emotions of surprise!

It is impossible to describe the enthusiasm with which I felt myself actuated on this occasion; all that I saw filled my mind with expectations of what was yet unseen. I prepared therefore eagerly for a tour through the country.[9]

The spectator is struck by the variety he sees, by what he seems to regard as transgressions of gender roles, but this is not enough. The people are not the face of the country, and the face is not the concealed identity. Madras and its people seem here to be like the partly clothed attendants of some classical deity, who direct the Englishman's curious eye, not to their own concealed nakedness, but to that of a figure yet unseen.[10] The spectator wants to look through, look beyond, to the interior of the continent, and not to be detained by that initial apprehension of the coastal border with its great distinction.

The first few pages of Hodges's *Travels in India* establish the importance of notions of gender in constructing the relations of the European spectator and narrator to the peoples he observes. And they also demonstrate that the idea of the Hindu crowd as a feminine spectacle, which the narrator initially finds surprising and striking, quickly yields to his enthusiastic eagerness to see something else, beyond. The feminization of the Hindu people makes them visibly spectacular to the narrator, but it also seems to make them hardly worth contemplating, as though they were too visible to be worthy of his gaze, to gratify his curiosity, in comparison with the 'yet unseen'. Hodges is eager to get beyond Madras, to explore the interior, perhaps because, in his account, the recognition and identification of the people there seems overdetermined. Madras, he points out, 'was formed by the English' in the mid-seventeenth century, and since the wars of 1748–52 they 'may be considered as Sovereigns' there. But their presence doesn't have the interest of the exotic, and is for him 'more like a tale of enchantment than a reality'.[11] Their dominance over the local Hindu population seems absolute, though vaguely defined, and hostility, in the form of the 'torrent' of war, comes from an enemy perceived to have 'over-run' the country beyond. The Hindu people of Madras, he implies, are insubstantial, and somehow without depth, in their feminized submission. He comments that there is little here 'to illustrate the history or characters of the original inhabitants': their feminized presence, in the absence of tangible historical evidence, reveals to the European eye 'no Characters at all'.[12] Instead, it manifests their subordination and responsiveness, and the identification of that in terms of gender elides the distinctions between the various forms of their disadvantage, and effaces the differences between the positions of subordination accorded them in relations of commerce, or military government, or religious and cultural discrimination. Because the distinction of gender may accommodate and describe all of these, it tends to homogenize their different implications, and to blur any conflicts between them.[13] It is perhaps this attribute that makes gendered identification of primary importance in Hodges's account, but not itself the focus of interest. Instead it functions, as it were, as a lens, that enables the spectator to perceive or ignore further and apparently more complex objects of knowledge.

In Hodges's account of Madras, notions of gender describe the perceived relation between the population and the residues of its historical culture. They describe the visible strangeness of the people, rendered merely spectacular in the absence of indications of historical depth and substance; and those notions thus enable the elision, the glossing over, of the relationship between the perceived status of the 'original inhabitants', the licensed independence of the spectator, and the imperial and commercial ambitions of the British. Difference of gender was also a privileged notion in representations of the South Seas – both in Hodges's paintings, and in the writings of his fellow-travellers. The naturalist Johann Reinhold Forster, who accompanied Cook on his second voyage, along with Hodges, can be taken as broadly representative in his comment on the men of Tahiti that the 'outlines of their bodies are ... beautifully feminine'.[14] The predominance of this notion of difference as a means of describing the distinction between the European spectator and what he observes works to emphasize similarities, parallels, between European perceptions of the peoples of Polynesia, and of Asia. But it is the capaciousness of the notion of gender difference that gives it this importance, for it is in its complexity and flexibility that this notion is comparable to the ideological distinction that informs European perceptions. The terms in which the Polynesians of the South Seas, or the Hindu population of Madras, might appear feminine to the gaze of the European observer in the late eighteenth century may construct them in terms that are almost entirely disparate.[15] And indeed I think that *within* the terms in which Europeans construct their conceptions of *each* of these groups, the use of gendered discourses enables a degree of diversity, and of contradiction, which is significant to the development of commercial and imperial ambitions in this period.

II

I want to explore, in this essay, some of the implications of the construction of European perceptions of the exotic in gendered terms, and to suggest some of the ways in which we might understand these to be engaged or articulated in Hodges's paintings. But rather than attempting to discuss the whole range of Hodges's work, I want to focus my discussion on one place and one painting, for I think that the interaction of gender and exoticism in that one image will best indicate the complexity of the relation between these discursive categories in the late decades of the eighteenth century. This is Hodges's painting of *A View Taken in the Bay of Otaheite Peha* [*Vaitepiha*] (plate 17.2), now in Anglesey Abbey. It was probably produced in 1775–6, and intended to hang at the Admiralty with the pendant *View of Matavai Bay in the Island of Otaheite* (plate 17.1), now in the Yale Center for British Art at New Haven. Both paintings suggest the fertile abundance of vegetation, the physical or sensual ease, that made the idea of Tahiti, to European perceptions, an image of Paradise. The apparent leisure of the women in the foreground of *Otaheite Peha*, and the indolence of the men in the foreground of *Matavai Bay*, reinforce the conception of the island as a place where, in the words of Johann [John] Forster, 'the living' is 'easy & cheap'.[16] The image of Otaheite Peha, in particular, appeals to that idea of Tahiti that seems to have exercised a powerful attraction for the imagination of European men – a place where man might sweat in pleasure and not labour, a place which justified the conflation of the exotic and erotic. In the image of Matavai Bay, there is a similar luxuriance of foliage, of dripping paint, emphasized by the liquid expanse of water in the foreground, the oily plasticity of the sails and rigging. But the painting presents the waters that encircle the island as a masculine space, in contrast to the femininity of the interior landscape. The Tahitian men in their canoes may in a sense be feminized, contained within the terms of that gendered notion of the exotic, because of their indolent physicality, or because the aggressive finery of the warriors in the middle distance exemplifies that idea of exotic effeminacy that William Blake alluded to when he commented that 'Savages are Fops & Fribbles more than any other Men'.[17] But the pairing of this image with that of Otaheite Peha nevertheless confronts the European gaze with a striking contrast between manly boldness and feminine leisure.

The contrast between the paintings, then, points up the importance of gender in distinguishing the different social spaces that the landscapes represent. But for contemporary critics the contrast contained within each of these compositions, in the manner in which they are painted, seems to have been more remarkable. For contemporary responses to Hodges's work repeatedly comment on what they saw as the disparity between the topographical intentions of his images, their aim of making unfamiliar scenes known, and the apparent lack of accuracy and negligent concern for the known features of the landscape, implied by Hodges's generous use of broad brushstrokes and liquid paint. A reviewer commented, on the Pacific landscapes exhibited at the Royal Academy in 1777, that:

> The public are indebted to this artist for giving them some idea of scenes Which they before knew little of. It is rather surprising however, that a man of Mr. Hodges's genius should adopt such a ragged mode of colouring; his pictures all appear as if they were unfinished, and as if the colours were laid on the canvas with a skewer.

And these reservations are echoed by other eighteenth-century critics.[18] Hodges himself, however, believed that his work was distinguished by his genius for what he called 'accurate observation'. He argued, in his later

Plate 17.1 William Hodges, *A View of Matavai Bay in the Island of Otaheite*, 1776. Oil on canvas, 36 × 54″. Yale Center for British Art, New Haven, Paul Mellon Collection

writing, that 'every thing has a particular character', which he implied that the artist must discover and disclose if his work is to have any 'pretensions to reputation as characteristical' of the nation that is being portrayed. He concludes that pictures achieve their highest value when they are 'connected with the history of the various countries, and ... faithfully represent the manners of mankind'.[19] His success in achieving these aims may have been apparent to some of his contemporaries: Sir William Jones praised his aquatint *Views of India* for 'correct delineations', and they served as patterns and sources for artists working in India until well into the nineteenth century.[20] More ambiguously, perhaps, Sir Joshua Reynolds referred to his representations of Asiatic buildings with approval in his 13th Discourse, and commented that he produced the 'best landskips' in the Academy exhibition of 1786.[21]

The relation in Hodges's work, then, between accurate observation and boldness, between particular character and ragged colouring, was controversial, and I want to suggest that the features of his work that could arouse this debate can be understood to be intimately related to the function of gendered discourses in constructing European conceptions of the exotic in the late decades of the eighteenth century.[22] I can best demonstrate that relation by discussing Hodges's *View Taken in the Bay of Otaheite Peha* in a little more detail. The prominence and boldness of the figures of the two women in the landscape are immediately striking. The vivid pinkness and inflated form of the bathing woman in the centre, and the bluish-pink skin-colour of the seated woman on the right, give them prominence in contrast to the greens, blues and yellows of the landscape. Their position in the foreground of the painting seems to throw them into relief, to emphasize their presence, to a degree that is unusual in Hodges's work. The figures of the women seem to function as focal points for the landscape beyond, their familiar forms providing a point of reference that makes its unfamiliar and almost fantastic contours knowable, and drawing their own exotic interest from their place within it. But if the figures of the women make the scene somehow recognizable, they seem to do so because the image draws on several different and perhaps incompatible conventions: on theories about primitive and exotic societies as well as on images of economic and sensual paradises.

In their monumental study of *The Art of Captain Cook's Voyages*, Bernard Smith and Rüdiger Joppien suggest that this landscape represented a challenge to the way Cook wished to see the Society islanders portrayed after his second voyage. Cook had been dismayed by the emphasis on the apparently promiscuous sexual behaviour of the islanders in accounts of his first voyage, and wished to redress the balance in the account of his second. He asked for all reference to what he called 'the Amours of my people' to be expurgated, so that the edited and published account would be 'unexceptionable to the nicest readers'.[23] But Hodges's painting, I think, points up the pressures that made this chastening ambition unworkable. For the painting of Otaheite

Plate 17.2 William Hodges, *A View Taken in the Bay of Otaheite Peha*, 1776. Oil on canvas, 36 × 54″. National Trust, Anglesey Abbey, Cambridgeshire

Peha demonstrates the sense in which the intersection, the engagement of the discourses in terms of which European visions of the South Pacific are articulated involves ambivalences, contradictions which it is one of the functions of the notion of exotic sexuality to embody.

Perhaps the most obviously troubling aspect of the idea of the South Seas as it is represented in these paintings is the apparent ease of the inhabitants. For they enjoy a desirable but apparently unearned leisure and plenty that seem inevitably to question the values of industry and progress, the need for endeavour, resolution and adventure. And the manner in which that troubling ease is represented in this pair of paintings seems both to emphasize and to conceal this problem. On the one hand, the prominent position of the women in the landscape, and the implications of their gender, might work to lend a moral gloss to the idea of a natural Paradise. It was a commonplace of Enlightenment social theory that the position of women is the index to the degree of civilization achieved in any society, and their position, their behaviour and treatment, was judged according to what might be described as a bourgeois pastoral fantasy of the gendered apportioning of labour and ease. The leisure of women in the second half of the eighteenth century is understood in this context as a sign, a product and reward, of the labour of men. European explorers are insistently disapproving in their accounts of anything visible, recognizable, as female labour in the societies they observe, because they take it to be evidence of the degeneracy and tyranny of the men of that society.[24] On the other hand, however, the leisure apparently enjoyed by women might not be a sign of a society emerging into civilization from what Europeans saw as a primitive and barbarian state. For it may not indicate that the women are engaged in the easy consumption of whatever the men in the pendant canvas may have fished up or fought for. The indolence of those men may indicate that they enjoy a barbarous ease purchased as a result of the servitude, the commodification, of the women's sexuality. That ambivalence, about whether the women's leisure indicates an earned and moralized ease, or sexual abandon, is in a sense necessary to the terms in which these images represent Tahiti as the object of the curiosity and desire of the European spectator.

The different terms in which the women's leisure may be contextualized and thus articulated in this landscape, construct the rewards of resolution and adventure, the purposes of European exploration, in complex terms.[25] The view of Otaheite Peha claims comparison with the sub-genre of scenes of young women bathing, scenes which cast the European spectator both as the unintrusive admirer of women's secluded freedoms, and as Actaeon, only secured from animality by the composing frame, the self-conscious distancing and deferral of the pleasures he views.[26] In Hodges's painting, the necessity of that distance seems emphasized by the dissolution of the form of the bathing woman in the water that supports her: in order for her to achieve coherence, to become integrated into corporeality, the spectator must stand well away from the picture, and must see her within the landscape and the frame, he must recognize her exotic distance as the condition of her desirability. The subordination of the figure to the unity of the landscape as a whole, then, enables at the same time as it anaesthetizes curiosity and desire; it licenses these by assimilating and diffusing them to the compositional whole that offers to transcend physicality, to displace the pursuit of it on to the chaste idea of the whole landscape.[27] In these terms the painting seems to apply the conventions for the representation of a golden age that is erotic because it is innocent to the landscapes explored in the South Pacific: it exploits the deferred sensual promise of the exotic to represent the landscape and climate of Tahiti, the composition of the painting, as the necessary condition, and perhaps the diffused but comprehensive object, of desire. The bathing woman, viewed in this context, would seem to confirm the desirable salubrity of climate that dominates Hodges's smaller oil sketches (for example, *A View of the Islands of Otaha and Bola Bola with part of the Island of Ulietea* (plate 17.3), in the National Maritime Museum at Greenwich) and that climate would in turn confirm the innocence of the leisure that the Tahitian women enjoy.[28]

In those terms the lack of finish with which the bathing woman is painted seems to be necessary to the capacity of the image to give the spectator an idea of scenes he before knew little of; it seems to involve innocence in a kind of enforced distance. But it is not only because of its climate, most powerfully represented in Hodges's depopulated sketches, that Tahiti appeared to offer the attractions of Paradise to European explorers and armchair travellers. Though its pleasures could be understood in terms appropriate to classical Arcadias, they are also immediate, material. In this painting, the ambivalent relation between these different conceptions of the kind of Paradise Tahiti might offer can be perceived in the contrasting and perhaps incongruous representation of the two women in the foreground. The seated woman forms through her gesture a sub-group with the figure of the *tii*, the carved image to her right,[29] and both are painted with a degree of detail and finish that's conspicuously lacking in the central, bathing woman. They seem to invite a curious and close inspection that is at odds with the distance necessary to make sense of the form of the woman in the water.

Viewed from a distance, the figure of the *tii* seems to assume the familiar proportions of Priapus, and, by virtue of that classical allusion in its form, it might legitimize whatever sexual abandon the figures of the women might suggest. In a letter ostensibly written by Lord Lyttelton in the 1770s, the notoriously dissolute aristocrat discussed his collection of drawings and paintings of nude women and boys, and commented that while most of these had to be kept in his private dressing-room, scenes involving sacrifices to Priapus could be prominently displayed in the library, perhaps because the figure seemed to dispel the prurience provoked by what was described as his 'inanimate Seraglio'.[30] For Priapus's phallic form guarantees the

Plate 17.3 William Hodges, A View of the Islands of Otaha and Bola Bola with part of the Island of Ulietea, September 1773. Oil on canvas, 13 × 19¼". National Maritime Museum, London

heterosexuality of his worshippers, as well as the satisfaction of their desires within the social landscape of the painting. But the detail in which the carving of the image is represented seems to claim for the *tii* a scrutiny that reveals its specifically barbarous identity, an identity that resists assimilation to the more familiar classical idea of Priapus. And it invites a close inspection that discloses, to the right of the image, the elevated *tupapau*.[31] These two exotic curiosities, close together at the margin of the painting, are reminiscent of the kind of occasional and collectable objects whose scarcity value attracted virtuosi as well as scientists to the South Pacific.[32] They might fulfil a function similar to that of the curiosities and memorabilia from Cook's first voyage that surround Joseph Banks in Benjamin West's portrait (plate 17.4). The riches of Banks's collection, drawn from a dispersed variety of cultures, are organized to display his cosmopolitanism, their exotically random incoherence, as well as to indicate authenticity, the first hand and intimate experience that informs knowledge. The representation of these exotic *things* locates the sign of authenticity in material detail, removed from any indication of the more generalized effects of climate or topography.

The *tii* seems to work in this painting as a kind of doubled, middle term, between the two women, in so far as it might either fulfil a Priapic role, which emphasizes the subordination and containment of the women within the landscape, or serve as a sign of cryptic but nevertheless curious and authenticating exoticism – an exoticism that does not depend on context, but can be transposed, perhaps appropriated as it has been in the portrait of Banks. And the knowledgeable spectator who sees in the carved form of the *tii* a specifically exotic significance, rather than a culturally masking resemblance to Priapus, would perhaps also be sufficiently well-informed about its exotic context to recognize the *tupapau* behind it as an elevated stage bearing a corpse. The figure of the *tii*, then, in the context of the knowledge that published accounts of the voyages made available, seems to ward off the curiosity that the detail of the painting invites, for it seems to call attention to the dark and morbid superstitions that lurk in the intricacies of the exotic.[33]

Grouped with this image, the finished and quite elaborately detailed form of the seated woman poses a strong contrast to the diffusive and vague outline of the bather. The detailed representation of her tattoos invites the curious attention to detail that discloses the presence of the *tupapau* on the right, and it locates the exotic as the reward of that attention, rather than in the grasp of the landscape as a whole. And that curious exoticism of detail might be perceived to exercise a fascination that detracts from the kind of sensual pleasure that was involved in the perception of the bathing woman enveloped, half-submerged in the landscape. For my discussion has suggested that when the women are perceived in subordination to the landscape, their leisure a function of its luxuriant climate, they are susceptible to a humanizing appropriation that casts them as the innocent objects of the spectator's Actaeon-like gaze. So that the exotic inscription of this woman's detailed

Plate 17.4 Sir Joseph Banks, mezzotint by J. R. Smith, after a portrait by Benjamin West. British Library, London. (I reproduce this image, rather than West's oil painting, for its clarity of detail.)

tattooing might appear to clothe, fetishize and dehumanize her, in so far as it isolates her from the landscape and makes her an object of curiosity. It marks her with an inscription that was common to both sexes – it seems to be based on Hodges's drawing of a Tahitian man (plate 17.5) – and it may thus deny her innocent feminine desirability. Reynolds, in his seventh discourse, argued that 'All ... fashions are very innocent', because they have the sanction of custom, but he excluded from this pale 'some of the practices at Otaheite', which were 'painful, or destructive of health'. Accounts of the Tahitians had dwelt on the apparent painfulness of the tattooing operation, and Reynolds's comments locate it in a different register of exoticism from that which celebrates the healthy climate, the beauty and innocence of the islanders. In this register, the exotic seems identified with what Reynolds called 'circumstances of minuteness and particularity', which he observed, 'frequently seem to give an air of truth to a piece, and to interest the spectator in an extraordinary manner'.[34] This different register invites curious investigation, but the idea of exoticism that it represents encourages the spectator to peer into the canvas with a kind of distasteful fastidiousness. And this idea of the exotic precludes the distance and deferral that were necessary to the loose form of the bathing woman, diffused into the climatic richness of the landscape.

III

The representation of the two women in the foreground of Hodges's painting employs what we might think of as incongruous visual languages, incongruous because they make potentially incompatible demands on the position of the spectator, in implying different relations between the discourses of gender and the exotic. I have suggested that the problem that the relation between them poses illuminates the sense in which that reviewer whom I quoted earlier felt that Hodges's work did offer an 'idea of scenes Which [the public] before knew little of', though it was an idea that they gained by looking through, looking beyond, the paint on the surface before them. For what Hodges means by the capacity for 'accurate observation' on which he prides himself may have more to do with the way his painting demonstrates this doubled focus, than with the desire to produce the sort of cluttered but flat fidelity to human and material detail that other artists of the exotic, some armed with camera obscura, achieved in this period.[35] This is not, of course, only a matter of reconciling the representation of detail with what Hodges described, in writing of the work of his master Richard Wilson, as the 'broad bold and manly execution' of the whole;[36] for the disjunction apparent in this image may manifest instabilities in the matrix of discourses that inform theories about the nature of primitive and exotic societies in the late eighteenth century. What Europeans want from images of Tahiti, what made the idea of the place so attractive to them, may inform the combination of qualities

Plate 17.5 William Hodges, enlarged detail from *Studies of Tahitian Figures*, August, 1773. Pencil, pen and grey wash, $11\frac{5}{8} \times 7\frac{3}{8}''$. Yale Center for British Art, New Haven, Paul Mellon Collection

that Hodges's image demonstrates, and I want now to turn to some of the contemporary discussions of Tahiti, which illuminate the nature of the disjunction that characterizes this image, and also suggest the terms in which it can nevertheless be perceived to soothe rather than unsettle the spectator's eye.

The islanders of the South Pacific were usually perceived in terms of their similarity or difference to those classical or barbarian societies familiar to the educated European. The voyagers themselves made lengthy comparisons between the Tahitians and, usually, the ancient Greeks, and essayists discussed the resemblance of South Pacific customs to those of the Greeks and Romans, the North American Indians, the Goths and the ancient Hebrews. Vicesimus Knox, lucubrating on the custom of human and animal sacrifice, concluded that: 'I cannot but be struck with the wonderful similarity observable in the manners and superstitions of savage men throughout the world, and in all ages.'[37] In contrast to this perception of wonderful homogeneity, the barbarian or savage peoples observed by Europeans were thought not to perceive similarities between themselves and other groups. Barbarous and savage people are understood to be incapable of generalizing their ideas, and to be 'miserably deficient', in the words of Lord Kames, in the two mental powers necessary to reasoning – 'the power of invention, and that of perceiving relations'.[38] William Robertson wrote, of the 'rude and barbarous times' through which he believed every country passed, that:

> When the intellectual powers are just beginning to unfold, and their first feeble exertions are directed towards a few objects of primary necessity and use; when the faculties of the mind are so limited as not to have formed general or abstract ideas; when language is so barren as to be destitute of names to distinguish any thing not perceivable by some of the senses; it is preposterous to expect that men should be capable of tracing the relation between effects and their causes; or to suppose that they should rise from the contemplation of the former to the discovery of the latter, and form just conceptions of one Supreme Being, as the Creator and Governor of the universe.[39]

One of the distinguishing constituents of barbarism, as these comments indicate, is that barbarous peoples are thought to be limited, imprisoned, by a disconnected specificity – of place, superstitious belief, language – that excludes general ideas and just conceptions. It is this feature, for example, that Cook alludes to when he traces unacceptable barbaric behaviour, like cannibalism, to its root cause in the alienation or isolation of one primitive group from another, and in the failure or refusal, therefore, to acknowledge common human features, common humanity.[40]

This contrast between the diverse specificities that constitute barbarian society and thought, and the grasp of wonderful similarity which distinguishes the civilized, proceeds from the ideological construction of two contrasting subjects, of a barbarian or a civilized observer whose capacity to systematize what he sees in the context of general ideas is the index of his place and power in the social and natural hierarchy. But in the later decades of the eighteenth century the contrast between these two modes of perception is more complex than that distribution of talents would suggest. The massive scholarly investment in archaeological and anthropological research, the perceived need to unearth the authentic materiality of cultures historically or geographically remote from those of Europe, tended to appropriate to learned thought the absorption in specificity which had previously defined the objects of knowledge. Thus, for example, the accounts of Cook's second voyage produced by the naturalists Anders Sparrman and Johann Forster both make much of their distance from the comprehensive theories of moral philosophers, a distance substantiated by the detailed and specific nature of their knowledge, its intimate and empirical dependence upon particular things. The preface to Sparrman's account asserts that 'every authentic and well-written book of voyages and travels is, in fact, a treatise of experimental philosophy'. It is the mark of its authenticity that it should contain 'the best materials for the purpose of building ... systems', but should not develop those systems itself.[41] Forster's book demonstrates a similar commitment to the local and particular. His comments on the 'various stages' of mankind's development are, as it were, sustained by the contextual proximity of his detailed *Observations ... on Physical Geography, [and] Natural History*.[42] Their accounts do, to some extent, organize and systematize their materials, but they are nevertheless characterized by an absorption in diverse materials, a respect for the isolation and simplicity of the particular example, that indicates an instability in the contrast I described between barbarian and civilized observers.

Clearly, that contrast is reinforced by the purposive selectivity that the natural philosopher exercises in presenting the 'best materials'. The 'treatise of experimental philosophy' describes or implies relations of cause and effect which it is imagined to be beyond the capacity of the barbarian to trace, and the teleological project that informs those relations is essential to their authenticity and authority, as Robertson's conclusions indicated. But it nevertheless remains the case that in late eighteenth-century conceptions of knowledge, and most acutely in theories of art, the status of empirical research appeared problematically servile and lowly. Joshua Reynolds wrote that the landscape painter 'applies himself to the imagination, not to the curiosity, and works not for the Virtuoso or the Naturalist', and a similar sense of the lowliness of empirical curiosity in the context of heroic art informs James Barry's argument, that art arises:

from the disappointment of the human mind, sated, disgusted, and tired with the monotony of real persons and things which this world affords. ... In proportion to the serenity and goodness of the mind, it naturally turns away from such a state of things, in search of some other more grateful and consoling; and it has a natural horror of those atheistical cavils, which would malignantly deprive it of all other resource, by mercilessly chaining it down to the scene before it.

What Barry objects to, of course, is the particular state of the scene before the mind, a state that he perceives as miserable in its imperfection, but he also suggests that the mechanical condition of mind that is 'chained down to the specific properties of natural objects' may be atheistical in its opposition to ideal truth, and may therefore not be capable of entertaining those purposive projects that end in general ideas, and 'just conceptions' of the first cause.[43]

John Wesley's comments on the published account of Cook's first voyage provide an interesting example of some of the implications of this instability in the opposition between the barbarian and the civilized. He wrote in his journal for 17 January 1774:

> Meeting with a celebrated book, a volume of Captain Cook's Voyages, I sat down to read it with huge expectation. But how was I disappointed! I observed, 1. Things absolutely incredible: 'A nation without any curiosity;' and, what is stranger still, (I fear related with no good design,) 'without any sense of shame! Men and women coupling together in the face of the sun, and in the sight of scores of people! Men whose skin, cheeks, and lips are white as milk.' Hume or Voltaire might believe this; but I cannot. I observed, 2. Things absolutely impossible. ... A native of Otaheite is said to understand the language of an island eleven hundred degrees [*query*, miles] distant from it in latitude; besides I know not how many hundreds in longitude! So that I cannot but rank this narrative with that of Robinson Crusoe; and account Tupia [the Tahitian who acted as a guide and interpreter] to be, in several respects, akin to his man Friday.[44]

Wesley's huge expectation and disappointment, I think, are informed by that discursive opposition, though the terms in which his criticisms are articulated indicate its instability and redefinition. His comments suggest the expectation that physical, sexual behaviour should be common – the face of the sun, the sight of scores of people, should induce a universal and perhaps instinctive response – while intellectual behaviour, the articulation or understanding of language, should, his disbelief implies, indicate the social or topographical place and identity of the subject. In the barbarian, therefore, language should be limited in its specificity, it should express only the particular circumstances in which the islander is thought to be absorbed. Like the Indian in Pope's *Essay on Man*, who is represented as believing that his dog, bottle and wife will be found in heaven, the conceptions of the islander should be dictated by his immediate experience.[45]

Wesley's reaction to the transgression of this social or natural hierarchy involves a further inversion of the terms of that opposition between the civilized and barbarian subjects. For the discovery that the sexual behaviour of the islanders does not resemble what he can consider to be common and natural occasions Wesley to reflect on their physical similarity to Europeans – he remarks that the men's complexions are white as milk, apparently in order to underscore his alarmed disbelief. And he describes his expectation of their sexual behaviour in terms that seem to make this, and not any intellectual capacity, the basis of their claim to interiority, to recognizably human subjectivity: if they had not behaved in this disturbing way, he suggests that he would have been able to credit them, on the basis of the invisibility of their sexual activities and the visibility of their milky complexions, with a natural capacity for moral or social shame, and therefore with a subjectivity at least potentially civilized, and, in that context, common. As it is, the sign that they possess something resembling the systematic and abstract rationality of a civilized subject – their capacity to use a language which is apparently not tied to their immediate material circumstances – seems to him proof that they are 'akin to … man Friday', that they are fictive, and are, not civilized, but the possessions and servants, the subjects, of whose who are: *his* man Friday.[46]

Wesley's brief comments, then, register the shift from a construction of exotic barbarism in which the local particularity of language is a privileged constituent, to a construction which privileges what is social and specular, and which recognizes the regulation of sexuality as the prime indication of moral personality. His remarks demonstrate, in a conveniently concise form, the appropriation of humanist, universal value to the bourgeois construction of subjectivity in terms of a socially regulated and moralized interiority, and they indicate that the coherence of the interior and the social is manifested in sexual behaviour. Discussions of the South Sea islanders in the later decades of the eighteenth century return repeatedly, insistently, to the problematic issue of their sexuality, to the relation between the exotic and the erotic that troubles Hodges's painting, and, I think, this insistence can best be understood in terms of the instabilities of the network of discursive interconnections that define the opposition between the civilized and the barbarian, in the ideological context of bourgeois humanism.[47] Wesley's comments exemplify a more general discursive redefinition of the concept of the barbarian, which acknowledges the importance of his visible and intellectual attachment to a specific locality – the sense in which the barbarian is understood to be somehow more thoroughly and definitively indigenous, more distinctively native and enchorial – but which privileges his unacceptably exotic sexual behaviour as the determining constituent of his barbarous condition. And the significance of this is, I think, that it displaces and diffuses the force of the opposition between the civilized intuitive comprehension of the whole, and the barbarian absorption in detail.

This redefinition does not, of course, reject the terms of that opposition, but it enables the barbarian to be identified, discursively constituted, *either* in local and particular containment, confinement, in the inability to generalize or form coherent theories, *or* in libidinous abandon, in characteristically exotic sexuality. And the second of those identifications could be constructed through its opposition to bourgeois conceptions of the social subject, rather than in contrast to the ideal of the civilized man. The terms of that opposition place the kind of interest in material detail, in phenomena defined by their specific locality, that distinguished the work of naturalists like Forster, in contrast to the barbarian's failure to moralize his desires, his lack of curiosity and shame, and thus conceal the problematic nature of the comparison between their attachment to epistemological discontinuities, materials and not systems, and his. It's worth noting that in Wesley's remarks barbaric sexuality is associated with shamelessness but not with curiosity, not with the 'turn for experiment ... and disposition to enquire' that characterized both the endeavours of enlightened scientists and the reception of their works.[48] Thus the discursive gendering and eroticization of the peoples of the South Seas works to accommodate instabilities and incoherences in the ideological construction of bourgeois humanism. For emphasis on the sexual constituent of barbarism redefines the terms of its opposition to the civilized, and masks the tensions or contradictions involved in the appropriation of humanist attributes to the bourgeois subject.

The privileging of exotic sexuality functions to mask the opposition between contrasting ideological constructions of knowledge; between, on the one hand, the conception of civilized and civilizing knowledge, in which particulars are given form and meaning by their relation to the whole that is grasped in an intuitive act of comprehension, and on the other, the construction of a more bourgeois concept of knowledge as achieved in the progressive acquisition of diverse material facts. It glosses over the tension between the project of adventuring into an unknown new world, which has to be discovered and appropriated piecemeal, and the idea of enlarging the map of the known world, assimilating, drawing in, the details implicit in its design.[49] And it points up, and calls attention to the contrast between the amorality of barbarism, which is the object of curious fascination or chaste disapproval, and the moralized European subject. It can perform these demanding functions because, as Hodges's painting suggests, the object of erotic fantasy is constructed as diverse and formless, without chaste definition or containment except in so far as it is distanced and deferred, but at the same time it is, as Reynolds noted, the 'smaller objects' that 'serve to catch the sense', it is the curious attraction of detail that lends material and sensual substance to fantasy.[50] These two exotic registers find their focus, their expression, in the eroticized and feminized body of the barbarian.

This process, in which the matrix of discourses which construct civilized and humanist perceptions of exotic barbarism is, as it were, mapped on to the different discursive matrix informing bourgeois ideas of exploration, and where that complex relation between the two is manifested and mystified in the fantasy of barbarian sexuality, is perhaps most clearly demonstrated in

John Forster's *Observations made during a Voyage Round the World* (1778). I have already mentioned that Forster's account bases the authority for his lengthy disquisitions on '*Ethic Philosophy*' in the detailed empirical investigation of physical geography and natural history, and his remarks on the 'various stages' of mankind bear witness to the dominance of that rationalist methodology. In his account of the South Sea islanders, he stresses that a man 'born in a civilized nation' cannot envy the 'state of intoxication' – with its implications of physical and moral degeneracy – which the 'savage or barbarian', living in an inhospitable climate, independent of social regulations, mistakes for happiness.[51] But in Tahiti he believes he observes a society developing from barbarism into early civilization, free from the vices which corrupt its later and more fully formed stages, a society which is not only the appropriate object of moral disapprobation and empirically fastidious curiosity. The affection, and even admiration, that he feels for these people seems almost to take him by surprise, and to be experienced in spite of his methodology, with its implications of moral distance and distaste. The experience seems to force on him a kind of sentimental paternalism that is at odds with the principles of his work. He writes that:

> I felt for many of them emotions, which were not so far distant from paternal affection and complacency, as might be expected, when we recollect the great difference of our manners and our way of thinking. But I found likewise ... what a great and venerable blessing benevolence is ... when this best gift of heaven sits enthroned in the heart, fills the soul with gracious sensations, and prompts all our faculties to expressions of good nature and kindness: then only does it connect all mankind as it were into one family; youths of different nations become brethren, and the older people of one nation, find children in the offspring of the other.

Forster's feelings of benevolence, the gracious sensations of his soul, work to connect and assimilate the islanders to the family of mankind. And in that family structure, of course, he assumes the position of the paternal head and enjoys the enthronement of his own virtuous superiority to the Tahitians, whom he implies are childlike in their 'natural levity' and inattention.[52] But while this all-embracing affection and complacency do establish the distance between the mature civilized man and those who are emerging from barbarous adolescence into civilized youth, they do not insist on that distinction between the moral interiority of the perceiving subject, and the observed subjection or degeneracy of the amoral object of knowledge.

In later decades of the eighteenth century, however, as I have already suggested, this kind of benevolent paternalist humanism is adopted to the service of precisely that distinction. And Forster's discussion engages in this process of redefinition through situating this paternalist vision in the more immediate context of the bourgeois ideal of the domestic family. He writes, of the family unit, which he believes is the source of the civilizing development he traces in Tahitian society, that the 'father seemed to be the soul which animated the whole body of the family by his superior wisdom, benevolence and experience'. That difference between the soulful father and the bodily family, only animated by his 'gracious sensations', inscribes the generosity of Forster's paternalist vision with the distinction essential to his rationalist project.[53] Forster debates at some length in the course of his argument the controversial question of race: he considers, on the one hand, the theory, notoriously associated with Lord Monboddo, that the race of humanity extends to include orang-outangs, and on the other the theory that the race is divided into distinct species, which exclude those who are not European from kindred with those who are. And his refutation of both of these theories is based in a bourgeois concept of familial and marital relations. So that, in refutation of the first, more extensive theory, he asserts that it does not deserve serious argument; he writes:

> I appeal to an argument taken from the better half of our species, the fair sex; we all assent to the description which Adam gives of his partner: a creature

> So lovely fair,
> That what seem'd fair in all the world, seem'd now
> Mean, or in her summ'd up, in her contain'd,
> And in her looks; which from that time infus'd
> Sweetness into his heart, unfelt before,
> And into all things from her air inspir'd,
> The spirit of love, and amourous delight.
> Grace was in all her steps; heavn' in her eye,
> In every gesture dignity and love.

> I cannot think that a man looking up to this inimitable masterpiece, could be tempted to compare it with an ugly, loathsome ouran-outang!

The human family, for Forster, is circumscribed by ties of desire, like those bonding Adam to his wife, and he emphasizes the grounding of his argument in physical immediacy when he concludes that should any man persist in the first argument, 'may none but ouran-outangs vouchsafe and admit his embraces'.[54]

The importance that Forster gives to sexual desire as the defining term of the common human species is of course socialized, moralized, as it was in Wesley, by the regulations, limitations, implicit in that discourse: by the identification of body with what needs government, with what is spiritually inanimate or amoral, ignorant and not wise, innocent and not experienced, feminine and not paternal, desired and not desiring. He complains, only a few pages earlier, that:

> we are united in societies, where the constant intercourse with foreigners, makes it next to impossible to preserve the purity of races without mixture,

and pity it is, that the guiles of art and deceit are so great in one sex, and curiosity, levity, and lewdness, are so common in the other, in our enlightened and highly-civilised societies, that they contribute still more to make the preservation of races precarious. This depravation prevailed so far, that even OMAI [the Tahitian man who visited London] became the object of concupiscence of some females of rank.[55]

It is hardly surprising to find that it is not female sexuality or curiosity that define the extent or the boundaries of the human species, that for European women of rank to desire a Tahitian man is evidence of depravity. But for European men to see in the women of the South Seas something conformable to the desirable outline of Milton's Eve is at once less than serious, and the expression of the paternalist impulse – that confusedly incestuous impulse that is at once feared as transgressive and yet somehow recognized as inevitable, almost desirable, as the favoured means of animating the body of the narrative, in so many novels of the period.[56]

In Forster's *Observations*, then, his insistence that the bodies, the observed social forms, of the Tahitians, whatever their sex, are 'beautifully feminine', works to conceal any disjunction between the different terms in which they are perceived, for it provides a means of glossing over discontinuities in the construction of the European subject. On the one hand, his benevolent humanist paternalism defines the difference between the civilized and barbarian subjects in terms of a contrasting capacity for the assimilation of ideas. The comprehensive views of the civilized man indicate his paternal maturity, whereas the mercurial volatility and discontinuity of perception that characterize the barbarian subject define him as childlike and feminine. On the other hand, the distinction between the moralized bourgeois subject and the amoral barbarian defines the first in terms of his capacity for expectant curiosity or desire, and the second as the appropriate feminized object of that desire. An apparent congruence between the two is achieved by reference to the structure of the family, in which the soul of the father is contrasted with and animates the body of the family. Paternalism, therefore, appears to accommodate and to be appropriate to relations of animating desire, relations that focus in the feminine body of the barbarian.

In Hodges's *View of Otaheite Peha* I have argued that the figures of the women in the foreground present a doubled image of the femininity of the exotic. They indicate, as it were, the diverse identities that the idea of the exotic assumes within the terms of its discursive gendering. The prominence in the painting of their beautifully feminine but disparate bodies works to legitimate and moralize the desiring European gaze, for their doubling confuses its focus, its object, and articulates that confusion as a function of their exoticism and not of the European position. But in the context of accounts of Cook's voyages, and responses to them, the diverse meanings of the feminine exotic in this picture can be understood to articulate the ambivalent relation between paternalist assimilation and rationalist appropriation in defining the project of European exploration. The comments of the reviewer I quoted at the beginning of this essay suggest that the spectator responds to the doubled confusion of the image by attempting to look beyond and through the surface of the picture, with its embarrassing lack of finish, its peripheral detail. In doing so the spectator looks for a simplicity in the aims of exploration that his own position does not afford.

IV

In conclusion, I want to return to the detail, in Hodges's painting, of the tattoos marking the seated woman on the right (plate 17.2). For the representation of that exotic inscription can be understood to reiterate the ambivalence that I have argued characterizes the image as a whole, in terms that illuminate the relation between European visions of the exotic and the domestic ideal. I suggested earlier that the tattoos might clothe the figure of the seated woman, and deny her the innocent abandon that the bathing woman displays, their detailed inscription both attracting and repelling curiosity. The implications of the tattoos, the discursive and contextual meanings which we might understand them to articulate, are in a sense doubled, because the position of the woman seems to allude to two different and perhaps incongruous representational conventions. On the one hand, the position of the woman may confirm the casting of the spectator as Actaeon, gazing, in precarious innocence, at a golden age vision of secluded and feminine freedoms. For her posture alludes to that of Diana, in Titian's *Diana and Actaeon* (plate 17.6). The angle of her arm picks up the gesture with which Titian's goddess attempts to protect her modesty, a gesture repeated by the nymph in the centre of Titian's painting; and that allusion seems if anything to be emphasized by the lack of any narrative explanation for the apparent modesty of the Tahitian woman in Hodges's image, for there is no obvious intruder or voyeur within this composition.[57] But, on the other hand, the detailed representation of the tattoos may claim for the image the status of ethnographic portraiture: a practice best exemplified in the drawings and engravings that Sydney Parkinson produced as a result of Cook's first voyage, and which privileges those particular characteristics that distinguish one group of people from another.[58] In its allusion to that ethnographic tradition, the representation of the woman's tattoos might be perceived to interrupt, or to punctuate, the pleasure of the comprehensive gaze that gives desirable form to the bathing woman in the centre of the foreground.

These two different contextualizing allusions clearly imply very different claims for the status of the image – claims that may point up the problematic status of curiosity in the texts I have been considering. For curiosity describes, first, the investigative spirit of inquiry that, for Lord Kames, as well as for Forster and Anders Sparrman, is the basis of social virtue: it is thought to

Plate 17.6 Titian, *Diana and Actaeon*, c. 1556—9. Oil on canvas, 1.88 × 2.03 m. National Gallery of Scotland

promote a predilection for experienced truth, a desire to investigate the 'real qualities and properties of things' that leads to honesty and candour in human transactions.[59] But, second, curiosity describes a mode of investigative intrigue that is often sexually knowing rather than innocent or candid, and that is perceived as a social vice. It was in this sense, for example, that Forster used the term when he described the social corruptions that had led women of rank to treat Omai as the 'object of concupiscence'.[60] These ambivalent implications of curiosity seem as it were to be echoed in the doubled allusions of the position of the seated woman in Hodges's landscape. For these may seem either to privilege the distanced pleasures that the landscape of Tahiti offers to the Actaeon-like spectator, or to invite the more particular investigations of the ethnologist – roles which may each appropriate to the other the guilty knowingness of depraved curiosity. That ambivalent doubling of the spectator's interested pleasures is, I want to suggest, specifically appropriate to the representation of the tattoos, which puncture and mark the feminine foreign body, in ways that are indicated most intriguingly in Forster's *Observations*.

Forster writes more extensively on the subject of tattoos and comparable physical marks, in his published account of the second voyage, than any of his companions, and one of his anecdotes provides a key to his interest in the subject. He recounts that a young girl was brought to him by her brother and sister. He was asked to repeat a certain Tahitian phrase to her, and at each repetition the elder sister 'lifted up the garments of the younger, shewing she had the marks of puberty'. Finally, he asked the meaning of 'this transaction' or ceremony, and, he writes:

> I ... learnt, that in these isles, it is a kind of reproach, or want of dignity not to be of age, and to be destitute of the marks of puberty. As soon as they appear, the young women are obliged to undergo a very painful operation, viz. to have large arched stripes punctured on their buttocks: these curious marks are reputed honourable, and it is thought a mark of pre-eminence to be capable of bearing children. If therefore a man should reproach the person with the deficiency of these marks, she cannot in honour avoid refuting it by ocular demonstration. The origin of these strange customs, it is not in my power to investigate. I contented myself therefore with collecting and recording the fact.[61]

Forster sees in these marks a curious depth of customary significance, an origin that is mysterious, that prompts and frustrates investigation. The nature of this strange significance may be indicated in the ambivalent slippage in this passage between the marks of puberty and the marks of tattooing. For both mark the preeminent capacity for reproduction, and it is not clear whether or not this woman displays the arched stripes he describes.

These marks, he later goes on to explain, are for him important as evidence of the diversity of nations. He documents the various kinds of physical inscriptions mentioned in histories and travel accounts – the skin 'flowered like damask' of the 'great men' of Guinea, the thread sown into the faces of children by the Greenlanders and Tunguses, and so forth – and he introduces this catalogue with the comment that:

> we have ... collected ... these parallel customs; not always with a view to prove that nations, which chance to have the same custom, owe their origin to one another; but rather to convince ourselves that this similarity does not always give sufficient foundation for such a belief.[62]

The relations of similarity or of difference between nations are signalled by these bodily marks, whose origin and meaning are curious, but beyond investigation. Though Forster believes the human species to be unified, these marks, punctuating the physical surface, inscribe that universal homogeneity with cryptic differences. For the apparently widespread practice of marking the body in these ways defies belief in any shared historical origin, and its very universality, therefore, is perceived to be evidence of national diversity. The marks thus seem to authenticate the mysterious originality of these national cultures, and to indicate the fundamental definition of those origins in terms that physical or customary correspondences can only inflect or ornament. And Forster's transaction with the young Tahitian suggests that the distinctive origins of these marks may be preeminently natural or anatomical.

The caution with which Forster treats these marks, and his belief that they cannot be investigated, but should be collected, recorded, severally listed, seems to stem from the implication that they are the customary indices of essential differences, and that their trans-cultural correspondence is somehow the merely customary and superficial sign of deep ethnic and original disparities. Forster emphasizes the pride that he takes in his ability to construct for the peoples he observes histories of which they are themselves unaware. He writes that:

> these islanders having no other than vague traditional reports in lieu of historical records, it is impossible to know anything of their origin or migrations. ... A stronger proof of the advantages of civilization, cannot be given, than results from this total uncertainty, respecting the origin of these nations: if we have been able to produce any arguments that lay claim to probability, it is because our minds are improved by civilization, and our talents, natural and acquired, have enabled us to form a judgment as nearly approaching to truth as these subjects will allow. Our minds therefore should be impressed with the most unfeigned feelings and acts of gratitude to Providence for the blessings of a more exalted civilization and education, which give us in every respect so great a superiority over these nations, and assign us so high a rank in the scale of rational beings.[63]

The issue of tattoos and physical marks, which evidence historical and

Plate 17.7 Sydney Parkinson, *Black Stains on the Skin called Tattoo*, November 1769. Two pen drawings: (a) $11\frac{1}{4} \times 9''$ (b) $5\frac{7}{8} \times 4\frac{3}{4}''$. British Library, London

customary significance, but which he feels unable to judge or investigate, is I think the only outstanding case in which this civilized superiority of knowledge fails the natural philosopher, and the sense in which these marks are self-authenticating, the original and indecipherable self-inscription of alien and self-contained historical cultures, seems to be bound up with their intimate relation to marks which he perceives as essentially sexual.

Forster understands the Tahitians, as do other voyagers, to be set apart from the other peoples of the South Seas in so far as they appear to be emerging from barbarism into the early stages of civilization. The position of women in their society, he argues, is both the cause and symptom of this promising transition. And his account of their position exemplifies the combination of responses which I have argued characterize European constructions of the islanders. In a statement which is, as I have mentioned, almost a commonplace of Enlightenment social theory, he asserts that 'the more the women are esteemed in a nation, and enjoy an equality of rights with the men', the more the people are capable of those social virtues which 'naturally lead them toward the blessings of civilization' – and that reference to rights, which may imply political or public status, gives the statement a force that was not often present in the fantasy of feminine leisure that I mentioned earlier. In Tahitian society he believes that women are indeed esteemed, and exercise what he describes as 'a just and moderate influence in domestic and even public affairs', and he attributes this degree of equality to a peculiar combination of qualities. He writes that they

> are possessed of a delicate organization, a sprightly turn of mind, a lively, fanciful imagination, a wonderful quickness of parts and sensibility, a sweetness of temper, and a desire to please; all of which, when found connected with primitive simplicity of manners, when accompanied with a charming frankness, a beautifully proportioned shape, an irresistible smile, and eyes full of sweetness and sparkling with fire, contribute to captivate the hearts of their men.

I have quoted this description at length, not only because it is a striking example of the way feminine influence is perceived, in these decades, to depend on women's capacity to personify, to give physical form, to the abstract but apparently seductive virtues of justice and moderation, but because of its resemblance to the description of 'the unhappy situation of the females' among those peoples of the South Seas who are still sunk in savagery and barbarism.[64]

Forster writes, of the position of women among these peoples, that they are reduced to

> the most wretched beings; yet this very oppression, and the more delicate frame of their bodies, together with the finer and more irritable texture of their nerves, have contributed more towards the improvement and

perfection of their intellectual faculties, than of those of the males.

He argues that as a result of their physical attributes, 'their faculties ... become more capable of ... abstracting general ideas from their perceptions'. This capacity for 'cooler reflexion', accompanied by the habit of submission, and will to please, make the 'toilsome, laborious life' of the women easier, and 'naturally contribute' to introduce 'the first dawnings of civilization'.[65] Forster's account of the position of women in the societies of the South Seas asserts, in these passages, that the recognition of women's equal rights, and their wretched state of oppression, both contribute to the emergence of civilization. And these socially advantageous but contrasting conditions are not opposed, indeed they are juxtaposed in his text, because both are understood to depend upon capacities vested in the delicate organization of the female body.

That delicate organization, in Forster's arguments, results in the 'social virtues' necessary to the emergence of civilization either because it is not esteemed, in which case it generates the capacity to abstract general ideas, or because it is esteemed, in which case women can exercise an ambiguously sensible influence. Either way, the situation of women is understood to be 'productive of an advantage' for the state of the society they inhabit, for whether their organization is esteemed, or subjected to 'constant acts of indelicacy', it enables the transition from barbarism to civilization.[66] The different means by which it does so, in the two models of social progress that Forster describes here, could be understood in terms of those paired constructions of what distinguishes the barbarian from the European that I traced earlier, in so far as they privilege the intellectual capacity or sexual morality with which the female organization is understood to be inscribed. But it is the distinction of the feminine and exotic body that it can bear both of these discursive constructions, and that doubled burden acquires, I have argued, a peculiar importance in legitimating the European project of exploration. The Tahitian feminine body is marked with the intersections of paternal affection and appropriative curiosity, as well as of barbarism and civilization, oppression and equality, and in Forster's argument these intersections seem to converge in the signs of the preeminent capacity for childbearing. This capacity marks the complex of relations involved in those intersections as beyond investigation, beyond any power to contaminate the knowledge that evidences the superiority of the civilized mind, because it marks the coincidence of customary or cultural similarities, and national or natural differences, and identifies that mysterious point of coincidence with the legible proof of the desirable homogeneity of the species.

Forster's comments on bodily ornament and on the position of women in the societies of the South Seas suggest that tattoos were a focus for curiosity because they were perceived to inscribe the universality of the species with cryptic differences. Tattoos were understood to indicate the diversity punctuating the homogeneity of humanity, because the apparent universality of the custom seemed evidently improbable and misleading; it did not appear to be susceptible to the kinds of historicizing analysis, or the models of historical development, that it was the privileged duty of the civilized European to construct. Tattoos were perceived to mark an original diversity which in its mysterious ethnicity approximated to sexual difference. The relations between these readings of the tattoos, as marks of indecipherable historical origins, or as marks of sexual difference, were problematic, and could prompt in the observer, at least in Forster's case, only the desire to collect and record. I have suggested that the problematic obscurity, in the perceived relation between these different readings, was important as a means of legitimating the project of European expansion in the late eighteenth century. Clearly, for example, it could enable that gendering of the exotic that appropriated unfamiliar social structures to the moralized judgemental standard of the bourgeois domestic family. European voyagers, as I have already pointed out, judged the treatment of women in the societies they observed according to standards that were not necessarily perceived to be appropriate, say, to the position of servants or poor women in Europe.[67]

Tattoos were perceived to be indecipherable in ways that obscured the boundaries between national or ethnic diversity and sexual difference, as objects of civilized incomprehension or mystification, and they were perceived to mark the slippage between constructions of humanity as homogeneous or diverse, universal but not common in its knowable origins, because of their curiously acultural status. As a result tattoos might also punctuate the cultural distinctions between the exotic and domestic. They might be legible as the preeminent characteristics of a delicate feminine organization that was universal in its indecipherability. When, for example, Joshua Reynolds argued that the tattooing practices of the Tahitians were excluded from the acceptable pale of diverse national customs, he linked them with 'the straight lacing of the English ladies', categorizing both as 'painful or destructive of health'. The strange practices of the two groups remain discrete, in his account, and yet because both are denied the significance of custom as well as the sanction of nature, they are lent a kind of approximate status. It was this apparent correspondence between groups that were perceived to be incongruous and discrete that was exploited in the various satirical letters attributed to Omai, in the years immediately following Cook's second voyage. In these letters, Omai's contemplations on London polite society are represented as returning repeatedly to comparisons between the Tahitian practice of tattooing and the fashions, in dress, cosmetics, hair-style, adopted by European women. The satirists mock Omai for the inappropriate interpretations of the behaviour and dress of English women which they attribute to him, but they also employ the opinions with which he is credited as the vehicle for a universalizing misogyny.[68]

In *A Vindication of the Rights of Women* (1792), Mary Wollstonecraft cites

Forster's 'pertinent observations' on polygamy, and she alludes to his account again, I think, in her discussion of the 'art of pleasing', where she writes that:

> A strong inclination for external ornaments ever appears in barbarous states, only the men not the women adorn themselves; for where women are allowed so far on a level with men, society has advanced, at least, one step in civilization.
>
> The attention to dress, therefore, which has been thought a sexual propensity, I think natural to mankind. But I ought to express myself with more precision. When the mind is not sufficiently opened to take pleasure in reflection, the body will be adorned with sedulous care, and ambition will appear in tattooing or painting it.[69]

Wollstonecraft's argument here is problematic in ways which, I have suggested, characterize discursive constructions of the feminine and exotic in this period, and which focus on the legibility of the tattooed or painted body. For her argument clearly implies that what, in women, is a mark of preeminence, indicative of the dawn of civilization in their society, in men is the mark of barbarity, of the absence of civilization. For women to be absorbed in the ornamentation of their bodies, and dedicated to the art of pleasing, places them on a potentially civilized par with the men of their society in the indulgence of a natural propensity; but it is a propensity which in its naturalness contrasts with those of the civilized, reflective mind that entertains 'grand pursuits that exalt the human race'. Wollstonecraft goes on to argue that:

> An immoderate fondness for dress, for pleasure, for sway, are the passions of savages; the passions that occupy those uncivilized beings who have not yet extended the dominion of the mind, or even learned to think with the energy necessary to concatenate that abstract train of thought which produces principles. And that women from their education and the present state of civilized life, are in the same condition, cannot, I think, be controverted.

For women to enjoy 'an equality of rights' in attending to the natural propensity for self-adornment, then, is for Wollstonecraft a matter of ambivalent value.[70] For in the context of 'civilized life' the enjoyment of this propensity evidences the debased condition of both men and women, though in the context of barbarous societies, its manifestation or indulgence in women indicates the dawn of civilization. Thus in a sense the equality that is indicated in the tattooing practices of Tahiti is at once the sign of civilization and of barbarity. Its prevalence implicitly feminizes, softens, the harshness that characterizes barbarous men, and makes them comparable to middle-class English women, whose degradation is evidenced by the parallel.[71] In the women of Tahiti, it implies both equality and differentiated subordination, for it indicates the dawning civility of Tahitian men, but constructs this almost as a consequence of the women's uncivilized absorption in the body.

For Wollstonecraft, then, the value or status of male tattoos is clear, and the devalued naturalness, or barbarity, of the love of adornment shown by middle-class English women is also unambiguous in this section of the *Vindication*. What is problematic, and cannot be securely located in the complex discursive matrix of the argument, is the inscribed or adorned feminine and exotic body, and its elusive significance here may be best understood in the context of Forster's account. On the one hand, the tattooed Tahitian woman may be implicitly attributed a degree of reflective or moralized interiority that seems to set her apart from barbaric or savage men, and, implicitly, from middle-class English women. She then seems to occupy a position similar to that of the feminized soul, in Edward Young's lines:

Let *Indians*, and the Gay, like *Indians*, fond
Of feather'd Fopperies, the Sun adore:
Darkness has more Divinity for me;
It strikes Thought inward, it drives back the Soul
To settle on Herself, our Point supreme![72]

As a result of her oppression (her 'Darkness' perhaps), the Tahitian woman may be imagined to have developed the capacity to generalize her ideas, to turn her thought inward, and the punctuation of the surface of her body might indicate that blurring of boundaries that enables her reflective interiority to exercise sensible public influence. For her marks set her on a par with the men of her society, and signify the achievement of 'at least, one step in civilization'. But, on the other hand, those Indians and gay people in Young's lines, who lack the independent self-sufficiency that characterizes the feminized soul, demonstrate a spectacular propensity for self-adornment that is worldly in its dependence on admiration, and that may indicate in them a debased and immoral or uncivilized effeminacy. Their spectacular display is comparable to the narcissistic self-absorption that Wollstonecraft describes as resulting in the desire to 'please without the aid of the mind', the self-engrossed display of middle-class women. That pleasure in the adornment of the 'physical part', which means that 'women never forget their sex', is, in Wollstonecraft's argument, opposed to the civilized 'pleasure in reflection' that results in the 'moral art of pleasing'. The category of those who demonstrate an unreflective and 'immoderate fondness for dress' and self-adornment embraces all 'uncivilized minds' – the barbarous or savage man, and the tattooed Tahitian woman – whose condition is 'the same' as that of an English 'female beauty, and a male wit'.[73]

The problematic status of the tattooed and exotic feminine body thus marks the unstable relation between civilization and barbarism in the late decades of the eighteenth century. In the social or moral context of barbarism, the indulgence of the natural propensity for self-adornment in women evidences a degree of civilizing sexual equality, because it is understood to be inscribed with sexually differentiated value and significance. Whether or not tattoos are understood to imply a capacity for reflection, it is the sexuality of those who are adorned that determines the range of meanings legible in the inscription. In the context of the state of civilization in England, the fondness for adornment, for 'tattooing or painting' the body, evidences an uncivilized and savage or barbarous sexual inequality, because it is not legible in terms of sexual difference. Whether it is demonstrated by men or women, it is understood to indicate their failure or incapacity to 'take pleasure in reflection' – an incapacity that may be effeminate, but is not peculiarly female, and is not inscribed with a value that depends on the sexuality of the adorned person. The punctured or painted surface of what Wollstonecraft, quoting Forster, describes as the 'more irritable nerves, more sensible organization, and more lively fancy' common to the female constitution might therefore be understood to carry meanings which are culturally specific. When the marked body inhabits a barbarous and exotic space, it is legible in terms of the comparative and gendered evaluations of the domestic and public spheres. It indicates that the feminine influence exercised in the family has extended its civilizing powers into the public sphere. But when that adorned body is English, domestic, the 'sedulous care' it receives is understood to indicate exotic barbarism, and to demonstrate a propensity that is merely natural because its meaning or value is not sexually specific. But the implicit equation, in Wollstonecraft's argument, of the natural and the uncivilized, points up the slipperiness of those culturally specific meanings.[74] The potentially civilizing qualities that are attributed to Tahitian women are understood to be natural, to result from the delicate and sensible organization of their feminine constitution. Their propensity for self-adornment is not understood to be culturally specific. These ornamented women are therefore evaluated, given meaning, in terms appropriate to barbarism and civilization, to the exotic and the domestic.

The elisions as well as the explicit arguments of Wollstonecraft's discussion, in this section of the *Vindication*, exemplify both the peculiar importance and the elusive significance of the feminine and exotic body in the cultural discourses of the late eighteenth century. For that painted body – generalized in terms that are reminiscent of Knox's perception of wonderful homogeneity among exotic peoples – makes legible the congruence of the domestic and the exotic, but it also manifests an original and exotic significance that is indecipherable to the European gaze. In Hodges's painting of Otaheite Peha, the qualities that might make the representation of the seated woman incongruous, unsettling, can be perceived in the context of these arguments to confirm the curious but desirable ambivalence of her position. She gives exotic embodiment to those discursive instabilities that constitute and threaten the structure of the domestic family, and to those contradictions that inform debate about the status of women in these decades, and she provides a focus for the complex aims of explorative curiosity. The Hindu people of Madras,

I have suggested, could be understood to be diminished by the scale and magnificence of their legible history, of architectural and intellectual achievements in the past that made their physical presence and strangeness merely spectacular. The Tahitians, in contrast, are perceived to have no written past, but an ethnic history that it is the superior privilege of Europeans to reconstruct. The delicate configuration of their beautifully feminine forms is therefore more immediately the focus of European interest, for it is inscribed with the key to their curious originality, with the marks of their strangeness and familiarity.

In the various accounts of the South Sea islanders, and references to them, that I have discussed in this essay, European attention can be seen to return repeatedly, insistently, to the 'beautifully feminine' physical outline of the islanders. It is their outline that is perceived to be inscribed with the key to their historical, national and customary significance, with the meanings that the civilized investigate and decipher. And it is of course important that it is through this hermeneutic and historicizing activity that European observers were able to confirm their right to 'so high a rank in the scale of rational beings'. For the various representations of exotic peoples that I have discussed all, I think, make it clear that interest in those peoples was significant to European observers primarily for the light that it cast, however obliquely or unwittingly, on their own societies, their conceptions of themselves in terms of the ideology of bourgeois humanism – which is not only to say that knowledge is a self-conscious business. The particular nature of that curious knowledge of the peoples of the South Pacific may be evident in an idea that William Bligh recorded in his account of the *Bounty*'s sojourn at Tahiti. He noted that:

> we see among these islands so great a waste of the human species that numbers are born only to die, and at the same time a large continent so near to them as New Holland, in which there is so great a waste of land uncultivated and almost destitute of inhabitants.

To a man engaged in transporting breadfruit half-way across the world, in order to feed cheaply a displaced and enslaved people not known to have any taste for the crop, the thought that the excess population of Tahiti could be collected and replanted in the 'desert' of Australia seemed to be an advantageous means of 'forwarding the purposes of humanity and general convenience'.[75]

Bligh's plan, he explained, was formulated in response to the perception that the paradisical happiness of the islands was threatened by a 'super-flux of inhabitants', potentially 'an unlimited population'. It seemed to him 'so humane a plan' perhaps because, unlike those 'orders of celibacy, which have proved so prejudicial in other countries', or the methods of infanticide practised by some orders of Tahitian society, it accommodated or controlled the sexual behaviour of the islanders without apparently violating the ideal of the domestic family. Bligh acknowledged that his idea might be impracticable, because the quality of populousness, with all that that implied, which made the Tahitian people seem suitable candidates for transportation, appeared to him to be intimately related to the climate they inhabited. His plans for them were therefore tempered by his sense of their necessarily distanced place, their absorption in the landscape they inhabited, which he imagined they would only leave 'under the tyrannous influence of necessity'.[76]

In spite of these reservations, however, Bligh argued that his proposal was not merely fanciful, and it perhaps seemed 'to merit ... attention' because it worked through some of the implications of the mixed nature of that curious interest that European observers took in the peoples of the South Pacific. It demonstrates a paternalist concern for the purposes of humanity and convenience, or utility, and that concern finds its focus in the capacity for childbearing that is perceived, though not necessarily acknowledged, as the preeminent characteristic of the islanders: their contribution to 'general convenience', he suggests, resides in their potential to convert a 'great continent ... from a desert to a populous country'. His argument therefore implicitly identifies their character as a nation, their ethnic definition, with the customary inscription of their physical outline, the mark of their capacity for reproduction. This 'sedulous care' for the inscribed exotic body, I have suggested, tended to confuse any distinction between conditions of oppression and of esteem, of equality of rights, because in either of these conditions the delicate organization of the female body could exercise its civilizing influence.[77] And it also tended to blur the cultural boundaries between the domestic and the exotic, for it made it difficult to identify the propensity for adornment that was civilizing, and natural, in one of these spheres, as uncivilizing, and even corrupting, in the other. The implications of this doubly problematic attention may be apparent in the similarities between Bligh's proposal, and Lord Sydney's plan that women should be transported from the islands of the South Pacific to Australia, in order to 'preserve the settlement from gross irregularities'. When that plan came to nothing, because Arthur Philip, like Bligh, thought the women might not survive the transportation, female convicts from Britain were transported, to 'raise a native-born yeomanry'.[78] The two groups of women are interchangeable, and their role in preserving the settlement seems ineluctably determined. Bligh's idea, with its emphasis on the need to cultivate or control what the islanders might produce, and its implicit equation of the British relation to them and to the breadfruit plants he was responsible for collecting, is a significant indication of the terms in which the curious spectacle of the tattooed bodies of the islanders could be perceived to legitimate the European project of expansion in the South Pacific.[79]

NOTES

1 William Hodges, *Travels in India, during the years 1780, 1781, 1782, & 1783* (London, 1793), preface p. iv, pp. 2–3, 2. Hodges's *Travels* are not only intended for his private friends, but are, he writes: 'submitted to a tribunal, which I have ever regarded with awful respect ... THE PUBLIC', ibid., preface, p. iv. See also *Analytical Review, or History of Literature, Domestic and Foreign, on an enlarged plan*, 1793, vol. XV, p. 248. I am grateful to Andrew Hemingway and Neil Rennie, who read and commented most helpfully on drafts of this essay. I would also like to thank John Barrell, Norman Bryson, Alex Potts, David Solkin and Tony Tanner, who discussed some of these ideas with me. I was able to extend my research into this area as a result of a Visiting Fellowship awarded by the Yale Center for British Art at New Haven.

2 In the opening pages of his account, Hodges repeatedly represents his narration as that of a generalized European spectator, asserting a culturally defined narrative identity enabled by its opposition to the transcendently unified Asia that is the object of his gaze. See Edward W. Said, *Orientalism* (Harmondsworth, 1978, 1985), pp. 45–6, 77–81, 102–3.

3 See, for example, Hugh Murray, *Historical Account of Discoveries and Travels in Asia, from the earliest ages to the present time* (Edinburgh, 1820), vol. II (of 3), p. 313; William Robertson, *An Historical Disquisition concerning the knowledge which the Ancients had of India* (1791), in *The Works of William Robertson, D.D.* (London, 1821), vol. X (of 10), appendix, p. 262; Sir William Jones, 'The Third Anniversary Discourse, on the Hindus, delivered 2d of February, 1786', in *The Works of Sir William Jones. With the life of the author, by Lord Teignmouth* (London, 1807), vol. III (of 13), pp. 30–1. See also Said, op. cit., pp. 138, 180, 182, 187, 206–8, 309, 311; and P. J. Marshall and Glyndwr Williams, *The Great Map of Mankind: British perceptions of the world in the age of enlightenment* (London, 1982), p. 161.

4 Hodges, op. cit., pp. 3–4.

5 Muslim culture is implicitly constructed as masculine, in contrast to the femininity attributed to Hindu culture, in Hodges's *Travels*. Thus, for example, Hindu architecture is remarkable for its beautiful variety, whereas Muslim architecture is praised for its sublime magnificence and grandeur. Cf. op. cit., pp. 60–1, 126–7, and see pp. 33–5, 151–3.

6 Jones, 'An Essay on the Poetry of the Eastern Nations', in *The Works of Sir William Jones*, vol. X, p. 359.

7 William Robertson, op. cit., p. 246; on the gendering of sensibility, see James Barry, 'Lecture II. – On Design', in *Lectures on Painting, by the Royal Academicians, Barry, Opie, and Fuseli*, ed. Ralph N. Wornum (London, 1848), p. 105.

8 Hodges, op. cit., preface, p. iv. For an indication of the extent to which that combination was perceived as problematic, see [? Henry Mackenzie] *The Mirror*, no. 28, 1 May 1779. See also Ramkrishna Mukherjee, *The Rise and Fall of the East India Company: A Sociological Appraisal* (New York, 1974), chapter 5, and P. J. Marshall's discussion, in Marshall and Williams, op. cit., pp. 158–64. On the conditions for artists working in India, see Mildred Archer, *Early Views on India: The Picturesque Journeys of Thomas and William Daniell, 1786–1794* (London, 1980), p. 12; Isabel Combs Stuebe, 'William Hodges and Warren Hastings: a study in eighteenth-century patronage', *Burlington Magazine* CXV, October 1973, pp. 659–66.

9 Hodges, op. cit., p. 5. Hodges points out, in an earlier note, the connection between the dress worn in India, and the 'jam', 'well known in England, and worn

by children', implying, perhaps, the childishness as well as effeminacy of the spectacle he observes (ibid., p. 3, n.).

10 Hodges writes of the Hindu temples on the banks of the Ganges: 'To a painter's mind, the fine antique figures never fail to present themselves, when he observes a beautiful female form ascending these steps from the river, with wet drapery, which perfectly displays the whole person, and with vases on their heads, carrying water to the temples' (ibid., p. 33).

11 ibid., pp. 8, 9, 10. Hodges does not elaborate on the relation between this sovereignty, and the role of Madras as 'a place of no real consequence, but for its trade', perhaps because he believes that his readers will already be familiar with the issues involved. See ibid., p. 48.

12 ibid., pp. 5, 8, 10. I quote from Pope's 'Epistle II. To a Lady: Of the Characters of Women', *Moral Essays*, in *The Poems of Alexander Pope: A one-volume edition of the Twickenham text*, ed. John Butt (London, 1963, 1968), l. 2.

13 For a discussion of this function of gender differences in colonial discourses see Chandra Talpade Mohanty, 'Under Western Eyes: feminist scholarship and colonial discourses', in *Feminist Review* no. 30, Autumn 1988, pp. 61–88.

14 John [Johann] Reinhold Forster, *Observations made during the Voyage Round the World, on Physical Geography, Natural History, and Ethic Philosophy* (London, 1778), p. 234, cf. p. 230. As was the case in the largely implicit discursive gendering of the Hindu and Muslim peoples of India, which functioned to describe the relations Europeans perceived between them, the gendered terms in which European voyagers, as well as less widely-travelled writers, constructed their perceptions of the islanders of the South Seas work to distinguish one group of people or nation from another, rather than always directly to characterize views of any one group. Forster's account is representative of those of other travellers in so far as they contrasted the Society islanders to, for example, the New Zealanders, in gendered terms, rather than because other travellers also directly and explicitly identified their bodies as feminine. The voyagers usually distinguished between the islanders they encountered in implicitly gendered terms, seeing the 'Polynesians' as gentle, lighter coloured, friendly and more civilized, and the 'Melanesian' group as hostile, ugly, incurious and condemned to a barbarously laborious life. See Lynne Withey, *Voyages of Discovery: Captain Cook and the Exploration of the Pacific* (London, 1987), pp. 288–94.

15 For comparisons between the South Sea islanders and the Hindu people of Northern India, see Hodges, op. cit., pp. 26, 41–1, 66–7, 69. Hodges seems to find these occasions for comparison curious because they are surprising in the context of what he perceives as their very different cultures and 'stages' of civilization.

16 *The Resolution Journals of Johann Reinhold Forster, 1772–1775*, ed. Michael E. Hoare (Hakluyt Society, London, 1982), vol. II (of 4), p. 237. See Isabel Combs Stuebe, *The Life and Works of William Hodges* (New York, 1979), p. 146; and Rüdiger Joppien and Bernard Smith, *The Art of Captain Cook's Voyages: Volume Two: The Voyage of the Resolution and Adventure, 1772–1775, with a Descriptive Catalogue* (New Haven, 1985), p. 61. Hodges produced at least two versions of each of these paintings. The relation between the pair I have chosen to discuss and other versions is explored in Stuebe, pp. 36–9, 148–9, and, most illuminatingly, in Joppien and Smith, pp. 61–4, 211. See also Bernard Smith, *European Vision and the South Pacific* (1960; New Haven, 1985), pp. 64–5, 69, 80.

17 'William Blake's Annotations to Reynolds' *Discourses*', in Sir Joshua Reynolds, *Discourses on Art*, ed. Robert R. Wark (1959; New Haven, 1975), appendix I, p. 307.

18 *The London Packet or Lloyd's New Evening Post*, 25 April 1777, quoted in Smith,

op. cit., p. 75. The reviewer probably refers specifically to Hodges's *The War Boats of the Island of Otaheite*, now in the National Maritime Museum. For comparable assessments, see Fuseli's entry on Hodges, in Matthew Pilkington, *A Dictionary of Painters from the revival of the art to the present period* (London, 1910), p. 237; Edward Edwards, *Anecdotes of Painters who have resided or been born in England: with critical remarks on their Productions* (London, 1808), pp. 243–5; *The Works of the Late Edward Dayes*, ed. E. W. Brayley (London, 1805), p. 332, quoted in Smith, op. cit., p. 76; *The Diary of Joseph Farington*, ed. Kathryn Cave (New Haven, 1978–84), vol. I, July 1793–December 1794, p. 270; William Daniell, quoted in W. G. Archer, 'Benares through the eyes of British artists', *Apollo* XCII, August 1970, p. 102.

19 Hodges, op. cit., pp. 155–6. In *A Dissertation on the Prototypes of Architecture, Hindoo, Moorish, and Gothic* (London, 1787), Hodges makes it clear that though his works are 'the genuine productions of truth, candour, and justice', he has, in order to achieve these aims,

> foregone the very possibility of satisfying the natural historian, architect, antiquary, and politician, who look for no pictures of India and Indian affairs but what can be expressed in rhetorical or arithmetical figures, algebraic forms, or the shape of a cash book. These figures, and minuter particulars to which naturalists, architects, and some antiquaries attend, were totally out of my line.
>
> (p. 1)

20 Sir William Jones, quoted in Nicholas Cooper, 'Indian Architecture in England, 1781–1830', *Apollo* XCII, August 1970, p. 127. See Mildred Archer, *Company Drawings in the India Office Library* (London, 1972), pp. 6, 74; and R. W. Lightbown, 'India Discovered', in Mildred Archer and Ronald Lightbown, *India Observed: India as Viewed by British Artists, 1761–1860* (London, 1982), p. 30.

21 Reynolds, op. cit., Discourse XIII, p. 242. Letter, Reynolds to the Duke of Rutland, 29 August 1786, quoted in Stuebe, *Life and Works of William Hodges*, p. 86.

22 I use 'discourse' in this context to refer to a set of terms which work, through the 'logic' they define, to privilege certain aspects of the issue being addressed or articulated, and to exclude or silence others, in ways that are distinctive, or constitutive, of particular cultural collectivities at specific historical moments.

23 Joppien and Smith, op. cit., p. 61.

24 See, for example, William Duff, *Letters on the Intellectual and Moral Character of Women* (London, 1807), pp. 65–6; Jane West, *Letters to a Young Lady, in which the duties and character of women are considered, chiefly with a reference to prevailing opinions* (1806; this 3rd edn, London, 1806), vol. I (of 3), pp. 49–52, 60, and, on the specificity of this to middle-class women, pp. 199–201; George Gregory, 'Miscellaneous observations on the history of the female sex', *Essays Historical and Moral* (London, 1783), pp. 145–64. See, for example, James Cook [with the Rev. Canon Douglas], *A Voyage towards the South Pole, and Round the World. Performed by His Majesty's Ships the Resolution and Adventurer, in the years 1772, 1773, 1774, and 1775* (London, 1777), vol. II (of 2), p. 80.

25 This complexity is manifested in the relation between the arguments cited in note 24, and the comments of, for example, Anna Seward; see 'Letter to George Hardinge, Esq., Oct. 1, 1787', in *The Swan of Lichfield: being a selection from the Correspondence of Anna Seward*, ed. Hesketh Pearson (London, 1936), pp. 103–4. Voyagers were uncomfortably aware that it could be a function of the expansion of imperial and commercial European interests in the Pacific to displace on to the people there the luxury and indolence that might otherwise be the corrupting rewards of international trade for domestic society; cf. the arguments for mer-

cantile expansion in John Campbell, introduction to John Harris, *Navigantium atque Itinerantium Bibliotheca, or, a Complete Collection of Voyages and Travels* (1744), quoted in *Byron's Journal of his Circumnavigation, 1764–1756*, ed. Robert E. Gallagher (Hakluyt Society, Cambridge, 1964), introduction, pp. xxxiii–xxxvi; George Forster, *A Voyage Round the World, In His Britannic Majesty's Sloop, Resolution, commanded by Capt. James Cook, during the Years, 1772, 3, 4, and 5* (London, 1777), vol. I (of 2), p. 303; *The Journals of Captain James Cook on his Voyages of Discovery: The Voyage of the Resolution and Adventure, 1772–1775*, ed. J. C. Beaglehole (1961; Hakluyt Society, Cambridge, 1969), vol. II (of 3), pp. 174–5. See also Withey, op. cit., p. 411.

26 For a further discussion of the importance of Actaeon in this context see section IV below. On the cultural construction of the spectator see Louis Marin, 'Towards a theory of reading in the visual arts: Poussin's *The Arcadian Shepherds*', in *Calligram: Essays in New Art History from France*, ed. Norman Bryson (Cambridge, 1988), pp. 63–77; Peter de Bolla, *The Discourse of the Sublime: Readings in History, Aesthetics and the Subject* (Oxford, 1989), chapter 8.

27 It is, of course, an aesthetic imperative in this period for landscapes to represent 'subjects ... exactly adapted to the scene, without exercising the mind in any historical action'. My point here is that these conventional compositional structures acquire particular meanings, of the kind that I go on to discuss, in the representation of exotic subjects. In this image it might also be argued that the juxtaposition of the women may, in a sense, produce something comparable to the effect of the combination of genres, when, 'should the interest of the piece be at all equally divided, it is needless to say the eye must be distracted and unquiet'. (I quote from J. H. Pott, *An Essay on Landscape Painting. With Remarks General and Critical, in the different schools and masters, ancient and modern* (London, 1782), p. 26.)

28 On the importance of climate to theories of civilization in the later decades of the eighteenth century, see Joppien and Smith, op. cit., p. 63; Smith, op. cit., pp. 86–8. Accounts of the South Seas do frequently stress the role of climate as a social and physical determinant, but it is not always perceived to be itself beyond ideological or cultural definition. Hodges writes, in 'An Account of Richard Wilson, Esq. Landscape Painter, F.R.A.':

> From the close attention he had given to his studies, he had neglected to improve himself in the arts of modern politeness and policy.... This irascible habit has been supposed to be the effect of climate, as there is no word in the Welch language to express argument or ratiocination but contention.
>
> (*The European Magazine, and London Review*, June 1790, p. 404)

29 John Forster argues that the *tii* is a representation of an ancestor, and believed to be possessed by the inner beings of the dead, but he insists that the 'figure is not intended to be the real figure of the invisible soul', op. cit., p. 552, and see pp. 543, 567. George Robertson, who accompanied Wallis on the first British voyage to Tahiti, commented on the figures that the islanders 'are none of the finest carvers, but they take care to imitate nature so Exact, that no man can mistake the sex which they mean to represent'. He thought the figures were 'set-up to Commemorate some of their families after death'. *An Account of the Discovery of Tahiti: From the Journal of George Robertson, Master of H.M.S. Dolphin*, ed. Oliver Warner (London, 1955), pp. 85–6. George Forster observed that 'All these figures faced the sea', though the figure in Hodges's painting does not, Forster, op. cit., vol. I, p. 267. See Terence Barrow, *The Art of Tahiti and the neighbouring Society, Austral and Cook Islands* (London, 1979), pp. 41–4; Marshall Sahlins, *Islands of History* (Chicago, 1985), pp. 13–14; Dorota Czarkowska Starzecka,

'The Society Islands' in *Cook's Voyages and the Peoples of the Pacific* (London, 1979), pp. 48–52.

30 'Letter the Fiftieth', in [? William Combe], *Letters of the Late Lord Lyttelton* (4th edn, London, 1792), vol. II (of 2), p. 161. For an example of the sense in which slavery, femininity, childishness and emasculation become almost interchangeable attributes of those who live in the seraglio, see Hugh Murray, op. cit., pp. 192–3.

31 A *tupapau*, or platform bearing a shrouded corpse, is referred to in Forster's *Journal*, where he describes a walk taken at Vaitepiha with his son George Forster, Sparrman, Grindall and Hodges. He notes that the platform bore the corpse of a woman; op. cit., pp. 331–2. See also the account given by George Forster, op. cit., pp. 267–70; Sydney Parkinson, *A Journal of a Voyage to the South Seas. In his Majesty's Ship The Endeavour* (London, 1784), p. 26; and Starzecka, op. cit., p. 63.

32 On European attitudes to Pacific curiosities, see Adrienne L. Kaeppler, 'Pacific Culture History and European Voyages', in *Terra Australis: The Furthest Shore*, eds William Eisler and Bernard Smith (Sydney, 1988), pp. 141–6; P. J. P. White-head, 'Zoological Specimens from Captain Cook's Voyages', *Journal of the Society for the Bibliography of Natural History* 5, 1969, pp. 161–201. Cook's attempts to regulate trade between the islanders and the sailors reflect his concern that the interest that men as well as officers took in Pacific curiosities would drive up the exchange value of the provisions he needed. He comments at one point in his *Journals*, for example: 'by this time we had a great number of the Islanders aboard and about the sloops, some coming off in Canoes and others swiming off, bringing little else with them but Cloth and other curiosities, things which I did not come here for and for which the Seamen only bartered away their clothes. In order to put a stop to this and to obtain the refreshments we wanted, I gave orders that no Curiosities should be purchassed by any person whatsoever either aboard or alongside the Sloops or at the landing place on shore', op. cit., vol. II, p. 249; see also Cook, *A Voyage*, vol. I, pp. 304, 308, 318. John Forster's attitude to curiosity-collecting reflects his unease at the proximity between the interests of commerce and of the natural historian. He remarked on the islands of the Indian Ocean:

> what vast treasures of shell-fish their shores, massive rocks, and the bottom of their seas contain, may be gathered from hence, that for at lest a century that these seas have been frequented by *Europeans*, they have continuously been offering somewhat new to the curiosity of men whose avarice or vanity has prompted them to collect such stores from all parts.
> (John Reinhold Forster, 'An Essay on India, its boundaries, climate, soil, and sea', trans. from the Latin by John Aikin, in *Indian Zoology*, ed. Thomas Pennant (2nd edn, London, 1790), p. 12.)

33 The implications of the representation of the *tii* and *tupapau* are complex. If, as Joppien and Smith argue, this pair of paintings 'present Tahitian society in its pristine independence, untouched by European contact', then they might suggest 'a hint ... of the radical pessimism of George Forster' about the effects of the European presence (op. cit., p. 62). But they might also indicate the original imperfection of Tahitian society, or signal a threat to European pleasures in this idyll.

34 Reynolds, op. cit., Discourse VII, p. 137; Discourse IV, p. 58. On tattooing, see Wilfred Blunt, 'Sydney Parkinson and his fellow artists', in *Sydney Parkinson: Artist of Cook's Endeavour Voyage*, ed. D. J. Carr (London, 1983), pp. 34–5; Barrow, op. cit., pp. 27–30; Cook, *Journals*, I, p. 125. Parkinson, Sir Joseph Banks and other travellers on the first voyage were themselves tattooed in the South Seas, in what seems to have been the initiation of a seafaring tradition. See

Parkinson, op. cit., p. 25; and John Elliott's account, in *Captain Cook's Second Voyage: The Journals of Lieutenants Elliott and Pickersgill*, ed. Christine Holmes (London, 1984), pp. 20–1. The mutineers from the *Bounty* were almost all tattooed, according to William Bligh, who noted that Fletcher Christian was 'tattooed on his backside'. William Bligh and Others, *A Book of the 'Bounty'*, ed. George Mackaness (London, 1981), p. 275.

35 See, for example, the work of Tilly Kettle, and of Thomas and William Daniell. On the latter's use of camera obscura, see Archer and Lightbown, op. cit., p. 130.

36 Hodges, 'Account of Richard Wilson', p. 404.

37 Knox, *Winter Evenings; or lucubrations on life and letters* (1788; London, 1823), no. 125, vol. III (of 3), p. 152. See also Gregory Denning, 'Ethnohistory in Polynesia: The value of ethnohistorical evidence', in *Essays from the Journal of Pacific History*, compiled Barrie Macdonald (Palmerston North, NZ, 1979), esp. p. 53; and Smith, op. cit., chapter 3.

38 Henry Home of Kames, *Sketches of the History of Man* (Edinburgh, 1813), vol. II (of 3), p. 419, cp. p. 129, on the 'rustic'.

39 Robertson, op. cit., p. 239.

40 Cook, *A Voyage*, vol. I, p. 245.

41 Andrew [Anders] Sparrman, *A Voyage to the Cape of Good Hope, towards the Antarctic Polar Circle, and Round the World: but chiefly into the country of the Hottentots and Caffres, from the year 1772, to 1776* (London, 1785), vol. I (of 2), preface, pp. iii–iv. See Harriet Guest, *A Form of Sound Words: The religious poetry of Christopher Smart* (Oxford, 1989), pp. 252–60.

42 Forster, *Observations*, preface, p. ii, and title. George Forster's account of the restraining conditions imposed by the Admiralty on the nature of the text Johann Forster could publish suggests that these may, to some extent, have dictated its appearance as 'unconnected philosophical observations', but the elder Forster's 'Essay on India' is similarly 'unconnected'. George Forster, op. cit., vol. I, preface, p. vi; see pp. iv–vi.

43 Reynolds, op. cit., Discourse XI, p. 199; Barry, op. cit., 'Lecture I. On the history and progress of the art', p. 82, 'Lecture IV. On composition', p. 175.

44 *The Works of the Rev. John Wesley, A.M.* (London, 1872), vol. IV (of 14), p. 6. The query suggesting the substitution of miles for degrees is an editorial emendation. It was more usually the peoples of New Zealand, or of Tierra del Fuego, who were perceived to be savages and to lack curiosity.

45 Pope writes: 'Go, like the Indian, in another life / Expect thy dog, thy bottle, and thy wife', *An Essay on Man*, ed. Maynard Mack, in *The Poems of Alexander Pope* (1950; London, 1982), epistle IV, ll. 177–8; cp. Epistle I, ll. 99–112.

46 This fictive state is, of course, attributed to the voyagers as well as the islanders in Wesley's comments. On the difficulty of defining for Wesley a specific and stable position within mid-eighteenth-century culture, see Harriet Guest, op. cit., pp. 98–9, and the discussion of the conditions under which his *Journals* were produced and edited in Felicity A. Nussbaum, *The Autobiographical Subject: Gender and Ideology in Eighteenth-Century England* (Baltimore, 1989), chapter 4.

47 On 'bourgeois humanism', see Stephen Copley's introduction to his anthology, *Literature and the Social Order in Eighteenth-Century England* (London, 1984), pp. 3–7; J. G. A. Pocock, *The Machiavellian Moment: Florentine Political Thought and the Atlantic Republican Tradition*, chapter 13; see also John Barrell's use of the idea of bourgeois republicanism, in his *The Political Theory of Painting from Reynolds to Hazlitt: 'The Body of the Public'* (New Haven, 1986), pp. 130–6. For most theorists in the later decades of the eighteenth century, the 'stages' of animalism, savagery, barbarism and civilization are understood to be linked in a

progressive process in which phylogeny recapitulates ontogeny. This process can be represented either in terms of a gradual ripening and maturation, an organic development, or in terms of an advance achieved through cultivation, individual industry and interactive commerce – an advance understood in terms of the economic model of progress from savage hunting and gathering. It is in terms of this second model, privileging the economic activity of the private individual, and the disposition to trade, that the state of society among the peoples encountered on Cook's circumnavigations is most commonly evaluated, and which I take to be characteristic of the cultural ideology of bourgeois humanism. For some eighteenth-century writers, the opposition between civilized cultivation and uncivilized states is marked to a degree that overrides discrimination between the states of, most usually, savagery (childhood), and barbarism (adolescence), although the model of economic progress that I have outlined may be implicit to their arguments, and specifically to the privileged value of cultivation. The distinction between the states of savagery and barbarism is, therefore, not always clear. See, for example, the passages from Mary Wollstonecraft quoted below.

48 Sparrman, op. cit., preface, p. iii.

49 See, for example, Edmund Burke's letter to Robertson, quoted in Marshall and Williams, op. cit., p. 93. See also Paul Carter, *The Road to Botany Bay: An essay in spatial history* (London, 1987), chapter 1.

50 Reynolds, op. cit., Discourse III, p. 50.

51 John Forster, op. cit., p. 302. For fuller discussions of Forster's work, career and influence see Michael E. Hoare, *The Tactless Philosopher: Johann Reinhold Forster (1729–98)* (Melbourne, 1976), and J. C. Beaglehole, *The Life of Captain James Cook* (Hakluyt Society, London, 1974).

52 ibid., pp. 348, 231; while the familial structure Forster describes does emphasize the voyagers' position of paternal superiority, there were instances of filial sentiment towards the Tahitians. See Cook's *A Voyage*, vol. I, p. 163; George Forster, op. cit., p. 329.

53 op. cit., p. 352.

54 ibid., p. 255. In the passage that he adapts from Milton, Forster omits the lines in which Adam praises Eve as the perfect spouse – lines which might suggest that mutual obligation as well as assent is implicit in the relation described. Forster's presentation of paternalist feeling is typical of the language of sentiment, in its displacement of the role of physical sensations on to the feelings of the heart or soul. See, for example, the play on this in the description of the father in Mary Hamilton, *Munster Village* (1778; London, 1987), pp. 8, 18. Forster's argument here clearly alludes to the influential theories of Louis LeClerc, Comte de Buffon.

55 op. cit., p. 247. See also [? G. Kearsley], preface, *Omiah's Farewell; Inscribed to the Ladies of London* (London, 1776).

56 For example, in the novels of Anne Radcliffe, Horace Walpole, *The Castle of Otranto* (1764), Sara Scott, *Millenium Hall* (1762), Mary Hamilton, *Munster Village*, Samuel Richardson, *Pamela* (1740), etc., where fathers, or more usually those *in loco parentis* threaten the heroine's virtue. For an illuminating discussion of this apparent crisis in familial relations, see Jay Fliegelman, *Prodigals and Pilgrims: The American revolution against patriarchal authority, 1750–1800* (Cambridge, 1982).

57 The position of the seated woman in Hodges's painting is also similar to that of Susanna, in Tintoretto's *Susanna and the Elders* (Kunsthistorisches Museum, Vienna). This representation of the youthful Susanna, surrounded by mature voyeurs, and overlooked by the figure of Priapus, seems a clearly appropriate allusion for Hodges's image, in so far as it presents a society emerging from

barbarous adolescence to the gaze of a mature European civilization. See also Poussin's *The Triumph of Neptune and Amphitrite* (Philadelphia Museum of Art).

58 See Bernard Smith, 'Captain Cook's artists and the portrayal of Pacific peoples', *Art History* vol. 7, no. 3, September 1984, pp. 295–312.

59 Forster, *Observations*, p. 383. See Kames, op. cit., vol. I, p. 392.

60 See also Stanfield Parkinson's comments on his brother Sydney, quoted in Smith, 'Captain Cook's artists', pp. 300–1; and the anonymous 'Dedication. To Joseph B—NKS, Esq.', *An Historic Epistle, from Omiah, to the Queen of Otaheite: being his Remarks on the English Nation. With Notes by the Editor* (London, 1775).

61 John Forster, op. cit., pp. 433–4. Cook noted that 'these arches seem to be their great pride as both men and women show them with great pleasure', and it was also observed that the islanders applied the term 'tat-tow' 'to letters when they saw us write', *Journals*, vol. I, p. 125 and n. John Elliott's account indicates that tattoos were also perceived to mark masculinity, and it might therefore be taken to confirm the relation between tattoos and sexual difference, Elliott, op. cit., pp. 20–1. On the construction of the capacity to bear children as destiny, see William Duff, *Letters, on the Intellectual and Moral Character of Women* (Aberdeen, 1807), pp. 290–2.

62 ibid., pp. 589, 587, 586.

63 ibid., p. 608. Forster did construct for the islanders a tentative 'history' based on their apparent physical or racial correspondences to Oriental peoples. His account does not, however, suggest that he perceived this as an adequately historicizing analysis of their customs and culture.

64 ibid., pp. 421, 422, 419. Forster's reference to 'an equality of rights' might, of course, be taken to allude to the public rights of women recognized in the marriage contract. On Forster's shift from radicalism to conservatism in the late decades of the eighteenth century, see Hoare, op. cit., pp. 40–1, 302–3.

65 ibid., pp. 419–20. Forster writes: 'Used implicitly to submit to the will of their males, they have been early taught to suppress flights of passion; cooler reflexion, gentleness, and every method for obtaining the approbation, and for winning the good-will of others have taken their place, and must in time naturally contribute to soften that harshness of manners, which is become habitual in the barbarous races of men', p. 420. On the connection between civilization and submission, see John Forster, 'An Essay on India', in Pennart (ed.), op. cit., p. 12.

66 ibid., p. 419.

67 See, for example, Mary Wollstonecraft, *The Wrongs of Woman*, ed. Gary Kelly (1798; Oxford, 1980), p. 134.

68 Reynolds, op. cit., Discourse VII, p. 137. See [G. Kearsley] *Omiah's Farewell*, preface, p. iii, and pp. 2–4; *An Historic Epistle, from Omiah*, ll. 501–52; William Preston, *Seventeen Hundred and Seventy-Seven: or, a Picture of the Manners and Characters of Age. In a poetical epistle from a Lady of Quality in England, to Omiah, at Otaheite* (Dublin, 1777).

69 Mary Wollstonecraft, *A Vindication of the Rights of Woman*, ed. Carol H. Poston (New York, 1975), p. 186.

70 ibid., p. 187. Forster, *Observations*, p. 421.

71 See n. 65 above.

72 Edward Young, *The Complaint: or Night-Thoughts on Life, Death, and Immortality* (1742–6; this 8th edn, London, 1749), Night V, p. 124.

73 Wollstonecraft, *Vindication*, pp. 186–7.

74 ibid., p. 186; Wollstonecraft quotes these phrases, from Forster's discussion of polygamy, p. 70.

75 Forster, op. cit., pp. 234, 608. William Bligh, *A Voyage to the South sea, undertaken*

by command of His Majesty, for the purpose of Conveying the Bread-Fruit Tree to the West Indies, In his Majesty's ship the Bounty (1792), in George Mackaness, ed., *A Book of the 'Bounty'*, pp. 57, 58. The West Indians refused to eat the breadfruit, which was treated as animal food until after the abolition of slavery, when it became acceptable for human consumption.

76 Bligh, op. cit., pp. 57–8.

77 ibid., pp. 58, 57; Wollstonecraft, *Vindication*, p. 186.

78 Sydney's plan of settlement is quoted in Robert Hughes, *The Fatal Shore* (New York, 1986), p. 245. I quote from Hughes's comments on the role of the women convicts, p. 245; my argument is indebted to his discussion of transportation, pp. 244–58. Compare Robinson Crusoe's attitude to the need for women in his colonies, in Daniel Defoe, *The Life and Adventures of Robinson Crusoe*, ed. Angus Ross (1719; Harmondsworth, 1965), pp. 298–9.

79 For further discussion of some of the issues raised here, see Harriet Guest, 'Curiously marked: tattooing, masculinity and nationality in eighteenth-century British perceptions of the South Pacific', in *Painting and the Politics of Culture: new essays in British art 1700–1850*, ed. John Barrell (Oxford, 1992).

Chapter 18

'Because men made the laws': the fallen woman and the woman poet

Angela Leighton

In 1851, from her vantage-point in Florence at the windows of Casa Guidi, Elizabeth Barrett Browning looked towards an England that was confident and powerful, an 'Imperial England' (*Casa Guidi Windows*, II.578)[1] that had come through the Hungry Forties, and was embarking on the new decade with a Great Exhibition. Instead of rejoicing, however, she issued accusations:

> no light
> Of teaching, liberal nations, for the poor
>   Who sit in darkness when it is not night?
> No cure for wicked children? Christ, —no cure!
>   No help for women sobbing out of sight
> Because men made the laws?
>
> (II.634–9)

Quick to take up the cause of the downtrodden – the poor, children and women – she points accusingly to the dark underside of economic expansion, an underside of ignorance, crime and prostitution. The glittering facade of commercial prosperity only hides the need for 'God's justice to be done' (II.655).

Barrett Browning's message is neither new nor unusual. The Victorians were the first to acknowledge their double vision, as well as their double standards. The age which so thoroughly explored the underlying reaches of the individual subconscious was also one haunted by the social underworld of class. Doubleness was of its very nature. In some ways, Barrett Browning sounds a note of characteristically middle-class concern. She is conscience-stricken at the plight of the poor, and uses them to castigate the materialism of the age. Yet the last two lines mark a sharpening of her attitude. Her social criticism turns into a specific grievance over the condition of women in England's cities: 'No help for women sobbing out of sight / Because men made the laws?' The figure of the fallen woman elicits from the woman poet her most pointed accusation.

Yet prostitution at this time was not associated with specific laws. It was not a criminal offence, unless it entailed disorderly behaviour. The age of consent was twelve, until in 1875 it went up to thirteen. Only in 1885, partly as a result of W. T. Stead's sensational exposure of the white slave trade in the pages of the *Pall Mall Gazette*, did it become sixteen. Spooner's Bill, introduced in 1847 to suppress trading in seduction and prostitution, was itself quickly suppressed in the House of Commons, when the names of 'some of the highest and noblest in the land'[2] were in danger of being made public in it. The Contagious Diseases Acts, by which suspect prostitutes were subjected to forced medical examinations, and against which Josephine Butler waged her fierce campaign of repeal, were not passed until the 1860s. In general, as historians have often pointed out, 'prostitution does not seem to have threatened any fundamental principle of the state',[3] and on the whole the law tended to let it alone, if only for the reason that 'some of the highest and noblest in the land' had an interest in it.

When the French romantic socialist, Flora Tristan, visited England in 1839, she was astonished at the numbers of prostitutes to be seen 'everywhere at any time of day'.[4] In her *London Journal* she describes how they collected round the taverns and gin palaces – the 'finishes', as they were called – and she recounts in some detail the lurid sport that was enjoyed at their expense. The Englishman, she notes with disgust, is a sober prude by day and a drunken lecher by night (p. 87). She herself showed none of the shrinking horror of the middle-class Englishwoman in her investigations. She availed herself of some stout protectors, and went to the 'finishes' to have a look.

Tristan is passionate in her denunciations of two aspects of English life, which she blames for the prevalence of prostitution: the inequality of wealth between the classes, and the social and legal inequality between the sexes. She is full of indignation, above all, at the legal dependence of the married Englishwoman, who, at this time, had no right to sue for a divorce, to own property, to make a will, to keep her earnings, to refuse her conjugal services, to leave the conjugal home, or to have custody of her children if separated. Such overwhelming legal dispossession leads Tristan to a quite surprising conclusion in her defence of woman as a class: 'As long as she remains the slave of man and the victim of prejudice, as long as she is refused training in a profession, as long as she is deprived of her civil rights, there can be no moral law for her' (p. 82).

However, it is precisely in the area of the 'moral law' that the Victorian woman holds power. Deprived of 'civil rights' by the law of the land, hers are the compensatory rights of morality. She is the chief upholder and representer of morality, and also its most satisfying symbol. Thus, angel or demon, virgin or whore, Mary or Magdalen, woman is the stage on which the age enacts its own enduring morality play. The struggle between good and evil, virtue and vice, takes up its old story on the scene of the woman's sexual body. The 'moral law', as a result, has a glamorous simplicity as well as a fascinating secretiveness. Its simplicity is mythic, and its secrets sexual.

Yet this 'moral law' of woman's sexuality also relies on a hard core of technical fact. The woman's virginity on which, as Engels points out,[5] the whole social and familial system depends, is not a spiritual virtue, which can be constantly reclaimed, but a physical virtue, subject to proof. If, on the one hand, woman represents a last remaining absolute good in a world of threatening expediency and enterprise, she also, on the other hand, represents a perishable good, the misuse of which diminishes the value. The 'moral law' is not only feminized, but economized, and thus comes very close to the law of commodity.

The broad implications of this 'economizing' of sexuality are brought out in a notorious passage from William Lecky's *History of European Morals*, published in 1869: 'That unhappy being whose very name is a shame to speak ... appears in every age as the perpetual symbol of degradation and sinfulness of man. Herself the supreme type of vice, she is ultimately the most efficient guardian of virtue.'[6] It is in the interests of the very principle of morality to keep the 'type of vice' separate from the type of 'virtue'. The moral stakes of Lecky's opposition are high. The individual 'type' carries the burden of a whole system. Unsurprisingly then, for the Victorians the fallen woman is a type which ranges from the successful courtesan to the passionate adulteress, from the destitute street-walker to the seduced innocent, from the unscrupulous procuress to the raped child. To fall, for woman, is simply to fall short.

The logic of Lecky's statement is manifestly not moral; it is economic. The unspoken fact which makes women either types of 'vice' or types of 'virtue' is the unquestioned fact of male sexual need. Such a need justifies the supply and demand, by which the 'type of vice' offers what the type of 'virtue' necessarily abhors. Thus the 'moral law' erects its mythology of good and bad on a laissez-faire economics of male sexuality, which relies on a social apartheid between women. 'No help for women sobbing out of sight / Because men made the laws?'

More than any other poet, Barrett Browning probes the notion of the moral law as the mythologized superstructure of social inequality. In *Aurora Leigh*, the sexual fall of Marian Erle constantly entails a quarrel with that law. At times Marian's innocence seems too white to be true. However, the purpose of that innocence is not to indulge the squeamishness of the reader, but to deflect moral judgement from the personal to the social. The idea of the law, recurring throughout the poem, provides the connection between those two separate spheres.

Thus, for instance, in Book 3, Barrett Browning describes the birth of Marian, in a mud shack, liable, 'Like any other anthill' (3.836),[7] to be levelled by a ruthless landlord. The defiant mixture of physical detail and political reproach is typical:

> No place for her,
> By man's law! born an outlaw was this babe;
> Her first cry in our strange and strangling air,

When cast in spasms out by the shuddering womb,
Was wrong against the social code, —forced wrong:—
What business had the baby to cry there?

(3.841–6)

Here, 'man's law' is unequivocally the law of property rights, land ownership and class difference. This law casts out, from the start, the girl child born in poverty. The poor have no business to be giving birth to girls on other people's land. The 'social code' of wealth, class and, by implication, sex, makes Marian's life a kind of 'wrong' from the beginning.

The story of Marian Erle charts, every step of the way, the complicity between 'man's law' and moral law. For instance, the description of the mother's attempt to prostitute her daughter to that same 'squire' who also owns the land, is a continued indictment of 'the social code', as well as a rare reference in nineteenth-century literature to the scandal publicized in the *Pall Mall Gazette*. The trade in children for prostitution, both at home and abroad, was a thriving one, and one which had a singular appeal to the male customer afraid of catching venereal disease and willing to pay extra for virginity. As Flora Tristan noted, 'The demand for children is ... enormous' (p. 97). Yet, noticeably, even while Barrett Browning blames the mother, she traces her motives back to yet another kind of violence: 'Her mother had been badly beat, and felt / The bruises sore about her wretched soul' (3.1041–2). The temptation to 'Make offal of [our] daughters' (7.866) finds its originating cause in all men's violence: squires' or fathers'. Only because Marian Erle is 'poor and of the people' (4.845) is she more readily tradable than her wealthier sisters.

Marian's rape in a French brothel thus only continues a theme begun early. If Barrett Browning's account of the rape seems sensational, this is not because it is improbable. The trade in girls to continental brothels may have been exaggerated by Stead in 1885, but it was nonetheless a fact, and he witnessed the use of chloroform. Marian's unconsciousness is not a pretext to prove her innocent, but a truth to prove the guilt of the system. Barrett Browning constantly emphasizes the culpability of the system, and particularly, of course, the class system, involving 'some of the highest and noblest in the land'. Although she finally exonerates Lady Waldemar, her possible responsibility for Marian's fate lurks behind the story till the end.

Barrett Browning's deflection of moral responsibility from the personal to the social is then made clear in the dramatic encounter between Aurora and Marian in Paris. Accused by Aurora of being corrupt, Marian snatches up her child, and fiercely repudiates the morality by which she has been judged:

"Mine, mine," she said. "I have as sure a right
As any glad proud mother in the world,
Who sets her darling down to cut his teeth
Upon her church-ring. If she talks of law,

I talk of law! I claim my mother-dues
By law, —the law which now is paramount,—
The common law, by which the poor and weak
Are trodden underfoot by vicious men,
And loathed for ever after by the good."

(6.661–9)

Marian's self-defence consists in making a radical connection between the church law of marriage and the common law of oppression, between legalization of motherhood in a 'church-ring' and legalization of poverty by an accepted system. As law thus comes to seem less of a moral absolute, and more of a social commodity affordable by the rich, the very nature of virtue and vice becomes uncertain. Furthermore, there is an explicit gender shift to parallel the shift from sexual to social. The 'types of vice', here, are those 'vicious men' who tread the poor 'underfoot'. Thus the terms of Marian's own rape, 'being beaten down / By hoofs of maddened oxen into a ditch' (6.676–7), subtly echo the language of a more general beating down of a whole class of 'poor and weak'.

Against this continuing social protest one must read the end of *Aurora Leigh*, when Marian rejects Romney's offer of marriage, his ' "gift" ' (9.255) of law to her, as Aurora puts it, ironically echoing that earlier ' "gift" ' (2.1085) of money to herself, when Romney had tried to trap her in marriage, and make her family inheritance 'Inviolable with law' (2.1111). Both women repudiate the male gift that comes not as love but law. Against it, Aurora asserts her right to work. Now Marian asserts her right to live by a morality free of any Christian or social legitimacy: 'Here's a hand shall keep / For ever clean without a marriage-ring' (9.431–2). For all her adulation of Romney, she denies the law which he can confer, and rejects the fathering he offers. Her own child, she once asserted, is ' "Not much worse off in being fatherless / Than I was, fathered" ' (6.646–7). The law of the father is associated in her memory with the law of violence. Conveniently for Aurora, Marian has good reason to do without.

Once again, Barrett Browning is drawing general conclusions. The legalism of inheritance, property and blood is present in the best-minded of men. Even Romney, Marian declares, in marrying her, would be haunted by the law of birthright. The children on his knee would never be equal. ' "He is ours, the child" ' (9.409), she insists with passion, meaning mother's and God's. Fathers, even the best of them, will always have a taint of the other system, a system which excludes women: 'Because men made the laws.' It is interesting to remember that, at this time, by Victorian law, the fallen woman had automatic custody of her children; the legitimate wife did not. ' "He is ours, the child" ' gains added determination from the fact.

However, it is the actual encounter between Aurora and Marian which represents Barrett Browning's most obvious flouting of the moral law. The 'type of vice' and the type of 'virtue' meet and go together, in a liaison which is stressed at various levels in the text. Simply in terms of narrative, Aurora and Marian defy the conventions of class difference, sexual rivalry and moral discrimination which should separate them. This social alignment is then doubled by an alignment of voice, by which the virtuous poet and her vicious subject share a first-person narrative which is intimately gendered from the start. The speech of *Aurora Leigh* passes from woman to woman – from Barrett Browning to Aurora to Marian to Lady Waldemar. Each interrupts, and sometimes disproves, the authority of the others. This strategy of shared and relativized speech leaves little room for moral mediations, for charity, or disapprobation. The first person of this dramatic monologue secures her identity, not in opposition to, but in association with, the other women whose speech becomes closely allied to her own.

Thus *Aurora Leigh* asserts an identity of social and aesthetic purpose against the laws of difference between women. To say '"my sister" to the lowest drab' (5.789), as Lady Waldemar must in Romney's phalanstery, is a greeting repeated throughout this text. By the end, Aurora has sistered Marian: ' "Come with me, sweetest sister" ' (7.117), and even Lady Waldemar is begging to be recognized, as not so bad a sister as she has been judged. The class divisions which Romney so notably fails to bridge are bridged by this implicit sisterhood of women who, although they are rivals for the same man, are drawn to each other from a common bond of sexual powerlessness. As Sally Mitchell has pointed out, upper- and middle-class women in the nineteenth century had more in common with working-class women than with the men from their own class (p. 101). The trio of heroines in *Aurora Leigh*, though separated by class, share the common vulnerability of their sex.

The idea of sisterhood as a social liaison between women was given an impetus during the 1850s from a somewhat unexpected quarter. At this time, amid considerable controversy and opposition, the first Anglican Sisterhoods were established. Among those prominent in their support were Mrs Jameson and Florence Nightingale. Often the argument in favour of religious Sisterhoods in fact turns on the question of women's rights to education and to work, an argument which became all the more urgent as, from the middle of the century, the numbers of women rapidly outgrew the numbers of men. Mrs Jameson's lecture on *Sisters of Charity*, given in 1855, is a barely disguised advocacy of some 'well-organised system of work for women'.[8] Florence Nightingale, who gave her support to the new nursing Sisterhoods, roundly answered criticism of convent rules by declaring them preferable to 'the petty grinding tyranny of a good English family'.[9] The first issue of Emily Faithful's *Victoria Magazine*, which was set up as an enterprise run entirely by women, carried an article unequivocally in favour of Sisterhoods.[10]

Conservative opposition pointed not only to the Popish connotations of convents but also to the risk of moral contamination in those Houses which undertook social work among the poor, the sick or the fallen. An early article on 'Female Penitentiaries' in *The Quarterly Review* of 1848 gives a foretaste of the arguments to come. In general the reviewer lends his support to penitentiaries, but he balks at the idea of middle-class women undertaking any practical running of them. At this point his language becomes alluringly pious: 'We may express a doubt whether it is advisable for pure-minded women to put themselves in the way of such knowledge of evil as must be learnt in dealing with the fallen members of their sex.'[11] If the 'type of vice' meets the type of 'virtue', moral chaos might be loosed upon the world. The much more likely, and more injurious, contact between 'pure-minded women' and their rather less pure-minded husbands, fathers, brothers or sons, is a reality which never affects the myth. The scandal lies in the myth, in imagining the pure and the impure, nuns and prostitutes, living together. Such proximity seems a moral contradiction in terms.

II

'And whilst it may truly be urged that unless white could be black and Heaven Hell my experience (thank God) precludes me from hers, I yet don't see why "the Poet mind" should be less able to construct her from its own inner consciousness than a hundred other unknown quantities', wrote Christina Rossetti to Dante Gabriel, who had cautioned his sister against the inclusion of a particular poem in her new volume.[12] 'Under the Rose' is about an unmarried mother and her illegitimate child, a subject which, according to Dante Gabriel, might not be suitable for a woman. Licentious as he was in his own life, his moral protectiveness is roused by the possible impropriety of such a subject for a woman poet. Moral contamination, contrary to all the facts, is transmitted only from woman to woman, even when one of them is an imaginary creation. Christina insisted with due circumlocution on keeping the poem in her volume, and in later editions changed the title, perhaps pointedly, to 'The Iniquity of the Fathers Upon the Children'. Her reply at the time, however, clearly acknowledges the source of Dante Gabriel's anxiety: 'Unless white could be black and Heaven Hell'. Between herself and the unmarried mother of her poem there is a gulf as wide as that between heaven and hell. Yet the very extremity of these moral terms only throws into relief the nature of the task facing '"the Poet mind"'. In one place the bleak opposition between 'white' and 'black', 'Heaven' and 'Hell' might be overcome: '"The Poet mind" should be ... able to construct her from its own inner consciousness.' The 'inner consciousness' of a woman poet, as Dante Gabriel might have suspected, will be especially apt for the task.

Not only Christina's work in the refuge run by the Sisterhood of All Saints during the 1850s brought her into contact with the other sort of woman; her own imagination was unruly enough to throw into doubt and confusion the moral certainties of her own religious temperament. The clash in Rossetti's

work between the fixed moral reference of heaven and hell and the derange-
ment of that reference by an imaginative identification so strong it is anarchic,
is the hallmark of her greatness as a poet. All her best poems have the
intensity of a contradiction between the believer's knowledge and the imagination's desires:

> There's blood between us, love, my love,
> There's father's blood, there's brother's blood;
> And blood's a bar I cannot pass:
> I choose the stairs that mount above,
> Stair after golden skyward stair,
> To city and to sea of glass.
> My lily feet are soiled with mud,
> With scarlet mud which tells a tale
> Of hope that was, of guilt that was,
> Of love that shall not yet avail;
> Alas, my heart, if I could bare
> My heart, this selfsame stain is there.
>
> (ll. 1–12)[13]

Christina Rossetti wrote 'The Convent Threshold' in 1858. Like so many
poems about the fallen woman by women poets, it is a dramatic monologue,
in which the single speaking voice is both the self's and the other's, both the
poet's and the character's. The 'inner consciousness' of the text is a shared
one. Such an identification, however, entails, for Rossetti, a larger, terrifying
loss of bearings. Her poem sensationally blurs the distinctions, not only
between nun and lover, poet and fallen woman, but also, in the end, between
heaven and hell. Alice Meynell caught something of the emotional paradox
of the work when she called it 'a song of penitence for love that yet praises
love more fervently than would a chorus hymeneal'.[14] But it is not only love
which is at stake in this poem. On the threshold of the convent, torn between
sin and grace, world and refuge, earth and heaven, passion and renunciation,
the woman stands on a fine line between moral opposites she can barely keep
apart.

Such a border placing becomes radically displacing. This is the threshold,
not only of a convent, but of consciousness; it is a consciousness tormented
by white and black, heaven and hell, the 'skyward stair' and the 'scarlet
mud'. Whatever brought Rossetti's imagination to this pass, 'The Convent
Threshold' suggests that to cross from earth to sky, mud to stair, love to
grace, lover to nun, is to risk a passage into confusion and hallucination, in
which the 'inner consciousness' is wrecked by difference. This poem is rife
with a sensuality more lovely, but also more damnable, than anything in
Dante Gabriel. Rossetti's female imagination must always bear the cost of
its Romantic desires. To 'construct' the other is to yield the 'inner consciousness' to the moral opposite which that other represents.

Thus, although 'The Convent Threshold' seems to offer a choice between going in or staying out, that choice is soon lost in a disturbingly surreal narrative of visions and dreams, past and future, death and life. The threshold is not a single step, but a shifting subliminal line; it is not a place, but a boundary. This poem is full of thresholds, and consequently full of 'faults' of level and register. To cross into the convent is not, for Rossetti, a step into safety, but a nightmare plunge into vague, unconnected territories of the mind.

The penultimate section of the poem, which is spoken from within the convent, luridly contradicts the religious aspiration of the work. Having chosen the 'skyward stair', the nun dreams of being dragged down in mud. Having chosen eternal life, she hallucinates endless death. Having chosen renunciation, she enters a nightmare of lost love. Yet, the language of this section, contrary to all the moral purpose of the poem, sounds like a true homing of Rossetti's imagination:

> I tell you what I dreamed last night:
> It was not dark, it was not light,
> Cold dews had drenched my plenteous hair
> Thro' clay; you came to seek me there.
> And "Do you dream of me?" you said.
> My heart was dust that used to leap
> To you; I answered half asleep:
> "My pillow is damp, my sheets are red,
> There's a leaden tester to my bed:
> Find you a warmer playfellow,
> A warmer pillow for your head,
> A kinder love to love than mine."
> You wrung your hands; while I, like lead
> Crushed downwards thro' the sodden earth:
> You smote your hands but not in mirth,
> And reeled but were not drunk with wine.
>   (ll. 110–25)

'The Convent Threshold' seems to stage a sinner's progress on the way to grace; but in effect the poem founders in a hellish fantasy of decay and death. Distorted time and deranged dreams torment this latter-day Héloïse.

Yet Rossetti's sense of the macabre has a playful shiftiness about it. The thresholds of dream and waking, death and life, are unnervingly unstable in this poem. 'The Convent Threshold' opens up a strange hall of mirrors in which, by some bewildering logic, the living woman dreams of being dead and of dreaming nonetheless of him who asks: ' "Do you dream?" ' Instead of leading up to heaven, the poem leads downwards and inwards, to that typically Rossettian state of semi-consciousness, which is both heartless and fixated, both capricious and afraid. Certainly some deep and terrible doubt underlies this poem of religious penitence. Its passionate hallucinations seem closer to the imagination of an Emily Brontë than to that of the 'over-scrupulous'[15] Anglican, who, in her later years, would pick up pieces of paper in the street in case the name of God was written on them.[16] 'The "Poet mind" should be ... able to construct her from its own inner consciousness.' The evidence of 'The Convent Threshold' is that the 'inner consciousness' suffers as a result from some profound and brilliant incoherence.

The scene of encounter between fallen and unfallen woman, which 'The Convent Threshold' telescopes into the single figure of the lover-nun, recurs like an obsession in women's poetry. Its most obvious purpose is to forge a forbidden social liaison across the divisions of moral law and sexual myth. In a poem by Dora Greenwell called 'Christina',[17] the fallen speaker remembers her childhood friend Christina, with whom she still feels a sympathetic kinship: 'Across the world-wide gulf betwixt us set / My soul stretched out a bridge.'[18] The poem tells of a chance meeting between two women over the grave of Christina's dead child. In an interesting substitution of identities, Christina urges her fallen friend to come home, and take the place of her child: 'I call thee not my Sister, as of old' (but) 'Daughter' (p. 13). However, the 'world-wide gulf' proves too wide to cross, and the unnamed penitent returns to die in a refuge.

The religious sentimentality of Greenwell's poem keeps it from being anything more than a failed gesture of philanthropy. However, for other poets, the encounter between fallen and unfallen achieves the intensity of a recognition scene. The political sister is the psychic double, the social underworld into which the fallen disappear becoming associated with the subconscious in which the fallen re-emerge as the other self.

In a strange poem by Adelaide Procter, *A Legend of Provence*, a young nun runs off with a soldier, who then betrays and abandons her. After many years she returns to her convent, only to meet her double at the door:

She raised her head; she saw—she seemed to know—
A face that came from long, long years ago:
Herself.[19]

This is not a spectre from the past, but a real, other self, who has been living, all the while, in an unfallen state personated by the Virgin Mary. At the convent door, the two halves come together. Once again, the threshold of the convent seems to be a threshold of the self, marking a split of consciousness which echoes the moral divisions of the age. If the place of the Romantic imagination is that of a borderline between the known and the unknown, the borderline of the Victorian female imagination is the same, but fraught with social and sexual anxieties.

In *Aurora Leigh* the meeting between Aurora and Marian, as critics have noted,[20] has all the emotional urgency and narrative doubling of a recognition scene:

> What face is that?
> What a face, what a look, what a likeness! Full on mine
> The sudden blow of it came down, till all
> My blood swam, my eyes dazzled.
>
> (6.231–4)

Marian returns like the dead, but also like the repressed. When the two women finally meet, their uncanny doubling movements suggest a twinning of purpose beyond all the charities of social aid. First Aurora leads, and Marian 'followed closely where I went, / As if I led her by a narrow plank / Across devouring waters' (6.481–3). But a few lines later, as the moral authority is transferred to Marian 'she led / The way, and I, as by a narrow plank / Across devouring waters, followed her' (6.500–2). These 'devouring waters' are another 'world-wide gulf'. Unlike Greenwell, however, Barrett Browning goes across. That it is a crossing both ways emphasizes the egalitarian nature of the relationship. This is not rescue work. It is self-recognition.

Such doubling effects are taken a stage further in Rossetti's *Goblin Market*. Not only are the two sisters, Lizzie and Laura, hard to distinguish; they also enact the same drama though with different intentions. Laura pays for goblin fruit with a curl of her hair, and pines away. Lizzie gets fruit without paying, and so revives her sister. 'The moral is hardly intelligible', Alice Meynell complained.[21] Rossetti herself, it seems, did not intend a moral.[22] Certainly, as Jerome McGann has argued, a 'middle-class ideology of love and marriage' underlies the story,[23] and the cautionary figure of the fallen woman, Jeanie, 'who for joys brides hope to have / Fell sick and died' (ll. 314–15), casts a realistic shadow across the fairy tale.[24] Nonetheless, *Goblin Market* singularly fails to press home the moral of Jeanie. Laura knows she should not loiter and look, but she does. Lizzie knows she should not take without paying, but she does. The only rule pertaining at the end is that sisters should stick together. Only together will they be a match for the goblins. Jeanie died, not because she ate the fruit, but because she had no sister to rescue her.

If *Goblin Market* is a feminized myth of Christian redemption, it is redemption through a willed confusion of fallen and unfallen. 'Undone in mine undoing / And ruined in my ruin', Laura wails (ll. 482–3). Yet, it is precisely through this shared fall, this transgression of the rule of difference, that sisterhood becomes a match for brotherhood, and the goblins are beaten at their own tricks. 'We may express a doubt whether it is advisable for pure-minded women to put themselves in the way of such knowledge of evil as must be learnt in dealing with the fallen members of their sex', wrote the *Quarterly* reviewer. Such 'knowledge of evil', for Christina Rossetti, is not only advisable, but also awakening and saving. Lizzie, the rescuing sister, goes 'At twilight, halted by the brook: / And for the first time in her life / Began to listen and look' (ll. 326–8). The two girls desire, loiter and look, in a gesture that combines a Romantic hovering on the threshold of strange knowledge with the purposeful delay of the street-walker.

In the end, it seems that Rossetti brilliantly displaces the message of this poem on to the two terms of the title. *Goblin Market* is the place of magic and marketing. Far from being representers of the moral seriousness of the Fall, these mischievous and childish creatures play by the rules of magic and money. They thus uncannily echo the commodity morality of nineteenth-century myths of sexuality. Moral downfall is linked to market exchange. By not paying, Lizzie tricks the market and resists not so much the fruit as the law by which fruit turns to poison because, Rossetti seems to say, goblins made the laws. There is a sense in which *Goblin Market* hoodwinks the moralizers as well.

'After much hesitation and many misgivings, we have undertaken to speak of so dismal and delicate a matter', writes W. R. Greg.[25] He begins his 1850 article on 'Prostitution' with elaborate cautions and apologies. Even William Lecky slips at times into coy circumlocutions: 'That unhappy being whose very name is a shame to speak.' When it comes to speaking, 'shame' is a constant obstruction. When it comes to women speaking, a whole complicated magic of sin and contamination comes into play. 'I am grateful to you as a woman for having so treated such a subject', wrote Barrett Browning to Elizabeth Gaskell, on the publication of *Ruth*, as if she were speaking as one of the fallen herself.[26] Certainly, the connection between writing and sinning is a close and involved one. The doubling of sisters in these texts hints at the way in which the poet is verbally implicated in the fall. Writing and sexuality double each other. 'There has always been a vague connection', writes Simone de Beauvoir, 'between prostitution and art.'[27] Such a connection is both more probable and more inadmissible when the artist is a woman. A sign of the sheer inhibitory power of the taboo imposed on women is that, as late as 1929, Virginia Woolf, in *A Room of One's Own*, looks forward to a time when the woman writer will be able to meet 'the courtesan' and 'the harlot' without 'that self-consciousness in the presence of "sin" which is the legacy of our sexual barbarity'.[28] Woolf looks forward, but she might also have looked back.

One voice from the nineteenth century which speaks out with brave shamelessness on the subject of the fallen is a voice which has been unaccountably lost to the poetic canon. 'By-the-by', wrote Christina Rossetti to a friend, 'did not Mr. Gladstone omit from his list of poetesses the one name which *I* incline to feel as by far the most formidable of those known to me.'[29] The name she gave was that of Augusta Webster.

Webster's poem, *A Castaway*, was published in 1870, in her volume *Portraits*, and was almost certainly known to Rossetti. A long dramatic monologue, spoken by a relatively high-class courtesan who muses on the strange course of her life, the poem becomes a magnificent and panoramic indictment of contemporary society. Webster makes the connection between the moral and the mercantile overtly and persistently, so that all trades are levelled to the same kind of value: that of profit and loss. In a narrative that is strikingly free of myths and metaphors, the Castaway judges the ways of the world. Hers is a stark and literal language, a language of the market without any goblins:

> And, for me,
> I say let no one be above her trade;
> I own my kindredship with any drab
> Who sells herself as I, although she crouch
> In fetid garrets and I have a home
> All velvet and marqueterie and pastilles,
> Although she hide her skeleton in rags
> And I set fashions and wear cobweb lace:
> The difference lies but in my choicer ware,
> That I sell beauty and she ugliness;
> Our traffic's one—I'm no sweet slaver-tongue
> To gloze upon it and explain myself
> A sort of fractious angel misconceived—
> Our traffic's one: I own it. And what then?
> I know of worse that are called honourable.
> Our lawyers, who with noble eloquence
> And virtuous outbursts lie to hang a man,
> Or lie to save him, which way goes the fee:
> Our preachers, gloating on your future hell
> For not believing what they doubt themselves:
> Our doctors, who sort poisons out by chance
> And wonder how they'll answer, and grow rich:
> Our journalists, whose business is to fib
> And juggle truths and falsehoods to and fro:
> Our tradesmen, who must keep unspotted names
> And cheat the least like stealing that they can:
> Our—all of them, the virtuous worthy men
> Who feed on the world's follies, vices, wants,
> And do their businesses of lies and shams
> Honestly, reputably, while the world
> Claps hands and cries "good luck," which of their trades,
> Their honourable trades, barefaced like mine,
> All secrets brazened out, would shew more white?[30]

A Castaway presents the fact of prostitution bare of any myth or magic. Its causes are unremittingly social, and so are its effects – penury, poor education, an imbalance of the numbers of women against those of men, and a shortage of work for both sexes. Webster, who was a lifelong campaigner for women's suffrage (though she failed to convert Christina Rossetti to her cause) as well as for women's education, issues a moving reminder in this poem of how the education of girls is stinted to pay for the training of their luckier brothers: 'The lesson girls with brothers all must learn, / To do without' (p. 56). Never having been fitted for anything except marriage, what can girls do to keep alive except carry out that trade which so darkly resembles marriage, and yet is its moral opposite.

Most of the fallen women who play any prominent role in nineteenth-century literature are only variations on the real theme. Seduced, raped, betrayed, or simply fickle, they are either innocent girls led astray, or sensational adulteresses. Their actions thus remain largely within the parameters of romance. They are motivated by feeling, not by economic exigency. But Augusta Webster gives us the professional. As a result, she can point to the real unmentionable of Victorian prostitution: the male client. The endlessly elaborated discourse on the tantalizing secret of female sexuality, like any other taboo, in fact serves to disguise another, more deep-seated taboo which creates the silence on the other side of all this speech. Sexuality is not just, as Michel Foucault claims, the well-exploited 'secret' of the modern age;[31] woman's sexuality provides a gratifying decoy from the thing that is no secret at all and yet remains curiously unspoken. Gladstone, who was himself, like Dickens, a keen rescuer of fallen women, inclined to take them home to talk with his wife, confessed in his diary that his motives were suspect: he feared in himself some ' "dangerous curiosity & filthiness of spirit" '.[32] By writing about the professional courtesan, Webster dares to mention the men who in reality provide the rationale of prostitution. These are not the figures of literary romance, dark seducers or passionate rakes. These are, quite simply, other women's husbands, for whom the illicit is routine:

> And whom do I hurt more than they? as much?
> The wives? Poor fools, what do I take from them
> Worth crying for or keeping? If they knew
> What their fine husbands look like seen by eyes
> That may perceive there are more men than one!
> But, if they can, let them just take the pains
> To keep them: 'tis not such a mighty task
> To pin an idiot to your apron-strings;
> And wives have an advantage over us,
> (The good and blind ones have) the smile or pout
> Leaves them no secret nausea at odd times.
> Oh, they could keep their husbands if they cared,
> But 'tis an easier life to let them go,
> And whimper at it for morality.
>
> (pp. 39–40)

Webster exposes, with scornful simplicity, the other hidden and forbidden topic which lies behind the Victorians' obsession with fallen women. If men are the arbiters of virtue and vice, they are also the go-betweens. For them the passage from one to the other is a secret passage between separate spheres. But for women the difference is not so certain. The passage which divides the 'type of virtue' from the type of 'vice' can turn into a mirror, to reflect the self. The very nature of womanhood is split by a mirror stage, mandated by man's law. Thus, the doubleness of the social order serves to match a doubleness within. The very nature of female subjectivity is founded and wrecked on this law of opposites. Not only is the pure woman divided from 'the other'; the very self is split from its own history.

At one point, the Castaway remembers her girlhood:

> So long since:
> And now it seems a jest to talk of me
> As if I could be one with her, of me
> Who am ... me.

(p. 36)

When she looks in the mirror it seems to reproduce the doubleness. Between 'me' and 'me' falls the shadow of the moral law. Against that law, however, the dramatic monologue asserts its single voice. The pronoun doubles poet and outcast, speaker and actor, in a drama which is transgressively sistering from the start. The voice of the poem is both act and consciousness, both object and subject, both 'me' and 'me'. The gender-specific nature of this poet's voice makes a common cause of the fact of womanhood.

One of the saddest poems on the fallen woman is Amy Levy's 'Magdalen'. In reality a poem of seduction, its note of bitter and sceptical despair as the girl prepares to die in a refuge is a sign of the continuing power of the myth as late as the 1880s. Like Rossetti before her, Levy finds in the event of the fall a mockery of all creeds and of all ethical systems:

> Death do I trust no more than life.
> For one thing is like one arrayed,
> And there is neither false nor true;
> But in a hideous masquerade
> All things dance on, the ages through.
> And good is evil, evil good;
> Nothing is known or understood
> Save only Pain.[33]

Levy was only twenty-eight when, five years after the publication of this poem, she killed herself in her parents' house without explanation. Her 'Magdalen' is an immature poem, and its language is too limply melancholy; it does, nonetheless, betray the strain of that social morality which founds its whole system of good and evil on the sexual propriety of women.

Charlotte Mew – a poet who was, in many ways, herself a last Victorian – was one of the last poets to write about the Magdalen. In 1894, Mew published a story in *The Yellow Book* called 'Passed', describing an encounter between the narrator and a destitute young girl whom she meets in a church, and whose sister has killed herself following some sexual betrayal. Behind the vivid melodrama of Mew's language, the story traces a rather interesting psychological story. The moment when the narrator takes the girl in her arms is one of extreme bewilderment and hallucination. Thinking of her home, she finds it 'desolate'; imagining a mirror, she sees no 'reflection'; opening a book, she finds the pages 'blank'.[34] All the usual signs of her sheltered identity have been erased. In this encounter with the homeless, distraught girl, she seems to have lost her own self. In terror, she cruelly throws the girl off, and makes her escape; but when, many months later, she glimpses the girl on the arm of the same man who betrayed her sister, the meaning of the encounter flashes on her mind. The last lines of the story confirm the suspicion that the girl is the speaker's lost reflection, her alter ego, forfeited to the differences of moral law and class division: 'I heard a laugh, mounting to a cry.... Did it proceed from some defeated angel? or the woman's mouth? or mine?' (p. 78).

The 'woman's mouth or mine?' The sound of that confused 'laugh' or 'cry' comes from an 'inner consciousness' which is woman's, in general, not hers or mine, but both. Sexual morality and social difference have split the very nature of female subjectivity. For women in the nineteenth century, the Romantic split, 'I is another', carries the added penalty of a sexual transgression: 'I is the other.' The mirror, for women, is also a gulf. Yet to pass from one side of the gulf to the other is to undertake an act of social protest which is also an act of daring self-recovery.

By the time Mew came to write her own dramatic monologue of the fallen woman, the schizophrenia of Victorian morality had largely been overcome. 'Madeleine in Church' was published in 1916, and is, in spite of its title, an uninhibited love poem. The idea of the fall as a psycho-sexual event which splits subjectivity into 'me' and 'me' is missing in it. Instead, its rich evocation of passion affirms that the self is consistent with itself, and coherent with its history:

We are what we are: when I was half a child I could not sit
Watching black shadows on green lawns and red carnations burning in the sun,
Without paying so heavily for it
That joy and pain, like any mother and her unborn child were almost one.
I could hardly bear
The dreams upon the eyes of white geraniums in the dusk,
The thick, close voice of musk,
The jessamine music on the thin night air,
Or, sometimes, my own hands about me anywhere—
The sight of my own face (for it was lovely then) even the scent of my own hair,
Oh! there was nothing, nothing that did not sweep to the high seat
Of laughing gods, and then blow down and beat

My soul into the highway dust, as hoofs do the dropped roses of the street.
I think my body was my soul,
And when we are made thus
Who shall control
Our hands, our eyes, the wandering passion of our feet.

(pp. 23–4)

This poem, in some ways, marks the end of a tradition. By the time women come to write openly about sexual passion, the figure of the fallen woman ceases to haunt their imaginations. For she is the ghost of what has been forbidden, denied, divided. She is the Victorian woman poet's familiar, the double that returns like herself, the other that beats against the internalized social barriers of the mind. She is the vivid emblem of a social and sexual secrecy which is still clamorous with self-discovery.

The figure of the fallen woman is also, however, a sign for women of the power of writing. Her wandering, outcast state seductively expresses the poet's restlessness and desire. To summon her is not only to assert a political purpose which breaks the moral law, but also to claim the power of writing as necessarily free of control, of rule. The fallen woman is the muse, the beloved – the lost sister, mother, daughter, whose self was one's own. In poetry, above all, the social gesture of reclamation and solidarity becomes also an imaginative gesture of integration and identity.

Barrett Browning, at the beginning of this tradition, invokes the fallen woman, not only as her sister, but also as her muse. Only if the poet takes the 'part' of the other, and speaks with her cries, will she find her own voice. The political other is the poetic self. To speak from the 'inner consciousness' of being a woman is to speak from that which has been divided, disen-franchised, but which, for that very reason, needs to be recovered. The 'depths of womanhood' may have been kept 'out of sight', but only from such 'depths' can the poet challenge men's laws:

"Therefore," the voice said, "shalt thou write
My curse to-night.
Some women weep and curse, I say
(And no one marvels), night and day.

'And thou shalt take their part to-night,
Weep and write.
A curse from the depths of womanhood
Is very salt, and bitter, and good.'

('A Curse for a Nation', ll. 41–8)[35]

NOTES

1 Elizabeth Barrett Browning, *Casa Guidi Windows*, in *The Complete Works of Elizabeth Barrett Browning*, ed. Charlotte Porter and Helen A. Clarke (New York, 1900), vol. 3, pp. 249–313.

2 Quoted in Sally Mitchell, *The Fallen Angel: Chastity, Class and Women's Reading 1835–1880* (Bowling Green, Ohio, 1981), p. 340.

3 Vern Bullough and Bonnie Bullough, *Women and Prostitution: A Social History* (New York, 1987), p. 197.

4 *The London Journal of Flora Tristan 1842 or The Aristocracy and the Working Class of England*, trans. Jean Hawkes (London, 1982), p. 83.

5 Frederick Engels, *The Origin of the Family, Private Property and the State*, intro. Eleanor Burke Leacock (London, 1972), pp. 125–46.

6 William Lecky, *History of European Morals*, 2 vols in one (New York, 1955), vol. 2, p. 283.

7 Elizabeth Barrett Browning, *Aurora Leigh and Other Poems*, intro. Cora Kaplan (London, 1978).

8 Mrs Jameson, *Sisters of Charity: Catholic and Protestant, Abroad and at Home* (London, 1855), p. 13.

9 Quoted in A. M. Allchin, *The Silent Rebellion: Anglican Religious Communities 1845–1900* (London, 1958), p. 115.

10 Rev. F. D. Maurice, 'On Sisterhoods', in *The Victoria Magazine* 1, August 1863, pp. 289–301.

11 'Female Penitentiaries', in *The Quarterly Review* 83, 1848, pp. 375–6.

12 *Three Rossettis: Unpublished Letters to and from Dante Gabriel, Christina, William*, ed. Janet Camp Troxell (Cambridge, Massachusetts, 1937), p. 143. Letter from Christina to Dante Gabriel, 13 March 1865.

13 Christina Rossetti: 'The Convent Threshold', in *The Complete Poems of Christina Rossetti: A Variorum Edition*, ed. R. W. Crump (Baton Rouge, 1979), vol. 1, pp. 61–5.

14 Alice Meynell, 'Christina Rossetti', in *The New Review* NS, 12, 1895, p. 203.

15 William Michael Rossetti, 'Memoir', in *The Poetical Works of Christina Georgina Rossetti* (London, 1904), p. lxvii.

16 Katharine Tynan, *Twenty-Five Years: Reminiscences* (London, 1913), p. 161.

17 The poem was written in 1851, almost certainly before Greenwell had met Rossetti or had read any of her poems.

18 Dora Greenwell, 'Christina', in *Poems* (Edinburgh, 1861), p. 4.

19 Adelaide A. Procter, 'A Legend of Provence', in *The Poems of Adelaide A. Procter* (Boston, 1877), p. 189.

20 See, for instance, Dolores Rosenblum, 'Face to Face: Elizabeth Barrett Browning's *Aurora Leigh* and Nineteenth-Century Poetry', in *Victorian Poetry* 26, 1983, pp. 321–38, and Angela Leighton, *Elizabeth Barrett Browning* (Brighton, 1986), chapter 7.

21 Alice Meynell, 'Christina Rossetti', in *Alice Meynell: Prose and Poetry*, intro. V. Sackville-West (London, 1947), p. 147

22 Note to *Goblin Market*, by William Michael Rossetti, in *The Poetical Works of Christina Georgina Rossetti*, p. 459

23 Jerome J. McGann, 'Christina Rossetti's Poems: A New Edition and a Revaluation', in *Victorian Studies* 23, 1980, p. 248.

24 Christina Rossetti, *Goblin Market*, in *The Complete Poems*, vol. 1, pp. 11–26.

25 W. R. Greg, 'Prostitution', in *Westminster Review* 53, 1850, p. 448.

26 *Letters Addressed to Mrs Gaskell by Celebrated Contemporaries*, ed. Ross D. Waller (Manchester, 1935), p. 42.

27 Simone de Beauvoir, *The Second Sex*, trans. H. M. Parshley (Harmondsworth, 1972), p. 579.

28 Virginia Woolf, *A Room of One's Own* (Harmondsworth, 1945), p. 88.

29 *The Family Letters of Christina Georgina Rossetti*, ed. William Michael Rossetti (London, 1908), p. 175. Letter from Christina to William, 22 January 1890.

30 Augusta Webster, *A Castaway*, in *Portraits*, 3rd edn (London, 1893), pp. 38–9.

31 Michel Foucault, *The History of Sexuality*, trans. Robert Hurley (Harmondsworth, 1981), vol. 1, p. 35.

32 *The Gladstone Diaries*, ed. M. R. D. Foot and H. C. G. Matthew (Oxford, 1968–86), vol. 4, p. 51.

33 Amy Levy, 'Magdalen', in *A Minor Poet And Other Verse* (London, 1884), p. 71.

34 Charlotte Mew, 'Passed', in *Charlotte Mew: Collected Poems and Prose*, ed. Val Warner (Manchester, 1981), p. 71. Hereafter this edition is cited by page number in the text.

35 Elizabeth Barrett Browning, 'A Curse for a Nation', in *Aurora Leigh and Other Poems*, pp. 402–6.

Index